D1605778

Life Abounding

A Reading of John's Gospel

Brendan Byrne, SJ

LITURGICAL PRESS
Collegeville, Minnesota

www.litpress.org

1   2   3   4   5   6   7   8   9

Library of Congress Cataloging-in-Publication Data

Byrne, Brendan (Brendan J.)
    Life abounding : a reading of John's gospel / Brendan Byrne, SJ.
       pages   cm
    Includes bibliographical references.
       ISBN 978-0-8146-3574-2 — ISBN 978-0-8146-3599-5 (ebook)
       1. Bible. John—Commentaries.   I. Title.

  BS2615.53.B97   2014
  226.5'07—dc23

                                                            2014008777

In Memory of

Peter Daniel Steele, SJ

1939–2012

Priest, Poet, Companion, Friend.

In a sermon on John 1:1-18 he described

the Word made flesh

as

"The Eloquence of God"

Contents

Introduction

In 1963 Alan Walker, an Australian Methodist pastor ministering in Sydney, founded Lifeline, a telephone crisis counseling service. Lifeline rapidly spread across Australia and now exists in over thirty countries across the world. The original center was located in an old terrace house in Darlinghurst, inner Sydney. Inscribed on the modernized façade of the building was the text from the Gospel of John: "That they may have life and have it to the full" (10:10). In its present public face to the world Lifeline has moved on from describing its mission in such explicitly biblical terms. However, from the moment I saw that text inscribed on its original headquarters many decades ago, I could not help being struck by its appropriateness for the particular service that Lifeline has always aimed to provide. People who approach Lifeline are barely clinging to life; they simply exist, with no joy or hope or vitality. Lifeline exists to help them discover the possibility of a "more abundant" measure of life, a richness of relationship and satisfaction beyond mere existence.

I have recalled Lifeline and the particular text at the beginning of this book because I am convinced that the distinction between life as mere existence and more abundant life is central to the theology of the Fourth Gospel and opens a fruitful way into appreciating it at depth. In its very opening lines the gospel speaks of the Word through whom all things were made—that is, came into existence (1:3). It goes on immediately to speak of a mission of the Word into the world to draw human beings from mere existence into a more abundant life that is nothing less than a share in God's own "eternal life" (1:4).

Some time after the composition of the Fourth Gospel some members of the community that gave rise to it wrote the following account of what they had experienced and wanted to share:

1

> We declare to you what was from the beginning, what we have heard, what
> we have seen with our eyes, what we have looked at and touched with our
> hands, concerning the word of life—this life was revealed, and we have seen
> it and testify to it, and declare to you the eternal life that was with the Father
> and was revealed to us—we declare to you what we have seen and heard so
> that you also may have fellowship with us; and truly our fellowship is with
> the Father and with his Son Jesus Christ. We are writing these things so that
> our joy may be complete. (1 John 1:1-4)

These opening lines from the First Letter of John sum up admirably,
to my mind, what the Fourth Gospel wishes to commend to its audience.
My aim in the present work is to help facilitate that for readers of the gospel
today so that it may achieve today what it has always aimed to do: move
human beings from mere existence to a conscious sense of sharing the divine
eternal life—and the joy that goes with it.

What I am offering is a commentary in the sense that it follows the text
of the Fourth Gospel through from beginning to end. Unlike classic commentaries on biblical books, however, it has a more immediate pastoral aim
and so avoids detailed analysis of virtually every point at issue and sustained
engagement with the wealth of scholarly literature on the gospel. At the
same time the debt I owe to that literature should be patent on every page,
especially in the notes where acknowledgment of debt to other scholars is
principally to be found.

Though there may be touches of originality here and there in the reading of John that I offer, by and large I have relied upon a selection of representative commentaries and monographs. In this connection I should mention
the classic twentieth-century commentaries of Rudolf Bultmann, Raymond
Brown, Rudolf Schnackenburg, and C. K. Barrett,[1] and the more recent
commentaries of Francis Moloney, Gail O'Day, Ugo Schnelle, and Andrew
Lincoln.[2] As regards monographs, I should acknowledge the incomparable

---

[1] Rudolf Bultmann, *The Gospel of John: A Commentary* (Oxford: Blackwell, 1971); Ray-
mond E. Brown, *The Gospel According to John*, 2 vols., Anchor Bible 29–29A (Garden City,
NY: Doubleday, 1966–70); Rudolf Schnackenburg, *The Gospel According to St. John*, 3 vols.
(New York: Crossroad, 1968–82); C. K. Barrett, *The Gospel According to St. John*, 2nd ed.
(London: SPCK, 1978).

[2] Francis J. Moloney, *The Gospel of John*, Sacra Pagina 4 (Collegeville, MN: Liturgical
Press, 1998); Gail O'Day, "The Gospel of John," in *New Interpreter's Bible* IX (Nashville:
Abingdon, 1995), 491–865; Ugo Schnelle, *Das Evangelium nach Johannes*, 4th ed., Theolo-
gischer Handkommentar zum Neuen Testament 4 (Leipzig: Evangelische Verlagsanstalt,
2009); Andrew T. Lincoln, *The Gospel According to Saint John*, Black's New Testament
Commentary (New York: Hendrickson, 2005).

classic of C. H. Dodd, *The Interpretation of the Fourth Gospel*,[3] and the works of R. Alan Culpepper,[4] Robert Kysar,[5] and my colleagues, Dorothy Lee[6] and Mary Coloe.[7] Doubtless, readers conversant with the vast range of high quality scholarly literature now available on the Fourth Gospel will note many areas where I might have consulted more widely. However, I trust it will be appreciated that in a work of this kind a high measure of selectivity was unavoidable.[8]

My aim throughout has been to offer a reading of the Fourth Gospel that is sensitive to its enigmatic qualities and is at the same time sympathetic to the difficulty that it presents in many places and on many grounds for readers today. Unless necessary for interpretation, by and large, I avoid detailed discussion of historical matters to concentrate on helping readers derive from the text its theological and spiritual riches. Where I find the text impossibly obscure, or so captive to the concerns of its original context as to have little to say to our present situation, I do not hesitate to point this out. There are aspects, too, above all the gospel's characterization of the world that becomes irrevocably hostile to Jesus as "the Jews," where responsible interpretation—let alone public proclamation—must proceed with great caution and sensitivity. I have attempted to confront a range of the difficulties that the Fourth Gospel presents in the following chapter, "Read Me First," a perusal of which, as the title suggests, I do commend prior to further reading.

Some Presuppositions

It is not my intention here to offer at any length discussion of the issues that are customarily treated in considerable detail in the introductions to

---

[3] C. H. Dodd, *The Interpretation of the Fourth Gospel* (Cambridge: Cambridge University Press, 1953).

[4] R. Alan Culpepper, *Anatomy of the Fourth Gospel* (Philadelphia: Fortress, 1983).

[5] Robert Kysar, *John: The Maverick Gospel*, 3rd ed. (Louisville, KY: Westminster John Knox, 2007).

[6] Dorothy A. Lee, *The Symbolic Narratives of the Fourth Gospel: The Interplay of Form and Meaning*, JSNTSup 95 (Sheffield, UK: JSOT Press, 1994); *Flesh and Glory: Symbolism, Gender, and Theology in the Gospel of John* (New York: Crossroad, 2002).

[7] Mary L. Coloe, *God Dwells with Us: Temple Symbolism in the Fourth Gospel* (Collegeville, MN: Liturgical Press, 2001).

[8] An attractive new monograph by Francis J. Moloney, *Love in the Gospel of John: An Exegetical, Theological, and Literary Study* (Grand Rapids, MI: Baker Academic, 2013) arrived too late to be included in this work. Its quality and congruence with the overall theme pursued here lead me to commend it strongly to the reader.

standard commentaries. For an up-to-date, comprehensive, fair-minded, and admirably clear example of such an introduction I can do no better than recommend that provided by Andrew Lincoln.[9] The same can be said of Raymond Brown's *Introduction to the Gospel of John* as retrieved from his notes, critically edited and brought up to date by Francis Moloney.[10] Here I shall simply indicate the understanding of the Fourth Gospel that I presuppose in this reading.

Literary Integrity

First of all, I shall take the gospel as a complete whole in its final canonical form, rarely pausing to discuss sources or traditions that might be thought to lie behind the present text. I acknowledge that for several reasons—principally the presence at the close of chapter 20 (vv. 30-31) of what seems to be an ending to the entire work—the material contained in chapter 21 likely represents an addition to the main body of the gospel. However, as I shall indicate at the appropriate place, I believe that the material in the chapter is very much integral to the gospel and should be treated accordingly. The same consideration applies even more strongly to the Prologue (1:1-18), which provides the reader with information vital to an appreciation of the remainder of the gospel as a whole. There are grounds for holding that the so-called sacramental conclusion to the Bread of Life discourse, 6:51b (52)-59, is also a later addition to the text. However, while not denying the likelihood of this, I shall try to offer an overall interpretation of John 6 that sees it as integral to the sequence as it now stands. The truly "foreign body" in the gospel, Jesus' liberation of the woman accused of adultery (7:53–8:1-11), I shall consider in its present place.

Authorship: The "Beloved Disciple"

My understanding is that the Fourth Gospel is the product of a Christian community that evolved over the course of several decades with a highly distinctive view of Jesus Christ and understanding of itself as a community gathered around his memory and ongoing presence. This community also treasured the memory and traced the origins of its belief to the witness of one whom it refers to anonymously as "the disciple whom Jesus loved" (13:23; 19:26-27; 20:2; 21:7; 21:20; cf. 18:15; possibly 1:35). At one point,

[9] Andrew T. Lincoln, *The Gospel According to Saint John*, 1–91.
[10] Raymond E. Brown, *An Introduction to the Gospel of John*, ed. Francis J. Moloney (New York: Doubleday, 2003).

21:24, the gospel attributes the authorship of its narrative to this figure, though this need not mean that he literally wrote it any more than a similar statement about Pilate's "writing" the inscription placed on Jesus' cross (19:19) meant that the governor actually inscribed the placard himself; authorship in a broader sense is in view. Longstanding church tradition, based especially on the writings of Irenaeus toward the end of the second century CE, identified the Beloved Disciple, whom it understood to be the author of the Fourth Gospel, with John, the son of Zebedee, one of the twelve original disciples of Jesus. While still held by some, mainstream Johannine scholarship has increasingly distanced itself from this identification. The only mention of the sons of Zebedee in the Fourth Gospel occurs in the list of the seven disciples who experienced a meeting with the risen Lord in Galilee (21:2). It later emerges (21:7) that the Beloved Disciple is a member of this group but the way the story is told makes it very unlikely that he is to be thought of as one of Zebedee's two sons. Moreover, if the author of the gospel was one of the Twelve and an eyewitness to much of Jesus' ministry, it is inexplicable that so little of his account parallels in any way the Synoptic tradition in which the Twelve are so prominent, whereas in the Fourth Gospel the Twelve as a group rate barely a mention (only 6:67; 20:24). Attempts to identify the disciple with other known figures in the early tradition (Lazarus, Thomas, Nathaniel, John Mark) have been even less successful. It seems we must let the figure referred to as the Beloved Disciple remain in the anonymity with which the gospel itself, for its own purpose, presents him.

What might that purpose have been? First of all, the anonymity allows the figure of the disciple to have a key symbolic role within the narrative. Readers of later generations can identify with the disciple—in his fidelity, in his faith, and in his privileged intimacy with Jesus (especially, in the depiction of his position, lying upon the breast of Jesus at the Last Supper [13:23-25; cf. 21:20], an intimacy that echoes the description of Jesus' own intimacy with the Father [1:18]). In this sense the disciple functions as the point of insertion for later generations into the heart of the saving events told in the gospel.

That the disciple has this key symbolic function does not at all mean that he is a purely symbolic figure without any link to a historical figure in early Christianity. The statements about his witness in 19:35 and 21:24 would lack all credibility if he were not a historical figure, of whose identity the gospel presumes its original readers were aware, even if for its own good reason it has withheld that knowledge from us. In terms of historical reality it seems best to understand that the figure later represented as the Beloved Disciple was an early disciple of Jesus but not a member of the Twelve and insufficiently significant to find a place within the Synoptic tradition. In the post-Easter phase of the church a particular community of believers in Messiah Jesus, still very much frequenting the Jewish synagogue, grew up around the witness and teaching of this individual, evolving under his influence its own distinctive view of Jesus.

The Community behind the Fourth Gospel

In due course, the high claims that the community was making for the status of Jesus led to increasing tension with the synagogue authorities. This tension increased to a point sufficiently acute to lead to the expulsion of members of the community from the synagogue, a bitter and painful experience, the impact of which can be read in virtually every page of the later gospel narrative.[11]

At some stage, presumably on the known models provided by at least one and possibly more of the extant Synoptic gospels, a decision was made by the community, possibly during the lifetime of the disciple and at his instigation (cf. 21:24), to compose its own narrative. If it is unlikely, as we have seen, that the actual author was the disciple himself, then we must presuppose that the community found within its ranks a highly talented individual to complete this task. We may call this writer "the evangelist," the narrator whose voice we hear not only in the overall reportage about Jesus but also in frequent explanations and asides to the reader.

At a later stage in the community's history the material contained in chapter 21 and possibly that in 6:51-58, along with perhaps the comment about the reliability of the one "witnessing" the flow of blood and water from Jesus' side in 19:35, was added to the primary text. Whether all or some of these additions were made by the original evangelist or, as is perhaps more likely, by another member of the community (the "Redactor"), we do not know. It is reasonably clear from the remarks about the Beloved Disciple toward the end of John 21 that he had died in the meantime. This event appears to have caused something of a crisis in the community and led to its seeking a closer relationship to the wider church that cherished the memory of the pastoral leadership and heroic death of Peter (21:18-19).

Together with the traditional ascription of authorship of the Fourth Gospel to the apostle John has been the tradition of Ephesus as its place of composition. This tradition, which owes much to the ancient association of

---

[11] On this see especially the classic work of J. Louis Martyn, *History and Theology in the Fourth Gospel*, 3rd ed. (Louisville, KY: Westminster John Knox, 2003); for an updated survey, see Francis J. Moloney, in Raymond E. Brown, *Introduction*, 69–85.

the gospel with Revelation (Apocalypse), cannot be verified with any degree of certainty. While the origins of the community are undoubtedly Palestinian Jewish—shown especially by the prominence given to the Jewish feasts and also by certain quite concrete geographical references (3:23; 4:5; 10:22-23; 18:1)—it seems likely that by the time of the composition of the gospel, the community lived in a Greek-speaking milieu where there was also a sizable representation of the Jewish Diaspora. Along with Ephesus, several other great cities of the eastern Mediterranean world—Antioch and Alexandria, for instance—come into consideration in that connection, though the claim of Ephesus is perhaps more plausible than any other. The fact that the evangelist feels obliged to explain certain Jewish customs (2:6; 19:40) and translate some terms (1:38; 4:25; 19:17; 20:16) suggests that the gospel was written for an audience now living outside Palestine.

More significant for interpretation than the locale or even a precise date—though somewhere between 90 and 110 CE would seem to be most likely—is the consideration that members of the community were in a situation where they had emerged from a close and increasingly bitter relationship and "dialogue" with the local Jewish synagogue. In many ways, especially in its setting of so much of Jesus' ministry against the background of the principal Jewish feasts, the gospel reflects the community's struggle to forge its own distinct identity now that its erstwhile Jewish identity has been lost and, in more sociological terms, been physically stripped from it through expulsion from the synagogue. There is evidence, too—especially in the portrayal of figures such as Nicodemus (3:1-10; 7:50-52; 19:39), Joseph of Arimathea (19:38), and the parents of the Man Born Blind (9:22-23)—that a key purpose of the gospel was not only to strengthen the faith of those who had already made the break with the synagogue but also to summon across to full commitment those who were sympathetic but for various reasons had not yet made the transition to wholehearted discipleship (cf. 12:42-43).

The above outline represents the basic understanding of the Fourth Gospel presupposed in this project. I trust that the journey upon which I invite the reader to be my companion will confirm its validity. To keep the book within reasonable size and expense I have not, except very occasionally, set out the text of the gospel in English translation. The translation that I basically presuppose and quote is that of the New Revised Standard Version. I would urge readers to have this translation by them as they consult or read their way through the commentary.

Structure of the Fourth Gospel

The basic structural pattern of the Fourth Gospel is fairly easily discerned. The Prologue (1:1-18) obviously stands apart as an overture or prelude, providing the reader with essential information concerning Jesus' origin and status. Within the main body of the gospel, there is a clear break between the end of chapter 12 and the beginning of chapter 13. At this point Jesus' public revelation of the divine "glory" to the world, specifically to "his own" people, Israel, comes to an end (cf. 1:11), as the "Hour" of his "glorification" arrives. From here on "his own" (13:1) refers to the intimate band of disciples, whom he instructs at length (chapters 13–17) for their future life and mission in the world, following his departure to the Father. This departure is accomplished through Jesus' arrest, trial, and crucifixion (chapters 18–19), which paradoxically represent both divine victory over the world and the supreme revelation ("glorification") of God as love. In his risen life (chapters 20–21) Jesus empowers his disciples for their mission to the world in continuance of the mission that he had received from the Father (cf. 20:21-23; 21:15-19). (I have already indicated my reluctance to separate chapter 21 as an epilogue to the main body of the gospel.) In the outline of the Structure of the Gospel below I have given this second great division the unwieldy title: "The 'Hour' of Jesus' Glorification: the Disciples Empowered to take up his Mission." These two aspects are so entwined together in the continuous account of the Last Supper, passion, and risen life of Jesus as to rule out separation.

Much of the activity of Jesus in his public ministry (2:12–12:50) takes place explicitly in the context of several major feasts of the Jews: Passover (1): 2:13-25; the Sabbath: 5:1-47; Passover (2): 6:1-71 (cf. 6:4); Tabernacles: 7:1–10:21; Dedication: 10:22-39; Passover (3): 11:55–19:42. The prominence of Passover—located at the beginning, middle, and end—is clear, imprinting an overall "Passover" framework upon the whole. This goes along with John the Baptist's indication of Jesus as Passover Lamb at the very beginning (1:29, 36) and the similar associations of his death upon the cross at the end (19:36-37). Setting much of Jesus' ministry in the context of the Jewish feasts allows the evangelist to make rich christological use of imagery proper to each feast (e.g., "light" in the context of Tabernacles) and also to suggest to the community that in his Person they have everything and more that celebration of the feasts provided for Judaism.

Without trying to press everything into a rigid and overly systematic structure, we can set it all out as follows:

The Prologue: 1:1-18

JESUS REVEALS HIS GLORY TO THE WORLD (ISRAEL): 1:19–12:50
   John's Witness to Jesus: 1:19-51
   Cana to Cana: The Early Signs and Conversations of Jesus: 2:1–4:54
      Jesus' Reveals His Glory at a Wedding: 2:1-12
      Where God Dwells: Jesus at the Temple: 2:13-22
      Summary: Response to Jesus in Jerusalem: 2:23-25
      Jesus' Conversation with Nicodemus: 3:1-21
      John the Baptist's Last Witness: 3:22-36
      Jesus and the Woman of Samaria: 4:1-42
      Jesus Heals the Son of a Royal Official: 4:43-54
   Like the Father, the Son Must Give Life: 5:1-47
      Sabbath Healing of the Paralyzed Man at the Pool: 5:1-18
      Discourse A: Jesus: Life-giver and Judge: 5:19-30
      Discourse B: Jesus' True Testimony and Glory: 5:31-47
   The Bread of Life: 6:1-71
   The Light of the World: 7:1–10:21
      Jesus in Jerusalem at the Feast of Tabernacles (1): 7:1-52
      [Jesus and the Woman Taken in Adultery: 7:53–8:11]
      Jesus in Jerusalem at the Feast of Tabernacles (2): 8:12-59
      The Light of the World Heals the Man Born Blind: 9:1-41
      The Good Shepherd: 10:1-21
   Dedication: Jesus, Consecrated and Sent into the World: 10:22-42
      Contest at the Feast of Dedication: 10:22-39
      Jesus Withdraws across the Jordan: 10:40-42
   The Gathering Conflict: 11:1–12:11
      The Raising of Lazarus: 11:1-46
      Plot of the Sanhedrin against Jesus: 11:47-54

Read Me First

Any attempt to find meaning in a biblical text requires some degree of readiness to enter imaginatively into the world from which it originates and the worldview that it presupposes. To prepare the way for a fruitful reading of the text I propose to address characteristic features of the Fourth Gospel under two headings:

- Features that are likely to cause difficulty for contemporary readers;
- Literary features or devices that play a central role in the developing drama of the narrative.

In addition, readers will find at the end of the commentary a glossary of distinctive Johannine words and phrases to supplement what is offered here.

Difficult Features of the Fourth Gospel

Repetitions, Inconsistencies, Lack of Direction

There are a few sequences in the Fourth Gospel that are outstanding dramatic narratives by any standard. The perfectly proportioned drama of the man born blind in chapter 9 and Jesus' dialogue with the Samaritan woman in chapter 4 come readily to mind—perhaps too the sequence leading up to the raising of Lazarus in chapter 11 and the skillfully arranged trial before Pilate as the centerpiece of the passion. There are others that seem to go nowhere, like the conversation with Nicodemus in chapter 3, while the healing of the paralyzed man at the pool in chapter 5 degenerates into a sharp exchange between Jesus and the authorities in Jerusalem. The dialogues in chapters 7 and 8 soon become polemical monologues—with Jesus reacting rather than responding to the questions and difficulties raised. The discourse at the Last Supper comes to a close at the end of chapter 14, only to resume immediately in a way that repeats and in some respects contradicts what has been said earlier (cf. 16:5 with 13:36 and 14:5). Likewise we seem to have two juxtaposed versions of the "Bread of Life" discourse in chapter 6.

In this we have to reckon with the fact that the evangelist, as an ancient author, did not feel constrained to harmonize material received from the tradition but, on the contrary, thought it right to let different "voices" stand and have their say. Likewise, the fact that Jesus is more or less on trial from the beginning of the narrative means that he is depicted at many points as countering accusations that in the Synoptic accounts are reserved for a more formal process before the Jewish authorities at the end of his life. In this the gospel is reflecting and attempting to address the painful experience of its original readers as well as that of Jesus. As readers and interpreters we have to recognize and bear patiently with these features stemming from the gospel's original aim and context.

Dualism

More so than perhaps any other New Testament document the Fourth Gospel displays a sharply dualistic divide between the community of believers and the outside "world" (*kosmos*). This comes to a head in the second half of chapter 15, where Jesus' sublime instruction to the disciples about abiding in his love, the fruit of which will be their love for one another, gives way to warning about the hatred and persecution to be expected from the world. It is important to recognize that the gospel uses "world" in a variety of meanings even if the predominant sense is the negative one of depicting that part of humanity that has definitively said "No" to the saving mission of the Son and has responded with unbelief and hatred (15:18-19; 17:14). Aside from those locked into that decision in the most negative sense, the "world" denotes the human world, created by God to share the divine eternal life but factually fallen into the grip of forces alien to God, which is why it needs to be saved (3:16; 17:6, 11, 17). This is the world that God loved so much as to give the only Son that it might not perish but find life through him (3:16), the world that God continues to love and to which Jesus sends the disciples in continuation of the life-giving mission he himself has received from the Father (15:16; 17:20; 20:21-23). When encountering the more dualistic statements in the gospel, it is important to keep in mind this overarching sense of the Father's love for the world and the entire "missionary" impulse of the gospel stemming from it.[1]

---

[1] On Johannine dualism, see Robert Kysar, *John: The Maverick Gospel*, 3rd ed. (Louisville, KY: Westminster John Knox, 2007), 71–80; on dealing with it in contemporary interpretation,

Portrayal of Jews and Judaism

Perhaps the most regrettable aspect of the Fourth Gospel is the fact that the chief representatives of the "world" in the most severely hostile sense are the Jewish authorities. In a sense this was inevitable: if the divine Son was to become incarnate, this could not come about save in a particular time and ethnic context—and in the divine economy of salvation that context was the Jewish world of the early first century CE. What accentuates the difficulty in the case of the Fourth Gospel is its regular designation of the authorities hostile to Jesus as "the Jews"—as though he could be extradited from and set over against his own people. The tragic consequences for the Jewish people of this separation and depiction down the ages need no elaboration. Responsible reading, interpretation, and proclamation of the Fourth Gospel today must be acutely sensitive to its potentiality for anti-Jewish or anti-Semitic interpretation and recognize that the phrase "the Jews" regularly indicates the hostile authorities and rarely—and then in a neutral (e.g., 12:11) or even positive sense (e.g., 4:22)—the nation as a whole.[2]

Christology

Jesus is predominantly a heavenly figure in the Fourth Gospel. His humanity, to be sure, is not in doubt: he is tired and thirsty (4:6-7; cf. 19:28); he weeps (11:35); he becomes troubled and distressed (13:21); even upon his risen body he bears the marks of the nails and the spear (20:27). But essentially he enters the world from a "before" with God (1:1-2; 17:5, 24) and to that "glory" he is destined to return (16:28; 17:13). This presentation of Jesus—omniscient, in control, constantly in communion with the Father— stands somewhat at odds with Christology in vogue in recent decades which has been at pains to recapture the humanity of Jesus after centuries in which, while not denied, it has been overshadowed by emphasis upon the divine. That John's Gospel is somewhat out of sync with this tendency cannot be denied. At the same time, we can recognize the immense theological significance of its "high" Christology precisely in the context of its explicit stress from the very start (1:14) upon incarnation. The God whose essence is revealed when Jesus washes the feet of his disciples—God at our feet—is equally the God revealed when Jesus dies the most shameful death imaginable upon

---

see David Rensberger, *Johannine Faith and Liberating Community* (Philadelphia: Westminster, 1988), 135–54.

[2] See further, Andrew T. Lincoln, *St. John*, 70–81; Raymond E. Brown, *Introduction*, 157–72; Terence L. Donaldson, *Jews and Anti-Judaism in the New Testament* (Waco, TX: Baylor University Press, 2010), 81–108.

the cross. The key question here is not so much, "How can this man Jesus be God?" but "Who must God be if this man Jesus, in his actions and words, is God's revelation?" That is the question that must accompany any journey through the narrative.

Predestination

In not a few passages of the Fourth Gospel we encounter a tension between statements suggesting that no one can come to Jesus unless drawn by the Father (6:37, 44, 65) and the much more prevalent tendency to insist upon full human responsibility (e.g, 3:19-21). Likewise, failure to respond in faith is attributed to not belonging to the "flock" that the Father has given Jesus (10:26-29) or—quoting Isaiah 6:9-10—to a divine "blinding" or "hardening" rendering belief impossible (12:39-40). This tension between divine choice and action, on the one hand, and human responsibility, on the other, was something that biblical writers were far more at ease with than we are today. They tended to have recourse to statements of a predestinatory character when grappling with the phenomenon of unbelief, especially—and most poignantly—the failure on the part of the bulk of the Jewish people to believe in the One sent by God as Messiah. Without canceling human responsibility, attributing such failure to divine action was a way of seeing it enclosed within a wider divine plan of salvation and hence not necessarily foreclosed to a more positive final outcome. It is all ultimately a way of saying that, despite and indeed through human failure, God and God's grace will have the last word.[3]

Argument and Logic

Not infrequently the Fourth Gospel presents sequences where the order of statements seems to run in reverse order to the logic (e.g., 1:16-17; 1:30-34; 13:13-16), or where a premise seems to be missing or has to be supplied (3:25-26; 6:43-50; 10:34-38), or where cause and effect are wantonly exchanged (cf. 14:21-24 with 14:15). Notoriously in this gospel Jesus gives answers that seem to bear no relationship to the questions being asked or else dismisses them altogether (3:4-8; 4:12-14; 6:25-26; 10:24-25; 14:22-23). In a sense we are dealing here with a form of discourse happy to associate

---

[3] See further, Rudolph Schnackenburg, *The Gospel According to St. John*, 3 vols. (New York: Crossroad, 1968–82), 2:259–74 ("Excursus II: Personal Commitment, Personal Responsibility, Predestination and Hardening"); Robert Kysar, *Maverick Gospel*, 84–88.

ideas without too strict a regard for niceties of logic (e.g., 10:47). From another angle, we have to recognize that often the narrative allows questions, issues, and concerns that are those of the later community rather than of Jesus' original audience to intrude into the drama of the narrative—or else it presupposes knowledge that, at our distance from the time of composition, we simply do not have today.

Eschatology

The most glaring example of the Fourth Gospel's capacity to hold together seemingly inconsistent ideas arises in the area of eschatology, that is, hope or speculation about what is to happen at the "end-time," the final act in the cosmic drama of God's dealing with the world. In places the Fourth Gospel asserts the "futurist" eschatology characteristic of many strands of Judaism at the time: belief in a definitive "day" in which God, through the Son, will institute a final judgment of the world, which will involve a general resurrection of the dead, the good rising to (eternal) life, the evil to condemnation: 5:25-29; 6:39-40, 44, 54; 11:24; 12:48. Other passages, often in close association with these just mentioned, feature the "realized" eschatology that is particularly characteristic of the Fourth Gospel. Here the key "events" of the "end"—judgment, resurrection, (eternal) life—are brought forward, so to speak, so as to become present realities in the lives of believers: 3:18-19; 5:24; 11:25-26. A fresh species of the future eschatology appears at 14:2-3 in the sense of a heavenly dwelling place awaiting believers to which, after their death, Christ will come and fetch them. The evangelist is content to leave these various strains of eschatology jostling and indeed entwined with each other (e.g., 5:25: "the hour is coming and is now here"), allowing each one to have its say.[4]

Literary Devices Characteristic of the Fourth Gospel

Irony

The Fourth Gospel can exploit the simple ambiguity present in several key terms and expressions, for example, the Greek word *menein*, which can mean both "dwell" (1:38) and "remain" (1:39), or *anōthen*, which can mean both "again" and "from above" (3:3, 7). Irony takes ambiguity a step further

---

[4] See further, Robert Kysar, *Maverick Gospel*, 118–26; Raymond E. Brown, *Introduction*, 234–48.

in the sense that readers, possessed of privileged knowledge already communicated to them (especially through the Prologue [1:1-18] in the case of the Fourth Gospel), become conscious that characters are saying or doing something that has a meaning beyond that of which they are aware, a meaning that is in fact at odds with their explicit intention. The classic example in the Fourth Gospel occurs when the High Priest Caiaphas advises the council, "It is better for one man to die for the people than to have the whole nation destroyed" (11:50), unaware that he is in fact spelling out the meaning of Jesus' life-giving death. In this case the evangelist explicitly draws the attention of the reader to the irony being expressed (11:51). More frequently, however, irony is something that readers have to be alert to as they pursue the narrative of the gospel, for example, Nathaniel's prejudiced retort: "Can anything good come out of Nazareth?" (1:46). "Yes, indeed!" we readers say to ourselves, having read the Prologue. Irony, then, is a device whereby the narrator makes readers informed "insiders" in their observation of the unfolding story. It is a "wink" in the direction of the reader.[5]

Misunderstanding

Closely associated with irony is the Fourth Gospel's use of misunderstanding. This usually occurs when Jesus makes a statement that is ambiguous or open to a metaphorical meaning, and a character latches on to the simple or literal meaning or goes off on a tangent of thought away from the more profound meaning that Jesus is attempting to communicate. A classic instance in the gospel occurs when the Samaritan woman is perplexed by Jesus' offer to provide her with "living water" (4:10) because, as she points out (v. 11), he has no bucket and the well is deep. She does then go on to ask whether he is "greater than our father Jacob" (v. 12), presumably implying the answer "No," whereas we readers, discerning the irony, will again answer to ourselves, "Yes, indeed!" (cf. 1:50-51). The evangelist uses misunderstanding as a kind of fork in the road to point the reader away from simplistic or prejudiced understandings and in the direction of the more mysterious and profound revelation that Jesus communicates to those of adequate faith.[6]

---

[5] See further, R. Alan Culpepper, *Anatomy of the Fourth Gospel* (Philadelphia: Fortress, 1983), 165–80.

[6] Ibid., 152–65.

Symbolism

This feature of the Fourth Gospel is again closely connected with the preceding one in the sense that instances of misunderstanding Jesus' words or actions frequently arise out of a failure to perceive that in referring to everyday things such as water or bread, for example, Jesus is actually speaking of more transcendental realities (for example, the Spirit; himself as come down from heaven like the manna) of which such things are signs or symbols to those who perceive them with faith. The long narratives or discourses attached to many of the miracles in the gospel (5:1-47; 6:1-71; 9:1-41; 11:1-44) are designed to draw out this deeper, symbolic meaning and so lead the reader to appreciate the miracles not simply as miraculous remedies of various human needs but as signs disclosing this deeper meaning, the revelation from heaven that Jesus brings.[7] Other sequences, while not proceeding from a miracle but having a point of departure that is puzzling or seeming to require a miracle, are equally designed to "unpack" a symbolic meaning for the benefit of those with whom Jesus is in conversation (2:13-22; 3:1-15; 4:7-42). The Fourth Gospel makes copious use of symbolic language and technique because it is the only language adequate to convey the revelation from the heavenly world that Jesus, who belongs primarily to that world, has come into our world to convey (3:31; 17:16). It is a revelation that the Paraclete Spirit will continue to impart to the disciples following Jesus' return to the Father.[8] Johannine symbolism whereby the ordinary and everyday is made a symbol of the divine is essentially bound up with the fundamentally incarnational and sacramental theology of the Gospel.[9]

---

[7] See esp., Dorothy A. Lee, *The Symbolic Narratives of the Fourth Gospel: The Interplay of Form and Meaning*, Journal for the Study of the New Testament, Supplement Series 95 (Sheffield, UK: JSOT Press, 1994), 14–20.

[8] Cf. Raymond E. Brown, *Introduction*, 289.

[9] In this sense "flesh" (*sarx*) is the fundamental symbol of the gospel; cf. Dorothy A Lee, *Symbolic Narratives*, 48–50.

The Prologue: 1:1-18

The majestic, hymnlike Prologue standing at the beginning of the Fourth Gospel functions like the overture to a classical opera. It airs several of the themes that will be prominent in the drama that is about to unfold. Above all, it informs us about the true status of the gospel's central character, Jesus of Nazareth. Truly human, he is at the same time the incarnate Son of God, sent into the world to bring human beings to the fullness of life.

For all its theological richness and poetic quality, the Prologue presents quite a challenge for most readers. It yields its full riches only when a number of motifs that it is evoking from the biblical (Old Testament) tradition are fully recognized. Moreover, while its basic symmetry is clear, determining its structure in detail is more complex and many analyses are on offer. Particularly difficult to incorporate within a neat pattern are the two clusters of statements about the witness of John the Baptist (vv. 6-8; v. 15), which seem so intrusive and disturbing of the content and poetic structure that otherwise prevails. Likewise intrusive is the prose expansion in vv. 12b-13 in connection with the rebirth of believers as children of God. A progression of thought from creation to incarnation to human response is clear in a general kind of way. But there is dispute about when exactly the motif of incarnation first appears or is at least presupposed: certainly at v. 14, but is it there already at v. 9 or even v. 5? The Prologue does not in fact progress in a linear systematic way: it recapitulates major themes as it progresses, while also revolving around a central pivot (v. 12b), as I shall explain.

An integrated sense of the Prologue will, I trust, emerge from a closer examination of the text. In the meantime I propose the following structure as something reasonably well-founded in the text. The Prologue begins (vv. 1-2) and closes (v. 18) with statements about the Word's relationship to God. About a third of the way through (vv. 6-8) and then towards the end (v. 16)

21

there are the statements about John's role as witness. These and other less obvious features lend to the Prologue a chiastic structure: that is, a pattern where the first element corresponds to the last, the second to the second last, and so forth, to construct a framework around a central "hub" where the sequence of thought "crosses over" to proceed in reverse direction. The central hub of the Prologue would be the motif of "rejection/reception" by human beings (vv. 11-13), pivoting around the motif of "power to become children of God" (v. 12b). Remaining elements of the chiasm would be: a correspondence between the content of vv. 3-5 and v. 14 around the idea of benefit brought to human beings by the Word, and a further correspondence between vv. 9-10 and v. 14 around the motif of the Word's incarnation.

We can set it out as seen on the following page.

I would not claim that the author of the Prologue had this precise structure in mind when composing the hymn. Some of the correspondences may seem arbitrary. I propose the structure as a means of coming to grips with a complex text and, in particular, of highlighting what appears to be a central concern: the bestowal of the privilege of being "children of God" upon those who respond positively to the Word (believers) (vv. 12a).[1] In a major "inclusion" spanning the gospel (John 1-20) this privilege returns when the risen Lord says to Mary Magdalene, "Go tell my brothers (and sisters) that I am ascending to my Father and your Father, to my God and your God" (20:17; cf. 11:52). The privilege is nothing less than that of believers having a share in the eternal relationship between Father and Son (Word) with which the Prologue begins (vv. 1-2) and ends (v. 18). The Prologue "pivots" around the sense of this divine gift.

"In the beginning . . .": The Word with God: 1:1-2

It is hard to overestimate the significance of the opening phrase of the gospel. "In the beginning" (*en archēi* [1:1]) echoes the first words of the creation story with which the Book of Genesis and indeed the entire Bible begins. "In the beginning," we are told (Gen 1:2), the earth was a formless void and darkness covered the face of the deep. God creates the world and all living beings by speaking over and over a creative word: "Let there be."[2]

---

[1] Several other reconstructions are on offer. What I propose here is a simplified version of the analysis presented by R. Alan Culpepper in a well-accepted study, "The Pivot of John's Prologue," *New Testament Studies* 27 (1980–81): 1–31.

[2] The English phrase, "Let there be," translates a single word in the Hebrew (*yĕhî*) and LXX Greek (*genethētō*) of Genesis 1.

1. In the beginning was the Word; and the Word was with God and the Word was God. 2. This was in the beginning with God.	**A.** Word and God

3. Through him all things came to be, and apart from him there came to be not a single thing of all that has come to be. 4. In him was life and this life was the light of human beings. 5. And the light shines on in the darkness and the darkness has not overcome it.	**B.** Benefit from Word

6. There came a man sent by God whose name was John. 7. This one came as a witness to the light, so that through him all people might come to believe. 8. He was not the light—(he came) only to bear witness to the light.	**C.** John, the Witness

9. The true light that enlightens every person was coming into the world.	**D.** Incarnation

10. He was in the world and the world was made through him, and yet the world did not know him. 11. He came unto his own but his own people did not accept him. 12. But all those who did accept him—he gave them the power to become children of God, those, that is, who believed in his name, 13. who were born not of blood, nor of the desire of the flesh, nor of the will of man, but of God	**X.** (Pivot) Rejection/ Reception Result: Divine Filiation

14. And the Word became flesh and pitched his tent among us, and we have seen his glory, glory as of the only son of a father, the fullness of grace and truth.	**D.** Incarnation

15. John bore witness to him and cried out, saying, "This is he of whom I spoke, 'The one who comes after me ranks before me because he existed before me.'"	**C.** John, the Witness

16. Because from his fullness we have all received, grace in place of grace. 17. For while the law was given through Moses, this grace and truth came about through Jesus Christ.	**B.** Benefit from Word

18. No one has ever seen God. It is God, the only Son, who is in the bosom of the Father, who has revealed him.	**A'.** Word and God

The very first act of creation is the conquest of the prevailing darkness by God's word: "Let there be light" (Gen 1:3). What the Fourth Gospel does, here at its very beginning, is to personify this creative word of God—to let emerge, as the Prologue unfolds, that the creative word God spoke and continues to speak is God's eternal Son who took flesh in the person of Jesus of Nazareth, Messiah of Israel. To put it the other way around, the gospel presents Jesus Christ as God's creative Word. From this identification established in the Prologue, wherever Jesus speaks or acts in the story told in the gospel we are to understand that it is God saying, "Let there be": "Let there be life," "Let there be light," a Light that conquers the darkness. In other words, the Fourth Gospel is reclaiming the original account of creation told in Genesis for its story of Jesus. It is not so much putting him "back there," so to speak, as saying, "What is told as something that happened back there is here coming true for the first time." Creation is now. It is God's reaching out to human beings in the Person of the Son to draw them out of the darkness into life-giving light.

All this is suggested by the gospel's evocative opening phrase, "In the beginning." We have, however, got a little ahead of the actual wording of the text. Before speaking of creation, the Prologue tells of the Word's existence with God in eternity before the world was made: the Word was "with God" (v. 1b; cf. 17:5) and "the Word was God (v. 1c). The first phrase (*pros ton theon*) has the sense not only of being "with" God but also of being "turned toward" God in relationship, a note that returns in v. 18.[3] The second, which is more literally translated "What God was the Word was," asserts the Word's divine status. It wards off simple identification between the Word and God while retaining a sense of the oneness that flows from their intimacy (cf. v. 18).[4]

A concluding line, "This was in the beginning with God" (v. 2; cf. v. 1a), seals off this sense of the Word's existence in divine eternity prior to and independent of the created world. The enclosure of the divine in the heavenly realm prepares the way for the enormity of the incarnation soon to be proclaimed. As readers of the gospel, we know from this point on that the human person who will be identified as "the Word" is also One who has entered the world from a divine "before" where he has enjoyed eternal life with God. We shall see those who encounter him during his human life wrestle with

[3] Cf. Francis J. Moloney, *The Gospel of John*, Sacra Pagina 4 (Collegeville, MN: Liturgical Press, 1998), 35.

[4] Cf. C. K. Barrett, *The Gospel According to St. John*, 2nd ed. (London: SPCK, 1978), 155–56; Francis J. Moloney, *John*, 35.

the entwined mysteries of his origin, status, and destiny. Not until the hitherto doubting Thomas confesses the risen Jesus as "My Lord and my God" (20:28) shall we see his divine status acknowledged as fully and as simply as here.[5]

Creation: The Word of Life and Light: 1:3-5

From eternal existence with God, the Prologue moves to speak of the Word's agency in creation—first, more generally, in regard to creation ("all things") as a whole (v. 3)[6] and then in the specific sense of communicating life (*zōē*) to human beings (vv. 4-5).

What is this continued gift of life—especially in view of the fact that the Prologue goes on to describe it as "the light (*phōs*) of human beings" (1:4b)? We must think of "life" here as something going beyond the mere existence common to all created things. It is the "more abundant" life about which Jesus speaks later when he claims: "I have come that they may have life and have it in abundance" (10:10b). This enhanced life is in effect the very life of God communicated to human beings. To have it is to share here and now, as well as across the barrier of death, God's "eternal life."[7]

In describing this life as "the light of human beings" (v. 4b) the Prologue continues to evoke the creation story (Gen 1:3-5), portraying the gift of life as a renewed conquest of the darkness. It prepares the way for seeing the public life of Jesus as a sustained ministry of the Word bringing light where darkness has hitherto prevailed. The gospel will describe Jesus simply as "the Light" (1:8-9) or "the Light of the world" (8:5; 9:5) and portray the opposition that he is destined to encounter as "Darkness."

---

[5] John 1–20 is thus "framed" inclusively by these acknowledgments of Jesus as "God" at beginning and end.

[6] Contrary to the NRSV (but with the NIV; C. K. Barrett, *John*, 156–57; Rudolf Schnackenburg, *St. John*, 1:239–40; Gail O'Day, "The Gospel of John," 520; Andrew T. Lincoln, *St. John*, 92), I take the final phrase of v. 3, *ho gegonen*, with what precedes rather than with what follows (as Raymond E. Brown, *John I–XII*, 6; Francis J. Moloney, *John*, 42–43), so as to read: "Through him all things came to be, and apart from him there came to be not a single thing of all that has come to be." The convoluted couplet expresses the absolute exclusivity of the Word's agency in creation.

[7] The phrase "eternal life" appears seventeen times in the Fourth Gospel: 3:15, 16, 36; 4:14, 36; 5:24, 39; 6:27, 40, 47, 54, 68; 10:28; 12:25, 50; 17:2, 3; and six times in the First Letter of John: 1 John 1:2; 2:25; 3:15; 5:11, 13, 20. Usually, however, when the gospel refers simply to "life" (or in verbal form, "live") without qualification, it has this enhanced sense of life in view, e.g., 11:25-26.

Jesus comes to invite people to be drawn to this new source of life. But, again and again, the gospel will show people preferring to remain in the darkness because "coming to the light" means conversion, having their lives exposed to the searching—though ultimately saving—light and truth of God (3:18-21).

In the end the powers of darkness will prevail and seemingly extinguish the Light by putting Jesus to death. His resurrection and ascension to the Father, however, will disclose a different outcome. The darkness of unbelief and hostility to God will not have prevailed. As in the original creation, the light will shine on. Beyond the ministry of Jesus, it will continue to shine, unextinguished, in the life and mission of the church. Despite the continuing prevalence of "darkness" in so many aspects of human life, the fundamental and continuing victory of light over darkness has not been and will not be reversed (v. 5b).[8]

With this expression of hope, the Prologue introduces the "light" and "darkness" imagery that will feature so prominently in the gospel. As we have seen, that imagery represents the appropriation by the evangelist of the creation story told in Genesis 1–2. The divine work of creation is not over and done at the beginning of time. It came to a head in the person and ministry of Jesus Christ. It continues through the proclamation and living out of the Gospel today.

John's Witness to the Light: 1:6-8

At this point we encounter the first of the Prologue's two references to John (not called "the Baptist" in the Fourth Gospel) (v. 6; cf. v. 15). Intrusive as it seems at first sight, the indication of John's appearance as a "man sent from God" serves to focus the divine intervention upon a particular time and context. Though wholly within the confines of the human, John is "sent from God" as the vanguard of the divine invasion into the darkness. He is not himself "the Light." His role in this gospel is solely to bear witness to the Light, to point to and disclose the presence of the divine Light there where human beings will not expect to find it: in the human person ("flesh") of Jesus

---

[8] This interpretation attempts to catch the precise sense of the Greek verbs in v. 5: the present tense of *phainei* ("shine on") in the case of the light; the aorist sense of *ou katelaben* ("has not overcome") in the case of the darkness, with primary reference to the death and resurrection of Jesus. An alternative interpretation of *katelaben* as "master"/"comprehend" in the sense of "grasp intellectually" is possible but does not suit the hostile sense of "darkness" in the present context. See further, Raymond E. Brown, *John I–XII*, 8.

(1:29-36). The scope of the witness is universal: the purpose is "that all may believe" (v. 7c). But John's personal ministry will be confined to Israel. And in this context, introducing a motif that will run throughout the gospel, "witness" introduces a legal or forensic tinge. From virtually the beginning of his ministry Jesus will be on trial before the leadership of his people, and John will be a key witness in his cause (5:33; cf. 10:41).[9]

The Coming of the Light into the World (Incarnation 1): 1:9

Reference to John has brought the whole perspective "down" from the heights of the Word's eternal existence with God to a concrete moment of human history. The Prologue now points to the Light's presence in the world as a process already under way: "The true Light that enlightens every person was coming into the world" (v. 9).[10] "World" (*kosmos*) refers not to the entirety of creation but to the human world in general. While the term at this point may not carry the negative overtones of hostility to God that for the most part attach to it in the Fourth Gospel, the fact that every person needs to be "enlightened" by the Light suggests that, apart from and prior to that enlightenment, the human world sits in darkness. The Light is not coming into neutral terrain, "no man's land," so to speak. In extension of the divine act of creation, the Light is coming to conquer the darkness and draw all human beings into the light and "more abundant" life that is the life of God.

The Word in the World: Human Response: 1:10-13

Now, at the center of the Prologue, we move from the divine to the human pole. The sense of the Word's mission to "enlighten" all human beings (v. 9b) leads naturally to consideration of human response—first negative (vv. 10-11), then positive (vv. 12-13)—to the coming of the Light.

---

[9] Cf. especially, Andrew T. Lincoln, *St. John*, 100, 450. In the Johannine passion narrative, in contrast to the Synoptic accounts, the trial of Jesus before the Sanhedrin is not a trial properly so called but a simple arraignment before the high priest. The Fourth Gospel "retrojects" the Jewish trial, with its panoply of accusation and counteraccusation, back into the ministry of Jesus, portraying him as "on trial" throughout.

[10] This sense of process is conveyed in the Greek by the periphrastic formulation "*ēn . . . erchomenon*," which in turn rests upon taking the participle *erchomenon* ("coming") as a neuter nominative referring to the "Light" rather than as a masculine accusative qualifying "every person" (*pan anthrōpon*), as in several traditional translations (e.g., Vulgate, KJV, Douay-Rheims); see C. K. Barrett, *John*, 160–61.

The note of hostility or rejection, first struck in reference to the "darkness" (v. 5), sounds again (v. 10) as the Prologue underlines a supreme irony. The Word[11] was in the world, a world that had come into being through him (v. 3)—and yet, by and large, that world has chosen not to "know" him. "Know" here has the biblical sense that goes beyond mere recognition to involve a relationship of intimacy and love.[12] "World" (*kosmos*) appears in this verse in two senses: first, in a neutral sense as before (v. 9) where the reference is to the human world brought into being to share such relationship with God; second, in the more pejorative sense where it denotes the same human world under the aspect of having rejected the divine overture of love and so existing in a state of alienation from God.[13] How human beings got into this situation the Fourth Gospel does not explain.[14] But it seems that what is in view is a long-standing pattern of human rejection of God, of which the world's rejection of Jesus would be simply the culmination.

The focus on rejection becomes more specific with the statement that the Word came "to his own domain" (*eis ta idia*) but "his own" (*hoi idioi*) did not receive him" (v. 11). Because of the Word's agency in creation (v. 3; v. 10) the entire world could well be described as "his own domain." However, in the second more personal formulation, "his own" must refer to Israel, a people frequently described in the biblical tradition as the Lord's "possession" (e.g. Exod 19:5; Deut 4:20; 9:26; 14:2; Ps 135:4; Mic 7:18). Israel was "his own" in the sense of being a people chosen out from all other peoples on the face of the earth to be the "laboratory" or "beachhead," as it were, of God's design to draw human beings into "more abundant" life. Contrary to all expectation, "his own" in this sense "did not receive him."

Foreshadowed here is the tragic development whereby, as the ministry of Jesus unfolds, "the Jews" (primarily the Jewish leadership) in their rejection of Jesus their Messiah function as the representatives of the world's rejection of God.[15] By the time Jesus' unsuccessful appeal to his own people concludes at the end of John 12, "his own" will have acquired a new meaning. From this point on the phrase will refer to the intimate band of disciples

---

[11] The subject of the sentences here has shifted from "Light" (vv. 5-9) back to "the Word" (reflected in the Greek in the change from neuter pronouns and adjectives to masculine)—though of course the identity of the subject remains the same.

[12] Cf. C. K. Barrett, *John*, 162.

[13] Cf. Andrew T. Lincoln, *St. John*, 102.

[14] The existence of the human world in this alienated situation prior to the redemptive mission of Christ, later elaborated in the Christian doctrine of Original Sin, is a presupposition of Johannine theology—as also of Pauline theology (cf. 2 Cor 5:18-21; Rom 3:23; 5:12).

[15] Cf. Andrew T. Lincoln, *St. John*, 102.

and the community of believers into which they will evolve (13:1; cf. 10:3, 4, 12; 19:27).

It is to these that the Prologue turns (vv. 12-13), to take up, by contrast, positive response to the Word. In the biblical and postbiblical tradition a unique privilege of Israelites was that of being known as "children (or sons [and daughters]) of God" (Exod 4:22-23; Deut 14:1-2; 32:5-6; Hos 1:10; 11:1; etc.; cf. Rom 9:4).[16] In the face of Israel's failure to receive the Word, the Prologue—at its very center or "pivot" (v. 12a)—presents this privilege as the key benefit bestowed upon all who "believe in his name," who believe, that is, in the person of Jesus and in the revelation of God that he brings.[17] Without regard to race or nation or status, those who come to faith in this way receive from him the capacity to become children of God (*tekna theou*), along with the intimacy with God that such status entails.

Whereas Israelites enjoyed this privilege simply on the basis of natural birth and ethnic origin, believers acquire it through a mysterious process of birth that will later form the subject of a conversation between Jesus and the Jewish teacher Nicodemus (3:1-10). At some length, though with considerable rhetorical effect, the Prologue excludes (v. 13) three purely natural explanations of birth, before climactically stating the positive truth. Believers are not born "from blood" (v. 13a), that is, through the natural process of conception as understood in the ancient world,[18] nor in a birth instigated through human sexual desire (literally, "the will of the flesh"), nor through "the will of man" in the sense of fulfilling the patriarchal male will to continue the family line.[19] On the contrary, beyond and above all human capacity, they are "begotten by God" (*ek theou egennēthēsan*). Through this divine begetting—to be understood metaphorically, of course, rather than literally—they acquire the status of "children of God," with the intimacy and share in the divine life ("eternal life") that such status implies (cf. 11:52; 20:17; 1 John 3:1-2, 9; 4:7; 5:2-4).

The actual phrase "children of God" occurs only twice in the Fourth Gospel (here and in 11:52). However, its position at the "pivot" of the Prologue, along with the later discussion of being "born from above/born again"

---

[16] I set out the evidence for this motif extensively in Brendan Byrne, *'Sons of God'—'Seed of Abraham': A Study of the Idea of the Sonship of God of All Christians in Paul against the Jewish Background*, Analecta Biblica 83 (Rome: Biblical Institute Press, 1979), 9–78.

[17] Cf. Andrew T. Lincoln, *St. John*, 103.

[18] Lit., "of bloods" (plural). Procreation was understood to come about through the male sperm, seen as derived from blood, mixing with female blood to form the fetus; cf. Andrew T. Lincoln, *St. John*, 103.

[19] Ibid.

between Jesus and Nicodemus (3:1-10), and above all the instruction of the risen Jesus to Mary Magdalene toward the end of the gospel ("Go, tell my brothers [and sisters] that I am ascending to my Father and your Father" [20:17]), signal its centrality in the mind of the evangelist. The bestowal of this status upon human beings—more specifically upon believers—is the chief consequence of the victory achieved by Jesus on the cross. Beyond the gospel itself the First Letter of John makes even more play of this distinctive privilege in which believers share the life and future of God:

> See what love the Father has given us, that we should be called children of God; and that is what we are. . . . Beloved, we are God's children now; what we will be has not yet been revealed. What we do know is this: when he is revealed, we will be like him, for we will see him as he is. (1 John 3:1-2; cf. 4:7; 5:2)[20]

In the gospel as also in 1 John the goal of the mission of the Son is to draw human beings out of the darkness of alienation from God into this familial relationship with its promise of enjoying forever the fullness of life with God.

The Word Became Flesh: 1:14

The unambiguous statement of the incarnation of the Word is the Prologue's most familiar and significant assertion. It heads a long and rich sentence (v. 14) that merits quotation in full:

> And the Word became flesh and pitched his tent among us,
> and we have seen his glory,
> the glory as of a father's only son,
> full of grace and truth.

First, we should note the change into the first person plural ("pitched his tent among us" . . . "we have seen"). The recital of the Prologue has moved from description into testimony, the testimony of a community speaking out of its experience, which it wants to share.

Accustomed as we are to the statement, "The Word became flesh" (v. 14a) we can miss the sharpness of the paradox it represents. "Flesh" (*sarx*) in John's Gospel retains the biblical sense denoting human existence in its fragility, transience, and mortality in contrast to all that is spiritual and di-

---

[20] On "children of God" in 1 John, see Raymond E. Brown, *The Epistles of John*, Anchor Bible 30 (New York: Doubleday, 1982), 388–91.

vine.[21] It is one thing for the Word to be "in the world" in some undefined way (v. 10). It is quite something else—especially after the stress upon the divine origin of the Word in vv. 1-2—for the Word to be in the world in the full sense of identity with the human connoted by "The Word became flesh." In a gospel that otherwise tends to portray Jesus as unambiguously divine, the statement safeguards the incarnation by firmly nailing down the truth of his humanity from the start. It also establishes the essential sacramentality that runs through the gospel: the revelation of the divine, not aside from or through the humanity of Jesus, but precisely *in* the humanity, not excluding but in fact culminating in his death upon the cross.[22]

Having become "flesh," the Word "pitched his tent among us" (v. 14b). "Pitched his tent" is a very literal translation of the Greek verb *eskēnōsen* (*skēnē* being the Greek noun for "tent"). More commonly the meaning is simply "dwell." The literal sense is justified here because the Prologue at this point is evoking the biblical motif of God's dwelling among the people of Israel. This divine dwelling began during the forty years of Israel's wandering in the desert of Sinai. It involved the construction of a "tent of meeting" upon which the divine presence would descend in a pillar of cloud (cf. Exod 33:7-11).[23] A remarkable parallel to the Prologue's presentation of the Word appears in a passage of Ben Sirach (Ecclesiasticus). In this passage Wisdom speaks of leaving her abode in the highest heaven to seek a resting place on earth and of then receiving the following instruction from the Creator:

> Then the Creator of all things gave me a command,
> and my Creator chose the place for my tent (*skēnē*).
> He said, "Make your dwelling (*kataskēnōson*) in Jacob,
> and in Israel receive your inheritance." (Sir 24:8)

In view of these associations it is not unreasonable to see the Prologue presenting the Word's becoming flesh as the divine presence coming to share the fragile, "tent-like" existence of humanity in the world.[24]

---

[21] Cf. Rudolf Schnackenburg, *St. John*, 1:267; Dorothy A. Lee, *Flesh and Glory*, 34.

[22] "The *doxa* is not to be seen *alongside* the *sarx*, nor *through* the *sarx* as through a window; it is to be seen in the *sarx* and nowhere else" (Rudolf Bultmann, *Gospel of John*, 63 —though Bultmann may not have been at ease with the description of this as "sacramentality"); cf. also C. K. Barrett, *John*, 165; Dorothy A. Lee, *Flesh and Glory*, 35–36.

[23] Cf. Raymond E. Brown, *John I–XII*, 33–34. In later rabbinic theology this divine presence descending upon and dwelling with Israel would be known as the *shekinah*.

[24] It is quite likely that the Prologue's origins lie in such speculations about Wisdom (*sophia*) in the biblical and postbiblical tradition. The preference for "Word" rather than Wisdom would

The biblical background furnished by Israel's Sinai experience also makes it understandable why, immediately after speaking of the Word's "enfleshed" presence in the world, the Prologue goes on (v. 14b) to record the community's claim "to have seen his glory" (v. 14b). In the biblical tradition "glory" (*doxa*) refers essentially to a visible manifestation of the presence and power of God. While no human beings can look upon God and live, the "glory" of God, in the sense of divine presence and power, can be discerned from the beauty of the created world and from events that show God's hand at work. Human beings "glorify" God when they acknowledge the divine presence in such things. Conversely, God can display "glory" or "glorify" someone or something to make the divine presence known. When Moses completed the tent of meeting (Tabernacle) the cloud came down upon it and it was filled with the glory of the Lord (Exod 40:34); the same phenomenon was repeated at the dedication of the temple by Solomon (1 Kgs 8:10-11). Just prior to the destruction of the temple by the Babylonians, the prophet Ezekiel saw the glory of the Lord depart from the city of Jerusalem (Ezek 11:23); in a vision of the restored temple he saw the same glory return (Ezek 44:4).[25]

These rich scriptural associations lie behind the community's claim to have seen the Word's glory. Whereas once the tabernacle in the desert and later the temple in Jerusalem became the dwelling place of God's glory, in the incarnation of the Word that dwelling place is to be found in the "flesh" or body of Jesus. As will soon be made clear (2:13-22), he—no longer the temple—is the place where God's presence and power are to be found. Jesus will display God's glory—be "transparent" to God in this sense—in the miracles and symbolic actions that he performs (cf. 2:11; 11:5, 40). Above all, he will display God's glory (= "be glorified") when, "lifted up" upon the cross (3:14; 8:28; 12:32, 34), he reveals the very essence of God to be love.

The first of two added phrases (v. 14d), "the glory as of the only son of a father" underlines the accuracy of Jesus' revelation of God.[26] While in a general way it can be said that children transmit the image of their parents, when a man has only one son, that "only son" is the sole image of the father

---

then be explained by the masculine *logos* being more appropriate than the feminine *sophia* for expressing the incarnation of God's Son as a Jewish man; cf. Gail O'Day, "The Gospel of John," 519.

[25] Cf. Raymond E. Brown, *John I–XII*, 34.

[26] While the reference is clearly to Jesus who is the only Son of the Father, it seems best, especially in view of the lack of definite articles in the Greek original, to take the phrase first as a simple image before applying it to Jesus; cf. Andrew T. Lincoln, *St. John*, 105.

before the world. As God's only Son, Jesus in his humanity is the unique revelation of the Father in the world.[27] Later in response to a plea from Philip, "Lord, show us the Father," Jesus will exclaim, "Whoever has seen me has seen the Father" (14:9).

The rich theology of this verse is rounded off with a phrase (v. 14e) that reads literally, "full of grace and truth" (*plērēs charitos kai alētheias*). Behind this phrase lies a sense of contrast with and superiority to the covenant received by Moses at Sinai, a contrast now running strongly in the Prologue. What Moses received was for its time a covenant embodying God's favor (*charis*) and faithfulness (*alētheia*). But what has come about through the incarnation of the Word is such "fullness" of divine favor and faithfulness as to render the earlier dispensation partial and overtaken. Moses had asked to see the divine glory (Exod 33:18) but had been denied. To look upon God's face would have meant death. Hidden in the cleft of the rock, he had to be content with seeing "the back" of God, as the divine glory passed by (Exod 33:21-23). But the Johannine community—and believers of subsequent generations—do see the divine glory in the human flesh of Jesus. In contrast to what was merely provisional and passing, this final revelation embodies the fullness of God's grace and truth.

While "grace" (*charis*) does not appear in the gospel beyond the Prologue (cf. also 1:16, 17), in the final word of the phrase, "truth" (*alētheia*), we meet a term destined to play a significant role in the story. For the present we may simply say that while "truth" in John can simply have the sense more familiar to us of "true," "corresponding to reality," as opposed to "false" or "not corresponding to reality," the Fourth Gospel inherits the biblical sense where "truth" refers to the divine faithfulness to covenant commitment. More distinctive still, "truth" in this gospel has to do with the revelation of the divine essence and faithfulness present in the person of Jesus, the incarnate Son. So in the present context, the incarnate Word is the "fullness of truth" in the sense of being the definitive revelation of God, as distinct from the earlier, partial revelation accorded to Israel.

John's Witness Again: 1:15

A second statement of John's witness seems more intrusive than the first (vv. 6-8) since the content of vv. 16-17 would follow on very naturally from v. 14. It is odd, too, in that John is made to refer to a testimony he is

---

[27] The Greek preposition *para* before "Father," while functioning as a simple genitive can also convey the sense of the Son being sent *from* the Father to image God on earth.

yet to give (cf. 1:30) as something he has already stated or is at least presently giving.[28] But John, who is the first witness to the presence of the Word in the world, actually underlines the reality of the incarnation that has just been proclaimed (v. 14). The One who is coming "after" him in terms of historical human existence ranks "before" him because that One had an existence before him in the eternity of God. John's "crying out" (*krazein*) of this witness will ring through early scenes of the gospel (cf. 1:19-36; 3:28-30).[29]

Jesus Christ: the Fullness of Grace and Truth: 1:16-17

The community continues its own testimony across that of John, picking up the sense of "fullness" from the final phrase of v. 14. The logic, as is often the case in the gospel, is not exactly linear. The revelation and covenant given by God to Moses was indeed a gift of God's grace (cf. v. 17a).[30] But what the community ("we all") has received in the person of the Word is a fullness of grace surpassing and replacing that earlier gift (*kai charin anti charitos*) (v. 16).[31] The superiority is made explicit in a final sentence (v. 17) when at last the protagonists in each case—Moses and Jesus Christ—are named. The law was something given "through Moses": that is, Moses was simply a mediator passing on the gift of the law from a God who remained unseen and unseeable. But the fullness of God's "grace and truth," in the sense of these words explained above, has been embodied (literally, "come about" [*egeneto*]) in the world through the man Jesus Christ. The law was indeed a gift valid for its time; in the course of the gospel it will bear Scripture's witness to Jesus. But it is only in and through his person that the definitive revelation of God has come to the world.

---

[28] Interpreters take this as evidence that the references to John had been added to a preexisting form of the Prologue, cf. Andrew T. Lincoln, *St. John*, 106–7.

[29] The verb, *kekragen*, though formally in the perfect tense, has a present reference; cf. C. K. Barrett, *John*, 167.

[30] "Grace" (Hebrew, *ḥēn*; Greek, *charis*) appears six times across Exod 33:12–34:9, the scriptural passage describing Moses' sojourn on Mt. Sinai presupposed throughout this section of the Prologue.

[31] A sense of "replacement" ("instead of") is unavoidably communicated by the Greek preposition *anti*; cf. Francis J. Moloney, *John*, 46; Andrew T. Lincoln, *St. John*, 107. This rules out the more general sense often proposed (cf., e.g., C. K. Barrett, *John*, 168; Rudolf Schnackenburg, *St. John*, 1:275–76) of a cumulative flow of grace: "grace upon grace."

From the Bosom of the Father: 1:18

The Prologue sweeps to a majestic conclusion returning us to where it began in the eternity of the Word's dwelling with God (1:18; cf. 1:1-2). First we have an axiom of the biblical tradition: "No one has ever seen God" (v. 18a; cf. Exod 33:20). In view of the running comparison with the Sinai revelation, "no one" seems designed to rub in Moses' failure to obtain a sight of the glory of God (Exod 33:18). In the face of this failure, the superiority of the revelation enjoyed by believers stands clear: "(It is) God, the only Son, who is in the bosom of the Father, who has made him known" (v. 18b).[32] The statement recalls what was said of the Word at the start of the Prologue: that the Word was "with God" prior to the act of creation (1:1-2). Here in conclusion, the Prologue sets out the Son's abiding relationship with the Father in terms of great intimacy. It is the Son who is "in the bosom" (*eis ton kolpon*)[33] of the Father who has made known the God whom humans cannot see.

What is being suggested here is in fact the central notion of the gospel. The entire human life of Jesus Christ will be a playing out—literally, an "exegesis" (*exēgēsato*)—in the field of time of the divine communion of love that exists between the Father and the Son. Played out in the human sphere it will be accessible to human beings, so that they, as "children of God" (1:12; 20:17), may be drawn into Jesus' filial communion of love with the Father and so come to share the divine eternal life.

This will become clear in light of the position of the "disciple whom Jesus loved" (the "Beloved Disciple") at the final Supper when he is said to be reclining in the bosom (*en tōi kolpōi*) of Jesus (13:23; recalled also in 21:20). In the closing chapters of the gospel this disciple functions as the model and "entry point," so to speak, for all subsequent generations of believers. Through their belief in the witness contained in the gospel, believers gain access to the intimacy with Jesus enjoyed by this privileged disciple. Through him and with him they "recline in the bosom (*kolpos*)" of Jesus,

---

[32] "God, the only Son" (NRSV) is something of a translation compromise between two textual traditions here: one, by far better attested in the manuscript tradition, reading *monogenēs theos* ("only God"); the other, *monogenēs huios* (only Son), giving a more natural sense in line with similar phrases in the Johannine tradition (3:16, 18; 1 John 4:9); cf. Raymond E. Brown, *John I–XII*, 17.

[33] The Greek preposition *eis* has the same meaning as *en*, giving the sense "in"; cf. C. K. Barrett, *John*, 169. If *eis* retains something of its directional nuance this would convey the sense of the Son's being at all times turned toward the Father, in obedience and love, throughout the story of his human life that is about to unfold; cf. Francis J. Moloney, *John*, 46–47.

the only Son who is always "in the bosom" of the Father. It is through this "chain of intimacy" that the Fourth Gospel portrays its remarkable vision of human beings drawn into the very life of God.

The Prologue, as we have seen, functions as an overture to the Fourth Gospel. It introduces us to the true identity and status of the chief character, Jesus, and gives more than a hint of the conflict that he will face in his mission from the Father to give eternal life to the world. It invites us to view the mission of Jesus against two scriptural backgrounds in particular: (1) as the definitive realization of the creation story in the opening chapters of Genesis; and (2) as a surpassing of the partial revelation of God's identity and will for human beings given through Moses at the time of Israel's wandering in the desert of Sinai (Exod 33-34). Again and again, as the narrative proceeds, aspects of these two backgrounds (light and darkness; law and Moses) will emerge from time to time and play a significant role in the story. It will greatly enrich understanding and appreciation of that story if we can keep them in mind.

As we move now from the Prologue to follow the human career of the Word in the narrative of the gospel, it is appropriate, I believe, to cite at length the concluding paragraph of C. H. Dodd's discussion of the motif "Son of God." Composed sixty years ago, it remains unsurpassed in my view as a summary exposition of the narrative theology of the Fourth Gospel.

> The relation of Father and Son is an eternal relation, not attained in time, nor ceasing with this life, or with the history of this world. The human career of Jesus is, as it were, a projection of this eternal relation (which is the divine *agapē* ["love"]) upon the field of time. It is such not as a mere reflection, or representation, of the reality, but in the sense that the love which the Father bore the Son "before the foundation of the world," and which He perpetually returns, is actively at work in the whole historical life of Jesus. That life displays the unity of Father and Son, . . . in the sense that the love of God in Christ creates and conditions an active ministry of word and deed, in which the words are *pneuma kai zoē* ["spirit and life"] and the deeds are *sēmeia* ["signs"] of the eternal life and light; a ministry which is also an aggressive conflict with the powers hostile to life, and ends in a victory of life over death through death. The love of God, thus released in history, brings men into the same unity of which the relation of Father and Son is the eternal archetype.[34]

[34] C. H. Dodd, *The Interpretation of the Fourth Gospel* (Cambridge: Cambridge University Press, 1953), 262. Enclosed within brackets are my English translations of terms written in Greek in the original.

JESUS REVEALS HIS GLORY
TO THE WORLD (ISRAEL):
1:19–12:50

John's Witness to Jesus: 1:19-51

From the theological heights of the Prologue we come down to earth as the narrative proper opens with John's witness to Jesus. We have, of course, been prepared for this by the two references to John and his role as witness that "intruded" into the Prologue (vv. 6-8, v. 15). Now we are to learn how John discharged this task: first, by deflecting any claims to messianic status from himself; then, by asserting the unrecognized presence of a figure vastly superior to himself; finally, by pointing to Jesus as that figure when, simply and quietly, he makes his entrance onto the scene (v. 29).

As readers of the gospel today, we might think that we know Jesus and do not need to have him pointed out to us through the witness of John. But knowing Jesus is a lifelong project rather than a simple coming to faith once and for all. The unfolding discovery of Jesus and the series of interlocking invitations described here, in which people enter into discipleship and recruit others to do so, have much bearing upon Christian discipleship and life in community today.

The sequence unfolds in a series of scenes that take place on four distinct "days" (cf. v. 29; v. 35; v. 43).[1]

1. John first (vv. 19-28) clarifies his own status: he is not the Messiah, nor Elijah, nor the prophet but a "voice" making straight the way for the "Lord," already present but unrecognized.

---

[1] The "days" serve simply as chronological markers dividing the scenes. Some see the four days of 1:19-51 linked with the time marker "on the third day" at the start of the first Cana episode (2:1) to form a "week" in which the revelation of Jesus' "glory" on the seventh day (2:12) evokes the sequence leading up to the giving of the law as described in Exodus 19 and celebrated in later Jewish tradition in the feast of Pentecost. Appeal to this background lends rich theological overtones to the Cana revelation of Jesus' glory (cf. Francis J. Moloney, *John*, 50–51) but is perhaps something interpretation brings to the text rather than something read out of it; cf. Andrew T. Lincoln, *St. John*, 116, 126.

2. On the second day (vv. 29-34), when Jesus appears, John points to him as Lamb of God, the Son of God, who will baptize with the Spirit.

3. On the third day (vv. 35-42) John bears witness about Jesus to two of his disciples, leading them to transfer their discipleship to Jesus.

4. On the fourth day (vv. 43-51), with John receded from the scene, Philip and Nathanael become disciples of Jesus.

Across the four days what begins as John's witness is gradually transformed into the gathering of disciples around Jesus—as John will later evince: "He (Jesus) must increase, but I must decrease" (3:30).

Day 1: John's Witness to Emissaries of the Jewish Authorities: 1:19-28

John begins his witness in response to a delegation that approaches him on behalf of the Jewish authorities (literally, "the Jews from Jerusalem").[2] The approach comes in two "waves" of interrogation (vv. 19-23; vv. 24-28). First, emissaries described as "priests and Levites," seek to fix his identity in terms of three figures destined, according to popular expectation, to rise up in the messianic age and herald its arrival: the "Christ" or Messiah (that is, an ideal ruler of David's line who would restore the fortunes of the people in a political, social, and religious sense); the prophet Elijah (whose return at the dawn of the messianic age was anticipated on the basis of the prophecy in Mal 3: 23 [4:5][3]; cf. Sir 48:10); a prophet like Moses (expected to arise on the basis of the assurance given to Moses in Deut 18:18[4] [cf. John 6:14]). John emphatically disclaims identification with any of these three figures (vv. 20-21).[5] When pressed (v. 22), he identifies himself (v. 23) as the one

---

[2] This terminology reflects the situation at the time of the gospel's composition toward the close of the first century CE when the Jewish and Christian communities had gone their separate ways. This is the first instance of the use of the phrase "the Jews" in its most frequently occurring sense in the Fourth Gospel to indicate the Jewish leadership, who will become the chief adversaries of Jesus and be, in the historical location of the drama, the representatives of "the world" that will reject him. Their headquarters are in Jerusalem.

[3] "Lo, I will send you the prophet Elijah before the great and terrible day of the LORD comes" (Mal 3:23 [4:5]).

[4] "I will raise up for them a prophet like you from among their own people" (Deut 18:18).

[5] The overloaded sequence of threefold assertion/denial in v. 20 lends a forensic (legal) tone to John's witness; cf. Andrew T. Lincoln, *St. John*, 111. Jesus is already on trial before his actual appearance in the story.

dubbed by Isaiah "the voice of one crying out in the wilderness, 'Make straight the way of the Lord,'" (Isa 40:3).

With this identification of John, the Fourth Gospel aligns itself not only with the Synoptic Gospels (Matt 3:3; Mark 1:3; Luke 3:4) but also with a broader Jewish tradition that looked to the second part of Isaiah (Isa 40–66) as a repository of promise concerning the messianic age. (Deutero-)Isaiah's message of liberation, which originally referred to the homecoming of those taken in captivity to Babylon in the sixth century BCE, was being read in Jewish circles at the time of Jesus with reference to the hopes for national liberation and restoration entertained for the messianic era. The early Christian tradition in particular found in the opening words of Isaiah 40 a key expression of the role and status of John the Baptist in relation to Jesus: John was the "voice" summoned to prepare the "way of the Lord." Thus, in this opening round of his interrogation by representatives of the Jewish leadership John has signaled the onset of the messianic era while disclaiming any identification of himself with a known messianic figure. His role is to "straighten the way" for One who will bear the exalted title "Lord."

A second "wave" of interrogation (vv. 24-28) from emissaries now specified as "the Pharisees" focuses on John's activity as baptizer.[6] Why, if he is not one of the three mentioned messianic figures, is he baptizing? At the time of Jesus the Jews practiced baptism as a rite of repentance in preparation for the messianic age. It is through baptism—an outward enactment of inner conversion of heart—that John "prepares" (literally, "makes straight" [v. 23]) the "way of the Lord," the "way" no longer being understood as the road back from Babylon but as the repentant human heart.

To this fresh interrogation John responds (vv. 26-27) that he is baptizing with water not for his own sake but in view of the presence in their midst, albeit unrecognized, of a personage of immensely superior status. Though technically "senior" to this person in terms of temporal priority, John himself is not worthy to untie even the strap of his sandal.[7]

An added comment characteristic of the gospel informs us that all this happened in Bethany across the Jordan where John was baptizing (v. 28; cf.

---

[6] With reference to the Jewish authorities, the Fourth Gospel speaks of "the Pharisees" more or less interchangeably with "the Jews," reflecting the fact that at the time of the gospel's composition the successors of the Pharisees, the rabbis, were the dominant force in Judaism; cf. Gail O'Day, "The Gospel of John," 528.

[7] Whereas students might carry their teacher's sandals as a mark of respect, to bend down and untie them was a task reserved for slaves; the same phrase occurs in Mark 1:7; Luke 3:16.

also 10:40).[8] Later, we shall learn that, whereas Galilee and the trans-Jordan region are safe for Jesus, Judea is the place of hostility and danger (11:7-8, 16). The fact that those interrogating John came from Jerusalem (1:19) is a first hint of that hostility.

Day 2: "Behold the Lamb of God": 1:29-34

On the following day, John sees Jesus "coming toward him"[9] and begins to make his positive witness: "Behold, the Lamb of God (*ho amnos tou theou*) who takes away the sin (*tēn hamartian*) of the world" (v. 29b). Stated in these terms, the title and the role break somewhat unexpectedly into the messianic expectation raised by the questions of the emissaries from Jerusalem. "Lamb of God" was not a title with messianic connotations in Jesus' day, nor was the Messiah expected to deal with the removal of sin. Jesus will shortly be acknowledged as Messiah (v. 41; v. 49). But his introduction as Lamb of God destined to take away the world's sin signals from the start that he will play the role according to a script seriously challenging to conventional messianic hopes. Rather than political liberation or national restoration, his messianic role will focus upon the overcoming of the human alienation from God brought about by the world's sin.

We should note that the text here speaks of taking away the world's sin (*hamartia*) in the singular, rather than "sins." While Johannine theology does take account of human sinning in the sense of particular acts of moral transgression (murder, lying, theft, etc. [cf. 8:24; 9:34]), its primary concern is the radical evil and alienation from God in the human heart of which particular "sins" are simply the outward expression. The gospel portrays such alienation above all through the image of "darkness." Archetypal human sin has primarily a christological reference in that when God sends "the Light" (the Son of God) into the world for its salvation, human beings reject the Light, preferring to remain in the darkness lest their misdeeds be exposed (3:18-21). The divine remedy for overcoming the world's sin in this global sense is the outpouring of love displayed in the incarnate mission of the Son,

---

[8] This Bethany across the Jordan must be distinguished, it seems, from the Bethany, the home village of Martha, Mary, and Lazarus, mentioned in 11:18 (cf. 11:1; 12:1) as only two miles distant from Jerusalem. Its location has not been identified.

[9] "Coming" (*erchomenon*) recalls the identical term in the Prologue: "The true Light . . . was coming (*erchomenon*) into the world" (1:9).

culminating in the self-sacrifice of the cross, the "victory" of light and love over darkness and sin (16:33d).[10]

It is to liberation from sin in this radical sense that the unusual title "Lamb of God" points. According to the Johannine chronology Jesus will die at the hour when the priests are slaughtering the lambs in the temple in preparation for Passover. Like the Paschal Lamb, none of his bones will be broken (19:33, 36; cf. Exod 12:46; Num 9:12). While these associations will emerge explicitly only at the end of the gospel, the Baptist's hailing of Jesus as the Paschal Lamb establishes here at the start that the primary task of his messianic mission will be that of lifting the collective burden of sin weighing upon humankind and reclaiming human beings for life in the divine communion of love.[11]

The description (vv. 30-34) of the remaining witness of John hardly flows in logical sequence. John first addresses once more the issue of Jesus' superior status (v. 30; cf. v. 27). Despite coming later ("after") in the temporal order, Jesus ranks before him because, as we know from the Prologue, he "*was* before (*prōtos*) him." With considerable repetition and argument in reverse order, John then elaborates on his own role in relation to this superior figure (vv. 31-33). He, John, was sent by God to reveal this One (the Lamb of God) to Israel (v. 31bc). His being sent to baptize with water was part of this overall mission (v. 31c)—indeed its sole purpose. He did not know beforehand the identity of the One he was to reveal (v. 31a; v. 33a). But the

---

[10] For an excellent summary of the Fourth Gospel's presentation of "sin," see Dorothy A. Lee, *Flesh and Glory*, 188–90.

[11] Association of the title "Lamb of God" with the Paschal Lamb is a matter of some controversy in Johannine scholarship since the Paschal Lamb ritual in Judaism was not a sacrifice nor was it connected with the removal of sin. Some favor association with the "Servant" figure of Isaiah 53, who is described as like a "lamb" (*amnos*) dumb before its shearers (53:7). While the Old Testament background to the title is difficult to pin down precisely, there is a clear association of the Passover Lamb with removal of sin in the early Christian tradition: cf. 1 Cor 5:7, as well as the location of the Eucharistic celebration in a Passover context (cf. Matt 26:27). Within a developing Christian tradition along these lines it is understandable that the Fourth Gospel should portray Jesus as the (Paschal) Lamb of God who takes away the world's sin. See further Raymond E. Brown, *John I–XII*, 58–63; C. K. Barrett, *John*, 176–77; Rudolf Schnackenburg, *St. John*, 1:297–301; Dorothy A. Lee, "Paschal Imagery in the Gospel of John: A Narrative and Symbolic Reading," *Pacifica* 24 (2011): 13–28, esp. 15–19. The controversy over the meaning of "Lamb of God" is part of a wider discussion as to whether Jesus' death has an expiatory function in the Fourth Gospel; see further, Craig R. Koester, "The Death of Jesus and the Human Condition: Exploring the Theology of John's Gospel," in *Life in Abundance: Studies of John's Gospel in Tribute to Raymond E. Brown*, ed. John R. Donahue (Collegeville, MN: Liturgical Press, 2005), 141–57, esp. 145–48, 156, n. 15.

One (God) who had sent him to baptize with water had told him that the moment of recognition would arrive when he saw the Spirit descend like a dove from heaven and remain upon one of those who came to him for baptism. That one was destined to baptize with the Holy Spirit (v. 32, v. 33). The Johannine Gospel presupposes here on the part of its readers knowledge of the Synoptic tradition of Jesus' baptism (Mark 1:9-11 and parallels). It refrains from mentioning explicitly that Jesus was among those who received baptism at the hands of John. It focuses entirely on the motif of the descent of the Spirit upon Jesus, which in the Synoptic tradition follows immediately upon his emergence from the water.

The link between the title, "Lamb of God, who takes away the sin of the world" (1:29b) and the role of baptizing with the Spirit becomes clear in light of a scene toward the end of the gospel. Jesus, who has died as Paschal Lamb, appears as risen Lord to the disciples and breathes the Spirit upon them to empower them for the forgiveness of sins (20:22-23). Though bearing the Spirit throughout his earthly mission, Jesus will not impart the Spirit in this cleansing sense until he is glorified (cf. 7:37-39; esp. v. 39b). It is as the crucified and risen Lord that he will baptize believers with the Spirit and empower them to carry on this ministry of reconciliation.

With this clarification of roles—both his own and that of the Lamb—John formally concludes his witness: "Now I have seen and have borne witness that this One is the Son of God" (v. 34).[12] In light of the Prologue it is not surprising that John should hail Jesus with this title (which in the Synoptic tradition appears in the Father's address to Jesus following his baptism [Matt 3:17; Mark 1:11; Luke 3:22]). In itself the title is ambiguous. In the Jewish tradition "Son of God" can refer to the messianic king, with no connotation of divinity or unique filial relationship to God.[13] By concluding on this note, John at least acknowledges that Jesus will fulfill the role of Israel's Messiah. It is safe to announce him in such terms now that the nature of his fulfillment of that role is clear: it will have to do with reconciliation of the world to God rather than political liberation.

[12] An alternative reading in the Western textual tradition, "Chosen One (*eklektos*) of God," has good claims to originality; cf. C. K. Barrett, *John*, 178. On balance "Son of God" is to be preferred; cf. Bruce M. Metzger, *A Textual Commentary on the Greek New Testament*, 2nd ed. (London: United Bible Societies, 1975), 200.

[13] Cf. Brendan Byrne, *'Sons of God,'* 59–62, 223.

Day 3: John's Disciples Transfer to Jesus: 1:35-42

John has borne public witness to Jesus. Now he bears more specific witness to his own disciples. Standing with two of them and seeing Jesus passing by, John once again points him out as the Lamb of God (vv. 35-36). What the two disciples make of this title we do not know. But they are sufficiently intrigued on hearing John's witness to begin a new life of discipleship by "following" Jesus (v. 37).

Sensing that he is being followed, Jesus turns around, sees them following, and, as his first utterance in the gospel, puts to them the question: "What are you looking for?" (v. 38a). At an ordinary human level this is an understandable question for someone being followed to ask. But little in the Fourth Gospel operates simply on one level. Beneath the ordinary and everyday, there runs the deeper level of meaning of which the ordinary is often a symbol. The question asks the disciples—and through them all readers of the gospel—concerning their deepest desires. What are you really looking for? What do you want out of life? Even on the surface level of the story the fact that the disciples have attached themselves to a prophetic figure such as John shows that they are already dissatisfied with the status quo and searching for the messianic renewal of their people.

The two disciples anticipate many figures in the gospel who will bring their desires and wants to Jesus. He will uncover and draw out from them a thirst for life in a more fundamental sense. But he can only communicate this life to those who sense their need for it, who have gone beneath their surface desires to discover and own a more basic longing. Hence the programmatic nature of Jesus' initial question, "What do you want?" The mission of Jesus, now beginning, will expose the inadequacy of their initial desires and lead them on a costly journey toward the fullness of life that they—and all human beings—really want.[14]

The inadequacy of the disciples' understanding is shown by the way they address Jesus in response (v. 38b). Though he has been pointed out to them as "Lamb of God" (v. 35), they address him simply as "Rabbi"—a title which simply means "Teacher"—and go on to ask, "Where do you live (*menein*)?" At one level the question is natural: they presume that, like other Jewish rabbis, Jesus has a place where he gathers his pupils for instruction.[15] But, again, things are not so simple. The Greek word *menein* has a significant

---

[14] The question is particularly pertinent for those who enter upon the program of retreat contained in the *Spiritual Exercises* of St. Ignatius Loyola.

[15] Cf. Francis J. Moloney, *John*, 54.

range of meaning in this gospel. It can mean "live" or "dwell," as here, but it also has the sense of "remain" (as in the Spirit's "remaining" after its descent upon Jesus [v. 32, v. 33]). At one level Jesus has a temporary place where he is currently staying here in Bethany across the Jordan. At another level entirely, the Prologue has made clear that from "the beginning" he has had an eternal dwelling with the Father (1:1, 4), a being "in the bosom" (*kolpos*) of the Father that, even as incarnate Son, he never leaves (1:18).

When, then, Jesus responds to the disciples with the phrase "Come and see" (v. 39a), the invitation is also operative on two levels and programmatic. The disciples are being invited to come and see where he lives in his present dwelling, a simple booth perhaps or shelter along the banks of the Jordan. On a deeper level they are being invited to embark upon a life of discipleship that will involve "seeing" where he truly lives: "ever in the bosom of the Father" (v. 18). In other words, they—and all readers of the gospel—are being invited to go on the journey that will enable them to make their own the affirmation in the Prologue: "we have seen his glory, glory as of an only son of a father, full of grace and truth" (1:14c-e). In a truly sacramental way, the human life of Jesus, when seen with the eyes of faith, will disclose the presence and power ("glory") of God. By coming and seeing where Jesus dwells, and by "remaining" (*emeinan*) with him all that day (v. 39bc), the two disciples set the pattern for all who will follow in their footsteps, sharing their calling and experience.[16]

The two disciples—one of whom is identified as Andrew,[17] the brother of Simon Peter, while the other remains unnamed[18]—now (vv. 40-42) set in train a pattern whereby disciples recruit others to share the experience of what they had seen and heard in the company of Jesus (cf. 1 John 1:1-4). Andrew goes off to find his brother Simon and when he has done so tells him, "We have found the Messiah" (the narrator once again [cf. v. 38] trans-

---

[16] The intriguing time marker, "It was about the tenth hour" (= 4 p.m.) has defied explanation. The sense may be that, fascinated with their newly discovered Master and reluctant to leave, the disciples remained with Jesus as long as they could throughout the day right up till when they had to leave so as to be home before dark.

[17] Andrew plays a more prominent role in the Fourth Gospel than in the Synoptics: he testifies to Jesus as the Messiah, recruiting his brother Peter; later he plays a role in the miracle of the loaves (6:8) and facilitates the coming of the Greeks to Jesus (12:22); cf. Andrew T. Lincoln, *St. John*, 117–18.

[18] That one disciple remains unnamed leaves the way open for identifying him as "the disciple whom Jesus loved" ("Beloved Disciple"), who plays so prominent a role toward the end of the narrative (13:23-25; [18:15?]; 19:26-27; 20:2-10; 21:7, 20-23). If the evangelist intended this identification, he might have made it more explicit.

lating this as "Christ"). Messianic hope, it seems, has been central to their discipleship of John. Acknowledging Jesus as fulfilling that hope does not mean, however, that they truly know him or understand the implications of John's hailing him as "Lamb of God." A "merely messianic" knowledge of Jesus has to be greatly deepened if his full stature and role is to be grasped.

It is characteristic of the Fourth Gospel that Simon Peter, clearly the first-called and first in rank among the disciples in the Synoptic tradition, enters upon discipleship here in this secondary way, recruited by his brother Andrew. It agrees with the portrayal of Peter at the time of the trial, death, and resurrection of Jesus, where he is consistently upstaged by "the disciple whom Jesus loved," until rehabilitated and established in the role of chief pastor following his triple protestation of love (21:15-19). It is presumably in view of this later role that, when Andrew brings Simon to Jesus (v. 42), Jesus looks at him and makes a solemn pronouncement: "You are Simon, son of John. You will be called Cephas" (which the narrator again translates for us as "Peter"). It is only as one who has plumbed the depth of his own weakness and come to know the forgiving love of Jesus that Simon will function as chief pastor and the "rock foundation" ("Cephas") of the church.

Day 4: Jesus Calls Philip and Nathanael: "Greater things . . .": 1:43-51

With John the Baptist entirely receded from the scene, Jesus himself, prior to setting out for Galilee, recruits two more disciples, Philip and Nathanael. Whereas Jesus "finds" Philip and directly calls him to discipleship ("Follow me" [v. 43]), Philip himself finds Nathanael, just as Andrew had recruited Simon Peter. The detail (v. 44) that Philip is from the same town, Bethsaida, as the other two, along with the plural formulation "we have found" (v. 45), suggests that Philip sees himself as part of a community formed by the three already called. The roundabout formulation, "the One whom Moses wrote about in the law and the prophets (spoke of) too, we have found: Jesus, son of Joseph, from Nazareth" (v. 45b), again (cf. v. 41) locates the discovery within the aura of messianic hope. The "law" (= Pentateuch) and "the prophets" indicate Scripture in a global sense.[19] No specific messianic text is in view—just the sense, widespread in Judaism at the time, that Scripture points to what will occur in the messianic age. Philip's

---

[19] Cf. Luke 16:29, 31; 24:27; Acts 26:22; 28:23; also Matt 5:17; 7:12; 11:13; 22:40: Luke 16:16; 24:44; Rom 3:21; cf. Rudolf Schnackenburg, *St. John*, 1:315, n. 97.

statement, then, repeats the balder formulation of Andrew: "We have found the Messiah" (v. 41b).

Ignoring Philip's claim to have found the Messiah, Nathanael fastens solely upon the mention of Nazareth (v. 46a). The expostulation: "From Nazareth! Can anything good come from there?" introduces a note of irony that will recur again and again throughout the gospel. At a surface level Nathanael simply gives voice to the kind of small town prejudice common in all human societies. By the same token, Nathanael's exclamation raises the issue of Jesus' origins: where has he come from? On a human level, he has come from Nazareth; on a divine level, we know from the Prologue that he has come from an eternal life with God. The double level of allusion once again instances the sacramentality that pervades the story. That Jesus should come from such an ordinary, unremarkable town as Nazareth of Galilee is part of the incarnation, the disclosure of the divine in the human. Very soon in fact the Son will display "his glory" in another small town in Galilee— Cana—which just happens to be (though we only learn this toward the close of the gospel [21:2]) the hometown of Nathanael!

Philip does not argue with Nathanael but simply repeats the earlier invitation: "Come and see" (v. 46b). Like the others, Nathanael is invited to enter upon a life of discipleship ("come") where he will "see" the divine presence ("glory") disclosed in the humanity of Jesus. He will learn that out of Nazareth can come very great "good" indeed.

Seeing Nathanael coming toward him,[20] Jesus ignores his cynical comment and instead makes an entirely positive pronouncement: "Behold, an Israelite in whom there is no guile" (v. 47b). "Israelite" is an honorable title.[21] Nathanael's lack of "guile" (*dolos*) sets him favorably off against the archetypal biblical "trickster" Jacob (Gen 27:35-36), to whose dream at Bethel (Gen 28:12) Jesus will shortly allude (v. 51). In contrast to Jacob, the eponymous ancestor of old Israel, Nathanael will model what being an "Israelite" will mean in the era now dawning with the presence of Jesus.

That is a promise for the future. For the present, surprised by Jesus' comment and the claim to supernatural knowledge that it implies, Nathanael exclaims: "Whence (*pothen*) do you know me?" [v. 48a]).[22] Jesus, again,

---

[20] "Coming to Jesus" is a more or less technical expression in the Fourth Gospel for entering upon a life of faith and discipleship: 3:26; 4:30; 5:40; 6:35, 37, 44, 65; 7:37; 19:39.

[21] Occurring only here in the gospel, "Israelite" carries none of the ambiguity that attaches to "Jew"; cf. Gail O'Day, "The Gospel of John," 532.

[22] The interrogative pronoun "whence" (*pothen*), rather than—as we might have expected— "how" (*pōs*) keeps alive the issue of Jesus' origins. Jesus' supernatural knowledge about Nathanael stems from his origin with the Father.

does not answer directly but gives yet a further example of special knowledge: "Before Philip called you I saw you under the fig tree" (v. 48b). Proof of ability to see beyond the ordinary limits of space and time guarantees the truth of his previous pronouncement. Whether any significance is to be attached to Nathanael's being "under a fig tree" is unclear. In Micah 4:4 and Zechariah 3:10 sitting under the fig tree is a symbolic expression of messianic peace and prosperity; later Jewish traditions pictured rabbis under fig trees teaching or studying the Torah.[23] The suggestion could be that before Philip called Nathanael, Jesus already knew him as one who was searching the law for signs that the age of the Messiah had arrived (cf. v. 45b). Nathanael, though at first having difficulty with Jesus' origins (Nazareth), would then represent all Israelites cherishing messianic hopes who are promised the sight of "greater things" (v. 51) if only they can expand those hopes beyond what they now imagine.

This is to wring a lot out of the simple phrase "under a fig tree." It does, however, account well for Nathanael's enthusiastic response: "Rabbi, you are the Son of God, you are the King of Israel" (v. 49). As in the case of the testimony of John (v. 34), "Son of God" here lacks the transcendent, more-than-human sense that will emerge as the narrative unfolds (and of which we who have read the Prologue are already aware [1:18]).[24] On the basis of Jesus' more than human knowledge, Nathanael hails him as Israel's long-awaited Messiah-King. But his faith will have to go on a long journey to be adequate to the full mystery of Jesus.

More than a hint of this is contained in Jesus' final response, which is also a promise (vv. 50-51). Nathanael has come to believe in Jesus on the basis of his seemingly miraculous knowledge.[25] He is now promised "sight" of "greater things" than wonders such as this (v. 50). In a solemn pronouncement ("Amen, Amen, I say to you" [v. 51a),[26] Jesus promises a "seeing" of "heaven opened and the angels of God ascending and descending upon the Son of Man" (v. 5ab). As has long been recognized, there is an echo here of Jacob's dream at Bethel:

---

[23] Cf. Raymond E. Brown, *John I–XII*, 83.

[24] Cf. also Martha's confession of Jesus in 11:27; also 20:31; see further, Francis J. Moloney, *John* 56, 61–62.

[25] His level of faith at this point corresponds to those who believe on the evidence of "signs" (miracles)—a level for the most part not rated highly in the gospel: 2:23; 4:48.

[26] Here and throughout this commentary I use the more literal "Amen, Amen" translation rather than the NRSV's "Very truly."

> And he dreamed that there was a ladder set up on the earth, the top of it reaching to heaven; and the angels of God were ascending and descending on it. (Gen 28:12)

While allusion to this text is clear, there are also differences. In Jesus' promise "heaven lies open" and the angels of God ascend and descend, not upon the ladder (as in Gen 28:12) but upon the Son of Man—that is, upon Jesus here designated for the first time in the gospel in this enigmatic way.[27]

Jesus, in other words, is the vehicle of the "commerce" between heaven and earth. For Nathanael—and all who will share his journey of faith[28]—the barrier between heaven and earth will fall away; heaven will "remain open"[29] in a constant revelation of God. Like Jacob awaking from his dream, believers will exclaim, "Surely the Lord is in this place—and I did not know it!" (Gen 28:16); "this is . . . the house (temple) of God" (Gen 28:17c; cf. John 2:19-21); "this is the gate of heaven" (Gen 28:17d; cf. John 10:7-10).

The distinction between a correct but inadequate level of faith and a mature faith that sees "greater things" is one that will recur throughout the gospel. The lesser level is prompted by and rests upon the miraculous, the marvelous: in this case Jesus' accurate knowledge of Nathanael's situation before actually meeting him. Mature faith, paradoxically, moves "back," so to speak, from the marvelous to the ordinary and everyday. It pierces the barrier between heaven and earth to find the divine depth in the "Nazareth" of one's own life. The pervasive sacramentality of the Fourth Gospel—the disclosure of the divine in the earthly and physical—begins and ends around his person: the open "gate" of Heaven.[30]

Earlier (v. 31) John had described the purpose of his coming and baptizing with water so that he (Jesus) might be revealed to Israel. In the revelation of Jesus to Nathanael, the "Israelite without guile" (v. 47), this task has been discharged.[31] Nathanael, in contrast to the trickster Jacob, is the

---

[27] The origin, meaning, and use of the phrase "Son of Man" in the gospel tradition are matters of long-standing controversy. The phrase represents not so much a title as a role. For the present it will suffice to say that Jesus refers to himself in this way in connection with his mysterious role and destiny in which both suffering and exaltation are entwined.

[28] In the transition from v. 50 to v. 51, there is change of subject from singular (*opsēi*) to plural (*opsesthe*) in "you will see."

[29] The sense of remaining open is conveyed by the use here of the Greek perfect participle: *aneōigota*.

[30] The poem "In No Strange Land" by the nineteenth-century British poet Francis Thompson gives admirable expression to this sense of the divine presence behind the ordinary and familiar.

[31] Cf. Raymond E. Brown, *John I–XII*, 87.

model Israelite who overcomes his initial prejudice ("Nazareth!") to accept Jesus as the fulfillment of his search for the Messiah (v. 49), even if his journey of faith is at this point far from complete (1:51). We will not hear of Nathanael again until we find him included among the seven disciples who join Peter in a fruitless fishing expedition prior to an encounter with the risen Lord (21:2-3). But the presentation of this "true Israelite" at the beginning and end of the narrative should blunt something of the force of the Fourth Gospel's negative characterization of "the Jews" in general.[32] Though the narrative does not draw attention to the fact, it is significant that it is at Nathanael's hometown, Cana in Galilee (cf. 21:2), that Jesus will begin his ministry and for the first time display his "glory" (2:11), an initial fulfillment of the pledge regarding the "greater things" that Nathanael and all the disciples will "see" (1:51).[33]

Reflection. In the person of the disciples, a number of idealistic individuals, each in their own way cherishing hopes for the renewal and freedom of their people, have attached themselves to a genuinely prophetic figure: John the Baptist. John knows who he is and who he is not. He plays a classic mentor role, not holding on to his disciples but pointing them toward Jesus. The disciples approach Jesus through the lens of their messianic hopes and expectations. He does not impose himself but asks them first to examine and state their desires: "What do you want?" "What are you really looking for in your life?" In answer to their halting question, "Where do you live?" he invites them into his "home," so to speak, to "come and see" where he lives, which is in the world laid open to the presence of the Father (1:51). Disciples today have to put aside preconceived categories and prejudices ("Nazareth!") to begin to enter into the knowledge of his person. Like Nathanael, they learn that he already "knows" them with mysterious insight and has a future for them ("Cephas"!). Jesus' invitation, "Come and see," draws them into an ever-widening web of discovery and witness.

---

[32] Cf. R. Alan Culpepper, *Anatomy*, 123.

[33] If it is correct to see Nathanael played off as "true Israelite" over against the "trickster Jacob," then it is possible that lying behind the "seeing" promise in 1:51 is a postbiblical Jewish tradition of Jacob-Israel as "the man who sees God." The tradition is based upon a linguistically false but popular etymology of the Hebrew of "Israel"; cf. Brendan Byrne, *'Sons of God,'* 54, n. 275.

Cana to Cana:
The Early Signs and Conversations of Jesus:
2:1–4:54

Jesus Reveals His Glory at a Wedding: 2:1-12

One of the most attractive features of the Fourth Gospel is the fact that Jesus begins his ministry in the context of something so homely as a village wedding where the wine runs out. Nothing could underline more effectively the reality of the incarnation than this revelation of the divine "glory" (1:14) in such a down-to-earth human context.[1]

Somewhat later in the story, in the same Galilean village, a grievously ill child will be restored to health at the word of Jesus (4:46-54). These two Cana miracles enclose, like bookends holding volumes on a shelf, a sequence of scenes in this early part of the gospel. All the scenes touch upon the motif of faith at various levels: lack of faith, partial but inadequate faith, faith that is truly adequate to the revelation of Jesus.[2]

As well as looking forward, the display of Jesus' "glory" (2:11) in the abundance of wine that he creates at Cana is a first fulfillment of his promise to Nathanael about seeing "greater things" (1:50-51). Jesus does begin his ministry here but it is not strictly speaking the beginning of his *public* ministry. He is still very much within the ambit of his family (vv. 1-2, 12) and local origins in Galilee. The scene thus forms something of a bridge between the gathering of disciples in 1:35-51 and the truly public ministry that begins with his going up to Jerusalem at Passover in 2:13.

---

[1] Cf. Ugo Schnelle, *Johannes*, 59.

[2] Francis Moloney has notably identified the significance of this "Cana to Cana" inclusion in his work; see Francis J. Moloney, *John*, 63–65.

The scene falls easily into a pattern typical of miracle stories in the gospels: vv. 1-5 describe the situation of need: a wedding at which the wine has run out; vv. 6-10 describe Jesus remedying the situation by providing the "best wine"; in v. 11 the evangelist comments upon the effect of the miracle on the disciples; in v. 12 Jesus and his party transfer to Capernaum.

Wine Runs Out at a Wedding: 2:1-5

It is easy to pass over the time marker "on the third day" with which the scene opens (v. 1).[3] The phrase "on the third day" appears over and over in the description of the revelation of God (theophany) Israel experienced at Mt. Sinai in connection with the giving of the Torah (Exod 19:3-25; see v. 11, v. 15, v. 16). YHWH descends upon the mountain in the form of a "thick cloud" (v. 16), a terrifying revelation of God's glory. Forbidden to approach the mountain under pain of death, the people witness it all from afar. This theophany at Sinai provides a dramatic scriptural background and contrast to the Cana miracle, which ends, as we have noted, with the comment that here Jesus "revealed his glory" (v. 12).[4] The Lord who once communicated the divine presence in such a remote and terrifying form, now reveals it in an event as human as a village wedding.[5]

The episode itself is told in a rather cryptic way that leaves many puzzling features. Clearly the mother of Jesus is important. (She is never identified by name in the Fourth Gospel.) She is the first named among those invited (v. 1b); the invitation to Jesus and the disciples (v. 2) seems secondary. It is the mother too who begins the action by pointing out to her Son that the wine has run out (v. 3). Jesus' response (v. 4) is enigmatic in more than one sense. Why does he call her "Woman," rather than "Mother," and appear to brush her off with the phrase, "Why do you bother me with that?"[6]

---

[3] For readers of the gospel, mention of "the third day" also brings to mind the tradition of Christ's resurrection on "the third day" after his death (cf. the very early tradition in 1 Cor 15:4); cf. Ugo Schnelle, *Johannes*, 59. However, the Fourth Gospel makes no explicit mention of this tradition, locating the resurrection appearances as beginning on "the first day of the week" (20:1).

[4] Cf. Andrew T. Lincoln, *St. John*, 126.

[5] Wedding festivities could last an entire week. They would be occasions when villagers would have the otherwise rare opportunity to eat and feast on a generous scale, hence the disappointment—and embarrassment for the host—of a situation where the wine runs out.

[6] This distancing sense appears to be the correct interpretation rather than the more unifying, How is that our (i.e., yours and my) concern?; cf. Raymond E. Brown, *John I–XII*, 99.

Why does he protest that his "hour has not yet come" and yet go on eventually to remedy the situation and so disclose his glory (v. 11)?

In itself the address "Woman" implies no disrespect. Jesus addresses the Samaritan woman in this way (4:21), and also Mary Magdalene at the empty tomb.[7] It is unusual, though, for a son to address his mother in so distancing a fashion. To my mind, the best explanation amongst the many on offer remains that of an allusion to Eve. The first man, Adam, we are told, named the woman created for him as companion "Eve, because she was "the mother of all living" (Gen 3:20). Jesus addresses his mother as "Woman" because, as will emerge particularly from her second appearance in the gospel, at the foot of Jesus' cross (19:25-27), she plays the role of the New Eve.[8] Just before he dies, Jesus bequeaths her to the Beloved Disciple, instructing her to take as her children all those whom the disciple symbolically represents: the community of believers that is being born as the new family of God. Whereas the former Eve is simply the mother of all human beings who come into existence, the new Eve ("Woman") is to be the mother of all those who through God's grace and their faith will be "born again" with God's "eternal life" (1:12-13). It is appropriate, then, that her role in this respect is signaled in this opening scene featuring his "old family" ("his brothers") and his "new family" ("his disciples") (v. 12), and where she plays such a significant role in promoting their faith.

Harder to explain perhaps is the response: "Why do you bother me with that?" Despite the efforts of Christian piety down the centuries, it is difficult to understand this as anything but a distancing brush-off, at least in the first instance.[9] It seems designed (like the later response, 7:1-10, where Jesus refuses to act on "his brothers'" suggestion that he go up to Jerusalem for the feast [v. 10]), to signal from the start that divine power will not be prompted by occasions of human need such as arise from time to time. His mission operates solely on a program set by the Father to address human need at its most radical and fundamental (alienation from God), something that will come to a climax at the "hour" of his lifting up upon the cross. Hence his explanation, "My hour has not yet come" (v. 4b).

Yet his mother seems confident that this is not his final word. Her instruction to the servants, "Do whatever he tells you" (v. 5), while open-ended in expectation, suggests confidence that he will act. We are running into a

---

[7] Cf. C. K. Barrett, *John*, 191; Andrew T. Lincoln, *St. John*, 127.

[8] Cf. Raymond E. Brown, *John I–XII*, 109.

[9] Ibid., 99.

tension here that will surface from time to time: the divine agenda that drives Jesus toward his "hour" of glorification on the cross is interrupted by particular instances of human need. The latter inevitably win out and bring about, as here, an anticipatory disclosure of the glory that more properly belongs to "the hour." Through her instructions to the servants the mother of Jesus, who at that hour will become the mother of all believers, begins here her role of nurturing faith.

Jesus Provides the "Best Wine": 2:6-10

Jesus' remedying of the situation begins with a description of the six stone water jars that are at hand for the Jewish rite of purification, each holding twenty or thirty gallons (v. 6). His instruction to fill each with water "to the brim" (v. 7) ensures that an abundance of water—about to become wine—is at hand. It also, symbolically, conveys the sense that the Jewish rite has fulfilled its role. It is now to yield to a far deeper "purification" of human life that will renew relations with God (cf. 1:29).[10]

The miraculous transformation of water into wine is not described. All we know is that when the servants, on Jesus' instruction (v. 8), draw from the large jars, what they convey to the master of the feast is not water but wine in abundance. They know where it has come from—and are in this sense witnesses to the miracle.[11] But the master of the feast, having tasted the wine, is puzzled about its origins ("where it came from" [v. 9])—always a significant question in John. His puzzlement in this regard and mild protest to the bridegroom about having, contrary to custom, kept the best wine till last (v. 10) introduce the note of irony central to the dramatic impact of the scene. We, who have read the Prologue, know that the abundant wine is the gift of One whose true origins are with God (1:1-4, 18). We, likewise, know why the wine kept in reserve and only served now is the "best wine." It is best because, while the law (and its associated rites of purification) was given through Moses, the fullness of God's grace and truth, have now come into the world through Jesus Christ (1:14, 16-17).

---

[10] The number six, one less than the "perfect" number seven, could signify imperfection; cf. Andrew T. Lincoln, *St. John*, 129. At the same time, Jesus' provision of wine from water held in jars used for the Jewish rite retains an element of continuity: as Jesus will point out to the Samaritan woman, "salvation is from the Jews" (4:22c).

[11] "The miracle is not described but merely verified" (Rudolf Schnackenburg, *St. John* 1:333).

There is really present here another Bridegroom who has supplied the best wine and made it a "sign" of a deeper reality. The miraculous gift of ordinary (albeit best) wine in abundance signals the presence here at this Galilean village wedding of Israel's Bridegroom, fulfilling the divine promise recorded in the prophet Hosea:

> Therefore, I will now allure her, and bring her into the wilderness,
>   and speak tenderly to her.
> From there I will give her her vineyards,
>   and make the Valley of Achor a door of hope.
> There she shall respond as in the days of her youth,
>   as at the time when she came out of the land of Egypt.
> On that day, says the LORD, you will call me, "My husband,"
>   and no longer will you call me, "My Baal." (Hos 2:14-16)[12]

The water required for the Jewish rite of purification, now become an abundance of best wine, points to the onset of the messianic age when the marital relationship between YHWH and Israel is restored and indeed transcended in the person of Jesus.[13]

The abundance of wine provided here at Cana will be matched later by the abundance of bread Jesus will later provide when he multiplies the loaves (6:1-13, esp. v. 13). In view of the clear eucharistic allusions in the later miracle, it is not unreasonable to find at least a hint of a similar allusion in the provision here of wine.[14] All participants in the Eucharist become guests of the Bridegroom at the wedding feast of Cana.

Comment of the Evangelist and Transfer to Capernaum: 2:11-12

The disciples, we are told (v. 11), "believed in him." They have begun to see the "greater things" promised, the removal of the barrier between heaven and earth with the revelation of divine glory in the ordinary and mundane (1:50-51). They still have a long journey to make before their faith will be adequate to the display of divine glory when his "hour" will have truly come. The glimpse of glory that they—and we—have caught here at Cana can be likened to those moments before an opera or musical when the

---

[12] For similar depictions of YHWH as Israel's Bridegroom, see Isa 54:4-8; 62:4-5; Jer 2:2; Ezek 16:8; 23:4; Hos 2:21; etc.

[13] For copious references in biblical (OT) and postbiblical literature to abundance of wine as symbolic of the messianic age, see Andrew T. Lincoln, *St. John*, 129.

[14] Cf. Raymond E. Brown, *John I–XII*, 109; Gail O'Day, "The Gospel of John," 538–39.

audience is gathering and a gust of wind or the like creates a momentary gap in the curtain allowing a glimpse of the "glory" shortly to be disclosed on the stage.

Finally, Jesus and his entourage (literally, "his brothers and his disciples") go down to Capernaum and "remain there" (v. 12).[15] The location at this lakeside town corresponds to the Synoptic tradition (cf. Mark 1:21; Matt 4:13; Luke 4:31) but otherwise is not significant since in the following scene Jesus heads for Jerusalem (2:13). What is significant is the association of the disciples with the family of Jesus. As we have noted, at the climax of Jesus' "hour," his mother will take "the disciple whom Jesus loved" to herself and vice versa (19:25-27). In the person of this representative figure the blood family and the new family of Jesus will be fused under the overarching filial relationship to the Father (20:17), fulfilling the pledge sounded already in the Prologue: "He gave them power to become children of God" (1:12-13). The composition of the little entourage accompanying Jesus to Capernaum foreshadows this goal of his entire mission.

Excursus: Miracles as "Signs" (sēmeia) in the Fourth Gospel

In the mode characteristic of the Fourth Gospel the miraculous remedy Jesus has supplied in this situation is described (v. 11) as "the first—better, 'the beginning'—of his signs" (sēmeia). This terminology requires some comment. At one level the miracles Jesus works in the gospel are called "signs" because they point to the reality of his identity and messianic role and so promote faith in that reality. Hence the summary statement that represents a first conclusion to the gospel:

> Now Jesus did many other signs in the presence of the disciples which are not written in this book; but these are written that you may believe that Jesus is the Christ, the Son of God, and that believing you may have life in his name. (20:30-31 [NRSV])

In an understanding more characteristic of the gospel, however, the signs do not produce faith that is adequate to the reality of Jesus (cf. 2:23-25). On the contrary, they presuppose a measure of faith *already* present. When rightly apprehended, they take the believer to a new level of belief that is truly adequate to the revelation of the divine in the person and work of Jesus. In many instances (though not in this Cana miracle) they do this

---

[15] On the various explanations of the relationship of these "brothers" to Jesus and its bearing upon the tradition of the virginity of Mary, see Raymond E. Brown, *John I–XII*, 112.

through being accompanied by a discourse or narrative that brings out the symbolic meaning of the sign. Thus we find the following pattern:

A human **need** (e.g., wine run out at a wedding; bread lacking in a deserted place; etc.)

⟶   A **remedy miraculously supplied** by Jesus   ⟶

A **discourse** and/or **narrative** disclosing the divine reality *symbolically* represented by the remedy provided (wine in abundance; bread in abundance; etc.)

Imperfect faith stops at the second stage—the miraculous remedy—and draws inadequate conclusions regarding Jesus. Mature faith, drawn into a symbolic understanding, moves beyond the miraculous to discover the disclosure of the divine (the "glory") in the person of Jesus.[16] While appearing in a variety of shapes and completeness, this "sign" pattern can frequently be discerned in some form throughout the first half of the gospel ("The Book of Signs": 2:1–12:50). We shall return to it again and again in the course of the discussion.

Where God Dwells: Jesus at the Temple: 2:13-22

Jesus' stay in Capernaum with his family and his disciples is brief (v. 12). As the feast of Passover approaches he goes up to Jerusalem for the celebration (v. 13). This is the first of three Passover feasts that will have a significant place in the story. At the midpoint of his public ministry the feast of Passover will form the backdrop to the sequence on the Bread of Life (6:1-59; cf. v. 3). At the close of that ministry a final Passover will be the context of his arrest, trial, and execution (11:55–19:41); Jesus will in fact die as the Passover Lamb (19:36; cf. 1:29, 36). The feast of Passover, commemorating Israel's liberation from slavery in Egypt, forms the biblical

---

[16] Cf. Robert Kysar, *Maverick Gospel*, 95–102; Dorothy A. Lee, *Flesh and Glory*, 19–28.

background to the even more fundamental liberation under way in the ministry and death of Jesus.

For Jesus, as for all pilgrims arriving in Jerusalem, the focal point of the feast is the temple: God's dwelling place, and the locus of worship, reconciliation, and covenant renewal. Jesus, however, is no ordinary pilgrim. The temple is his Father's "house" (v. 16). When, on arrival there, he finds trade going on he takes vigorous prophetic action. What begins as a "cleansing" of the Jerusalem temple amounts in the end to a radical relocation of the divine presence in the world.[17]

It is presumably because of the Fourth Gospel's preoccupation with the motif of divine presence in the world ("the Word became flesh and pitched his tent among us" [1:14]) that it locates Jesus' action in the temple at the beginning of his ministry rather than at its close, as in the Synoptic tradition (Matt 21:12-13; Mark 11:15-17; Luke 19:45-46).[18] Here, the gospel presents the Word coming first to what is most distinctively "his own"—his "Father's house"— and experiencing a failure in acceptance from those ("the Jews") currently in charge (cf. 1:14a).[19] From the start, then, the gospel is signaling that the divine project to bring more abundant life will meet with resistance from those of his own people who enjoy power and honor ("glory") in the prevailing order.[20] The action in the temple functions as a narrative symbol, pointing to and foreshadowing the pattern of Jesus' ministry as it will unfold.[21]

The episode falls into two, roughly parallel sections: the first (vv. 14-17) concerns Jesus' interaction with the traders (vv. 14-16ab), followed by a word of explanation (v. 16c), and a concluding indication of a scriptural text that the disciples "remember" (v. 17); the second (vv. 18-22) describes an interaction between Jesus and the authorities ("the Jews"), who challenge him for a sign and receive an enigmatic word in response (vv. 18-21); all concludes with a further reference to a scriptural "remembering" on the part of the disciples (v. 22).

---

[17] Cf. Mary L. Coloe, *God Dwells with Us*, 65–84, esp. 84.

[18] Since it is unlikely that Jesus performed such an action in the temple on two occasions, more plausible is its location at the close of Jesus' ministry, as in the Synoptic tradition, where it is clearly the catalyst for his arrest and eventual execution. In bringing the incident forward and making the raising of Lazarus the ultimate provocation (11:45-57), the Fourth Gospel is following a theological rather than a historically based chronology; see further, Raymond E. Brown, *John I–XII*, 116–18; Ugo Schnelle, *Johannes*, 146.

[19] Cf. Andrew T. Lincoln, *St. John*, 136.

[20] Cf. Gail O'Day, "The Gospel of John," 543.

[21] Cf. Mary L. Coloe, *God Dwells with Us*, 82–84.

Jesus' Action in the Temple: 2:14-17

In comparison with the Synoptic descriptions the Johannine account of Jesus' action in the temple is at once more detailed, forceful, and radical. The animals being bought and sold are specified as "cattle" and "sheep" (v. 14, v. 15), as well as "doves" (cf. Matt 21:12; Mark 11:15); to drive them out Jesus fashions a whip out of cords; he spills the coinage of moneychangers as well as overturning their tables. Since he cannot drive out the doves in their cages, he tells those who sell them, "Take them out of here," adding the injunction that explains his entire action: "Do not make my Father's house a house of trade" (v. 16). At first glance, Jesus' aim appears to be a cleansing of the temple from the polluting effects of the trade being conducted in its precincts.[22] But to drive out the animals required for sacrifice (cattle, sheep, and doves [the offerings of the poor]) and to shut down the exchange of foreign coinage was in effect to shut down the temple as a place of worship per se.[23] Jesus' action amounts to a declaration that the function of the temple as the place of covenant renewal and reconciliation between God and Israel is henceforth null and void. In this connection the phrase "house of trade" (*oikon emporiou*) at the end of v. 16 could be an allusion to Zechariah 14:21: "And there shall no longer be traders in the house of the LORD of hosts on that day," an eschatological text the wider context of which points to a time when the sacrificial system will no longer be necessary because, in the presence in Jerusalem of YHWH as King, all aspects of life (even "cooking pots" [cf. vv. 20b-21a]) will have become sacred to the Lord.[24]

As Jesus will soon explain to the Samaritan woman, a time is coming —and now is—when those who truly worship the Father will do so, not in material temples or shrines, whether in Jerusalem or elsewhere, but "in Spirit and in truth" (4:23-24). And, as already hinted at in the Baptist's designation of him as "the Lamb of God who takes away the sin of the world" (1:29), the reconciling function of the temple sacrifices will be replaced once and for all by the saving effects of Jesus' death upon the cross. In this sense,

---

[22] The word *hieron* refers to the entire temple precinct, including the outer Court of the Gentiles, where presumably the trade referred to in this incident is taking place. In the second section of the episode, in vv. 19–21, *hieron* gives way to *naos*, a term which can also refer to the temple as a whole but has the more precise nuance of the dwelling place of God. On the significance of the change from one term to the other, see Mary Coloe, *God Dwells with Us*, 73.

[23] Temple dues had to be paid in Tyrian coinage, which, unlike Roman money, did not bear human images.

[24] Cf. Raymond E. Brown, *John I–XII*, 121; Andrew T. Lincoln, *St. John*, 138; Gail O'Day, "The Gospel of John," 543; Ugo Schnelle, *Johannes*, 64.

Jesus' cleansing action is an anticipatory sign of what will come into effect at the culminating Passover in which he will give his life for the life of the world (cf. 6:51; 10:15-18).

This hint of the passion is already present in the ambiguity of the scriptural text that the disciples, having witnessed Jesus' action, "remember" (v. 17): "Zeal for your house will consume me" (Ps 69:9).[25] At one level, this simply refers to a zeal for the purity of temple worship that could lead any prophetic figure to act as Jesus does here. At a deeper level (perhaps not evident to the disciples at this point), the text is a comment upon what is driving the entire mission of Jesus and will ultimately "consume" him in the most radical sense of encompassing his death:[26] a zeal to reclaim the world as the place where human beings, as "children of God" (1:12), are at home in their Father's house, recognizing and worshiping the divine presence and power ("glory") in line with Jacob's experience at Bethel (Gen 28:16-18) and Jesus' promise to Nathanael (John 1:51).

The Authorities Demand a Sign: 2:18-22

The second part of the episode (vv. 18-22) centers upon an understandable reaction from the temple authorities ("the Jews"). They demand from Jesus a "sign" (*sēmeion*), a miraculous event of some kind that would authorize the action he has just taken (v. 18). As will be the case throughout the narrative to come, Jesus will not accede to such demands. He does work signs (cf. v. 23) and these can arouse faith (v. 23), but faith based upon signs is imperfect (cf. v. 24; 4:48). An attitude that *demands* a sign puts God to the test; it blocks the revelation of God, which is always a gratuitous divine gift.

In the face of this hostile demand, Jesus' response is enigmatic: "Destroy this sanctuary (*naos*) and in three days I will raise it up" (v. 19). The authorities, taking his response on the literal level as a reference to the material temple in which they are standing, respond with incredulity: the temple was still being built after forty-six years (v. 20).[27] Jesus, however, as the

---

[25] The reference to Jesus' passion is enhanced by the change in the quotation from the past tense ("has consumed") in the original Hebrew and LXX to the future tense: *kataphagetai* (though there is some variation in the textual tradition, this seems to be the most assured reading; see C. K. Barrett, *John*, 198–99).

[26] Texts from Psalm 69 feature prominently in early Christian appeals to Scripture (OT) in explanation of the suffering and death of Jesus: besides John 15:25; 19:28-29, cf. Mark 15:36; Matt 27:34, 48; Luke 23:36; Rom 15:3.

[27] The Greek allows for the sense that the temple, which Herod began in 19 BCE is still being built. Calculating forty-six years after that gives the date 27 CE, which corresponds

evangelist tells us (v. 21), was speaking on a different level entirely: the "sanctuary" to which he was referring was his "body," which they would indeed "destroy" by clamoring for his death (19:6, 15) and which he would "rebuild" by rising "after three days" (v. 21; cf. 10:17-18).[28] Ironically, they will get the sign they demand by bringing about his death.

We meet here for the first time the Johannine literary device of misunderstanding.[29] This consistently serves to show how faith, in contrast to unbelief, goes beyond and beneath the literal and the mundane to arrive at the allusive and the symbolic. The disciples, we are told in conclusion (v. 22), arrived at this level of faith only after their experience of Jesus' (death and) resurrection. In light of that event they remembered Jesus' enigmatic statement ("Destroy this sanctuary") and now understood both its deeper meaning and also the deeper meaning of the scriptural text, Psalm 69:9, which Jesus' action had recalled (v. 17). Zeal for his Father's house, his dwelling place on earth, had indeed consumed Jesus. But that was not the end of the story since a new "sanctuary" for the divine presence, the risen body of the Lord, had been "built" in resurrection. By living in him through faith and baptism believers live continuously in the divine presence as in a new sanctuary, "at home" with him in his Father's "house."

In a somewhat confusing way the text, then, operates at two time periods: that of the incident itself, early in Jesus' ministry, and that of the time after his resurrection. The disciples in their first remembering (of Ps 69:9 [v. 17]) at the time of the incident arrive at a certain level of faith; only after the resurrection do they understand the full meaning of the incident and Jesus' words at the time.[30] We readers, however, in the light of our knowledge of the total story are invited to grasp those implications right here at this early stage of the narrative. We are being taught to read between the lines of the story, to grasp from the start the nonliteral, symbolic meaning, and to have our faith deepened by seeing now what the disciples saw only at the end: how Jesus' action, symbolically understood, foreshadows the contest that will climax at his "hour" (cf. 2:4b), fulfilling a script laid down in the Scriptures.

---

reasonably well to a plausible beginning date for Jesus' ministry; cf. Andrew T. Lincoln, *St. John*, 140.

[28] The time scale of the Johannine passion-resurrection story makes it clear that Jesus rises "on the third day," even if that expression does not appear in the Gospel.

[29] On this, see especially R. Alan Culpepper, *Anatomy*, 152–65.

[30] Later in the Gospel this remembering with fuller understanding is attributed to the influence of the Spirit-Paraclete, 14:26; cf. also 12:16.

Reflection. Christianity, when it emerged from the catacombs to become under the Emperor Constantine the official religion of the Roman empire, did begin to build churches and cathedrals and other sacred shrines. In this it initiated a religious and cultural heritage that today seems inseparable from its essence. Some distinction between sacred and secular does seem to be inevitable in multiple aspects of religious belief and practice. Nonetheless, focus upon the sacred (whether persons, buildings, objects, or texts) in a sense that sets them "apart" in an absolute way runs counter to the sacramental principle that is fundamental to Christianity, especially as a legacy of the Fourth Gospel. The sacred points to the "divine depth," the presence of the divine in physical reality as a whole. Jesus' action in the temple, in line with the prophetic traditions of Israel and especially in fulfillment of Zechariah 14:20-21, challenges all religious practice that absolutizes and consigns the presence and revelation of God simply to the realm of the sacred.[31] When the Word became flesh and dwelt among us, while remaining ever in the bosom of the Father (1:14, 18), he pointed to the presence of God in the everyday and ordinary—as at Cana—as well as in the sacred and set apart.

Summary: Response to Jesus in Jerusalem: 2:23-25

A brief summary of how people in Jerusalem at Passover are responding to Jesus forms a transition to the conversation with Nicodemus that follows (3:1-15). Many "believe in his name" on the basis of the signs that he performs (v. 23).[32] The following comments of the evangelist (vv. 24-25) reveal the inadequacy of such faith. "Many" believe (*episteusan*) in Jesus, but he does not respond by "believing" (*episteusen*) in them. The gospel is playing upon the dual meaning of the verb *pisteuein* in that it can mean both "believe in" and "entrust oneself to." While many may believe in Jesus, his supernatural knowledge through which he can discern beyond appearances what is truly "within" a person (vv. 24b-25; cf. 1:41-42 [Simon Peter]; 1:47-50 [Nathanael]; 6:64), means that he is not confident about the depth of their faith. The following conversation with Nicodemus will graphically illustrate the depth of conversion that truly adequate faith requires.

[31] Cf. Gail O'Day, "The Gospel of John," 545.

[32] Strictly speaking, the only "sign" that Jesus has performed in Jerusalem so far is his action in the temple just described—and whether that counts as a sign in the Johannine sense (which usually involves a miracle) is open to question. We are perhaps meant to take the statement as indicating that, following his action in the temple, Jesus has been engaged in working miracles of various kinds that the signs to be described later will illustrate. Nicodemus's opening words to Jesus certainly presume such to be the case (3:2c).

Jesus' Conversation with Nicodemus: 3:1-21

After two comparatively short scenes (the wedding at Cana and Jesus' action in the temple), we now encounter the first of the extended dramatic dialogues that are a feature of the Fourth Gospel: Jesus' conversation with the Jewish teacher and Pharisee Nicodemus. The scene is rather unsatisfactory from a dramatic point of view. After three exchanges with Jesus that fail to overcome his inability to understand, Nicodemus simply fades from view (vv. 1-10). The encounter becomes a monologue (vv. 11-21) in which Jesus appears to be addressing a larger audience. We seem, in fact, to be hearing the voice of the Johannine community addressing the difficulties its understanding of Jesus presents for the Judaism of its time.

Nicodemus is clearly a figure representative of this official Judaism: a Pharisee and "a ruler of the Jews" (3:1; cf. v. 10). In his person the gospel engages in conversation with someone who, while remaining within the synagogue, has been sufficiently impressed by the signs Jesus has worked to acknowledge him as a "Teacher who has come from God" (v. 2). He is an example of "the many" we have just heard about (vv. 23-25) who on the basis of signs have arrived at an inadequate level of faith.

Nonetheless, the portrayal of Nicodemus is not unsympathetic. While he fades from view in this scene, on a later occasion (cf. 7:50-52) he will go against the other authorities to point out that Jesus is not being treated with the justice required by the law. He will make a final appearance after the death of Jesus when, along with Joseph of Arimathea, he courageously attends to the burial of Jesus' body, bringing a very large mixture of myrrh and aloes (19:39). This suggests that, in the end at least, this teacher of Israel had moved from the darkness into the light of full faith and discipleship.[33]

After an introduction (vv. 1-2a), there follows a dialogue between Nicodemus and Jesus, consisting of three exchanges (vv. 2b-3; 4-8; 9-10); vv. 11-12 constitute a kind of bridge passage where, after Nicodemus has faded from view, Jesus reflects upon the failure of the conversation, before embarking upon a discourse, vv. 13-21, touching upon a variety of themes central to the gospel. Lending unity to the whole is the duality of light and darkness appearing at the beginning and end: Nicodemus comes to Jesus ("the Light" [cf. 1:4-5]) out of the darkness ("night" [3:2]) of unbelief). The discourse concludes with an analysis of what hinders and what encourages human beings to come out of the darkness to the light (3:19-21). Resuming the thought of the Prologue, not only in regard to the "light/darkness" duality but in several other respects as well, the scene goes to the heart of Johannine

---

[33] On the character of Nicodemus, see further, R. Alan Culpepper, *Anatomy*, 134–36.

theology and, especially in v. 16 ("God so loved the world that he gave his only Son"), contains one of the most significant statements in the gospel.

Jesus and Nicodemus: 3:1-12

The scene opens with Nicodemus—clearly a genuine searcher after truth within the tradition of Israel—coming to Jesus out of the darkness ("night") of unbelief (vv. 1-2a). On the basis of the signs he has seen, he is confident that Jesus is at least a teacher who has come from God and that God is "with him" (v. 2b-d). As readers of the Prologue we know that both statements about Jesus are true in a far more radical sense than Nicodemus presently comprehends. The descriptions could apply to any number of figures in Israel's history, including Moses or any of the classic prophets.[34] Nicodemus's confident "We know" simply seeks to encapsulate Jesus within standard, though wholly inadequate, categories of the Jewish tradition.

Brushing aside these patronizing compliments, Jesus confronts Nicodemus immediately and solemnly with the radical requirements of full faith: "Amen, Amen, I say to you, unless a person is born *anōthen* he or she is not able to see the kingdom of God" (v. 3). I have left the word qualifying "born" in Greek transliteration because once it is translated its ambiguity in the original is lost—and also lost in consequence is the misunderstanding central to the drama now under way.[35] The Greek adverb *anōthen* can have the temporal meaning "again" as well as the spatial meaning "from above."[36] Nicodemus's startled response to Jesus' statement (v. 4) shows that he is understanding the expression in the first sense ("again"), whereas Jesus' subsequent explanation (vv. 5-8) makes clear that he is speaking of being born "from above"—being reborn, that is, as "children of God," the status mentioned in the Prologue as the goal of the Son's mission (1:12-13).

Whereas the Prologue indicated that human beings acquire that status through "believing in his name" (1:12), here it comes about through "water and the Spirit" (v. 5b). John the Baptist had already pointed out Jesus as the One upon whom he saw the Spirit descend and who, in contrast to his own water baptism, would baptize with the Spirit (1:32-34). It is reasonable to see "water" here as referring to the Christian sacrament of baptism, the physical and communal enactment of the more interior disposition of faith.[37]

---

[34] Cf. Andrew T. Lincoln, *St. John*, 149.

[35] Cf. Francis J. Moloney, *John*, 92; Gail O'Day, "The Gospel of John," 549.

[36] Cf. BDAG, 92.

[37] In defense of this "sacramental" understanding, see Rudolf Schnackenburg, *St. John*, 1:369; David Rensberger, *Johannine Faith*, 58, 66–70.

In view of John's words, however, the primary emphasis would seem to lie upon the role of the Spirit. John baptized with water only; Jesus "baptizes" with a "water" that consists of the Spirit.[38] He is indicating to Nicodemus the radicality of the transformation required: it involves a symbolic rebirth brought about by the Spirit, allowing believers to "see" or "enter the kingdom of God" (v. 3; v. 5c).

This phrase, the "kingdom (or "rule") of God," is central to the message of Jesus in the Synoptic Gospels (cf. Mark 1:14-15; Matt 4:17; Luke 4:43; 8:1; etc.). It occurs here uniquely in John. Without any parallels the Johannine sense is not easy to pin down. It is best taken as referring to the heavenly sphere (cf. *ta ourania* [v. 12]), which is at once the abode of God removed from the world (cf. 14:3; 17:24) and at the same time the divine presence that is "invading" and reclaiming the world in the person and ministry of Jesus (cf. 19:36-37), where the barrier between heaven and earth falls away (1:50-51) and where believers can dwell, reborn, as children of God (1:12-13; 20:17). In this sense, like the gift of "(eternal) life" with which it is more or less synonymous, the kingdom is not simply a future destiny awaiting believers but a reality that they already "see" with the eyes of faith and into which they have already "entered" in the community of believers.[39]

Nicodemus's problem, as Jesus points out (v. 6), is that he is thinking of birth in purely human categories—literally "flesh" (*sarx*).[40] What Jesus is speaking of has to do with the realm of the Spirit, which the human mind, unaided, cannot grasp. To assist Nicodemus to see the distinction and to accept the necessity of a rebirth "from above"—that is, through the Spirit (v. 7)[41]—Jesus appeals (v. 8) to a little parable that plays, once again, upon a dual meaning in the original. The Greek word *pneuma* (like the Hebrew *ruach*) serves for both "wind" (or "breath") and also "spirit." Just as one cannot know where the wind comes from and where it is going, so it is with one who is born from the Spirit ("from above"). The origin and destination

---

[38] This is to take the second term in the phrase *ex hydatos kai pneumatos* in an epexegetic (explanatory) sense. In an interpretation along similar lines, Andrew T. Lincoln, *St. John*, 150, points out how water regularly functions as a symbol of the Spirit in the biblical and post-biblical Jewish tradition; cf. esp. Ezek 36:25-27, as also John 7:38-39.

[39] For a survey of the discussion of "kingdom of God" in John, see Francis J. Moloney, *John*, 98 99. It seems too reductive to see the kingdom as referring simply to the community of believers (so, Francis J. Moloney, *John*, 93).

[40] "Flesh" here simply denotes the human sphere distinct from and unaided by the divine; cf. Andrew T. Lincoln, *St. John*, 151.

[41] The "you" in the second half of v. 7 ("You must be born from above") is plural, indicating that Jesus is addressing the community represented by Nicodemus as well as the teacher himself.

of the agent of rebirth is wrapped in the mystery of God—God who is reaching out in the mission of Jesus to bestow upon human beings the filial status that has been from eternity the prerogative of the Son (1:18; cf. 20:17).

Jesus' parable does not help Nicodemus at all. He remains on the purely literal level ("flesh"), asking simply, "How can this be?" (v. 9). A final, somewhat sarcastic exclamation on Jesus' part ("You, a teacher of Israel, do not know these things!" [v. 10]) brings the dialogue to an end. It also leads into the following discourse in the sense that the difficulty a learned Israelite such as Nicodemus has experienced illustrates the difficulty Jesus—and the subsequent community of believers—have in communicating to the wider Jewish audience ("you") what they have experienced (vv. 11-12). So far the conversation has been about "earthly things" (*ta epigeia*). If such testimony has not resulted in belief, how much more difficult it will be when Jesus—or the Johannine community speaking through him—bears witness to what he has experienced of the "heavenly" (*ta ourania*). "Earthly things" would seem to refer to the physical realities to which Jesus has pointed—birth and the wind—as images of the divine operation ("birth from above"). If Nicodemus has failed to see through the images to the divine realities to which they point, how will it be when Jesus goes on to speak, as he now proceeds to do, of "heavenly" realities (the descent and ascent of the Son of Man) simply in themselves?[42]

No One Has Gone Up to Heaven: 3:13-15

The discourse moves very swiftly from one motif to another. We may be surprised by the opening denial that "no one has gone up to heaven save one who has come down from heaven, the Son of Man" (v. 13), followed by a reference to a saving, "lifting up," of the same Son of Man on the pattern of Moses' "lifting up" of the serpent in the wilderness (vv. 14-15). We are eavesdropping here on a long-standing conversation—more accurately, a dispute—between the Johannine community and contemporary Jewish leaders concerning the relative status of Jesus and Moses. In the Jewish tradition if any figure had access to the "heavenly world" it was Moses. His ascent of Mount Sinai to commune with God and receive the Torah (Exod 19:3-15; 24:12-18; 33:18–34:35; Deut 34:10) equipped him to be the supreme revealer of the "heavenly." Renewing a polemic already hinted at in the Prologue (1:17), the discourse challenges this tradition (v. 13a), insisting that "no one"—neither Moses nor any other notable figure of Israel's past—has

---

[42] Cf. C. K. Barrett, *John*, 212; Andrew T. Lincoln, *St. John*, 152.

ascended to the heavenly realm. But there is One who has descended from there (v. 13b) and who has truly ascended back there to the heavenly realm from which he came (1:1-2, 18):[43] namely, Jesus, once again denoted in his role as "Son of Man" (cf. 1:51).[44] As such, he alone—and the community that preserves his witness—is qualified to speak of the heavenly realm and the benefits that flow to human beings as a consequence of his descent therefrom.

Moses does indeed have a role, albeit one subservient to that of Jesus (vv. 14-15). According to Numbers 21:4-9, when Israel grumbled against God in the wilderness, the Lord sent serpents among the people, their poisonous bite causing many deaths. When Moses prayed for relief from this affliction, he was told to erect a bronze image of the poisonous serpent on a pole. When anyone was bitten, they looked at the bronze effigy and lived (21:9). The gospel sees this curious biblical incident as a type or anticipatory sign of the saving revelation later to come about through Jesus. It does so by once again exploiting verbal ambiguity. The Greek verb *hypsoun* can mean "to lift up" in a physical sense but also more generally "to exalt."[45] As such it enables the gospel to hold together Jesus' physical lifting up in crucifixion with his exaltation and return to the Father in glory. Moses' "lifting up" of the serpent in the wilderness foreshadows the "lifting up" of Jesus upon the cross (v. 14; cf. later 8:28; 12:34). The life-restoring effect of looking upon the bronze serpent anticipates and points to the gift of (eternal) life that flows from looking upon the Crucified with the eyes of faith and finding there, not simply crucifixion, but the supreme revelation of God (v. 15). While the death of Jesus will take place on earth and in this sense belong to the "earthly" sphere alluded to above, what it reveals to believers is "heavenly" *par excellence*: the truth that God is love, a love that the mission of the Son, culminating in his self-sacrificial death upon the cross, makes manifest on earth (cf. 1:18).

---

[43] It is curious that at this point of the narrative Jesus should speak of himself by implication as having already ascended (the force of the Greek perfect *anabebēken*), something that he *will* accomplish when "lifted up" upon the cross (v. 14b; 8:28; 12:32-34). The post-Easter perspective of the Johannine community emerges on the lips of Jesus here; cf. C. K. Barrett, *John*, 213; Gail O'Day, "The Gospel of John," 551.

[44] The "Son of Man" title is frequently associated in the gospel with the "descent-ascent" schema and the corresponding exchange between the earthly and heavenly realm: cf. C. K. Barrett, *John*, 72–73, 212; Andrew T. Lincoln, *St. John*, 152; John Painter, *The Quest for the Messiah: The History, Literature and Theology of the Johannine Community*, 2nd ed. (Edinburgh: T. & T. Clark, 1993), 319–33.

[45] Cf. Francis J. Moloney, *John*, 95; Gail O'Day, "The Gospel of John," 552; Andrew T. Lincoln, *St. John*, 153.

"God So Loved the World": 3:16-21

The mission of the Son as an expression of God's love comes to the fore in what is justly one of the most celebrated sentences of the Fourth Gospel:

> For God so loved the world that he gave his only begotten Son, so that everyone who believes in him may not perish but may have eternal life. (3:16)

The radicality of this assertion is striking when we consider the negative rating that normally attaches to "world" in the Fourth Gospel. Even here "the world" is not a neutral term. Before the divine mission the world belongs to the darkness that has sought and failed to "overcome" the light (1:5).[46] It is this world that is the object of the divine love and it is to rescue it from the darkness that God, in a supreme exercise of love, has sent the Son into the world to be its Light.[47] What God's "giving" of the Son adds to "sending" is the hint that the sending will end in death, death upon the cross. The incarnation described in the Prologue is to play itself out in redemption: the rescue of human beings from death so that they may have a share in the divine "eternal life."

Faith, then, is akin to the life-restoring "gaze" of the Israelites bitten by the serpents upon the image of the very thing that was afflicting them. Believers "gaze" at the Crucified One, compelled to confront the human evil, including their own evil, that has put him there. "They look upon the One they have pierced" (19:37; cf. Zech 12:10), who is at that very moment the Lamb of God who takes away the world's sin (1:29; cf. 1:36). Confronting at one and the same time their own evil and the supremely costly divine gift that takes it away, they come to know God revealed as Love, reaching out to draw them into the sphere of undying divine life.

The following verses (vv. 17-21) make clear that this vision of faith subverts any sense that the primary movement of the divine toward the (sinful) world is one of condemnation. The Son has not been sent to condemn the world but to bring it salvation (v. 17). There is judgment and condemnation,[48] but this is a function and an outcome transferred to human

---

[46] "[T]he world that is at enmity with God" (Rudolf Bultmann, *Gospel of John* 154, n. 3 [continued from previous page]).

[47] "The force is not, then, that the world is so vast that it takes a great deal of love to embrace it, but rather that the world has become so alienated from God that it takes an exceedingly great kind of love to love it at all" (Andrew T. Lincoln, *St. John*, 154).

[48] The Johannine text plays upon the ambiguity inherent in the Greek word stem *krisis/krinesthai*, which can mean both "judgment"/"judge" as well as (more negatively) "condemnation"/"condemn"; cf. Andrew T. Lincoln, *St. John*, 155.

beings, wholly dependent upon the attitude they choose to take toward the divine outreach to them in the person of the Son.[49] Those who respond with faith to the saving revelation of the cross are not judged by God; they have confronted their own sinfulness and had their sin "taken away" by the Lamb (v. 18a). Those, on the other hand, who have failed to respond in faith have condemned themselves through their failure to believe "in the name of the only-begotten Son of God." That is, they fail to acknowledge that in his person God is reaching out to them in their sin, seeking to remove it and draw them to eternal life (v. 18b).

In conclusion (vv. 19-21) Jesus reflects upon this divided outcome in respect to judgment, reverting to the "light"/"darkness" dualism character-istic of the gospel.[50] In his person "the Light" has come into the world (cf. 1:4-5, 9). The coming of the Light brings judgment because human beings do not come to the light but prefer to remain in the darkness for fear that their evil deeds should be exposed (vv. 19-20). This means that, rather than having their sins removed by the Lamb (1:29), they remain in the darkness and so bring down upon themselves judgment in the sense of condemnation. Those, however, who "do the truth" in the sense of being loyal to God and of living openly and without deceit in the divine presence are not afraid to come to the Light. The Light may have exposed their sinfulness but it also "takes it away." Living henceforth in the Light means living in such a way that adherence and loyalty to God are manifest in their entire pattern of life (v. 21).[51]

Reflection. Emerging from the discourse is a kind of discernment of spirits that flows from what is involved in the act of faith. The Israelites had to look at the image of the evil afflicting them and confront it in order to be saved

---

[49] Cf. C. K. Barrett, *John*, 216–17; Rudolf Schnackenburg, *St. John*, 1:393; Francis J. Moloney, *John*, 96; Gail O'Day, "The Gospel of John," 553. This "realized" understanding of judgment is characteristic of the gospel—though not to the total exclusion of a more tra-ditional perspective as in 5:25-29 where the Son is portrayed as destined to exercise judgment.

[50] It is possible to interpret vv. 19-21 in a "predestinarian" way in that the coming of the Light brings judgment in the sense of exposing or bringing to the surface what a person has been and is, implying that the distinction between the two groups has been fixed before the confrontation with Christ, with no sense of "conversion" possible; cf. C. K. Barrett, *John*, 218. As Barrett acknowledges, if this were the whole of John's meaning the overall salvific thrust of the gospel would be undermined. The presentation of judgment in a realized sense here does not imply removal of the capacity to make a decision in favor of the light; cf. Rudolf Schnackenburg, *St. John* 1:402–3; also Rudolf Bultmann, *Gospel of John*, 157–60; Francis J. Moloney, *John*, 96, 102.

[51] The final phrases are an admittedly loose translation of the Greek which reads more literally, "that their deeds have been done in God" (*en theōi . . . eirgasmena*).

from its death-dealing bite. Likewise, faith involves confronting one's own evil as exposed by the Cross, bringing it in this sense out into the light. While the sequence as a whole confronts the radicality of the conversion required in initially coming to faith, conversion is not for most people a once-off affair. As believers we are summoned to a continuing conversion, a continual coming out of the pockets of darkness that remain in our lives, the areas of deceit and self-delusion that we erect as barriers to the light and prevent us living fully in the truth that would set us free (8:32). If Jesus' discourse in the present passage summons us to continual "judgment" in this sense, it does so only in the context of a sublime assertion of God's love (3:16).[52]

John the Baptist's Last Witness: 3:22-36

Considering Nicodemus in the preceding half of chapter 3, we noted that he is a representative figure standing in for Jews who, while sympathetic to Jesus, are unwilling to take the radical step toward full faith and commitment. In the remainder of John 3, we have something similar to this in that we hear a conversation between John the Baptist and his disciples in which John completes his witness to Jesus by pointing out to them the superiority of Jesus and the necessity for his own role to fade away. In allowing us to "overhear" that conversation the gospel is in all likelihood addressing disciples of John who continued their allegiance to his memory in their own time. The community behind the gospel is appealing to this further group within Judaism to hearken to their master's witness and make, as he indicated, the transition to the figure whose messianic status and superiority it was his role to point out. In other words, in both sections of John 3, we hear in sequence the gospel making an appeal to two groups continuing within the Judaism of its day to come to full faith and commitment to Jesus.[53] This direction of thought will continue in the immediately following chapter where Jesus will be in conversation with an even more marginal group in Judaism (the Samaritans) in the person of the Samaritan woman.

This means that as contemporary readers of the gospel we have to face the fact that considerable sections of the text represent places where the Johannine community is sorting out its relationship to representative sectors

---

[52] Those familiar with Ignatian spirituality will note how closely the entire Nicodemus sequence parallels what is asked of those making the First Week of the *Spiritual Exercises*: especially the confronting of their own sinfulness in the context of the saving revelation of God's love in the cross.

[53] For this analysis of the content and unity of John 3 I am particularly indebted to David Rensberger, *Johannine Faith*, 52–53.

of Judaism in the late first century CE, including a remnant of the disciples of John the Baptist. Such historical relationships and the issues they raised are not our concern today—which could mean that passages in the gospel where this process has left its mark hold less interest for us. Within them, however, we do find some nuggets of gold if we are prepared to look closely. One such passage is that containing the final witness of John the Baptist: 3:22-30.

Just as Jesus' conversation with Nicodemus (3:1-12) was followed by a discourse (3:13-21), so, in parallel fashion, the interaction between John and his disciples (3:22-30) is also followed by a discourse (3:31-36)—though whether we are to take the latter as spoken by the Baptist is a question to be discussed in its place.

John and His Disciples: 3:22-30

The scene for the conversation is set by information concerning the location and baptizing activity of Jesus and John (vv. 22-24). Their spheres of operation have grown apart. Jesus has left the city of Jerusalem and entered the more general surrounding area denoted by "Judea" (v. 22). John, it would seem, has moved to the northern part of Samaria (v. 23).[54] The comment that there was "much water" in the region reinforces the sense that he was very much a "water" figure, in contrast to Jesus, who "baptizes" with the Spirit (1:33). Nonetheless, uniquely in the whole gospel tradition, Jesus is said here to be himself baptizing (v. 22)—a point soon (4:2) to be "corrected" by the assertion that it was his disciples rather than he himself who was baptizing.[55] Be that as it may, the information sets up a scenario for rival—albeit geographically separate—baptizing activity on the part of both figures. This then becomes the context for John's final witness.[56]

The context is further specified by the otherwise curious statement to the effect that a dispute had occurred between the disciples of John and

---

[54] The geographical reference, "Aenon near Salim," while in itself precise, is not certainly identifiable today. A location in northern Samaria is widely accepted; cf. Rudolf Schnackenburg, *St. John*, 1:412–13.

[55] On whether in attributing baptizing activity to Jesus personally the Fourth Gospel has recorded an accurate historical tradition; see Andrew T. Lincoln, *St. John*, 162–67, who ultimately sees the evidence marginally against rather than in favor of historicity.

[56] The clarification (v. 24) to the effect that John had not yet been thrown into prison safeguards the contemporaneity of the two sets of baptizing activity—contrary to the Synoptic tradition according to which Jesus began his public ministry only after the imprisonment of John (Mark 1:14; Matt 4:12).

"a Jew" concerning purification (v. 25). To grasp the logic we have to read between the lines of a highly cryptic report. By "Jew" in this case we have to understand simply an inhabitant of Judea.[57] He has come from that region (Judea), where Jesus is active, to Samaria where John is similarly engaged. In the course of a dispute with the latter's disciples about Jewish purificatory rites (baptism, presumably, included[58]), this Judean figure has communicated the information that Jesus is also baptizing and in fact attracting a far greater number of people than their own master. The report sets the stage for John's witness when his disciples, alarmed at this threat to their master's preeminence, pass on to him this (to them unwelcome) news: "Rabbi, the one who was with you across the Jordan, to whom you testified, here he is baptizing, and all are going to him" (v. 26).

The narrative path to set up the scene for John's reply has been complex but the response when it comes (vv. 27-30) is one of the gems of the gospel. John begins to correct his disciples' suggestion of rivalry by stating what seems at first sight to be a general axiom but which actually reflects quite specifically the theology of the gospel.[59] A person (a religious leader such as Jesus or John himself) can only receive (as disciples) those who have been allotted to him "from heaven," that is, from God—a truth later reiterated by Jesus in terms of those whom the Father has given him (6:37, 65; 10:29; 17:6, 9, 24).[60] If, as the report indicates, more are flocking to Jesus, then that is simply the fulfillment of the divine design. The development is completely in accord with John's earlier statements, concerning which they themselves are in a position to bear witness (v. 28): namely, that he is not himself the Messiah but only the one sent (by God) to prepare his way (literally, "sent before him").

John further clarifies his role appealing to an image or allegory at once very attractive and revealing (v. 29). The bridegroom is the one who "possesses" (literally, "has") the bride; the "friend of the bridegroom" stands and listens to him, rejoicing at the sound of his voice. The "friend of the bridegroom"—in our parlance, the best man—has a significant and trusted role at a Jewish wedding, taking care of all the arrangements.[61] Chosen for his

---

[57] In all likelihood this would seem to be how we should understand the otherwise mysterious, but nonetheless textually preferable, reference to "a Jew" (*Ioudaios*) in this context.

[58] Cf. Rudolf Schnackenburg, *St. John*, 1:414; Francis J. Moloney, *John*, 109.

[59] The term *anthrōpos* ("a man/person") suggests an axiom; but "receive" (*lambanein*) draws it immediately into the Johannine sense.

[60] Cf. Raymond E. Brown, *John I–XII*, 155; Gail O'Day, "The Gospel of John," 557.

[61] Cf. Gail O'Day, "The Gospel of John," 558.

integrity, it is unthinkable that he would want to usurp the bridegroom's place and "have" the bride.[62] The mention of his rejoicing at hearing the bridegroom's voice may refer quite specifically to his welcoming the jubilant shout of the bridegroom from within the bridal chamber announcing the consummation of the marriage.[63]

The widespread biblical image of Israel as the bride or spouse of YHWH (Isa 54:4-8; 62:4-5; Jer 2:2; Ezek 16:8; 23:4; Hos 2:21; etc.) makes it appropriate, as earlier at Cana (2:1-11), to understand the image in an allegorical sense as well: Jesus is the Bridegroom; John is the Bridegroom's friend; Israel—or rather the renewed Israel being constituted by Jesus—is the Bride. The Johannine tradition here coheres with other strands of the New Testament where Jesus is "Bridegroom" (Mark 2:19-20) and the church, his bride (Eph 5:25-27; Rev 19:7; 21:9-10; cf. 2 Cor 11:2). The allegory reinforces the sense of impropriety in any attempt on John's part to take the bride (the community of believers) for himself. On the contrary, just as the bridegroom's friend rejoices at the voice of the bridegroom signaling the consummation of the marriage, so John rejoices at the "consummation" of the marriage between God and Israel signaled by the numbers flocking to Jesus. John's "joy," then, is "fulfilled" (*peplērōtai*, v. 29d) because that development is also the sign that his own role is complete.[64]

More correctly, since some overlap between his own ministry and that of Jesus will continue for a time, it is a matter of Jesus "increasing" while he "decreases" (v. 30). Elsewhere in Greek such language appears in respect to the waxing and waning of heavenly bodies. As the light of other heavenly bodies, notably the moon, wanes with the rising of the sun, so John must wane in the presence of the One he has pointed to as "the Light" of the world (1:7).[65]

John will be mentioned again in the course of the narrative (5:33, 36; 10:40-41). But his active share in the story comes to a close at this point. We leave him impressed with the sense of one who knows exactly his place in the scheme of salvation, who can rejoice not simply that his own task is complete but that the One to whom he has borne witness is enjoying greater following and allegiance than he. How much contention, jealously, and strife would have been spared the Christian church down the ages if latter-day disciples had taken this last instruction of John more deeply to heart.

[62] Cf. Raymond E. Brown, *John I–XII*, 152.

[63] Cf. Rudolf Schnackenburg, *St. John*, 1:416; Andrew T. Lincoln, *St. John*, 161.

[64] John's sense of completeness of his mission foreshadows the final words of Jesus as he dies upon the cross (19:30).

[65] Cf. Rudolf Schnackenburg, *St. John*, 1:417; Andrew T. Lincoln, *St. John*, 161.

The One Who Comes from Heaven: 3:31-36

This small paragraph builds up to a climax containing some of the most exalted statements of Johannine theology. As such it forms a fitting conclusion to the entire sequence making up John 3. The most natural understanding is to hear John continuing his witness here—and certainly there is no indication of a change of speaker in the text. On the other hand, the high statements of trinitarian theology, especially in the concluding verses are theologically more attuned to the content of Jesus' discourse in 3:14-21 rather than to John's concerns as aired in vv. 22-30. Certainly it is hard to hear them as stemming from the John the Baptist of history. Most likely we have here what is basically a reflection of the evangelist on the uniqueness of Jesus and the absolute necessity of responding wholeheartedly to him if salvation ("eternal life") is to be gained. By positioning the reflection at this point and giving the impression—without actually stating as much—that it continues John's witness, the evangelist lends it authority. It also serves as a solemn conclusion to John's witness to Israel, a witness adumbrated in the Prologue (1:6-8, 15) and made to a variety of groups within Judaism, not excluding his own disciples. They should look exclusively and definitively to Jesus if they wish to gain rather than lose (eternal) life.[66]

The text makes the unique status and role of Jesus unequivocally clear from the start through the disjunction that it proposes between "the One who, coming from above (*anōthen*) is above all" and the one who comes "from the earth" and hence speaks simply of earthly things" (v. 31ab). The One who comes from above ("from heaven" [v 31c]) is clearly the Son. Having been "with" God from the beginning (1:1-2, 18), he and he alone is in a position to testify to the "heavenly" things that he has seen and heard in that divine sphere (v. 32a). The one who, by contrast, is "from the earth" (*ek tēs gēs*) refers to human beings in general, including, as the context suggests, exalted teachers of Israel such as Moses and John.[67] Unlike the Son, they have not been in heaven. While their witness has its value—and indeed

---

[66] For an identification of the speaker along these lines, see C. K. Barrett, *John*, 224; Gail O'Day, "The Gospel of John," 558; Andrew T. Lincoln, *St. John*, 158–59, 161. The tendency of scholars of an older generation to alter the sequence of the text in order to more naturally hear the voice of Jesus here (e.g., Rudolf Bultmann, *Gospel of John*, 131–32, 160; Rudolf Schnackenburg, *St. John*, 1:360–62) is now largely abandoned.

[67] "Earth" here is a neutral term, more or less corresponding to "flesh" (*sarx*) and reflecting the description of the creation of human beings in Gen 2:7. It does not carry the negative loading normally attaching to "world" (*kosmos*) in John. The sense of incapacity attaching to "earth" as distinct from "heaven" (cf. 3:12) corresponds to the distinction between "flesh" and "Spirit" (cf. 6:63); cf. Raymond E. Brown, *John I–XII*, 160–61.

its necessity—it cannot compare with the sublime witness of Jesus, who can speak of what he has seen and heard in the realm of his Father.

The text then takes up (vv. 32b-33; cf. v. 36) the response this witness receives on the human level. The initial assessment is very pessimistic: "No one accepts his testimony" (v. 32b). In mind is probably nonacceptance on the part of even well-disposed Jews such as Nicodemus. Matching this immediately, however, is a positive statement of what is involved when people *do* accept the witness:[68] they "seal" (*esphragisen*) "that God is true" (v. 33). That is, as if signing a legal document, they commit themselves solemnly and irrevocably to the definitive revelation of God incarnate in Jesus. They are prepared to do this because they recognize him as One sent by God to impart with unique authority the revelation that God wishes to communicate to human beings (v. 34a). Whereas other figures (Moses, John the Baptist) may have displayed spiritual authority to some degree, only the Son imparts the Spirit "without measure" (v. 34b; cf. 1:32, 33).[69]

Mention of the Spirit, followed immediately (v. 35) by an assertion of the Father's love for the Son, opens up a theological vision that is genuinely trinitarian. The theme of the Father's love for the Son, while explicit here for the first time (v. 35a; cf., however, 1:18), will become increasingly prominent in the gospel (5:20; 10:17; 15:9; 17:23-24, 26). The entire mission of the Son is to draw human beings (rendered through faith and baptism "children of God") into the divine communion of love made palpable by the experience of the Spirit communicated by Jesus.

In furtherance of this divine project, the Father has given all things "into his hand" (v. 35b), including the role of judgment. As in the earlier sequence in 3:16-21, judgment in Johannine thought is not so much something exercised by the Son at the end of time as an outcome that human beings can decide for themselves in the response they make to the revelation of God made manifest in Jesus. The person who believes in the Son "has eternal life" here and now (v. 36a). The person who disbelieves (literally, "disobeys" [*apeithōn*]) will not "see life"; on the contrary, "the anger of God remains upon such a person (v. 36b).

---

[68] Cf. the similar transition from negative to positive acceptance across 1:10-12.

[69] The logic running through the various elements of vv. 33-34 is not at all clear. It is equally possible to read the text of v. 34b as implying that God (the Father) is the giver of the Spirit and the Son the recipient, a reading supported by a textual variant supplying "God" as subject; so, C. K. Barrett, *John*, 226; Rudolf Schnackenburg, *St. John*, 1:386; Gail O'Day, "The Gospel of John," 559; Andrew T. Lincoln, *St. John*, 162. The overall thrust of Johannine theology, however, is to portray the Son as the One who imparts rather than receives the Spirit: see 1:32, 33; 7:38-39; 20:22; cf. Raymond E. Brown, *John I–XII*, 161.

The starkness of this dichotomy concluding the whole sequence—especially perhaps the apocalyptic language on the negative side—comes rather suddenly upon us. "Eternal life," as we have seen, is a share in the life of God that begins here and now but which will extend beyond the barrier of physical death into the undying life of God.[70] Those who respond negatively to the revelation of God and display that rejection in their pattern of life[71] will never "see life" in the sense that they will not enjoy in the life to come the eternal life that believers possess as a real, albeit unseen, gift here and now.[72] In the words of Jesus to Nicodemus, they will not "see the kingdom of God" (3:3, 5). The "anger of God" will remain upon them in the sense that the alienation from God, which is the whole purpose of the Son's mission to dispel, will have become a fixture of their existence through their rejection of the offer of life.[73] Since human beings are created to live in vital relationship with God, such a standoff has ruinous consequences and so becomes an expression of ultimate loss, the very opposite of sharing the divine "eternal life."[74]

We might regret that the sequence, which has certainly had its theological highpoints, should end on this sharply negative note. While emphasizing the far more dominant stress upon the positive, we should also recognize that what the entire sequence in John 3 is aiming at is a firm decision (a "sealing" [3:33]) of adherence to Jesus from parties within Judaism—those represented by Nicodemus and the disciples of John—who have come halfway, so to speak, but not made a final, unequivocal commitment. Hence the starkness of the decision—and the respective outcomes in either case—that the sequence puts before them. The decision for faith is one that has to be ratified daily in one's pattern of life. The passage as a whole can still speak powerfully to us through its sense of God's love (3:16; 3:35a)

[70] Cf. Rudolf Schnackenburg, *St. John*, 1:389–91.

[71] This is the sense of the term "disobeys" (*apeithōn*) used only here in the Fourth Gospel. "John is not thinking of a single act but of a pattern of life" (Raymond E. Brown, *John I–XII*, 162).

[72] Cf. 1 John 2:2: "Beloved, we are God's children now; what we will be has not yet been revealed. What we do know is this: when he is revealed, we will be like him, for we will see him as he is."

[73] Reference to the "anger" of God occurs only here in John. As elsewhere in the New Testament, it denotes not so much an emotion of God but a standoff in divine-human relations, which, rendered permanent by disbelief, becomes eschatological judgment.

[74] David Rensberger, *Johannine Faith*, 63, n. 30, suggests that the phrase "wrath of God" is used here to give a particularly "Baptist" coloring to an otherwise very Johannine passage; cf. the account of the Baptist's preaching according to Matt 3:7; Luke 3:7.

drawing human beings to surrender, not only once but again and again and ever more deeply, to that divine love made manifest in Jesus.

Jesus and the Woman of Samaria: 4:1-42

The meeting and conversation between Jesus and the woman of Samaria would be many readers' favorite episode in the Fourth Gospel. The first of the really long episodes in the story, it unfolds as an engaging dialogue between the two characters, in the course of which many key themes and symbols of the gospel are aired. It also evokes a number of biblical (OT) episodes, awareness of which adds greatly to understanding and appreciation.

Jesus' Encounter with the Samaritan Woman: Structure

The length of the sequence makes it all the more necessary to appreciate the carefully contrived structure that it displays. The dialogue between Jesus and the woman (4:7-26) is framed by two passages: one (4:1-6) sets the scene by explaining Jesus' presence in Samaria; one (4:27-30) concludes it by recording the reaction of the characters. In an aftermath (4:31-38) Jesus reflects on the episode, pointing out how it anticipates the wider mission the disciples will take up. Finally, foreshadowing the success of this mission "many Samaritans" come to faith on the basis of the woman's testimony (4:39-42).

Within this broader structure, the central dialogue between Jesus and the woman divides into two distinct dramatic moments: in the first (A: 4:7-15) the discussion centers around Jesus' enigmatic offer to provide "living water"; in the second (B: 4:16-26), within the overall theme of "worship," the woman wrestles with the interconnected issues of the truth about Jesus and the truth about herself. Each of these two main sections (A and B) opens with a request/challenge from Jesus (vv. 7-9; vv. 16-18), followed by a sequence divided into two subsections. In section A, each of these two subsections (vv. 10-12 and 13-15) is initiated by Jesus, who introduces the topics, and each concludes with misunderstanding on the part of the woman. In section B, each of the two subsections (vv. 19-24 and 25-26) is initiated by the woman, followed by a correction/revelation on the part of Jesus, who thus has the last word.

This analysis may seem overcomplicated and contrived but it has a genuine foundation in the text and, I would maintain, serves to throw light upon it as an unfolding dramatic dialogue. We can set it out schematically as follows:

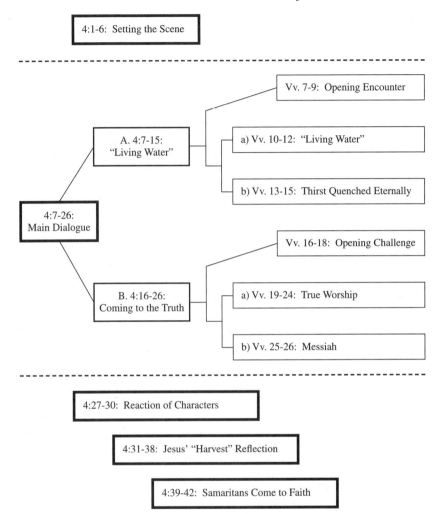

4:1-6: Setting the Scene

Vv. 7-9: Opening Encounter

A. 4:7-15: "Living Water"

a) Vv. 10-12: "Living Water"

b) Vv. 13-15: Thirst Quenched Eternally

4:7-26: Main Dialogue

Vv. 16-18: Opening Challenge

B. 4:16-26: Coming to the Truth

a) Vv. 19-24: True Worship

b) Vv. 25-26: Messiah

4:27-30: Reaction of Characters

4:31-38: Jesus' "Harvest" Reflection

4:39-42: Samaritans Come to Faith

Historical and Scriptural Background

Before considering the text in detail it will help to be aware of certain background information that it presupposes. Following the conquest of the northern kingdom of Israel by the Assyrians in 721 BCE and the deportation of many of its inhabitants, there was an influx of foreigners into the region of central Palestine known as Samaria (2 Kings 17). While these newcomers to some extent preserved the religion of the previous occupants of the land, the remaining Jews regarded their belief and practice as polluted by paganism and hence illegitimate. A particular source of aggravation was the setting up on Mount Gerizim of a rival place of worship to the temple in Jerusalem.[75] This and other factors led to the hostility and social separateness summed up in the brief explanation "Jews do not share things in common with Samaritans" (4:9b).

Likewise significant for interpretation is an awareness of certain biblical (OT) motifs and episodes that Jesus' encounter with the woman evokes. A particularly rich source of allusion is a pattern in the patriarchal stories where "courtship meetings," leading eventually to marriages, take place at wells. In Genesis 24:1-27, the servant whom Abraham has sent to Aram-naharaim to find a wife for his son, Isaac, meets Rebekah at a well and asks her for a drink. Generously, she offers to draw water for his camels as well.[76] In Genesis 29:1-14 Jacob is beside a well when his future wife Rachel approaches to water the sheep that she tends. Recognizing her as the daughter of his uncle Laban, Jacob removes the stone that covered the well, enabling her sheep to be watered; then he kisses her, his cousin and future wife. These biblical associations hover around the meeting between Jesus and the Samaritan woman.[77] Already present as "Bridegroom" (of Israel) at the wedding of Cana and explicitly named as such by John (3:21), Jesus comes now to "woo," in the person of this woman, a people (the Samaritans) beyond the confines of Israel, anticipating in this way the first mission of the later church (cf. Acts 8:1b-25).

Setting the Scene: 4:1-6

It is time for Jesus to leave Judea and return to Galilee (v. 3). Increasingly as the story proceeds, Judea emerges as a region where he experiences hostility from the religious leadership, here indicated as "the Pharisees" (v. 1). The rather convoluted statements in vv. 1-2 imply that the Pharisees, already unhappy about the crowds seeking baptism from John, are even more disturbed at learning that greater numbers are flocking to Jesus—though the text (in some tension with 3:22, 26) is careful to note that it was his disciples rather than Jesus himself who baptized (v. 2). The clarification preserves the distinction that, whereas John baptized with water, Jesus will baptize with the Holy Spirit (1:33).

---

[75] Cf. C. K. Barrett, *John*, 231.

[76] Also in common with John 4:7-30 is the fact that the woman is carrying a water-jar (*hydria*; Gen 24:15, etc.; cf. John 4:28) and that the success of the mission leads the servant to "worship" the Lord (Gen 24: 26-27; cf. John 4:19-24).

[77] Cf. Jerome H. Neyrey, "Jacob Traditions and the Interpretation of John 4:10-26," *Catholic Biblical Quarterly* 41 (1979): 419–37.

There were two routes to Galilee from Judea. The shorter and more direct passed through Samaritan territory; the longer and, for Jews, more secure route deviated to the east on the other side of the river Jordan.[78] The "necessity" (*edei*) for Jesus to take the more dangerous route through Samaria (v. 4) does not stem from geography. A divine necessity is driving his mission beyond Israel.

The journey through Samaria brings Jesus, accompanied by his disciples (cf. v. 8), to the town of Sychar. The exact location of this town is uncertain.[79] More important, however, is the fact that Jesus is in the territory that Jacob gave to his son Joseph (cf. Josh 24:32)—and, in the Samaritan view, to them as a people.[80] Included in the bequest was a well, "Jacob's well" (v. 6a).[81] When we learn (v. 6b) that Jesus, wearied by his journey, rests by this well at noon,[82] comparisons and contrasts with Jacob are strongly in play.

A. *"Living Water": 4:7-15*

Opening Encounter—the Divine "Thirst": 4:7-9. The arrival of a Samaritan woman at the well to draw water evokes the biblical "courtship" meetings already mentioned. It is a strange hour for a lone woman to be out in public approaching a well. When Jesus, by himself at this time since his disciples have gone to buy food (v. 8), asks her to give him a drink (v. 7b), he crosses two social barriers: (1) a gender barrier in that he, a lone male at a public place, requests a favor of her, a lone woman in a similar position; (2) an ethnic barrier in that he, a Jew, goes against the customary standoff between Jews and Samaritans (v. 9c). The crossing of the first barrier is later a matter of astonishment for the disciples when they return with food (v. 27). The transgression of the second is the subject of immediate remark on the part of the woman: "How is it that you, a Jew, ask a drink of me, a woman of Samaria?" (v. 9b). At this point in her understanding Jesus is simply "a Jew,"

---

[78] Cf. Francis J. Moloney, *John*, 116.

[79] It is usually identified with the present town of Askhar close to Shechem and the site traditionally identified as Jacob's well; cf. C. K. Barrett, *John*, 231.

[80] There is nothing in Gen 29:1-14 about Jacob providing a well for anyone. The Johannine sequence seems to presuppose a buildup of traditions based upon Gen 48:22, where the dying Jacob bequeaths the city of Shechem and its surroundings to Joseph.

[81] In Raymond E. Brown's view (*John I–XII*, 169) the traditional site of Jacob's well at the foot of the Samaritan temple on Mt. Gerizim "can be accepted with confidence."

[82] Lit. (v. 6c), "at the sixth hour," reckoning the twelve hours of daylight as beginning at 6 a.m.

a Jew moreover out of place and asking a favor that in view of the ethnic divide she is doubtless inclined to regard with disfavor and contempt.

The meeting begins, then, on a low note as regards her attitude to Jesus. For us as readers, however, awareness of the biblical background—courtship meetings at wells—enhances the dramatic tension. Is Jesus' bold request for a drink beginning a process of "wooing" on his part—a wooing through her of the Samaritan people whose true Bridegroom he longs to be? We recall, too, that "I thirst" will be his penultimate word before expiring in love upon the cross (19:28).

The Gift of God: "Living Water": 4:10-12. Whether the woman acceded to Jesus' request we do not know. His response to her exclamation turns the whole exchange around. Though she does not realize it, *she* is the one who is "thirsty"; *he* is the One who has "water" to slake her thirst: "If you knew the gift of God, and who it is that is saying to you, 'Give me a drink,' you would have asked him, and he would have given you living water (*hydōr zōn*)" (v. 10). In its double reference to what the woman might "know" the statement airs the two topics around which the rest of the conversation will unfold: the nature of the gift ("living water") that Jesus has to offer (vv. 11-15) and the identity of the One who is offering it (vv. 16-26).

The woman, becoming now (v. 11) more respectful ("Sir" [*kyrie*]) but remaining on a purely literal level of understanding, points out the difficulty. Jesus has no bucket and the well is deep; he cannot get water from it to give her to drink (v. 11a). Whence (*pothen*), then—if she takes up his suggestion and asks him for a drink—is he going to get this "living water"? (v. 11b). Since, as she has explained, there can be no question of his obtaining water from the well at hand, what mode of providing water does he have in mind? Instead of like Jacob providing a well with its inert water, is he by the phrase "living water" hinting at providing water that would bubble up from a spring, and not require a bucket or similar apparatus to draw it to the surface?[83] This explains her subsequent remark, "Are you greater than our ancestor Jacob, who gave us the well, and with his sons and his flocks drank from it?" (v. 12). As formulated in the original Greek (*mē*), her question expects the answer "No," whereas we readers know the answer is "Yes" and can pick up the irony.[84] As provider of "water" symbolically understood, Jesus is indeed "greater than Jacob" (cf. already 1:51). We also know "whence" he has such powers (1:1-2). But her question, though something of a retort, does suggest some movement in understanding. Her journey of faith is under way.

---

[83] Her understanding of "water" has moved on but remains on the material level.

[84] Cf. Andrew T. Lincoln, *St. John*, 174.

Thirst Quenched Eternally: 4:13-15. Leaving the comparison with Jacob hanging in the air, Jesus proceeds (v. 13) to prompt the woman to a symbolic understanding of "living water." [85] The difference between the water she has in mind—whether it be the inert water of a well or the bubbling up water of a spring—and the "water" he proposes to give revolves around capacity to slake thirst. Ordinary water slakes thirst only for a while; one soon becomes thirsty again and needs more. The "water" of which he is speaking will slake "thirst" eternally (v. 14a); it will be like a never-ending spring within a person, gushing up to eternal life (v. 14b). On the symbolic level on which Jesus is now speaking, "thirst" is no longer thirst for ordinary water but radical human "thirst" for God and for the life with God that all human beings were created to share. The "living water" that slakes that thirst and leads to that life is the Spirit, a gift that Jesus will give "without measure" (3:34b; cf. 1:33; 7:37-39; 19:30; 20:22-23).[86] At this point what he is offering is a promise; the reality has to await the completion of his mission, in particular his death upon the cross (cf. 7:39).

The woman's response (v. 15) is disappointing. Still wrapped up within her own world and her own needs—though realizing that Jesus has something to give her in addition to what she might give him—she asks for this gift. But her understanding remains on the material level. She simply asks for the provision of (ordinary) water to satisfy her (everyday) thirst and obviate her need to come day after day to the well. She still lacks a sense of her deeper thirst and the gift of Jesus that could slake it.

B. *Coming to the Truth: 4:16-26*

Opening Challenge: 4:16-18. The conversation has arrived at an impasse—something familiar to all engaged in spiritual direction. The woman cannot enter into a deeper appreciation of who Jesus is and the gift he has to offer her until she has transcended her own immediate needs and come to recognize her "thirst" at this deeper level. She cannot move from the literal to the

---

[85] Cf. Dorothy A. Lee, "The Story of the Woman at the Well: A Symbolic Reading (John 4:1-42)," *Australian Biblical Review* 41 (1993): 35–48.

[86] This is a traditional interpretation, based on the references to Jesus as giver of the Spirit in the gospel, as well as the widespread biblical imaging of the Spirit as water (e.g., Isa 44:3; Ezek 36:25-26; Joel 2:28; cf. Rom 5:5; 1 Cor 12:13); cf. Rudolf Schnackenburg, *St. John*, 1:431–32; C. K. Barrett, *John*, 233–34; Gail O'Day, "The Gospel of John," 566; Andrew T. Lincoln, *St. John*, 174. An alternative is to see a reference to the gift of revelation (Francis J. Moloney, *John*, 117, 122) or to the gift of eternal life (Ugo Schnelle, *Johannes*, 100). For a full discussion, see Raymond E. Brown, *John I–XII*, 178–179, who sees no reason to choose between the meanings Spirit or revelation since both can be present.

symbolic level until she has explored her own personal situation more profoundly. To begin this process Jesus turns the conversation in a new direction, saying: "Go, call your husband and come back" (v. 16a). The command brings to the forefront the biblical "courtship/marital" aura that has been hovering in the background since the conversation began. The woman's reply, "I have no husband (v. 16b)," draws from Jesus an informed knowledge of her marital experience and current status: she has had five husbands; the one she has now is not her husband; hence—ironically—she has spoken "well" and expressed the "truth" (vv. 17-18).

We have to tread carefully here. Feminist exegesis has rightly taken male interpreters to task for letting their imagination run riot in detailed reconstruction of the woman's sinful way of life.[87] On the other hand, it seems impossible to avoid all sense of scrutiny of her way of life—albeit with Jesus as conversation partner rather than master and judge. Dorothy Lee observes, "These verses function, not to expose moral guilt, but to uncover the pain of the woman's life in her relationships with men."[88] True, but such pain in human relationships is perhaps a symptom of the deeper "thirst" that Jesus is attempting to uncover, a longing for "life" that only the experience of intimacy with the divine can give. It is hard to eliminate from the conversation all sense of a need for conversion from a way of life that is to some degree morally suspect.[89] The woman's dismissive disclaimer, "I have no husband" (v. 17a), has expressed the truth (vv. 17b-18). She has had five husbands and, unsuccessful in all relationships, is ironically now free to be "wooed" and brought to the truth by Jesus.[90]

True Worship: 4:19-24. Jesus' mysterious knowledge of the woman's private life prompts her to conclude that he must be a prophet (v. 19).[91] This leads her to bring up an issue of hot contention between her people and the Jews:

---

[87] Gail O'Day, "The Gospel of John," 567, n. 106, takes even Raymond E. Brown (*John I–XII*, 171) to task in this connection.

[88] Dorothy A. Lee, "The Woman at the Well," 40–41.

[89] Cf. Andrew T. Lincoln, *St. John*, 175–76.

[90] The scarcely credible notion that the woman has in fact had five husbands has led many to interpret her personal history as symbolically representative of the religious situation of the Samaritans in Jewish eyes: that is, as an allusion to the false gods that they had previously worshipped and to the illegitimacy of their present attempt to worship the true God in their temple at Mount Gerizim (cf. v. 20). Both the literal and the symbolic meaning in this latter sense can be present.

[91] According to the biblical tradition prophets had access to knowledge, including knowledge about the interior and hidden life of persons, not otherwise accessible to human beings; cf. 1:48 (Jesus' knowledge of Nathanael's previous situation); 2:24-25; also Luke 7:39.

the question of the proper place for worship (v. 20).[92] If he is a prophet—perhaps "the Prophet" (Deut 18:15; cf. John 6:14)—maybe he can sort the matter out. Jesus, however, cuts through the issue by speaking of a coming "worship" of the Father that will completely transcend locale: "neither on this mountain (Mount Gerizim) nor in Jerusalem" (v. 21). Speaking as a Jew, he asserts for a moment (v. 22) the priority of Jewish worship over the Samaritan. The Samaritans have an inferior knowledge of God ("You worship what you do not know" [v. 22a]). Presumably, this is because they know God only from the Five Books of Moses (the Pentateuch), which is all that they recognize to be Scripture, rather than from the more complete Jewish canon that includes the Prophets and the Wisdom literature.[93] It is from this more widely informed "knowledge of God" that "salvation" (for the world) will emerge "from the Jews."[94] But, continues Jesus (vv. 23-24), overtaking this Jewish priority, a time (literally, "the hour") is coming—"and indeed now is"—when those who worship as God wants will do so "in spirit and in truth" (v. 23). A rather labored sentence explains why this must be the case: God is "spirit" (*pneuma*); hence those who worship according to the divine will must do so "in spirit and truth" (v. 24).

Worship characterized in this way implies at one level a distinction between the kind of material worship (the sacrificial ritual) offered in both the Jerusalem temple and its Samaritan counterpart on Mount Gerizim, on the one hand, and a more "interior" and spiritual worship appropriate to the immaterial being of God, on the other. Jesus had, after all, effectively suppressed material worship by driving from the temple the animals destined for sacrifice (2:14-22). But "spirit" (*pneuma*) in the Fourth Gospel means more than immaterial being. The Bible speaks of "spirit" in connection with the communicative and enlivening impact of God. Hence a worship that corresponds to the nature of God as "spirit" would be one that, aside from the ritual of sacrifice, is open to receiving life-giving communication from God within a truly personal relationship.

This is where the second member of the phrase, "and in truth," comes in. The Johannine sense of truth has to do with the definitive revelation of

---

[92] The woman's introduction of the issue of worship is not a stratagem to divert the conversation from the embarrassing details of her private life. The topic flows naturally from the understanding of Jesus as prophet and addresses a key issue between her people and the Jews; cf. C. K. Barrett, *John*, 236; Francis J. Moloney, *John*, 127–28.

[93] Cf. Gail O'Day, "The Gospel of John," 567.

[94] The assertion that "salvation is from the Jews" is a significant acknowledgment of the Jewish role in the scheme of salvation. Any consideration of the attitude of the gospel to Jews and Judaism must take note of this statement; cf. Andrew T. Lincoln, *St. John*, 177.

the reality of God (the Father) communicated to human beings through the Son. To "worship in spirit and in truth" involves, then, in the first instance responding in faith to this revelation. However, "truth" in the Johannine sense has also a human pole. Those who in faith commit themselves to the revelation of the truth allow their lives to be explored, enveloped, and shaped by it, beginning a life project in which they "do the truth" (3:21; 1 John 1:6). In this more complete sense, "worship in spirit and in truth" means a worship that proceeds from a truly converted heart, a heart that is "coming to the truth" about one's personal life, as is the case with this woman of Samaria. This is the kind of "worship" that the Father "now"—in this age of salvation—"wants." The (formerly correct) Jewish worship in the temple at Jerusalem and the (wrong) Samaritan worship at Mount Gerizim have both alike been overtaken by worship in the new "temple" that is the person of the Son (2:19-20). In her conversation with Jesus the Samaritan woman, like every believer committed to a life of prayer, is already beginning to "worship" the Father in this way.

Messiah: 4:25-26. The woman's progress in self-knowledge leads to deeper knowledge of Jesus as well: to know not only "the gift of God" but also "who it is who is speaking" to her (cf. v. 10). Failing to grasp Jesus' hint that true worship is attainable here and now, she expresses a conventional belief of her people: a Messiah is coming who will sort it all out (v. 25).[95] Jesus brings this vague hope back to the present with a climactic self-revelation: "I, the One who is (presently) speaking with you, am (he)" (v. 26). With these words Jesus is identifying himself as the messianic figure of her expectation but doing so in a way that transcends conventional categories, Jewish or Samaritan. The expression "I am" (*egō eimi*), echoing the self-identification of God to Moses at the Burning Bush (Exod 3:14), will play a significant revelatory role in the gospel (6:20; 8:24, 28, 58; 13:19; 18:5-6). The motif is notably developed in (Second) Isaiah, where *egō eimi* becomes in the LXX translation virtually a technical term to express the supremacy and saving activity of Israel's God (cf. Isa 41:4; 43:10, 25; 45:19, 22; 46:4, 9; 48:12; 51:12; 52:6).[96] Jesus is not merely the Jewish Messiah; he is the One in whom the presence and power of the unseen God is disclosed and communicated to the world (cf. 1:18).

---

[95] The woman could be giving expression to a Samaritan expectation of a messianic figure known as the Taheb. But the evidence for such a messianic belief is comparatively late; cf. Francis J. Moloney, *John* 129, 133–34.

[96] Association with this motif is especially brought out if Jesus' words are translated " 'I am' [is] the one speaking to you"; so, Francis J. Moloney, *John*, 130.

Reaction of the Characters: 4:27-30

The dialogue between Jesus and the woman has come to an end. The disciples, who have been offstage buying food, now return (v. 27) and are amazed to find him breaking the proprieties of gender relations: a lone male talking to a lone woman (cf. v. 9). The evangelist formulates for us the un- stated questions that arise: "What are you seeking?" and "Why are you speaking to her?" The questions prepare the way for Jesus' "harvest" reflec- tion shortly to follow (vv. 32-38). As he will explain (v. 34), his "food" is to do the will of the One who sent him. The divine will to communicate life without restriction impels him to cross and cast aside gender and ethnic barriers of the older dispensation.

The woman does not linger but goes off immediately to share her dis- covery with her townsfolk (vv. 28-30). The abandonment of her water jar (v. 28a) suggests that she is no longer interested in the ordinary water it was designed to carry. She is beginning to find within herself a thirst for the (symbolic) "water" that Jesus is offering. The way she voices her discovery and seeks to share it with her Samaritan townsfolk reveals the progress she has made on her journey: "Come and see a man who has told me all I have ever done. Can this one be the Christ?" (v. 29).

"Come and see" echoes the invitation of Jesus to the first two disciples (1:39), as also Philip's invitation to the initially reluctant Nathanael (1:46). More significant still is the reason the woman gives for coming to see the one with whom she has been speaking: he has told her all she has ever done (v. 29b). That is the literal meaning of the Greek and doubtless refers to Jesus' knowledge of her private life that led to her regarding him as a prophet. But to leave the statement there would miss something of a possible wider meaning. I have seen it translated, "Come and see a man who has told me the story of my life," a rendering far more truly expressive of the conversion that the woman has undergone. Jesus has taken the broken fragments of her life and shown that they can be part of a wider pattern of meaning in which her personal story and that of her people can be gathered up into the tran- scendent narrative being worked out in his mission from the Father. Her life, in its failures and deviations no less than in its strengths and successes, has meaning and value within the wider "great story" of salvation.

Also remarkable is the fact that it is while she is still asking questions, still wondering about the status of Jesus ("Can this be the Christ?" [v. 29c]),[97]

---

[97] The opening Greek negative particle, *mēti*, need not necessarily foresee a negative answer. It can express a cautious opinion designed to stimulate reflection; cf. Rudolf Schnackenburg, *St. John*, 1:444.

that the woman begins to attract people to Jesus. Her journey of faith is far from complete. Yet already, as her townsfolk come out from the city and approach him, it is having an apostolic effect (v. 30). True conversion of heart necessarily draws in others as well, and a faith still asking many questions is no less effective to that end.

Jesus' Harvest Reflection—the Divine "Hunger": 4:31-38

The story now reverts to the disciples, who urge Jesus to eat the food they have brought (v. 31). When he replies that he has food to eat of which they know nothing (v. 32), they wonder aloud whether some party other than themselves has brought him food (v. 33). Like the woman in regard to water at the beginning of her journey, they are fixed in a purely literal understanding of food. Again, the misunderstanding prompts Jesus to seek to move them beyond the literal and material to the symbolic: his "food" is to do the will of the One who sent him and complete (*teleioun*) his work (v. 34; cf. 17:4; 19:30b). He already "has" this food in the success of his outreach to the woman and in the movement of the Samaritans toward him that her witness has evoked (v. 32). The divine "hunger" for human salvation being satisfied in this way, he has no need of the food brought by the disciples.

The imagery of food now changes to the related one of harvest, a familiar biblical image to express completion.[98] Jesus takes up and turns to his purpose a series of proverbial sayings about harvest. The first, "four months more and then the harvest" (v. 35a), is not otherwise attested. The sense seems to be "Don't look for results before the time."[99] In the present case, however, the proverb does not apply: if the disciples lift up their eyes and see the Samaritans coming toward Jesus they will see "fields" already white in readiness for harvesting. The time gap between sowing and harvest has largely collapsed. That is why, contrary to what is usually the case, sower and reaper can rejoice together (v. 36).[100]

But who is the "sower" and who the "reaper," and who are "the laborers" in the sentences that follow (vv. 37-38)? Mention of "gathering harvest for eternal life" (v. 36a) suggests that the "harvest" image has now become an allegory of mission—the mission of Jesus, the Sower, and that of the post-Easter church that will reap what he has sown. As Jesus points out (v. 37), despite the collapse of the time between sowing and reaping, there

---

[98] Cf. Andrew T. Lincoln, *St. John*, 180.

[99] Perhaps a bit like "Rome wasn't built in a day."

[100] This is to see v. 36 as extending the imagery of the harvest in the direction of collapsing the space between sowing and reaping; cf. Gail O'Day, "The Gospel of John," 570.

is truth in the contention that the roles are distinct. The roles are distinct in that, whereas he has both sown and reaped (witness the response of the Samaritans), he is sending the disciples to reap where they have not performed the "labor" of sowing (v. 38a). "Others" (certainly Jesus, possibly John the Baptist,[101] or even the Samaritan woman[102]) have labored and the disciples "have entered into their labor" (v. 38b). The mission of the church to the end of time draws directly upon the mission of Jesus. It draws also upon the labors of those who like the Samaritan woman become themselves missionaries to their people through radical conversion in Spirit and truth.[103] They have caught the divine "hunger" to share with others the gift of life (3:16; 10:10).

The Samaritans Come to Faith: 4:39-42

The fruit of the Samaritan woman's witness is now displayed as her townsfolk stream out of their city to Jesus (v. 39). In response to their request Jesus "remains" (*menei*) with them two days (v. 40). Beyond mere presence, this "remaining" of Jesus has a truly salvific effect (cf. 1:38-39). "Many more" Samaritans come to believe in him on the basis of his word (v. 41). Somewhat ungraciously perhaps to our ears, they assure the woman that they no longer believe on the basis of her speech but because, having heard (Jesus), they (who previously did "not know what they worshipped" [v. 22a]) now know (*oidamen*) that he is "truly the Savior of the world" (v. 42). Unkind or not as it may be, their remark brings out a significant distinction. The woman's witness, like that of John earlier (1:19-36), had brought to Jesus people who were looking for a Messiah figure. But her witness, again like that of John, has to yield to the experience of his actual presence (cf. 3:29-30). The result is far deeper faith[104]—a faith that acknowledges that Jesus, beyond merely messianic categories (whether of Jewish or Samaritan kind), is indeed "the Savior of the world."[105] Transcending the role of the Jewish

[101] Cf. Francis J. Moloney, *John*, 140–41.

[102] Cf. Andrew T. Lincoln, *St. John*, 180.

[103] "This Samaritan woman with a dubious past has, ironically, brought Jesus his true food, in contrast to the disciples (cf. vv. 31-34), by her receptivity to his revelatory mission and by becoming the catalyst for the belief of other Samaritans" (Andrew T. Lincoln, *St. John*, 180).

[104] On the movement from one level of faith here to a deeper level, see esp. Francis J. Moloney, *John*, 146–47, 149.

[105] The title "Savior" (*sōtēr*) is redolent more of the Greco-Roman rather than the biblical-Jewish background. When applied to Jesus it asserts a claim to universal supremacy in the face of the claims made by the Roman emperor and other rulers (cf. 1 John 4:14; Luke 2:1; Phil 2:9-11; 3:20; 1 Tim 4:10).

Messiah, he is the One sent by the Father that "the world"—not just Israel—may not perish but have eternal life (3:16-17).

*Reflection.*The conversation between Jesus and the woman of Samaria begins with a request on his part for a gift of water to slake his thirst. His need for this simple service becomes the occasion for bringing the woman to an awareness of a much deeper need that she has, a "thirst" for life, which he alone can satisfy:

> Jesus thirsts; his asking arises from the depths of God's desire for us. Whether we realize it or not, prayer is the encounter of God's thirst with ours. God thirsts that we may thirst for him.[106]

As the conversation proceeds and deepens, Jesus leads the woman to ever-deeper self-knowledge, knowledge of himself and knowledge of the gift he has to give her—a gift so much greater than anything she can do for him. The woman allows Jesus to "tell her the story of her life." Running beneath all the disjointed and unsatisfactory aspects of her life has been a story of divine grace. Jesus has brought this story to the surface in the context of his wider mission to her people.

All this makes the episode such a wonderful paradigm of progress in prayer and spiritual transformation. Spiritual direction aims to allow Jesus to tell us "the story of our life" in the sense of gathering up all the fragments, the twists and turns, the false steps and failures, so that we can see them woven into a coherent and meaningful narrative of grace. The Lord can then lead us, as he led the woman, across constricting barriers of prejudice and fear, to a "worship in Spirit and truth" that is both liberating and apostolic.

Jesus Heals the Son of a Royal Official: 4:43-54

This episode, like the first Cana miracle (which it explicitly recalls [v. 46; cf. v. 54]), is attractive in its brevity and human interest. Preceding the miracle story proper, a short prelude (vv. 43-45) tells of Jesus' departure from Samaria and arrival in Galilee (v. 43), where he receives a welcome from the Galileans who had gone up to Jerusalem for the feast (Passover) and witnessed all he had done (v. 45).

---

[106] *Catechism of the Catholic Church*, 2nd ed. (Vatican City: Libreria Editrice Vaticana, 2000), §2560, with citation: "Cf. St. Augustine, *De diversis quaestionibus octoginta tribus* 64, 4: PL 40, 56."

Difficult to understand is an intervening statement (v. 44). It purports to give a reason (cf. *gar*) for Jesus' movements on the basis of a proverbial belief that a prophet receives no honor in his own land.[107] But isn't Jesus of Galilean origin—as the gospel makes clear (cf. 1:45; 2:1; 7:41, 52; 19:19)? If he is "welcomed" by the Galileans (v. 45), how can the proverb apply? An explanation would seem to be that, while Jesus' family origins may indeed be Galilean, the narrative of the gospel has already located much of his ministry in Judea and Jerusalem, the center of his people's life. In his interactions with the leaders of the people in Jerusalem, he has "come to his own" (*eis ta idia* [1:11]) and received at best a lukewarm response (2:14-23; cf. 4:1-3). In this wider sense, as the center of national life, Judea is the "homeland" (*patris*) that Jesus now leaves for the time being since his reception there has borne out the truth of the proverb (v. 44).[108]

The miracle story itself (vv. 46-54) falls into two main sections (vv. 46c-50) and (vv. 51-53), framed by introductory and concluding comments (v. 46ab and v. 54). We can set it out as follows:

Introductory indication of Cana as setting: 4:46ab

A. Encounter between Jesus and the Official: 4:46c-50

B. Verification of the miracle and effect upon participants: 4:51-53

Concluding comment: This was Jesus' second (Cana) sign: 4:54

Jesus arrives once again in Cana in Galilee (v. 46a), where—we are reminded (v. 46b)—he had changed the water into wine. The reminder hints at features that will parallel the first Cana sign. During his stay this time in the village Jesus is approached by a royal official who has a son grievously sick in Capernaum. The title *basilikos* suggests a military officer in the employment of a local ruler—Herod Antipas at the time of Jesus. Whether the man is a Jew or a Gentile is not clear from the title itself. The wider context, however, makes it more likely that we are to see in him a representative of the Gentile world.[109] In the course of the narrative so far Jesus has moved from the center of the Jewish world (Judea and Jerusalem) to the borderline non-Jewish milieu of the Samaritans, many of whom have come

---

[107] Cf. also Matt 13:57; Mark 6:4; Luke 4:24.

[108] For explanations of v. 44 along these lines, see C. K. Barrett, *John*, 246; Francis J. Moloney, *John*, 152; Gail O'Day, "The Gospel of John," 574. For Raymond E. Brown, *John I–XII*, 186–87; Andrew T. Lincoln, *St. John*, 184–85, the proverb anticipates the unsatisfactory faith of the Galileans; cf. 48.

[109] Cf. Francis J. Moloney, *John*, 153, 160–61; Ugo Schnelle, *Johannes*, 109.

to faith (4:39-42). Taking this man to be a Gentile goes along with the pattern of belief extending more and more beyond the confines of Judaism.[110]

Aware apparently of Jesus' fame as a healer and hearing of his arrival in Galilee, the official approaches to present his urgent plea. He begs Jesus to "come down" (to Capernaum) and heal his son, who is at the point of death (v. 47). The first Cana sign had simply remedied an embarrassing failure of wine at a village wedding. Now Jesus is confronted with the far more serious issue of life or death.

As in the first Cana miracle, the initial response is not positive (cf. 2:4). The man is desperate that something be done for his dying son. Jesus talks about faith. He does not even address the man's own level of belief but simply lumps him along with a collective weakness of faith: "Unless you (plural) see signs and wonders you will not believe" (v. 48). The collective reference is presumably to the kind of faith present in the Galileans who had welcomed him on the basis of what they had seen in Jerusalem during the feast (v. 45). Such faith may arouse interest in Jesus as one who can address more immediate human needs. It is a far from adequate basis for an engagement with him as he truly is ("I am" [4:26]).

The official does not protest or argue. Like the mother of Jesus (2:5), he simply presses his plea, speaking now even more desperately as a loving parent: "Sir, come down before my little boy (*paidion*) dies" (v. 49).[111] We are standing on the threshold of death.

Jesus still does not accede to the man's plea; he does not himself "go down" to save the child. He simply instructs (v. 50a) the man to go, assuring him that his son lives (*zēi*). With remarkable trust in Jesus' word, the man goes on his way (v. 50b). Only when in the course of his journey he is met by servants with the joyful news that his boy lives (v. 51 [*zēi*]) does he have confirmation that Jesus' assurance is true. He has not believed on the basis of seeing miracles ("signs and wonders" [v. 48]). He has first believed and then learned that what he so ardently longed for has come about.

But that is not all. The subsequent discovery (vv. 51-53) that the boy's recovery had occurred precisely at the moment when Jesus had assured him,

---

[110] Cf. Francis J. Moloney, *John*, 153, 160–61. The scene has strong parallels with the story of the healing of a centurion's son/servant in Matt 8:5-13 and Luke 7:2-10. All three accounts feature healing at a distance, and, of course, the centurion is a Gentile; see further, Raymond E. Brown, *John I–XII*, 192–93.

[111] The use of the diminutive *paidion* in the father's direct speech here (contrast *huios* in v. 46 and *pais* in v. 51) conveys the sense of parental love and desperation. It also confirms the fact that the son is a child.

"Your son will live," reveals the power of Jesus' word.[112] Transcending limits of distance, his word gives life in the face of death (cf. 1:3-4).

The healing constitutes a "sign" in the full Johannine sense. The restoration of the child to present physical life points to Jesus as One who can communicate in a more radical sense the "eternal life" that it is his mission to bring to the world. Moreover, as the first Cana miracle revealed "his glory" so that his disciples believed in him (2:12) and as the faith of the Samaritan woman, despite its hesitant beginnings, resulted in the faith of "many" of her townsfolk (4:39), so the faith of this official extends beyond him personally to draw in his entire household (*oikia*) (v. 53). From another aspect his faith foreshadows and models that required of later Gentile communities. In the post-Easter situation of Jesus' physical absence, they, like him, have to believe simply in the power of his life-giving word.

Reflection. The royal official deserves a place among the heroes of this gospel. In a human way we resonate with his anguish as a parent as Jesus coolly responds to his desperate plea with a generalization about the inadequacy of "miracle-based" faith. All the more admirable, then, in the face of this rebuff, is his decision to "walk" in faith, trusting simply in Jesus' assurance and the power of his word. There are likewise times in the lives of all believers when we simply have to "walk" in faith, trusting and believing that God can bring life out of what seems perilously close to death. The episode suggests, perhaps, that it is precisely at such times that we come to know God as the Giver of Life in a more transcendent sense, beyond our more immediate needs and wants, however pressing these may be.

---

[112] The synchronicity is a notable point of agreement with Matthew's account of the healing of the centurion's son; cf. Matt 8:13.

Like the Father, the Son Must Give Life: 5:1-47

At this point we come upon one of the less appealing areas of the Fourth Gospel. The sequence follows a regular pattern where a miraculous heal-ing—the cure of a long-paralyzed man—triggers a narrative or discourse that brings out the symbolic meaning. The cure of this particular person becomes revelatory of the more fundamental gift of "life" that Jesus has to offer. Aside from his being cured, however, there is no indication of any growth, human or spiritual, on the part of the man himself, and the following narrative consists largely of a polemical exchange between Jesus and his principal adversaries, unhappily termed "the Jews." For the first time we confront here the "shadow side" of the Fourth Gospel: the fact that so much of what it wants to say positively about Jesus emerges over against a nega-tive portrayal of the leading authorities of his people, who are regularly called simply "the Jews," as if Jesus himself were somehow abstracted from his own people and set over against them as a non-Jew.[1]

The polemic that we meet here—and will confront at greater intensity later on—reflects, of course, not so much Jesus' historical interaction with the authorities of his people but the later hostility between the community responsible for the Fourth Gospel and the larger body of Judaism from which they had recently—and painfully—separated.[2] The gospel explores the mo-tives and reasons behind the failure of the larger body to come to faith in Jesus as Messiah. The failure has a great deal to do with the claims being made for the status of Jesus, especially in regard to his unique and exalted

---

[1] It would correspond to setting a figure such as Martin Luther King, Jr., over against "the Americans." In this connection, note the very helpful words of Gail O'Day: " 'The Jews' in this story are not Jesus' enemies because they are Jewish (cf. Jesus' assertion, "salvation is from the Jews," 4:22), but because they reject Jesus. That is, their Jewishness is not the issue; their response to Jesus is" ("The Gospel of John," 581).

[2] Cf. C. K. Barrett, *John*, 250, and the long quotation from Rudolf Bultmann that he cites.

94

relationship to God. This is why so many richly theological statements about Jesus appear in polemical contexts unattractive, unappealing, and irrelevant to our present-day concerns. Contemporary interpretation has to confront and deal responsibly with this fact—and chapter 5 is where the task really begins in a sustained way. That said, there are nuggets of gold to be found here, especially in the central section (vv. 19-30), where Jesus presents himself over and over as the beloved Son sent by the Father to be both life-giver and judge.

The chapter falls into three main sections, in which an opening narrative featuring a miracle ("sign") is followed by a discourse in two parts:

1. Narrative: 5:1-18: Jesus cures a paralyzed man at the pool of Bethesda (vv. 1-9a), an action that attracts the critical attention of the authorities ("the Jews) since it has been performed on the Sabbath (vv. 9b-15); the man's identification of Jesus to the authorities leads to a sharp polemical exchange, raising the christological issues that will be central to the entire discourse to follow (vv. 16-18).

2. Discourse A: 5:19-30: Jesus, as his Father's "apprentice" (vv. 19-20), is life-giver and judge, in the sense of both "realized" (vv. 21-25) and "final" (vv. 26-30) eschatology.

3. Discourse B: 5:31-47: in a polemical defense Jesus points to the multiple witness sustaining the truth of his claims.

Sabbath Healing of the Paralyzed Man at the Pool: 5:1-18

The Healing at the Pool: 5:1-9a

In a setting of occasion (v. 1) and place (vv. 2-3), we learn that Jesus has gone up to Jerusalem for a Jewish feast. The notice about a feast initiates a large section of the gospel (5:1–10:42) where a sequence of feasts forms the setting for each episode. In some cases—Passover in the case of chapter 6, Tabernacles in chapters 9–10—the feast provides a background central to the story. In others it seems to be simply a device accounting for Jesus' presence in Jerusalem. The latter seems to be the case here. More important than any feast will be the fact that the cure takes place on a Sabbath.

The locale for the scene is a pool in Jerusalem, called Bethesda.[3] Within the five porticoes surrounding this pool lie many sick people, all seeking to

---

[3] The name of the pool appears variously in the textual tradition. Evidence from the Dead Sea Scrolls seems to confirm "Bethesda" as most likely to be original. Archaeologists have

be healed by its curative waters. An explanation later given by the paralyzed man to Jesus (v. 7) seems to imply a general belief that when there is a "disturbance" of the water the first person into the pool is the one destined to benefit from its curative effects. An addition to the text appearing in some late manuscripts (vv. 3b-4) attributes the healing "disturbance" to the action of "an angel of the Lord." What the original text has in mind, however, is probably simply a regular inrush of water from the source of the pool, in all likelihood a spring welling up from the depths of the Holy City, to which life-giving qualities were attributed.[4]

At this scene Jesus comes upon a man who had lain there for thirty-eight years (v. 5). The number seems to have no significance other than to indicate a great length of time and, consequently, the extremity of the man's need. Since Jesus, we are told, knows how long the man has been lying there, his questioning him (v. 6b) about whether he wants to be healed seems otiose. Why else would the man be there? But maybe the long years of fruitless waiting have extinguished hope and with it even the desire to be healed. The man may be paralyzed in spirit as well as body. Jesus' question may be seeking to arouse in the man the interior dispositions necessary for an adequate response to the One standing before him.

The man's response (v. 7) does not auger well. He does not reply directly to Jesus' question but simply points to the recurring pattern that has long since ruled out hope of finding healing: he has no one to help him get into the water; someone else always gets there before him. He may still "want" to be healed in a vague kind of way, but hope has been extinguished.

Jesus circumvents the issue with a word of command (v. 8): "Get up, take up your stretcher, and go on your way" (literally, "walk"). Instantly, the man becomes "whole" and does exactly as Jesus had said (v. 9a). That is the end of the episode as far as the miracle is concerned. Unlike other scenes in the gospel, there is no hint of faith or even of wonder about the status of the One who has just transformed his life beyond all expectation. The man simply goes on his way.

---

excavated near St. Anne's church a pool in Jerusalem with five porticoes, corresponding to the description in John 5:2; see further, C. K. Barrett, *John*, 251–52; Gail O'Day, "The Gospel of John," 578n.

[4] Such a belief might have some connection with Ezekiel's vision of life-giving water flowing from the sanctuary (47:1-12). If so, behind the healing that Jesus works may be an implied contrast between the power of his simple word (v. 8) and the efficacy of the water flowing from the temple, which is now being superseded by Jesus (2:19-21).

Controversy: Breaking the Sabbath: 5:9b-18

An aftermath to the miracle arises from the fact that healing has taken place on the Sabbath, which technically the man has violated by going off carrying his stretcher (v. 9b). Challenged on this account by the authorities ("the Jews") the man defends himself by claiming that this is what he was told to do by a man who had healed him (vv. 10-11). Ignoring the remarkable fact that a man paralyzed for thirty-eight years now stands before them healed, the authorities remain fixed upon the Sabbath violation and seek to pin down the identity of the one ultimately responsible. Already they are moving in a direction where a blinkered pursuit of religious law blinds them to a divine enhancement of life before their eyes. They seek to know the identity of Jesus, not as healer but as violator of the Sabbath (v. 12).

This information the man cannot presently supply. Jesus has vanished in the crowd (v. 13). But later, finding the man in the temple, Jesus moves to take him beyond mere physical healing to a deeper conversion (v. 14). Healing is one thing but let him sin no more, lest something worse befall him! This is one of the more troubling statements of Jesus in the gospel and has been variously interpreted. It is easy to find here an implication that the man's long-standing sickness has been a divine punishment for sin.[5] Later, in connection with the man born blind (9:2-3) Jesus will explicitly reject a suggestion along these lines. But even here the implication is neither necessary nor appropriate. The man has been physically restored to health. He must complete that restoration with a renewed moral life, lest "something worse" than the physical ailment he so long endured befall him—that "something" being, presumably, condemnation and loss of eternal life at the judgment (cf. 5:29).[6] The warning is admittedly couched in negative terms. But it can be seen as an effort on Jesus' part to stretch the moral horizons of the man toward a deeper experience of salvation.[7]

How, then, are we to interpret the man's immediately going off and identifying Jesus to the authorities (v. 15)? Ingratitude at worst, foolish naivety at best? Perhaps neither. A negative view of his action, looking only to its consequences, may attribute to him a motivation unwarranted by what the text actually says. The man "announces" to the authorities that Jesus is the One who had healed him. Elsewhere in the gospel the Greek verb

---

[5] So, Rudolf Bultmann, *Gospel of John*, 243.

[6] Cf. C. K. Barrett, *John*, 255.

[7] "(Jesus) urges that the man's healing should be more than physical. The man needs to be spiritually healthy also, as the expression 'be made well' suggests" (Gail O'Day, "The Gospel of John," 579).

anangellein has a positive sense (cf. 4:25; 16:13-15). The man no longer refers to Jesus as one who had caused him to violate the Sabbath (cf. v. 11) but solely as the person who had brought him healing. Like the Samaritan woman (4:28-29), he may be beginning to "live out" his deeper conversion by identifying Jesus to others as one who brings healing and enhancement of life.[8]

The consequence, however, is trouble for Jesus (vv. 16-18). Emerging here for the first time is a theme that will intensify as the gospel proceeds: Jesus does not provide healing and enhancement of life without cost to himself (cf. 10:10-18), a cost that stems in the present case from the narrowness of the categories in which the authorities view his activity. Blind to the gift of life, seeing only the violation of law—in this case the Sabbath—they set in motion a pattern of persecution or, more strictly, of legal accusation.[9] From this point on Jesus is explicitly on trial.[10]

In the face of this accusation Jesus moves to portray the Sabbath within a totally new horizon: his unique relationship with God and the fact that all his activity is simply the extension of the life-giving work of the Father (v. 17). As his Father (God) is continually at work, so is he. Presupposed here is a Jewish belief, reflected in rabbinic literature, that the statement in Gen 2:2-3 that God "rested" on the Sabbath could not mean a complete cessation of activity. Creation would simply collapse if the divine giving of life ceased even for a time. So Jesus justifies his work on the Sabbath by saying that, like his Father, he cannot refrain from "working."[11] He is the Word through whom all things were made, through whom they are held in existence, and through whom human beings are offered "life" in the fullest sense (1:3-4). His restoring the paralyzed man to health on the Sabbath is a symbol or sign pointing to this continual work of creation.

The authorities ("the Jews") are not slow to grasp the theological import of Jesus' claim. They react with extreme hostility, seeking to kill him. This threat will hang over him from this point on, especially when he is present in Jerusalem or Judea (7:1, 19, 20, 25; 8:37, 40). For the authorities it is no

---

[8] For this positive interpretation I am indebted to Gail O'Day, "The Gospel of John," 580. For a negative evaluation, see Francis J. Moloney, *John*, 173; Andrew T. Lincoln, *St. John*, 196.

[9] This sense of an action beginning and continuing indefinitely is conveyed by the imperfect tense of the Greek verb *ediōkon*, which can mean both "persecute" and "bring a charge against" in a legal sense.

[10] Cf. Francis J. Moloney, *John*, 169–70.

[11] On the Jewish tradition concerning the divine activity continuing on the Sabbath, see C. H. Dodd, *Interpretation*, 320–22; Dorothy A. Lee, *Flesh and Glory*, 116–18.

longer simply a question of violating the Sabbath. By speaking of God as his Father and defending his own "working" as simply extension of the divine giving of life, Jesus is "making himself equal to God" (v. 18).

Reflection. While the claim Jesus makes here is undoubtedly a challenge to Jewish monotheism in the strictest sense, we may rightly be shocked at the extremity of the response it provokes. How are we to read the episode today? Certainly, we must avoid any identification of the Johannine "the Jews" with the Jewish people as such. It is one amongst many episodes in the gospels as a whole where attempts on Jesus' part to restore or enhance life burst the categories of conventional observances, attracting the hostility of those who derive power and significance from keeping such observances in place. Conflict and oppression on this account can arise in many areas of socio-political life and, needless to say, is not something from which the Christian church has itself been immune. "Jesus brings God into human experience in ways that transcend and transform human definitions and categories"[12]— even, we might add, categories and observances that may appear to be of divine institution and sanction. In Judaism nothing is more sacred than the Sabbath. Without sweeping it away, Jesus' healing of the man at the pool of Bethesda represents a drastic reclaiming of the Sabbath in light of a more radical view of the divine gift of life.[13]

Discourse A: Jesus, Life-giver and Judge: 5:19-30

Jesus has defended his Sabbath activity on the basis that it is simply an extension of the continual activity of his Father (v. 17). He furthers this defense in a discourse expanding upon this work common to Father and Son. The discourse mines one of the richest veins of the theology of the gospel. At the same time it features ambiguities in both terminology and eschatology that, while adding to its richness, pose challenges for interpretation.[14]

Jesus has been accused of setting himself up as a rival "god" to the God of Israel ("making himself equal to God" [v. 18]). The central point of the

---

[12] Gail O'Day, "The Gospel of John," 581.

[13] Jesus' further defense of the healing later in the gospel brings this out: "If a man receives circumcision on the Sabbath in order that the law of Moses may not be broken, are you angry with me because I healed a man's whole body on the Sabbath?" (7:23).

[14] The chief terminological ambiguity concerns "judgment" in that the underlying Greek term *krisis* can indicate both the *process* of judgment in a neutral sense and also the negative *outcome* of such a process in the sense of "condemnation."

discourse is to refute this charge by insisting on the Son's complete dependence upon and unity with the Father in the "work"—giving life and judging—that is peculiar to God. This emphasis is pursued (vv. 19-20) in an attractive image, based perhaps upon a parable or proverb, portraying the Son as "apprentice" to his Father. In the world presupposed by the gospel, sons commonly followed the trade of their fathers, who were their first instructors. To cite C. H. Dodd,

> In John vv. 19-20a . . . we have a perfectly realistic description of a son apprenticed to his father's trade. He does not act on his own initiative; he watches his father at work, and performs each operation as his father performs it. The affectionate father shows the boy all the secrets of his craft.[15]

The image counters any sense of rivalry or competition. The Son does nothing save what he sees the Father doing. And it is from the love that the Father has for the Son that his willingness to show him what he does proceeds.

A statement following the image, "He (the Father) will show him greater works than these, so that you (the adversaries) will be amazed" (v. 20c-d), refers to the eschatological divine works of "giving life" and "judging" that are now to be discussed. They will be "greater" in comparison to the "work" that Jesus has already performed in restoring to bodily wholeness the paralyzed man at the pool. That physical restoration (vv. 8-9), together with the later pastoral warning ("Sin no more," v. 14), has provided a symbol of a more radical giving of life and pronouncement of judgment that the discourse is now to unfold. If the adversaries had been put out by that earlier healing, let them be warned that they will be even more radically "amazed" at what Jesus is yet to accomplish.[16]

Giving life to the dead and judging are divine prerogatives. But, as Jesus now insists (vv. 21-22), they are roles that the Father has entrusted, with complete discretion (cf. "to whomever he wishes" [v 21b]), to the Son. The upshot is that, instead of attacking Jesus for presenting himself as a rival to God (v. 18), all should honor the Son as they honor the Father. To refuse honor to the Son—as in the present case—is to refuse honor to "the One who sent him," that is, God (v. 23). Jesus is no independent agent: behind him and all his activity stands the Father's saving will.

---

[15] Cf. C. H. Dodd, *Historical Tradition in the Fourth Gospel* (Cambridge: Cambridge University Press, 1963), 386, n. 2; see also, Dorothy A. Lee, *Flesh and Glory*, 115.

[16] "Amazement" does not reflect a positive response in the Fourth Gospel: see also 3:7; 4:27; 5:28; 7:15, 21. I am taking the *hina* clause in a consecutive rather than a final sense.

With two solemn affirmations ("Amen, amen" [v. 24; v. 25]) Jesus turns to address the impact of his "work" on the human side. To truly hear Jesus' word and thereby come to faith in God as the One who sent him[17] is to "have eternal life" here and now. There is no question of "coming to judgment" since the person who has arrived at such belief has already passed out of "death" into "life." It is not that judgment has simply been bypassed. Rather, the process of hearing Jesus' word and coming to faith has involved a "coming to the light" in the sense explained in 3:19-21. The result being that one "has" the divine "eternal life" here and now.

The process just described reflects the "realized" eschatology characteristic of the Fourth Gospel. By contrast, a second solemn affirmation (v. 25) seems to locate it all in the future: "an hour is coming" when the (physically) dead are to hear the voice of the Son of God and rise to life—though the added phrase, "and now is" maintains the sense of present gift. The Son's "voice" will have this life-giving effect because the Father has communicated to the Son his own life-giving power (v. 27; cf. 1:3-4). Likewise communicated to the Son is the associated divine role of exercising judgment (v. 27a), a role the Son will discharge in virtue of being "Son of Man" (v. 27b). Earlier (1:51; 3:14-15) Jesus has applied this designation to himself in reference to his earthly ministry that will culminate in death. Now it designates his role as end-time judge.[18]

A concluding couplet (vv. 28-29) spells out Jesus' exercise of this role in terms that reflect the account of the general resurrection in Daniel 12:1-2. Because the Father has given the role of judgment to the Son, the adversaries are not to be surprised (to learn that) "an hour is coming" when all the (physically) dead (literally, "all in the tombs") will hear his voice and issue forth to receive judgment on the basis of how they have lived (literally, whether their deeds have been good or evil). This unambiguous statement of a judgment "according to works" comes as something of a surprise since, as already noted, "sin" in the Fourth Gospel more characteristically appears as refusal to believe in Christ—just as, on the positive side, righteous living is reduced almost entirely to the "new commandment" of love (13:34; 15:12).

---

[17] On the coordination of "hearing" and "believing" here, cf. C. K. Barrett, *John*, 261.

[18] As in Dan 7:13, but uniquely as far as the entire occurrence of "Son of Man" in the New Testament is concerned, the title appears here without an article; cf. Francis J. Moloney, *John* 180, 183–84. The "Son of Man" figure in Dan 7:13 does not exercise judgment. However, in the development of the motif in the post-Danielic tradition, the Son of Man does exercise this role, e.g., in the book of Enoch see, Rudolf Schnackenburg, *St. John*, 2:107; John Painter, *Quest for the Messiah*, 321–23.

Nonetheless, Jesus has already been presented as "the Lamb of God, who takes away the sin of the world" (1:29) and, after his resurrection, the risen Lord will breathe the Holy Spirit upon the disciples to empower them to remit sins (20:22-23). Such texts, along with the evocation of judgment in the present passage, show that repentance and conversion of life remain central to the Johannine sense of Christian existence.

A final sentence (v. 30) restates the central theme: Jesus' complete unity with and dependence upon the Father. Previously (v. 19) he had insisted that he "did" only what he "saw" the Father do. In the same vein, he now insists that his judgment is just because it does not derive from his own will but is entirely dependent upon what he "hears" from the One who sent him. We have returned, in effect, to the "apprentice" image with which the sequence began (vv. 19b-20).

Reflection. Looking back over the sequence, we can admit that its repetitive nature and its oscillation in time reference between present and future make for difficulty in following a consistent line of thought, let alone finding a unified meaning. We might well think that the evangelist would have done better to opt entirely for the sophisticated realized eschatology, letting go the futurist eschatology that presumably reflects earlier tradition.[19] But collapsing all sense of the "not yet" into the "already" would have impoverished the meaning. Reminder of a judgment still to come (vv. 27-29) can serve as a salutary warning that conversion must be lived out, that believers remain accountable for their deeds, whether "good" (v. 29a) or "bad" (v. 29b).[20] Moreover, the motif of the Son's voice calling all out of the tombs offers a powerful symbolic representation of what, from a more realized perspective, the voice of Jesus is doing now: summoning all to leave the "tombs" of darkness and sin to rise in faith to a present sharing in divine life. The subtle interplay of present and future in this passage will find ultimate resolution when Jesus summons his friend Lazarus from the tomb—a pledge of future resurrection but also a sign and symbol of the eternal life communicated to believers here and now (John 11:1-44; esp. vv. 25-26).

---

[19] Older commentators, in historical-critical mode, devoted much effort to the detection of the various levels of tradition lying behind the present text. As Gail O'Day remarks, too much focus upon source theories of this kind obscures the theological issues (cf. "The Gospel of John," 585). Like her, I take the final text as the basis of discussion.

[20] Cf. Paul in Rom 2:6-10; 2 Cor 5:10.

Discourse B: Jesus' True Testimony and Glory: 5:31-47

The second part of Jesus' discourse is a sustained polemical sequence in which it is hard to find anything attractive or edifying. Scholars will point out that the literary form operative here is that of a courtroom defense. That may assist understanding but courtrooms are hardly places where one goes to warm the heart. What we have to keep in mind is that what Jesus says here—or, rather, what the evangelist puts on his lips—reflects a time when the conversation between the Johannine community and representative Jewish authorities is well and truly over. To bolster its own identity and confidence the community is stating the superiority of its claims about Jesus. It is reflecting upon the failure—now conclusive—of the Jewish majority to accept Jesus as the definitive revelation of God and assigning reasons for that failure in terms of its distinctive understanding of sin.

All this means that when we read the passage we are listening to one side of a polemical exchange that was over and done with nearly two millennia ago. Despite the best efforts of commentators we have to work hard to find here some meaning for our time—though in places, as I hope to show, more positive theological insights can be discerned as the obverse of the complaints and accusations of which the passage largely consists. What emerges above all is the absolute centrality of Jesus in the gospel's understanding of God.

The passage begins (v. 31) with Jesus conceding that he cannot simply bear witness on his own behalf. In line with the traditional Jewish legal requirement of more than one witness (cf. Deut 19:15), for his defense to stand up the testimony of another is required.[21] But there is "another" who validly performs this role for him (v. 32) —though who that "other" is he does not for the moment reveal. An obvious candidate is John the Baptist. Jesus reminds his adversaries that they have already sought witness from John (cf. 1:19-26) and that the testimony they received from him was "true" (v. 33). But John is not that "other" witness about whom Jesus is speaking. He does not accept human witness (v. 34a), which is all that John could provide. John was a "lamp" that burned and shone for a time, giving forth a light in which they were happy to bask (v. 35). If Jesus mentions John, it

---

[21] "to stand up": I take this as the meaning of the adjective "*alēthēs*" at the end of v. 31, which in the present context refers to the validity of the witnessing rather than to "truth" in an absolute sense.

is only by way of concession to their regard for him—in the hope that it might aid their salvation (literally, "so that you might be saved" [v. 34b]).[22]

Greater than the testimony provided by John is that stemming from the "works" that his Father has given Jesus to perform.[23] When properly discerned by faith, these are "signs" that point to his true origins: namely, that he has been sent by God (v. 36; cf. 2:11; 4:46-54; 5:8, 17).[24] We now know who the "other" is who bears witness to Jesus: the Father himself (v. 37a).

At this point (v. 37b) Jesus shifts over to the offensive. Placing the authorities themselves on trial and under accusation, he sets out to expose why it is that they have failed—and continue to fail—to advert to the witness provided by the Father (vv. 37b-47). How could they have picked up the Father's witness when they have "neither heard his voice nor seen his form" (v. 37b)?[25] The gospel has already drawn attention to the biblical axiom that no one can see God (1:18a) and insisted, in the face of this, that it is the "only begotten Son, who is ever in the bosom of the Father, who has made him known" (1:18b). Apart, then, from acceptance of Jesus and belief in him, there can be no hearing or vision of God. That is why they cannot pick up the witness of the Father.

"The Jews" might well respond: "Agreed, we, like all other human beings, do not hear God's voice or see his form, but at least God has spoken to us in his word." Jesus moves (v. 38) to block this (unstated) line of argument as well. They (literally, "you") do not have his "word" (*logon*) dwelling (*menonta*) in them because they do not believe in the One whom God has sent. That is why their "searching" of the Scriptures fails to be productive of the eternal life they search them to find (vv. 39-40). Recalling the Prologue attunes us to the flow of Jesus' argument here. "The Jews" look to the Scriptures to hear God's word. But Jesus himself is the primary Word of God (1:1, 14), giving "life" to human beings (1:4). It is only when a person reads the Scriptures in the light shone by faith that one finds in them God's life-

---

[22] For the understanding of the tortuous logic of vv. 34-35, I am much indebted to Andrew T. Lincoln, *St. John*, 206.

[23] The "works" (*erga*) of Jesus include his whole earthly activity, not just his miracles; cf. Ugo Schnelle, *Johannes*, 125.

[24] Some interpreters see a duality of witness here: "the works" and the Father. I see a single witness. Since the witness of the unseen Father is not immediately accessible to human beings, one must first believe in Jesus and then discover the Father's witness shown in the works that he performs; cf. C. K. Barrett, *John*, 267.

[25] There could be an ironic allusion here to the experience of Israel at the foot of Sinai (Exod 19:9-25); cf. Gail O'Day, "The Gospel of John," 587.

giving Word. Then they too become instruments of the Father's witness to Jesus.

After this fairly unified sequence centered upon "witness," Jesus introduces the topic of "glory" (*doxa*). A somewhat cryptic excursus plays upon two meanings of the Greek word *doxa*: (1) the standard meaning in secular Greek as "reputation" or "opinion"; (2) the distinctive biblical usage in respect to the revelation of the presence and power of God. Human beings cannot see God but can detect and acknowledge ("glorify") the divine presence and power in creation and in saving acts on behalf of God's people; in these they see God's "glory." Chosen emissaries and instruments of God can also bear the divine glory as a sign of their authority to act and speak in God's name (human beings [Ps 8:5-6]; Moses [Exod 34:29-35; cf. 2 Cor 3:12-18]). When Jesus states (v. 41) that he does not accept praise ("glory") from human beings, he is using *doxa* in the first, everyday sense. It is not because he wants to enjoy human approbation that he is upbraiding his adversaries. He is upbraiding them for their failure to accept him as one who comes bearing the authority (literally, "in the name") of his Father, whereas they would accept (literally, "believe") someone who comes in his own name (v. 43). In this way they accept (or seek) honor (*doxa*) from one another but do not seek (or accept) the "glory" (*doxa*) of the "only God," the glory of the Father that empowers Jesus and is made manifest in him (1:14; 13:31-32; 17:5, 24).[26]

At one point in this diatribe Jesus claims to "know" that they "do not have the love of God in them" (v. 42). The reference to love—most likely, human love for God rather than vice versa—is, in this polemic context, unexpected. Yet we are probably meant to hear the accusation about lacking love as the ultimate explanation of the adversaries' failure to believe. The reference to "the only God" at the end (v. 44c) likely alludes to the kernel of Israel's faith contained in the Shema confession (Deut 6:4-8) with its command to love God "with all your heart, and with all your soul, and with all your might" (6:5). The implication would then be that it is because they approach Jesus from an adversarial stance rather than from the love that is God's core demand of Israel that the authorities fail to recognize in him the glory of the God they claim to worship.

The allusion to the Shema prepares the way for the highly polemic appeal to Moses with which the discourse concludes (vv. 45-47). Jesus will not be the adversaries' accuser at the time of the judgment. On the contrary,

---

[26] There is a similar play upon the two meanings of "glory" in 12:43; cf. also 7:18; 8:50, 54; see further, Francis J. Moloney, *John*, 364–65.

Moses, the one whom they look to as their key advocate (cf. Exod 32:7-14, 30-32; Ps 106:23), will in fact play this role.[27] Moses, author and promulgator of the Torah, will lead the prosecution against them for their failure to recognize that it was concerning Jesus that he wrote.[28] So, finally, the question is left hanging in the air: "If you do not believe what he wrote, how will you believe what I say?" (v. 47). The discourse ends on the line of division between the Johannine community and the synagogue over Scripture. For both communities Scripture is authoritative. The crucial point is how to read it. For the Johannine community it is all about Christ—with Judaism's key champion, Moses, recruited in that cause.

Reflection. The passage asserts the absolute centrality of Jesus in the revelation of God. It foreshadows his later claim to be "the way, the truth and the life" and that no one comes to the Father save through him (14:6). Only through surrendering to belief in Jesus has faith any chance of attaining God. No conditions can be set, no tests required before that surrender is made.[29] Such absolute claims sit uneasily with a contemporary theology more pluralistic in its understanding of salvation and open to finding ways to God in religions other than Christian. We must remember, however, that it is not so much what Christians believe *about* Jesus that is "the way." He, rather than any theological formulation, is the absolute.

The play upon "glory" (vv. 41-44) late in the passage may be an area where interpretation may escape the confines of the original polemic context. In the insecurity that is the general lot of humankind, we constantly rest our sense of identity in the good repute (*doxa*) that we enjoy in the eyes of others. This is unavoidable to some extent but it cannot lead to a security that is in any way absolute. Reputation, through our own fault or that of others, can soon fall away. Moreover, the effort to maintain or enhance our identity in this way will usually have within it a measure of selfishness or competitiveness incompatible with love. If we turn aside from this quest and, in faith, fix our eyes upon Jesus, we may discover in him a revelation of the

---

[27] In the biblical and later Jewish tradition Moses plays the role of key advocate for Israel before God; cf. Rudolf Schnackenburg, *St. John*, 2:129; Francis J. Moloney, *John*, 188.

[28] Particularly in mind may be Deut 18:15, 18-19 (cf. John 1:21d; 6:14), with its promise of the raising up of a "Moses-like" prophet: "I will raise up for them a prophet like you from among their own people. . . . Anyone who does not heed the words that the prophet shall speak in my name, I myself will hold accountable" (vv. 18-19).

[29] "The object of faith makes itself known only to faith; and this faith is the only means of access to its object" (Rudolf Bultmann, *Gospel of John*, 266).

glory (*doxa*) of God, a revelation of God as love, whose whole aim in our regard is to draw us into the love that has existed between Father and Son from all eternity, which to attain is to have "eternal life." The attempt to fit God—or Jesus as God's revelation—into confines dictated by our own constructed identity is doomed to failure; it is "sin" in the radical Johannine sense, the very opposite of faith. It is in being prepared to allow Jesus to shatter that construction that human beings find a secure identity in God.[30]

---

[30] My reflections along these lines owe something to the concluding "Reflection" of Gail O'Day on this passage, see "The Gospel of John," 589.

The Bread of Life: 6:1-71

At just over seventy verses John 6 comes in as the longest complete sequence in the Fourth Gospel. Despite its length and somewhat repetitive nature, it is held together by the motif of Jesus as the "Bread of Life" and the response this evokes from the crowds and the disciples. The sequence follows the Johannine pattern whereby a miracle (in this case the miraculous multiplication of bread) is followed by a discourse (at times a discursive interaction with the crowds) that unfolds the symbolic meaning of the miracle, rendering it a "sign" pointing to a deeper revelation of God in the person of Jesus.

The focus from the start upon the provision of bread and explicit allusions to the Eucharist in the final section of the discourse lead many, especially those from the Catholic tradition, to hear the entire sequence in purely sacramental terms: that is, as being from start to finish about the gift of the Eucharist, to the exclusion of all else. This is not entirely fruitful. While a eucharistic reference is indeed present in the opening scene (the multiplication of the loaves [vv. 1-15]), it recedes for a time as Jesus presents himself metaphorically as the Bread from heaven; here, faith in him in a revelatory sense rather than eucharistic participation is the required human response (vv. 35-50). Only in the final part of the discourse (vv. 51-58) does the eucharistic theme emerge explicitly once more, creating a Word + Sacrament duality across the sequence as a whole that admirably corresponds to the similar duality recaptured for the Roman eucharistic liturgy in the reforms of the Second Vatican Council (1962–67): life-giving revelation from heaven + life-giving "bread from heaven."[1] Faith in Jesus in a revelatory sense is

---

[1] Writing just before or in the early days of Vatican II, Raymond Brown, with great prescience, drew attention to this duality of Word and sacrament in the ancient liturgical tradition of the church (*John I–XII*, 290).

subtly woven together with other themes, including the eucharistic, to form a textual whole cloth of great theological richness. Only by adverting to the presence of all intertwined motifs can we truly appreciate the Fourth Gospel's distinctive presentation of the Eucharist, allowing it to complement the more familiar institution narratives of the Synoptic tradition (Matt 26:26-29; Mark 14:22-25; Luke 22:15-20) and Paul (1 Cor 10:16-17; 11:23-26).

The major building blocks of the long sequence are easily discerned:

1. The miracle (or "sign") of the multiplication of the loaves and fishes: 6:1-15

2. Jesus comes to the disciples walking upon the sea: 6:16-21

3. The crowd comes to Capernaum in search of Jesus: 6:22-25

4. Dialogue between Jesus and the crowd: 6:26-34

5. Discourse on the Bread of Life A ("Believe"): 6:35-50

6. Discourse on the Bread of Life B ("Eat"): 6:51-58(59)

7. Dialogue between Jesus and his Disciples: 6:60-66

8. Dialogue between Jesus and the Twelve: 6:67-71

Most interpreters recognize that Jesus' discourse to the crowd in vv. 35-59 falls into two distinct, and in several respects, parallel phases: one principally concerned with faith in him as the Bread come down from heaven; one where he identifies the bread with his flesh that must be eaten in a sacramental (eucharistic) sense in order to gain life. The second would seem to begin at v. 51 with Jesus' words "I am the living bread," which parallels his claim to be "the Bread of Life" in v. 35.[2] The relationship between the two phases—both from a literary point of view and from that of the evolution of the final text of the gospel—is one of the most discussed topics in Johannine scholarship.[3] Many interpreters of previous generations

---

[2] Aside from the two opening statements (v. 35 and v. 51a), remaining parallel features include: the reference to the hostile reaction of "the Jews" (v. 41 and v. 52); "raising up on the last day" (vv. 39, 40, 44, and 54); "Amen, Amen" (v. 47 and v. 53); concluding contrast between a bread eaten by the Israelites of old that did not prevent death and a bread provided by Jesus that is a remedy for death (vv. 49-50 and v. 58).

[3] For recent surveys, see Gail O'Day, "The Gospel of John," 605–7 ("Excursus: John 6:51c-58 in Critical Scholarship"); Marten J. J. Menken, "John 6:51c-58: Eucharist or Christology," in *Critical Readings of John 6*, ed. R. Alan Culpepper, Biblical Interpretation Series 22 (Leiden: Brill, 1997), 183–204.

tended to regard the second part of the discourse, vv. 51-58, as the work of a redactor with strong sacramental interests who composed and added to the gospel as we now have it in a fresh discourse, modeled on the first with many parallel features but with the "bread of life" now presented in explicitly eucharistic terms.[4] Most recent scholars interpret the discourse across vv. 35-58, including even the preparatory dialogue beginning at v. 25, as a unified whole.[5] Whatever the composition history of the text, I believe that a unified understanding makes good sense of John 6 and shall adopt it in this commentary.

1. The Sign: Multiplication of the Loaves and Fishes: 6:1-15

An account of Jesus miraculously providing food for thousands of people occurs no less than six times across the four gospels: twice in Matthew (14:13-21; 15:32-39) and Mark (6:30-44; 8:1-10), once in Luke (9:10-17) and John (6:1-15). This frequency, along with the rare coherence of the Synoptic and Johannine tradition in the matter, signals the extraordinary significance the episode had for the early generations of believers, a significance not unconnected with the fact that a banquet to which all are invited without reservation served for Jesus as a key image of the kingdom (rule) of God, so central to his preaching. The feeding of a multitude with food abundantly and freely supplied foreshadowed the banquet of the kingdom, to which it was Jesus' task to issue the invitations. More immediately, the feeding foreshadows the Eucharist, which is itself a sacramental anticipation of the divine hospitality of the kingdom.

The description of the feeding in John 6:1-15 falls into five distinct stages: (1) An opening setting of scene (vv. 1-4), locating the scene in time (Passover) and place (by the sea of Galilee [of Tiberias]); (2) a dialogue between Jesus and two disciples (Philip; then Andrew) establishing the problem that the miracle will address: how to feed the multitude that has followed Jesus (vv. 5-9); (3) the actual feeding itself (vv. 10-11); (4) the gathering of fragments left over (vv. 12-13); and (5) an unsuccessful attempt on the part of the crowd to make Jesus king (vv. 14-15).

---

[4] For a survey of the views of older commentators, see Raymond E. Brown, *John I–XII*, 272–74.

[5] E.g., Gail O'Day, "The Gospel of John," 605–7; Martin J. J. Menken, "John 6:51c-58"; Ugo Schnelle, *Johannes*, 145–46, 155–56. Francis J. Moloney, *John*, 207, sees vv. 25-59 as a unified "homiletic midrash on a text provided to Jesus by his interlocutors in v. 31: "He gave them bread from heaven to eat"; similarly, Andrew T. Lincoln, *St. John*, 223–25.

Setting the Scene: 6:1-4

Jesus is now back in Galilee, vaguely located by the lake of Galilee, which John specifies as "of Tiberias."[6] A large crowd has followed him there, having seen the "signs" which he has performed upon the sick—a motivation that has received a negative rating earlier in the gospel (2:23-25). People can benefit from Jesus' miracles without really seeing them as "signs" pointing to a deeper reality. While the account does not explicitly say so, the details that he ascended a mountain and sat down there (v. 3) suggests that he was engaged in teaching the crowd for some time before raising the issue about feeding them.[7]

Very significant for the following dialogue with the crowds is the information that the occasion was close to the Jewish feast of Passover (v. 4). Passover had been the context for Jesus' first appearance in Jerusalem (2:13-25); Passover will be the context for the climactic events of the end of his life (13:1); Passover now features at this midpoint in his ministry. All this establishes a "Passover framework" around the total ministry of One who will die as "the (Passover) Lamb of God" (1:29, 36; 19:36). In the more immediate context Passover prepares the way for the Exodus motifs (Moses; the "Manna," etc.) that will feature so strongly in the exchanges with the crowd following the feeding (vv. 31-32, 49, 58). It also goes along with the allusion to Jesus' death and the eucharistic references that become explicit in the second phase of the discourse (vv. 51-58).

*Dialogue between Jesus and the Disciples about
Feeding the People: 6:5-9*

The human need that Jesus addresses is aired at some length in a dialogue between Jesus and two of his disciples (vv. 5-9). He raises the issue himself: "Lifting up his eyes and seeing a great crowd coming toward him," he asks Philip, "Where are we to buy bread for these people to eat?" (v. 5). The issue is not whether the people are to be fed; the divine hospitality is already in play. The question—though Jesus already knows the answer (v. 6)—is where the food is to come from or, more literally, where it is to be bought. Jesus is deliberately raising the problem of feeding the people on a

---

[6] The Johannine specification (also 21:1) reflects the designation of the lake by the name of a town that Herod Antipas built on the western side of the Sea of Galilee and named for the emperor Tiberius in the 20s.

[7] Sitting was the posture of teaching; cf. Matt 5:1.

human level where food has to be worked for and bought. Philip, taking up the question on this level, points out the impossibly high cost involved even if each person were to get only a morsel (v. 7).[8] Moving away from the idea of buying food and fastening simply upon what is actually to hand, Andrew indicates the presence of a small boy with five loaves and two pieces of dried fish. Thinking on the same purely human level, he, too, points out the complete insufficiency of this in view of the multitude to be fed (vv. 8-9).

Feeding the Five Thousand: 6:10-11

In the face of this incapacity on the human side, Jesus addresses the problem on an entirely new level (vv. 10-11). His instruction to the disciples to make the people sit down (v. 10a) creates the expectation that they are about to be fed; there is no going back once that is done. The availability of grass on which to sit raises echoes of the opening of Psalm 23 ("The LORD is my shepherd. . . . He makes me lie down in green pastures" [vv. 1-2a]). The One who is later to describe himself as the "Good Shepherd" (10:11, 14) is here preparing to nourish his flock, who we are now told number five thousand.[9]

The gestures of Jesus in the actual feeding (v. 11) echo the Synoptic accounts of the institution of the Eucharist (save that the Johannine account omits reference to breaking the bread). In contrast to the Synoptic accounts of the feeding, Jesus himself distributes the bread and the pieces of fish directly to the people. Perhaps, granted the number to be fed, there is an implication that the disciples were involved in the distribution, but this is not explicitly stated. The Fourth Gospel seems to want to stress that the people receive the food immediately and abundantly from Jesus. There is no "rationing" in the divine prodigality; all receive "as much as they wanted" (v. 11e).

Collecting the Fragments: 6:12-13

Where the disciples have a role is in the collection of leftover fragments that Jesus commands after all have been fed (vv. 12-13). The twelve baskets that they fill are a first indication in the gospel of a select group of twelve making up the inner core of Jesus' disciples. They will emerge explicitly as

---

[8] A denarius amounted to a day's wages.

[9] Lit., "five thousand men." The restriction to the masculine suggests that, since women and children were not being counted, the full number was actually much larger; cf. Matt 14:21.

"the Twelve" at the close of the entire sequence (v. 67; cf. also 20:24). Here, their gathering of the fragments into twelve baskets foreshadows the sacrament of the Eucharist in the church, of which they will be foundational figures (cf. Rev. 24:14). They preserve the gift of Jesus for the life of the church following his departure to the Father. Put the other way around, in the eucharistic celebration of the church Jesus continues his ministry of the prodigal hospitality of God.

The Crowd Attempts to Make Jesus King: 6:14-15

An aftermath peculiar to the Fourth Gospel follows (vv. 14-15). The crowd interpret the miracle Jesus has performed as an indication that he is the "prophet who is to come into the world" (v. 14b). As part of his farewell address in Deuteronomy 18:15 Moses had told the Israelites that God would raise up a prophet like himself, to whom they should listen. This prophecy gave rise in the postbiblical period to the expectation of a Moses-like prophet in the messianic age.[10] Jesus has just performed a "Moses-like" sign in that, like Moses with the manna at the time of Israel's Sinai wandering (Exod 16:4-36; Num 11:4-9; Deut 8:3, 16; Neh 9:20; Pss 78:23-25; 105:40; Wis 16:20), he has miraculously provided food for the crowds. It is natural then for them to conclude that he is the awaited prophet. They have not seen the miracle as a "sign" in the true Johannine sense. They have taken it to indicate the presence of a savior figure along the lines of conventional messianic expectation.

In line with this understanding, they want to make Jesus their king (v. 15),[11] employing to this end the physical coercion characteristic of kingdoms of this world. The kingship theme will emerge significantly at the close of Jesus' life. Before Pilate he will acknowledge that he is a king, while immediately going on to disclaim a kingship of "this world" (18:36-37). In the face of the crowd's attempt to wrest him into such a role, he withdraws by himself to the mountain. When he emerges from that retreat, he will do so in a way revealing an identity far outstripping conventional messianic expectation (6:19-20).

Reflection. While the full significance of the feeding miracle remains to be drawn out in the remaining sections of John 6, the episode has its own wealth

---

[10] We recall that John the Baptist had to disclaim that he was "the prophet" (1:20-21).

[11] In some strands of the postbiblical Jewish tradition Moses is portrayed as a regal and military figure as well as a religious leader.

of meaning. With divine power Jesus remedies a human need on a material, physical level: he feeds the hungry crowds with ordinary bread and fish. Even though the physical serves as a "sign" pointing to a deeper spiritual truth—yet to be teased out—the spiritual does not engulf it. Moreover, the human resources at hand, inadequate though they be, are not swept aside but taken up into the exercise of divine power. The boy who makes available to Jesus the small amount of food that he has stands in for all prepared to offer their own meager resources to Jesus, allowing him to enhance them beyond all expectation. The reaction of the crowd, on the other hand, shows how difficult it is to receive a benefit from God without immediately confining it within one's own categories and expectations, and so missing its true import.[12] Much more significant than the gift of bread is the revelation that it will disclose to those prepared to go out on a bold journey of faith beyond their own wants and expectations.

2. Jesus Comes to the Disciples Walking upon the Sea: 6:16-21

While Jesus has been on the mountain communing with the divine,[13] the disciples have embarked on a difficult voyage to Capernaum (vv. 16-17). In the dark of nightfall, with a strong wind whipping up the sea (v. 18), they have progressed just three or four miles. Suddenly they see Jesus coming near the boat walking upon the sea (v. 19). Terrified, they hear him say: "It is I; fear not." At one level a simple formula of human reassurance, the phrase "It is I" (*egō eimi*) functions, as we have seen, as a vehicle of divine revelation in the Fourth Gospel, standing in continuity with the self-identification of God to Moses at the Burning Bush ("I am, who I am" [Exod 3:14]), developed in similar formulas in Second Isaiah (43:25; 51:12; 52:6; cf. John 4:26; 8:24, 28, 58; 13:19; 18:5, 7).[14] In the biblical tradition, to walk on the sea, trampling down the forces of primeval chaos and destruction, is a prerogative of YHWH alone (Job 9:8; 38:16; Ps 77:20; Hab 3:15; Isa 51:9-10). Jesus' appearance in this guise is a genuine theophany, the first unambiguous revelation of his divine status up to this point; hence the disciples' fear. The theophany confronts and corrects for their benefit the crowd's attempt to capture him within the inadequate and inappropriate category of worldly

---

[12] Here I am indebted especially to Gail O'Day, "The Gospel of John," 597.

[13] The association of mountains with the presence of God in the biblical tradition conveys this implication (cf. Exod 24:15-18 [Moses]).

[14] See the chart setting out these sayings (and the related predicative "I am" sayings) in Gail O'Day, "The Gospel of John," 602.

kingship. Reassured, the disciples are happy (literally, "willing" [*ēthelon*]) to take Jesus into the boat (v. 21)—whereupon, in contrast, to the hard going against the wind and stormy sea, they "immediately" reach the shore to which they were making.

The episode hardly amounts to a miracle or sign in the strict sense. But it does match the multiplication in that Jesus has miraculously remedied a human need (crossing the sea in the face of the storm) in a way revelatory of the divine. The One who is now with the disciples in the boat in a fully human way is the One who has just traversed the stormy sea revealing his oneness with God ("I Am"). The disciples cannot control Jesus' coming and going, his presence and absence. Likewise, the later church—down to the present day and especially when the going is hard—will often keenly feel the absence of the Lord. His coming to the disciples across the sea, his revelatory assurance ("It is I; fear not"), and his joining them in the boat remain a powerful symbolic reassurance that he will never allow adverse forces to prevail against his own.

3. The Crowd Comes to Capernaum in Search of Jesus: 6:22-25

It is not easy to discern what the evangelist is trying to convey in the tortured sentences with which he indicates the crowd's pursuit of Jesus. Although the action takes place "on the next day" (v. 22), what they see refers to what they had seen the day before.[15] They remember that there had been only one boat present the night before and that they had seen the disciples get into the boat unaccompanied by Jesus (v. 22). Presuming that he has somehow gone to Capernaum, they take advantage of the fact that some boats have arrived from Tiberias (vv. 23-24) to travel there by sea. The reminder that the boats came from the same place (Tiberias) where the crowd had been fed (v. 23) serves to link—albeit very awkwardly—the coming interaction between Jesus and the crowd (vv. 26-59) to the miracle of the multiplication. The crowd's question, "Rabbi, when did you come here?" (v. 25), shows how much they are at a loss to account for his movements. This highlights by contrast the privileged situation of the disciples. In their difficult passage across the sea, they have experienced from Jesus both revelation and assistance.[16]

---

[15] The verbs in v. 22, then, have to be understood in a pluperfect sense; cf. C. K. Barrett, *John*, 285.

[16] Cf. Ugo Schnelle, *Johannes*, 135.

4. Dialogue between Jesus and the Crowd: 6:26-34

The interaction between Jesus and the crowd presupposes from start to finish the biblical background of Israel's years of wandering in the wilderness of Sinai under the leadership of Moses. During this time the people survived on the manna rained down by God from heaven (Exod 16).[17] The manna that fell on the first five days became inedible after one day; only the manna collected on the sixth day was still edible on the seventh, that is, on the Sabbath when the work that would have been involved in collecting it was forbidden (Exod 16:20-21). The distinction emanating from this biblical background between food that lasts only for a time and food that endures is significant for the dialogue that now begins between Jesus and the Galilean crowd.

Jesus ignores the crowd's question about the time of his arrival (v. 25). More important for him is to convince them that they are seeking him for the wrong reason (v. 26). They have benefited from the multiplication of the loaves and are seeking him on that account. But that food, albeit miraculously provided, was still ordinary food, destined like the manna of old soon to grow stale. The crowd have not "seen signs" in that they have failed to see the miraculous provision of ordinary food as a sign pointing to food of a wholly different order: food that endures for eternal life (v. 27). For this food it is indeed worth "working," since the One who will give it is the one definitively accredited for this purpose: the Son of Man, upon whom God the Father has "set his seal."[18]

Against the biblical background, "working" inevitably brings to mind the Torah, promulgated by Moses at Sinai, with its plethora of commandments ("works") to be performed. When the crowd ask what they should be doing to do "the works (*erga* [plural]) of God" (v. 28), they are presumably thinking along these lines. Jesus replies that what God wants can be reduced to a single "work" (*ergon*): that of believing in the One whom God has sent (v. 29).

As a condition for believing, the crowd demand a sign (v. 30a-c). They ask Jesus what "work" he would perform to this end (v. 30d)[19] and go on to

---

[17] The classic study of the significance of this background for the interpretation of John 6 is that of Peder Borgen, *Bread from Heaven: An Exegetical Study of the Concept of Manna in the Gospel of John and the Writings of Philo*, NovTSupp 10 (Leiden: Brill, 1965).

[18] C. K. Barrett, *John*, 287, plausibly suggests that the Father's "setting his seal" upon Jesus refers to his baptism with the Spirit, which is not described but alluded to in 1:33-34. It is likely that a contrast with Moses is implied; cf. Andrew T. Lincoln, *St. John*, 226–27.

[19] "(The crowd) shift the burden of who is to work from themselves (vv. 27-29) to Jesus (v. 30)" (Gail O'Day, "The Gospel of John," 599).

suggest (v. 31) a biblical precedent: the provision of the manna which their ancestors ate in the desert, "as written 'He gave them bread from heaven to eat.' "[20] In the biblical text closest to this formulation, Ps 78 (LXX 77):24,[21] the one who gives the bread (manna) is God (cf. Exod 16:4). The crowd, however, seem to be attributing the action to Moses (cf. v. 32). Before they will believe that Jesus is truly sent by God they want him to establish his credentials by performing a genuinely Moses-like sign.

The True Bread from Heaven

Jesus responds with a solemn statement that provides the theme for the entire discourse to follow:

> Amen, Amen, I tell you: it was not Moses who gave you the bread from heaven, but it is my Father who gives you the true bread from heaven. For the bread of God is that which comes down from heaven and gives life to the world. (John 6:32–33)

The crowd's demand that Jesus repeat the Moses-like miracle is wrong on several accounts. It implies that he and Moses are comparable figures—continuing the misunderstanding of him as a Moses-like prophet (vv. 14-15). Moreover, it was God, not Moses, who rained down the original "bread from heaven" and it is God ("my Father") who is now—had they rightly seen the sign—giving them "the true bread from heaven" (v. 32).

"True" here has its characteristic Johannine sense of referring to the definitive revelation of the messianic age as distinct from what was purely anticipatory and provisional. The manna that God provided to Israel in the wilderness foreshadowed the "true bread of God" which was to come down from heaven and be life-giving beyond Israel for the entire world (v. 33). As in earlier sequences in the gospel (3:16; 4:42), a note of universalism is being sounded here.

Jesus' solemn statement about the "bread of God from heaven" is enigmatic. He has not at this point identified himself as the bread from heaven. He is teasing the crowd with these mysterious allusions, attempting to lead them to a deeper and more correct understanding.[22] But, their request, "Sir,

---

[20] Some see this text as the point of departure for the entire discussion to follow: so especially Peder Borgen, *Bread from Heaven, passim*; cf. also Francis J. Moloney, *John*, 207–8; Andrew T. Lincoln, *St. John*, 223–25.

[21] Cf. also, "For their hunger you gave them bread from heaven" (Neh 9:15a).

[22] On such anticipatory hints of motifs to be developed later, cf. Francis J. Moloney, "The Function of Prolepsis in the Interpretation of John 6," in *Critical Readings of John 6*, ed. R. Alan Culpepper, Biblical Interpretation Series 22 (Leiden: Brill, 1997), 129–48.

give us this bread always" (v. 34), shows that they are still thinking of a continuing provision of ordinary bread that will remove the need to "work" for daily sustenance.[23] Fixated upon the provision of ordinary food, they are far from any real appreciation of the life-giving "gift of God."[24]

5. Discourse on the Bread of Life A ("Believe"): 6:35-50

The dialogue between Jesus and the crowd has reached an impasse. It is time for him to identify himself outright. He is not one who will give manna ("the bread of life") in some new form. He is *himself* "the Bread of Life" that the Father is giving for the life of the world (v. 35a). With this self-revelation, we encounter the first of a series of predicative "I am" statements in the Fourth Gospel. These predicates ("Bread"; "Light" [8:12; 9:5]; "Gate" [10:7, 9]; "Good Shepherd" [10:11, 14]; "Resurrection and the Life" [11:25-26]; "Way, Truth and Life" [14:6]; "True Vine" [15:1, 5]) indicate how Jesus responds to a variety of human needs in ways that, while truly fulfilling those needs, also transcend them to disclose and fulfill a more basic human capacity: that of receiving and sharing the divine "eternal life."[25]

The first phrase of the discourse (Discourse A) devoted to Jesus as the Bread of Life follows in two parts (vv. 35-40 and 43-50), intersected by the objection of the crowd (vv. 41-42). Its primary focus lies upon the response that human beings need to make to this revelation: that of faith. To believe in Jesus is to accept him in his human person ("Word made flesh" [1:14]) as the definitive revelation of the unseen God.

Jesus, the Bread of Life (1): 6:35-40

Identifying himself as the Bread of Life, Jesus claims that those who believe and come to him will never know hunger or thirst again (v. 35). In the Wisdom tradition of Israel that provides a background to these statements (cf. Prov. 9:5), Wisdom herself had claimed: "Those who eat of me will hunger for more, and those who drink of me will thirst for more" (Sir 24:21).

---

[23] We recall a similar request at a comparable stage of understanding on the part of the Samaritan Woman (4:15).

[24] For all its non-inclusive language, Rudolf Bultmann's comment at this point merits quotation: "God's revelation destroys every picture which man's desires make of it, so that the real test of man's desire for salvation is to believe even when God encounters him in a totally different way from that which he expected" (*Gospel of John*, 228).

[25] The "I Am" sayings are set out in tabular form by Gail O'Day, "The Gospel of John," 602.

Jesus, by contrast, speaks of a "hunger" and "thirst" that faith in him will satisfy once and for all.[26] He alone can perfectly fulfill the most basic longing of the human heart: to see God as God truly is.

A sense of the crowd's failure to believe because they have "seen" him only superficially (v. 36) leads Jesus to press the invitation with a little excursus (vv. 37-40) featuring several Johannine themes. We seem to hear him speaking here already as the Good Shepherd (10:11-18). Those who come to him in faith will not meet with rebuff, as though they belonged to an alien flock. He will not drive them away because, by coming to him, they show that they are members of the flock drawn to him by the Father, and the sole object of his mission is simply to carry out the will of the Father who sent him, which is to lose none of those who come to him but to raise them up on the last day.

As modern readers we are perplexed by the ancient writer's easy assumption that human faith ("coming to Jesus") is at once the result of the Father's gift and a free human response to an invitation. Biblical thought can hold such tension together—just as without qualms it can interchange cause and effect.[27] The crucial consideration is that, confronted with Jesus' invitation, human beings—here the Galilean crowd—are not making a decision by themselves alone, on neutral terrain, so to speak. They are already held within the gracious will of the Father, whose only desire in their regard is to impart to them, through the mission of the Son, a share in the divine "eternal life."

The Crowd's Negative Response: 6:41-42

Jesus' exalted invitation has left the crowd well behind in understanding (vv. 41-42). The appearance for the first time in the sequence of the generally pejorative term "the Jews" signals growing hostility. The stumbling block, as usually in the gospel, is the incarnation: Jesus' claim to be the bread "come down from heaven." The crowd's complaining[28] reveals a very concrete awareness of his human origins: "Is not this Jesus, the son of Joseph, whose father and mother we know?" (v. 42b). Their knowledge is partially

---

[26] Cf. Rudolf Schnackenburg, *St. John*, 2:44–45.

[27] "Faith in Jesus is impossible without God's initiating will for the world, but human beings retain responsibility for the decision they make in response to God's initiative (cf. 3:16-21)" (Gail O'Day, "The Gospel of John," 603).

[28] The Greek *eggogyzon* echoes the murmuring of Israel during the Sinai wandering: Exod 15:24; 16:2, 7, 12; Num 11:1; 14:2, 27; Ps 105:24-25; cf. Gail O'Day, "The Gospel of John," 603.

correct; Jesus is, publicly at least, known to be the son of Joseph.[29] But they cannot see such ordinary human origin to be in any way compatible with heavenly origin as well. They lack the faith to see in and through his human flesh the "glory" of the only-begotten of the Father, the One who has indeed "come down from heaven" to impart life to the world (1:1-18).[30] Despite their claimed knowledge, they do not really "know" his parentage; they do not know the Father.

Jesus, the Bread of Life (2): 6:43-50

Jesus rebukes the crowd for complaining among themselves (v. 43) and goes on to reflect upon a key condition of faith: being drawn by the Father (v. 44). The logic is somewhat roundabout but it seems to run as follows. A text from Isaiah, "And they shall all be taught by God" (LXX Isa 54:13 [quoted v. 45]), promises a divine "teaching" to be given in the messianic age. The fact that the crowd are having difficulty in coming to faith shows that they are not listening to the Father, who would in fact "draw" them to Jesus in order that, in accordance with the Father's will, he might impart (eternal) life to them (literally, "raise them up on the last day" [v. 44c]).

A typical Johannine clarification (v. 46) hastens to insist that such "hearing" and "learning" from the Father does not mean "seeing" him—since no one has seen the Father except the One (Jesus) who is from God. Behind this clarification is probably the running contrast with Moses for whom certain strands of the biblical tradition could claim face-to-face converse with God (Exod 24:10; 33:11; Deut 5:4; 34:10; contradicted 33:20). For the Fourth Gospel the Son alone has seen God.[31] For everyone else knowledge and "sight" of the Father is given in the human flesh of Jesus discerned by faith (1:18; 14:7-9).

This clarification made, the discourse draws to an end where it began (vv. 47-50) with Jesus claiming again to be the Bread of Life (v. 48), belief in whom gives access to the gift of eternal life. Allusion to the Sinai com-

---

[29] Though the Fourth Gospel nowhere shows explicit knowledge of the virginal conception of Jesus, there is possibly here an ironical allusion to it: the complainants would not be voicing this objection if they knew the real truth about Jesus' origins; cf. C. K. Barrett, *John*, 295; Gail O'Day, "The Gospel of John," 603.

[30] Cf. Dorothy A. Lee, *Flesh and Glory*, 39–40.

[31] Cf. Marianne Meye Thompson, "Thinking about God: Wisdom and Theology in John 6," in *Critical Readings of John 6*, ed. R. Alan Culpepper, Biblical Interpretation Series 22 (Leiden: Brill, 1997), 221–26, see 242.

munity surfaces once more as Jesus, echoing an earlier claim made by the crowd (v. 31), contrasts (v. 49) the life-giving Bread that he himself is with the manna that the crowd's ancestors (the Israelites) ate in the wilderness. That food sustained them for a time, but eventually they died. Whereas (v. 50) he is the Bread that has come down from heaven so one may eat of it and not die but, on the contrary, have eternal life—a present possession (cf. v. 47) leading to resurrection on the last day (v. 40; v. 44).[32]

The motif of "eating" has been implicit in the discourse all along as a necessary connotation of the image of "bread." Here, for the first time (apart from the quotation in v. 31), it becomes explicit as a metaphor for faith, granted that we still refrain, as I think we should, from a eucharistic understanding.

Reflection. Appreciating the riches of the passage aside from a eucharistic understanding does require entering to some extent imaginatively into the symbolic world that it presupposes: God's provision of the manna to the Israelites in their Sinai wandering (Exod 16). If the gift of the "bread from heaven" (the manna) showed God's care for his people in their desert wandering, how much more does the gift of the Bread from heaven in the person of the Son. The Galilean crowd's difficulties with Jesus' claims ultimately stem from too constricted an image of God, an inability to believe in a God who has loved the world so much as to rain down from heaven "the Bread of life" in this so intimately personal form (3:16).

6. Discourse on the Bread of Life B ("Eat"): 6:51-58(59)

A new stage of the discourse is signaled by Jesus' opening claim to be "the living bread come down from heaven" (v. 51a), standing in parallel to the almost identical opening ("I am the Bread of Life") in verse 35.[33] Up till this point the response demanded by Jesus to his self-revelation had been belief in him, alternatively formulated as "coming" to him (vv. 35, 36, 37, 44, 45, 47). Now "eating" takes over from "believing" as the required human

---

[32] Here, in regard to "life," we see the easy oscillation between the future and present in the eschatology of the Fourth Gospel. Jesus' words to Martha (11:25-26) will play upon the same ambiguity.

[33] The new formula, "the living bread (*ho artos ho zōn*)" has the same active sense of "bread that gives (eternal) life" as "bread of life" (vv. 35, 48): eating this bread sets a person upon the path to eternal life; cf. vv. 51b, 57; cf. "living water" (4:10-11); cf. C. K. Barrett, *John*, 297.

response—though the distinction should not be pressed too vigorously since Jesus' image of himself as bread had implied at least a metaphorical understanding of faith as eating. Moreover, an explicit reference to eating had emerged in the very last clause of the preceding section (v. 50b), offering a clear bridge to the predominance of "eating" in the discourse to follow.

For all the continuity across the two sections, a surprising new element appears in the final clause of verse 51 when Jesus identifies the bread that he will give for the life of the world with "his flesh (*sarx*)." There is a striking similarity between this formulation and Jesus' words over the bread and the cup in the accounts of the institution of the Eucharist in the Synoptic Gospels (Matt 26:26-28; Mark 14:22-24; Luke 22:19-20) and Paul (1 Cor 11:23-25). Despite that similarity, we should hold back from immediately identifying "flesh" here with the eucharistic body—or at least, from making that the primary reference to the exclusion of all else. "Flesh" has its biblical sense, indicating human life as such in its material and mortal reality. The main thought now introduced is that the "Bread come down from heaven," that is, the Son of God incarnate, is also the One who gave up his human life to death in order to give life to the world (3:16). In short, the motif of incarnation (Word become flesh [1:14]) has been extended to take in Jesus' passion and death ("flesh given for the life of the world"). Up till this point we have understood Jesus as the "Bread" that God rained down—"manna-like"—for the life of the world. Now we know that that gift of life will come at the expense in love of his own life (10:11-18).[34]

As earlier (vv. 41-42), an uncomprehending objection from the crowd ("the Jews") interrupts (v. 52) the discourse and serves to spring it forward. They dispute among themselves, saying: "How can this man give us his flesh to eat?"[35] To eat human flesh (and drink human blood) is abhorrent and strictly forbidden in Jewish law (Gen 9:4; Lev. 3:17; Deut 12:23; Acts 15:20).[36] On the literal, material level of understanding, which is still that of the crowd, the objection stands. Jesus meets it on the only understanding that could render it acceptable: that is, as a reference to sacramental participation in the Christian eucharist, now made explicit and clear through the introduction of a fresh motif—that of drinking his blood—alongside that of

---

[34] Cf. C. K. Barrett, *John*, 298; Andrew T. Lincoln, *St. John*, 231.

[35] The sense of "disputing" among the hearers may prepare the way for the divided response that will be recorded in the concluding dialogue (vv. 60-71).

[36] Raymond E. Brown, *John I–XII*, 284.

eating his flesh.[37] First negatively (v. 53) and then positively (v. 54), Jesus insists upon the necessity of such "eating" and "drinking" for the gaining of "(eternal) life" (= "being raised by him on the last day").

While the eucharistic reference is clear, it should not be taken to mean that consumption of the eucharist will lead in a sacramentally "automatic" way to the gaining of resurrection (eternal) life. The necessity of eating and drinking in a eucharistic sense appears toward the end of a long discourse where faith has been stressed as the required human response, with the motif of "eating" first introduced (in v. 48) as a metaphor for faith and only subsequently (v. 53) passing over to a clearly literal understanding.[38] Moreover, the statement that the flesh to be eaten and blood to be drunk is that of the Son of Man (v. 53b) communicates the sense that, while pertaining to a real human person, they also belong to the One who has descended from heaven and will return there, having "given up" his "flesh for the life of the world" (v. 51c).[39] The overall sense, then, is that of a participation in the Eucharist where the literal eating and drinking is accompanied by a keen awareness of union with the One who came down from heaven to give his human life that the world might not perish but share his own eternal life (3:16).[40]

When Jesus insists (v. 55) that his flesh is "true" (*alēthēs*) food and his blood "true" (*alēthēs*) drink, the concern is not primarily to stress a literal rather than a purely figurative eating and drinking. Rather, in line with the

---

[37] So, most interpreters, e.g., C. K. Barrett, *John*, 299; Gail O'Day, "The Gospel of John," 609; Andrew T. Lincoln, *St. John*, 232. Some, while conceding that the evangelist may be making use of eucharistic language, consider that the metaphorical usage of response to the revelation of God in the incarnation and death of Jesus remains primary: so, e.g., Martin J. J. Menken, "John 6:51c-58"; Francis J. Moloney, "The Function of Prolepsis," 143. While "eating" can be an acceptable image for approaching Jesus in faith, as earlier in the discourse, it is hard to believe that an author in a Jewish context would pursue this metaphor in terms of "drinking his blood"; the realism and risk of misunderstanding would be too overwhelming.

[38] The use of the verb *trōgein*, often taken to place beyond doubt a reference to literal eating and so to the Eucharist here, should not be sharply distinguished from the other word for eating that appears: *phagein*. The *trog-* verb stem simply supplies the wanting present form of the stem *phag-*, which the gospel uses in other tenses; cf. C. K. Barrett, *John*, 299; Rudolf Schnackenburg, *St. John*, 2:62. Nonetheless, it is interesting that the only other place in the Fourth Gospel where *trōgein* appears is early in Jesus' discourse at the Last Supper (13:18), suggesting perhaps some linkage between the Johannine and the Synoptic eucharistic traditions; see Raymond E. Brown, *John I–XII*, 287; *John XIII–XXI*, 553, 571; also Francis J. Moloney, *John*, 381.

[39] This is the distinctive sense pertaining to the "Son of Man" title/role in the Fourth Gospel: cf. C. K. Barrett, *John*, 298.

[40] Cf. Raymond E. Brown, *John I–XII*, 292.

Johannine sense of "truth" the meaning is that of a food and drink that truly communicates life in distinction from a food—such as the manna (and perhaps the law of Moses)—that only foreshadowed such a gift.[41] The grounds for this are given in the following sentence (v. 56) where the distinctive Johannine motif of indwelling (*menein*: NRSV "abide") appears. Beyond mere presence in a purely spatial sense, "abide" has the connotation of living in a way that is determined by the milieu—or the person—within which or within whom one dwells. As Jesus explains (v. 57), the dwelling within him created by participation in the Eucharist is an extension of his own continual dwelling within the Father who sent him (cf. 1:18). As he has divine life because of his abiding within the "living" (= "life-giving") Father, so the abiding within him created by participation in the Eucharist creates a corresponding destiny to eternal life in the believer.

In conclusion (v. 58) Jesus resumes earlier themes, drawing the discourse together as a unified whole. He identifies the eucharistic bread ("this") with the "bread come down from heaven" that earlier in the discourse and here once again compares favorably with the manna that "the fathers" ate in the wilderness. That gift sustained their earthly life for a time but did not prevent their dying eventually—whereas (v. 58c) the person who eats the bread that Jesus is giving "will have life for eternity." In a characteristic Johannine afterthought (v. 59) the evangelist indicates that all this interaction and instruction took place not merely in Capernaum but in the synagogue there: the locus of worship and scriptural interpretation.

Reflection. Looking back over the discourse of Jesus as a whole, we can see a gradual unfolding of understanding whereby early enigmatic remarks and promises ("prolepses") gradually become clearer—to the reader, if not to the increasingly disaffected audience. All culminates in a rich understanding of Jesus as life-giving "Bread" given by the Father in a way that recalls, even as it fulfills and greatly surpasses, the gift of the manna to Israel. What Jesus offers here requires a faith that, first of all, sees in his human person One "come down from heaven," the revelation of the unseen Father, but which, beyond incarnation, is prepared to see that revelation extending into his self-sacrificial death upon the cross. Such a faith-inspired vision flows into a life-giving participation in the Eucharist, where sacramental communion with the flesh and blood of Jesus involves not only union with him

---

[41] Cf. Martin J. J. Menken, "John 6:51c-58," 197.

in a static sense but also being caught up in the rhythm of his sacrificial love for the world (13:34).[42]

7. Dialogue between Jesus and his Disciples: 6:60-66

Jesus' disciples now emerge once more, but only for some of them to join the now hostile crowd in its murmuring and rejection.[43] They complain that Jesus' "word" is "hard" (*sklēron*) and difficult to "hear" (v. 60). "Hard" here has the sense of difficult to accept and a stumbling block to belief, rather than difficult to understand in an intellectual sense.[44] What precisely the complaint is referring to is not immediately clear. Most obvious, because most immediately at hand, would be Jesus' insistence upon eating his flesh and drinking his blood in the final part of the discourse (vv. 51-58). But it is unlikely that the disciples, even those who are moving away from faith, are operating on such a crudely materialistic level of understanding, especially as the eucharistic allusions have already introduced a sense of eating and drinking in a sacramental sense under the forms of bread and wine.

In light particularly of Jesus' enigmatic response in v. 62 ("Then, what if you were to see the Son of Man ascending to where he was before?"), it seems necessary to regard the offense as arising particularly out of Jesus' original claim to be the Bread of Life "come down from heaven" (vv. 42, 50). If it was difficult enough to accept Jesus' claim to be the bread of life come down from heaven—that is, the incarnation (vv. 41-42)—how far more difficult it will be to accept that the One who has so descended is going to complete this divine "condescension" by giving himself up to death in order to give life to the world.[45] In other words, the "offense" presently taken is only part of a much wider challenge that will arise from the total sweep of

[42] This understanding of the Eucharist is not at all far from that to which Paul appeals in his pastoral remonstration to the faithful at Corinth in 1 Cor 11:17-34. When they eat the bread and drink the cup they are "proclaiming the death of the Lord" (v. 26) in the sense of a "death for others." The wider context in which the community is celebrating the Eucharist (v. 21) is not reflecting this self-sacrificing love of the Lord.

[43] The reference of "disciples" at this point must be somewhat wider than the band of twelve who were with him in the boat and to whom he turns in v. 67.

[44] Cf. C. K. Barrett, *John*, 302.

[45] This interpretation takes the incomplete conditional sentence making up v. 62 as meaning that the Son of Man's ascent to where he was before (via the cross) will add to the challenge already presented by the incarnation; cf. Rudolf Bultmann, *Gospel of John*, 445; Raymond E. Brown, *John I–XII*, 299; Andrew T. Lincoln, *St. John*, 236.

the saving "career" of the Son, with a particular focus upon the fact of his death as an act of self-sacrificial love. We do know that the crucifixion stood at the center of the "offense" that caused the bulk of the Jewish people to reject the proclamation of Jesus as Messiah (1 Cor 1:22-24; Rom 9:32-33). There is also abundant evidence in the Synoptic Gospels of the difficulty the prospect and actuality that Jesus should suffer such a fate held out to his closest disciples (Matt 16:21-23; 17:22-23; 20:17-19; Mark 8:31-33; 9:30-32; 10:32-34; Luke 9:43-45; 18:31-34; 24:25-27, 44-46). The Fourth Gospel is here accounting for the phenomenon, so painfully evident at the time of its composition, that the bulk of the Jewish people, including some who were initially sympathetic to Jesus during his historical life, ended up rejecting him and rejecting also the community that, after his death, continued to gather in his name.

Jesus' added comment addresses the same phenomenon: "It is the spirit that gives life; the flesh is useless. The words I have spoken to you are spirit and life" (v. 63). It is disconcerting to encounter such a negative usage of "flesh" when just so recently Jesus had spoken of "the bread" that he would give as "his flesh for the life of the world" (v. 51c). "Flesh" here is best taken in its normal biblical sense, indicating human existence as weak and mortal over against and to some extent alienated from God. Jesus' comment, then, is a reflection on human incapacity to grasp and accept matters for which the understanding of them requires the influence of the Spirit (1:13; 8:15; cf. 7:24). The revelation of himself as the Bread of Life come down from heaven and destined to return there via a self-sacrificing ascent upon a cross operates on a level that only Spirit-inspired faith attains and therein finds life. The fact that many of the disciples are complaining about his words simply shows the insufficiency of their faith ("among you are some who do not believe" [v. 64a]).

The presence of such failure to believe not only among "the Jews" but even among the disciples is a matter upon which the evangelist feels called to comment (vv. 64b-66). The abandonment of Jesus on the part of "many" disciples and, above all, the fact that one of them would ultimately prove traitor (v. 64c) were divinely foreseen. Such failure was also something that could be accounted for on the basis that faith requires being drawn by the Father (v. 65). The explanation presupposes once again that blending of human freedom and divine causality that causes difficulty for us but which biblical thought holds together without qualm. It is all a way of saying that dismaying developments in the community, not excluding betrayal in the inmost circle, are foreseen, held within, and ultimately gathered up into the saving plan of God.

8. Dialogue between Jesus and the Twelve: 6:67-71

Following the notice about the departure of many of the disciples (v. 66), Jesus turns to the inner group, the Twelve, mentioned here explicitly for the first time. Not without a note of pathos he asks them whether they too intend to go away (v. 67). Speaking on behalf of all, Simon Peter makes a response that has warmed Christian hearts down the ages (v. 68). If they were to go away, to whom else would they go? There may be other teachers, other figures offering some kind of salvation but only Jesus offers the "words" (*rhēmata*) that address the nub of all human longing: what this gospel terms "eternal life" (cf. 1:1-4; 20:31). Jesus' life-giving "words" in the discourse have led the disciples to believe and to know the truth they disclose: that he is "the Holy One of God" (v. 69).

This unusual title obviously transcends the categories elsewhere applied to messianic figures in the gospel.[46] As a response to all that Jesus has revealed in the discourse, the title would seem to designate him as the One who, having been with the Father from the beginning, has been consecrated and sent into the world (10:36; 17:11) to reclaim it for life.[47] We have arrived at a watershed moment in the narrative, closely parallel to the similar exchange between Jesus and his closest disciples at Caesarea Philippi in the Synoptic tradition (Matt 16:13-20; Mark 8:27-30; Luke 9:16-21).[48] The scene conveys the impression that from now on the band of Jesus' followers has shrunk almost to the Twelve, though this designation will not appear again in the gospel save, postresurrection, to indicate Thomas as "one of the Twelve" (20:24).

Yet even in this restricted band, as already noted (v. 64c), one will fall away (v. 70). Jesus has selected out the Twelve and yet one of them is "a devil," that is, not literally a devil but one who will become to such an extent the tool of Satan as to merit that designation (cf. 13:2). In a final comment (v. 71), the evangelist explains the allusion: Jesus "was speaking of Judas, son of Simon Iscariot, for he, one of the Twelve was going to betray him." At a key point of the discourse Jesus had identified the living Bread come down from heaven with "his flesh" that he would "give for the life of the world" (v. 51c). The offering in self-sacrificial love would be his gift

[46] Curiously, the exact form of the title is found elsewhere in the New Testament only upon the lips of the demon Jesus expels when teaching in the synagogue at Capernaum (Mark 1:24; Luke 4:34).

[47] Cf. Peder Borgen, "John 6: Tradition, Interpretation and Composition," in *Critical Readings of John 6*, ed. R. Alan Culpepper (Leiden: Brill, 1997), 111.

[48] Raymond E. Brown, *John I–XII*, 301–2, sets out the parallels at length.

and ultimately that of his Father, yet the external agent of that "giving up" (= "betrayal") would be Judas, one of the Twelve, acting as an instrument of Satan. Jesus' death will represent a conflict between divine love and diabolical evil. Though outwardly evil will prevail, penetrating even the intimate circle that Jesus has chosen, the light will shine on in the darkness and the darkness will not overcome it (1:5). All has been foreseen by Jesus and encompassed within the wider divine scheme. There are surely words of comfort and encouragement here for a church struggling to come to terms with abuse and betrayal even in the most sacred of her offices.

The Light of the World: 7:1–10:21

Jesus in Jerusalem at the Feast of Tabernacles (1): 7:1-52

We come now to what is frankly the most difficult and unappealing section of the Fourth Gospel. Save for two or three passages, I suspect there is little in chapters 7–8 that if omitted would cause grief. The content is polemical, with Jesus constantly in dispute and conflict with the authorities in Jerusalem, while the wider populace, like the chorus in a Greek drama, are puzzled and divided in their response. The interplay of narrative and theology that is a mark of the Fourth Gospel is skewed so much in the direction of theology that narrative coherence is sacrificed again and again. If the sequence brings little that is new but on the contrary repeats much of what has been said before, this is because it simply wants to drive home, by dint of repetition, a single central truth: that all hangs upon one's recognition of and response to Jesus as the one sent by God to make God visible and accessible to the world.[1] It highlights dramatically—if not totally successfully—Jesus' claims in this regard by setting them over against the hostility of the authorities and the incomprehension of the crowds, exploring again and again where the resistance is coming from. For all its comparative unattractiveness, John 7–8 has a place in the gospel and we need to make something of it.

One factor that does lend a measure of coherence to the sequence (including John 9) is the backdrop provided by the Jewish feast of Tabernacles, motifs of which appear from time to time. Interpretation requires some appreciation of what this feast involved at the time of Jesus. Tabernacles originally celebrated the gathering in of the harvest in late summer. The name derives from the fact that the harvest workers, taking advantage

---

[1] Cf. Gail O'Day, "The Gospel of John," 627.

of seasonal fine weather, slept out in the open in booths made of branches. In line with this practice, during the eight days of the feast (late September to early October) the men slept in the booths, reliving the wilderness experience of Israel at the time of the Exodus. Besides thanksgiving for the harvest, the feast also included prayers for rain, associated with daily processions in which water was brought to the temple from the Pool of Siloam and poured over the altar of sacrifice. On the first night of the feast the temple was brightly illuminated with torches and throughout the celebration pilgrims danced by night in the Court of the Women under the light of four large menorahs (seven-branched candelabras). This illumination of the temple in its high location led to its being described in some sources as "the light of the world." Both of these motifs—water and light—feature significantly in John 7–9.

The celebratory and joyous nature of Tabernacles led to its association in the later Jewish tradition with the hoped-for messianic era of salvation and peace. We find this already in a well-known passage from the prophet Zechariah:

> On that day living waters shall flow out from Jerusalem. . . . And the LORD will become king over all the earth. . . . Then all who survive of the nations that have come against Jerusalem shall go up year after year to worship the King, the LORD of hosts, and to keep the festival of booths. (Zech 14:8, 9, 16)

The understanding of Tabernacles as a harbinger of the messianic era led to an expectation that it would be during this feast that the Messiah would be revealed to Israel. Hence the prominence in John 7–8 of the issue as to whether Jesus is or is not the Messiah.[2]

The sequence in chapter 7 unfolds in four scenes in Jerusalem. Preceding these is a preliminary discussion in Galilee between Jesus and his brothers as to whether or not he will go up to Jerusalem for the feast (7:1-10), plus a short bridging notice that takes us to Jerusalem and gives notice of the controversy concerning him being already present among the crowds (7:11-13):

Preliminary Discussion: To Jerusalem or Not? 7:1-10.

Controversy in Jerusalem: 7:11-13.

Scene 1: Jesus' Teaches in the Temple and Interacts with the Crowd: 7:14-24.

---

[2] For greater detail on the celebration of Tabernacles and references to the relevant sources (some rather later than the time of the gospel), see Francis J. Moloney, *John*, 233–36.

Scene 2: Is Jesus the Messiah?: 7:25-36

Scene 3: Jesus, Giver of the Spirit: 7:37-44

Scene 4: The Authorities at a Loss as to What To Do about Jesus:
7:45-52[3]

Preliminary Discussion: To Jerusalem or Not? 7:1-10

The opening sentences provide background information in regard to both locale and time. Jesus has chosen to remain in Galilee because, as we know already from the sequence in chapter 5, Judea (including of course Jerusalem) has become a place of murderous hostility toward him (v. 1). Yet, the feast of Tabernacles is approaching (v. 2) and hence the question arises as to whether he will, like all observant Jews, go up to the feast.

Members of his family (literally, "his brothers") urge Jesus to go to Judea. In so doing they hardly want him to expose himself to danger. Rather, their prompting stems from an awareness of him as a messianic figure, if not in fact the Davidic Messiah himself. The "works" they allude to (v. 3) would be miracles such as the one they had seen him perform when the wine ran out at Cana. If he is Messiah, then he has to demonstrate his claim to this role on a larger stage: show himself "to the world" (v. 4).[4] What better place to begin than Jerusalem, at precisely the feast (Tabernacles) when the Messiah was expected to appear?

As the evangelist indicates (v. 5), any such belief in Jesus as Messiah, resting as it does upon miracles, is imperfect. His brothers do not believe in him in the full Johannine sense of a faith that penetrates beneath the merely miraculous to discover a deeper revelation. As Jesus explains (vv. 6-8), he is operating according to a time scale determined by God, rather than by human need or prompting. There will be an "hour" for his "going up" to Jerusalem and revealing himself to the world but it is not yet. In his brothers' understanding, "going up" refers simply to making the customary pilgrimage of "going up" to Jerusalem for the feast (Tabernacles). A "going up" does lie ahead for Jesus and it will occur in Jerusalem but it will involve an ascension to the Father that he will accomplish via death on a cross. On a conventional understanding, Tabernacles may be an appropriate time for a would-be messiah to "go up" to Jerusalem and reveal himself to the world.

---

[3] V. 53 is best seen as attached to the following episode in 8:1-11.

[4] The reference in v. 3 to "disciples" in Judea may refer to those in Jerusalem said in 2:23 to have believed in Jesus on the basis of the signs that he worked.

For the Messiah that Jesus is, the right time (*kairos*) and appropriate feast for his revelation will be Passover, where, as "Lamb of God" (1:29, 36), he will offer his "flesh for the life of the world" (6:51).[5]

It may be safe for Jesus' brothers to go up now to Jerusalem. It is not safe for Jesus. The world that prevails there is hostile to him in a way that it is not hostile to them. It is hostile to him—deadly hostile—because his role is to unmask its evil (v. 7). If he were to go up to Jerusalem now, the world would kill him before the time appointed by the Father.

We encounter here one of the most negative statements about the "world" to be found in the gospel. Yet we cannot forget the earlier comment that God so loved the world as to give up his only Son (3:16) to rescue it for life. What we have here is not the complete sense of "world" (*kosmos*) as understood by John but rather the current regime brought about by Satan in the world created and loved by God. It is to wrest the world in the wider sense from the hostile regime infesting it that Jesus will lay down his life. But the hour for this revelation and victory over the world (16:33) has not yet come. His brothers can go up to this feast because they are not part of his project nor are they operating on the same divine timescale as he (v. 8).

It is this complete disjunction that excuses Jesus from what seems like deception when, after telling his brothers that he was not going up to the festival, he does in fact do so secretly after a brief delay (vv. 9-10). As on two previous occasions at Cana (2:4; 4:48), his movements will not be prompted by human motivations or even—immediately at least—by human need. Responsive to a divine mission and program, he will not engage the world on its own terms and programs but rather undercut and overthrow them with radical freedom.

Reflection. Related to Jesus as we are—by discipleship rather than through family connection—we have needs that we would like God to address, and ideas and suggestions as to how and when divine assistance might work most effectively in our cause. Rarely, however, do we find our prayers and petitions answered in the terms in which we frame them. The redemptive mission of Jesus continues in our time along the same mysterious program displayed in the gospel. Our prayers will be heard, our concerns met—as Jesus will assure his disciples (14:13-14; 16:23-24, 26)—but only in the context of a more universal and radical divine mission, the traces of which we can barely discern but in which we are invited to place complete trust.

---

[5] "*Kairos*," occurring only here (vv. 6, 8) in the Fourth Gospel, has the same sense as "hour" (*hōra*); cf. C. K. Barrett, *John*, 312.

Controversy in Jerusalem: 7:11-13

This small passage acts as a bridge taking the action to Jerusalem and introducing the "third party"—the crowds—alongside Jesus and the authorities with whom he will be in dialogue and dispute. As stated, the crowds function like the chorus in a Greek drama, commenting on what is going on and displaying a divided response (v. 12).[6] At this point they share the view of Jesus' brothers that he is at least a claimant to the messianic role. Hence their expectation that he should appear and reveal himself at Tabernacles. The passage raises the messianic issue that will run through the sequence as a whole.

Scene 1: *Jesus Teaches in the Temple and Interacts with the Crowd: 7:14-24*

Halfway through the feast of Tabernacles Jesus goes up to Jerusalem and begins to teach in the temple (v. 14). We are not told of what that teaching consists. In any case, it is not so much the content of the teaching but the fact that this "unlettered" Galilean is presuming to teach that provokes reaction (v. 15).[7] The point is not that Jesus cannot read or write but that his credentials for teaching are not derived from having studied under a recognized rabbi and learned how to interpret ("read") the law. Since he is wanting in this respect his teaching proceeds simply from himself, lacking authority.

Jesus addresses the reaction head on (vv. 16-18). His teaching does not proceed from himself but from the One who sent him, the Father, the One whose will they should seek to do. Those who genuinely want to perform the will of God will recognize that his teaching is from God and not purely from himself (v. 17). The argument seems circular but rests upon a basic principle of divine revelation: recognizing whether a particular teaching comes from God requires a prior commitment to do God's will. In human terms it is natural to want to hear and assess a proposition before being prepared to recognize and surrender to its authority. But divine revelation does not work like that. Only through a prior commitment of living faith is

---

[6] The "murmuring" (*goggysmos*) (v. 12) does not reflect complaint, as in 6:41, 43, 61, but rather the fact that, through fear of the authorities, discussion about Jesus proceeded as a suppressed murmur; cf. Andrew T. Lincoln, *St. John*, 245.

[7] The "amazement" (*ethaumazon*; also v. 21) is hostile, not just puzzled; cf. Francis J. Moloney, *John*, 242.

it possible to arrive at the certainty that Jesus' teaching is not spoken on his own authority but comes from God, who is then "known" in a new way.[8]

Jesus supports (v. 18) his claim by pointing out that those (literally, "the one") who speak on their own authority seek to enhance their own reputation (literally, "glory" [*doxa*]) rather than that of the one who sends them. This renders them unlikely to be scrupulous concerning the truth. Those on the other hand who seek the glory of the one who sent them speak truth rather than falsehood. Jesus is enunciating a general principle but one clearly meant to apply to himself. The Greek word *doxa* has the dual meaning of "reputation" and "glory." Jesus does not seek his own glory (that is, to enhance his reputation) but as he moves toward his passion and death the Father will glorify him with the glory that is his as "only Son of the Father, full of grace and truth" (1:14; cf. 13:31-32).

A paragraph about Moses and the law breaks sharply into the sequence (vv. 19-24). Going over to the offensive, Jesus charges that none of "them" are doing the law because they are looking for an opportunity to kill him (v. 19). To some degree we can sympathize with the exclamation of the crowd who respond, "You're mad.[9] Who is trying to kill you?" (v. 20). What Jesus has in mind is the controversy that erupted following his healing of the paralyzed man on the Sabbath at the Pool of Bethesda (5:1-18).[10] The authorities determined to kill him on that occasion because they saw his defense as tantamount to making himself equal to God (5:18). The same threat hangs over him throughout his presence in Judea (including Jerusalem). Recalling the episode (v. 21) and the continuing threat, Jesus points out that it is not he who transgressed the law of Moses—by healing a man on the Sabbath. On the contrary, they are breaking the law's prohibition of killing ("You shall not kill") by seeking to kill him. Moreover, employing a kind of *a fortiori* argument, Jesus insists that in healing the man on the Sabbath he was in fact fulfilling the law. He points out (vv. 22-23) that faithful Jews will circumcise a child on the Sabbath in order to fulfill the stipulation that circumcision be performed on the eighth day after birth (Lev 12:3). The

---

[8] Cf. Rudolf Schnackenburg, *St. John*, 2:133.

[9] Lit., "you have a demon!" Various forms of madness were attributed to demonic possession in the ancient world; cf. C. K. Barrett, *John*, 319.

[10] Understanding Jesus' attribution of the negative reaction of the crowd to his healing of the paralyzed man rests on taking the phrase "for this reason" (*dia touto*) at the beginning of v. 22 with the preceding sentence (v. 21), rather than, as the verse division suggests, with what follows; cf. Raymond E. Brown, *John I–XII*, 310, 312. The NRSV completely ignores the phrase.

circumcision rule, then, (which Jesus actually traces back [v. 22b] to the patriarchs [literally, "to the fathers"; cf. Gen 17:10]) overrides the Sabbath. On the *a fortiori* principle, if, the Sabbath notwithstanding, the law requires an operation (circumcision) on a single member of the human body (the lesser case), how much more (v. 23) should it require the restoration of the whole person to full health (the greater)? If his adversaries had only looked at the matter in depth, rather than judging by appearances (*kat' opsin* [v. 24]), they would realize that he was fulfilling the law, where they, in their murderous intent, are breaking it.[11] The Sabbath is about wholeness and the divine gift of life. To hedge it about with restrictions that stunt the flowering of human life is to frustrate its essential purpose and so in fact to break the law.

Scene 2: *Is Jesus the Messiah?: 7:25-36*

The threat to Jesus' life remains in the background as the messianic issue finally emerges. "Some of the people of Jerusalem" (v. 25), acting again like a Greek chorus commenting on the action, wonder out loud whether the failure of the authorities to arrest Jesus is because they really do believe Jesus to be the Messiah (v. 26). Counter to this, though (v. 27), is the widespread belief that when the Messiah appears, no one will know where he is from,[12] whereas Jesus' origins in Galilee are known to all. The problem is left hanging in the air but it raises again the question of Jesus' origins, a question central to the dispute between Jesus and his adversaries, and one soon to be joined by a corresponding issue in the opposite direction: namely, where is he going? (vv. 33-36). For Jesus, questions concerning his origin and his destination transcend such categories. As the Prologue has made clear, he has come from the Father and to the Father he will return (cf. 16:28). He concedes (v. 28) that at one level the crowd do know where he is from—from Galilee presumably (cf. v. 41). But concerning his ultimate origins they are ignorant. They do not recognize that behind his presence among them is the One who has sent him, the One (the Father) who truly exists (literally, "the one who sent me is true [*alēthinos*]").[13] Not to know Jesus in his true origins amounts to not knowing God.[14]

---

[11] Cf. C. K. Barrett, *John*, 320.

[12] C. K. Barrett, *John*, 322, indicates a number of Jewish sources testifying to such a belief.

[13] For this meaning of the word "true" (*alēthinos*) here (v. 28), see Rudolf Schnackenburg, *St. John*, 2:147.

[14] Cf. Andrew T. Lincoln, *St. John*, 251.

To accuse a Jewish audience of not knowing God is to strike at the heart of Israel's faith and self-understanding. The severe accusation reflects both the sharpness of the split between the Johannine community and the synagogue at the time when the Fourth Gospel was written, and also the conviction on the part of the community that the true revelation of the unseen God is to be found in the human flesh of Jesus. Jesus does not displace the God of Israel but in him, and only in him, has God truly become known (1:18).

The high claims that Jesus is making lead to an attempt to arrest him (v. 30a).[15] The authorities do not succeed in this purpose because "his hour" had not yet come (v. 30bc). At the same time, from "many in the crowd" a more positive approach emerges. They are moving to belief in him as Messiah on the basis of the signs he has done ("When the Messiah comes, will he do more signs than this man has done?" [v. 31]).[16] Here, as elsewhere in the gospel (2:23; 4:48), the implication is that this is inadequate faith, an enclosure of Jesus within conventional messianic categories that fails to penetrate beyond the miraculous to the divine reality which the miracle should disclose.

The divided response among the crowd alarms the Pharisees,[17] who decide to take more effective action (v. 32). Along with the chief priests, they send temple police to stone Jesus. They do not understand that in trying to eliminate Jesus from the world in which they hold sway, "their plot is being thwarted because there is another world where an ultimate authority reigns, and Jesus' story is determined by that world."[18] The Roman governor (Pilate) will confront the same dilemma when Jesus stands on trial before him (19:10-11). And every martyr in Christian history appeals, explicitly or implicitly, to the same "other world," which is not really a world separate from our world but its deepest reality and truth.

Prompted by awareness of the measures taken against him, Jesus begins (vv. 33-34) to speak of the "little while" that he will be with them—that is, with the crowds in Jerusalem at the feast and also with his people as a whole.

---

[15] The "they" who seek to arrest Jesus are presumably not the crowds in general but "the authorities" mentioned in v. 26.

[16] There is little or no evidence of an expectation that the Davidic Messiah would work miracles—though such is clearly implied by the Fourth Gospel. The expectation possibly arose from a blurring of the roles of Davidic Messiah and the Prophet like Moses of Deut 18:15; cf. C. K. Barrett, *John*, 323; Francis J. Moloney, *John*, 248.

[17] As already indicated, the inclusion of Pharisees among the adversaries of Jesus at this point reflects the antagonism between the Johannine community and the leading authorities in Judaism after 70 CE, who were predominantly the heirs of the Pharisee party of Jesus' day.

[18] Francis J. Moloney, *John*, 249.

He has come to "his own (people)" (1:11a) and remained with them for a time. But the time for their acceptance is running out. He will return to the One who sent him. They will search for him and not be able to find him, nor will they be able to follow to the place where he has gone. Just as the crowd had showed limited understanding in the matter of his origins, so now (vv. 35-36) they show similar limitation in regard to where he is going. In saying that he is going to a place where they will not find him, does this signal an intention to go "to the Dispersion (*diaspora*) among the Greeks"? "Greeks" here we should probably understand, in the first instance, to refer to the Greek-speaking Jews of the Diaspora beyond Palestine. Maybe he is going to take his teaching to that wider Jewish world? Though wrong in terms of Jesus' real destination (to the Father), the misunderstanding, with characteristic Johannine irony, prophetically states what eventually will be the case. After his "little while" in Israel, Jesus will "go to the Greeks" when, post-Easter, his disciples extend his mission not merely to the Jewish Diaspora but to the Gentile world as a whole.[19]

Scene 3: *Jesus, Giver of the Spirit: 7:37-44*

The sequence comes to a climax in what is possibly for most people the one truly attractive passage in the whole of John 7: vv. 37-39. On the "last and greatest day of the feast," that is, the eighth day of Tabernacles, Jesus stands in public and cries out an invitation:

> If anyone thirsts, let them come to me,
> and let the one who believes in me drink.
> As Scripture says, "Streams of living water shall flow from his heart."
>   (vv. 37b-38)

Set out in this way the translation attempts to render in good English an underlying Greek text that contains ambiguities upon which interpreters have been divided from ancient times. (For a brief indication of the issues and justification of the choice I have made here, see the notes.)[20] The notion

---

[19] Cf. later the similar irony in the unconscious prophecy of Caiaphas the high priest in 11:49-52.

[20] There are three interconnected issues concerning these verses: (1) The punctuation in vv. 37-38a; (2) the reference of the one from whom streams of living water flow: whether to the believer or to Christ; (3) the source of the alleged scriptural quotation in v. 38b. Placing a full stop after "drink" associates the phrase "who believes in me" (v. 38a) very closely with the scriptural quotation that follows and favors the interpretation that sees a reference to the believer as the source of living water. Placing a full stop after "come to me" creates a more

of "thirsting" for God has its biblical background in well-loved psalms such as Psalm 42:1-2:

> As a deer longs for flowing streams,
> so my soul longs for you, O God.
> My soul thirsts for God, for the living God.
> When shall I come and behold the face of God?

and Psalm 63:1:

> O God, you are my God, I seek you,
> my soul thirsts for you; my flesh faints for you,
> as in a dry and weary land where there is no water.

In line with such biblical texts, Jesus is inviting those who thirst in this way for a life-giving experience of God to come to him and "drink." As we have seen, "coming" to Jesus and believing in him are more or less synonymous in John. To come to Jesus in faith is to access the life-giving revelation that will slake the "thirst" for God expressed in the psalms.

The imagery of drinking that Jesus employs here draws upon the ritual of Tabernacles. As I noted earlier, each morning of the festival water was taken from the fountain of Gihon on the southeast side of the temple hill, the source for the Pool of Siloam, and carried in solemn procession up to the temple, where a priest poured it into a silver funnel on the altar of holocausts, whence it flowed down upon the ground.[21] The ritual evokes the vision of Ezekiel 47:1-12, where the prophet sees water flowing down from the temple, in all four directions and in ever-increasing volumes until it becomes a great river, flowing down to the sea, and bringing life and fertility

---

balanced couplet across vv. 37b-38a and favors the christological reference in v. 38b. Many ancient commentators going back to Origen adopted the former punctuation and interpretation. It is found today in translations such as the RSV, NRSV, NIV, and defended by scholars of stature such as C. K. Barrett (*John*, 326–28). While the issue cannot be resolved on grounds of punctuation or textual witness, considerations of context and Johannine theology have led to a more common acceptance of the alternative, christological view. It is true that, in conversation with the Samaritan woman, Jesus refers to living water becoming a spring within the believer (4:14). However, there is no suggestion that the believer becomes thereby a source where others may slake their thirst, as is said of Jesus in several places (4:10; 6:35). The flow of water (as well as blood) from the side of Christ when his body upon the cross is pierced by a lance (19:34) also supports a reference to Christ, which I have adopted here. See further, Rudolf Bultmann, *Gospel of John*, 303; Raymond E. Brown, *John I–XII*, 320–21; Francis J. Moloney, *John*, 256; Gail O'Day, "The Gospel of John," 622–23; Andrew T. Lincoln, *St. John*, 253–55. The third issue (source of the scriptural quotation) is discussed in the text below.

[21] Cf. Raymond E. Brown, *John I–XII*, 326–27.

in every aspect to a hitherto barren land. Jesus has, of course, already identified himself with the temple—or, more accurately, has indicated his own body as the replacement of the Jerusalem temple (2:21). It is likely, then, that, in inviting those who "thirst" to come to him to "drink," he is presenting himself as the source of the life-giving revelation of God, now to be found in his living flesh rather than in the physical temple of old.

The invitation is supported (v. 37b) by a scriptural prophecy: "Streams of living water shall flow from his heart."[22] No identifiable text of Scripture (OT) exactly corresponds to this sentence. While puzzling at one level, the uncertainty opens up a rich possibility of allusion to several scriptural texts in combination. I have already mentioned Ezekiel's vision of ever-increasing, life-giving water flowing from the temple (47:1-12). Fundamental would also seem to be the motif of Moses striking the rock in order to provide life-giving water for the Israelites during their wandering in the wilderness (Exod 17:6) and, more particularly, the reprise of this motif in Psalm 78 (LXX 77):16, 20:

> He made streams come out of the rock,
> and caused waters to flow down like rivers. . . .
> Even though he struck the rock so that water gushed out and torrents overflowed. (Ps 78:16, 20; cf. Ps 105 [LXX 104]:41)

And in several passages in (Second) Isaiah, especially 44:3, where the provision of water is associated, as here (v. 39), with the gift of the Spirit (cf. also Isa 43:20; 48:21).

The scriptural passage to which the quotation in John 7:38 would seem to be most indebted is Zechariah 14, already noted for its connection with Tabernacles, with its prophecy of "living water(s)" flowing out, as in Ezekiel 47, from Jerusalem in the age to come:

> On that day living waters shall flow out from Jerusalem, half of them to the eastern sea and half of them to the western sea; it shall continue in summer as in winter. (Zech 14:8)

A similar indebtedness to both Ezekiel and Zechariah is to be found in the vision of the New Jerusalem in Revelation (Apocalypse) 21–22, with the "river of the water of life . . . flowing from the throne of God and of the Lamb" (22:1). Like Revelation, but with an explicit forging of a scriptural

---

[22] Lit., "from his belly" (*koilia*). The reference is probably equivalent to "heart" and simply communicates the sense of the flow proceeding from inner depths of a person, the seat of profound emotion.

quotation, the Fourth Gospel has drawn together a rich tissue of scriptural texts to present Christ as the Rock providing life-giving water to the new Exodus community, just as in the previous chapter he presented himself as the true "Bread from Heaven," replacing the manna of old.[23]

The evangelist (v. 39) identifies the "streams of living water" with the gift of the Holy Spirit and then explains that this was something that believers were yet to receive because Jesus had not yet been glorified. While Jesus himself has received the Spirit, as reported by the Baptist (1:32-33), and while he could say to the Samaritan woman that the hour for "worship in Spirit and in truth" was already at hand (4:23-24), in the more regular view of the gospel the gift of the Spirit to believers follows upon Jesus' hour of "glorification": the moment, that is, of his expiry upon the cross when he breathes out the Spirit upon the community represented by the Beloved Disciple (19:30; cf. 20:22-23).[24]

Jesus' response leads the crowd to raise the issue of his identity once more (vv. 40-44; cf. vv. 25-31). As in the case of John the Baptist (1:19-21, 24), they discuss and disagree about the various messianic roles that he might fit: "the prophet" (v. 40b), that is, the "prophet like Moses" expected on the basis of Deut 18:15 (cf. 6:14); or "the (Davidic) Messiah" (v. 41a). The problem with the second suggestion, as others point out (vv. 41b-42), is that the Messiah is supposed to be of Davidic descent and born in David's town, Bethlehem in Judea, whereas Jesus, as far as they know, is from Galilee.

There is a double measure of irony present here. Though not stated explicitly anywhere in the text, the narrative seems to presume an awareness of the tradition (preserved in the infancy stories of Matthew and Luke) that Jesus was actually born in Bethlehem, thereby fulfilling, unbeknownst to the crowd, the Davidic messianic credentials. More deeply, however, the whole issue is otiose because, though truly the Jewish Messiah, Jesus transcends the category entirely because of his true origins—beyond Bethlehem or Galilee—in the eternity of God (1:1-2; 16:28). Faced with this perplexity, some of the crowd want to arrest him but—either through fear or incapacity—fail to do so (v. 44). Mere human resources, either of understanding or strength, are completely at a loss before the One who has come from the Father to complete the mission set before him.

---

[23] On the scriptural background to the quotation in 7:38, see Raymond E. Brown, *John I–XII*, 321–23; Andrew T. Lincoln, *St. John*, 255–56.

[24] While the identification of the "living water" with the Spirit reflects the mature theology of the gospel, it is not necessary to exclude reference to the more general revelation that Jesus brings. The Spirit brings home Jesus' life-giving revelation of the Father's love very personally to the believer.

Scene 4: *The Authorities at a Loss as to What To Do about Jesus:*
    7:45-52

Inability to cope with Jesus is not confined to the crowds. Earlier (v. 32) we had learned that the chief priests and Pharisees, disturbed by the crowd's mutterings about Jesus, had sent temple police to arrest him. Now these same police return empty-handed and make their report to those who sent them. The excuse they offer for their failure is, "Never has anyone (literally, "any man") spoken like this!" (v. 46). The response implies that the police, though servants of the authorities, are genuinely impressed by Jesus and share the inability of the crowds to cope with him. They are pointing to reality, to what they have experienced. In this they distance themselves from their employers (the authorities), who have simply made up their mind about Jesus and will not consider evidence to the contrary of any kind at all. Instead of further questioning the police about their experience, they attack them as gullible ("Surely you have not been deceived too, have you?" [v. 47b]) and mock them for siding with the ignorant and "accursed" common people rather than with the authorities or Pharisees, none of whom have believed in Jesus (vv. 47-49).[25] The irony is that the common people (including the police) are at least asking questions about Jesus, while the authorities by contrast, for all their knowledge of the law, are held back by malevolence from any inclination to give Jesus a hearing and possibly move toward faith. They will display a similar blind prejudice and simple resting on authority in regard to the testimony of the man born blind and his parents (9:28-29, 34).

    Nor are the authorities entirely accurate in regard to the attitude of their own class. One of them, the same Nicodemus who had come to Jesus by night but faded from the story on that occasion without coming to faith (3:1-9), speaks up (v. 50). He points out to these men of the law that the law forbids judging a person without first giving the accused a hearing (v. 51; cf. Deut 1:16; cf. 17:4). It is they, then, and not the common folk they despise who are actually breaking the law in their attitude to Jesus. The response Nicodemus receives simply confirms their prejudice. They insultingly take his defense of the Galilean Jesus to imply that he too is from that region. Well, then, let him go and "search" (the Scriptures) to see that no prophet

---

[25] The harsh judgment about the ignorance of the crowd concerning the law reflects well-attested attitudes of the Jewish religious authorities at the time toward what were known as "the people of the land," that is, those who were not educated in the law and hence did not follow it accurately; cf. C. K. Barrett, *John*, 332.

is to arise from Galilee (v. 52).[26] They share the prejudice of Nathanael in regard to Nazareth (1:46). But, unlike him, their chosen distance from Jesus removes any chance of overcoming blindness with faith. Nicodemus, who had at least given Jesus a hearing, exposes their ignorance.[27] He will make an even better showing at the end of the story (19:39-42).

Reflection. Aside from Jesus' invitation to those who "thirst" in vv. 37-39, there is little to nourish the contemporary reader in the remainder of John 7. The sequence is preoccupied with the contrast between the true reality of Jesus (as sent by the Father) and the difficulty experienced by the crowds, on the one hand, and the authorities, on the other, to grasp that true reality. The problem, as expressed again and again, is the attempt to capture him within the limits of preconceived categories, limits that the authorities in particular are loath to enlarge upon or abandon, despite the evidence plainly before them. They do not allow God's revelation of the "truth" in Jesus to redefine their world because their prestige and power very much rests upon the setup of the world as it is. In this sense at least the sequence holds out a perennial challenge for leadership in both church and society.[28]

Jesus and the Woman Taken in Adultery: 7:53–8:11

As is universally recognized, the account of Jesus and the woman brought to him accused of adultery is a foreign body in the Fourth Gospel. It is missing in the major early manuscripts; its tone, content, and language are characteristic more of Luke's Gospel than John's.[29] There are indications, however, of its existence early in the Christian tradition and what it records seems so typical of the ministry of Jesus as known from other sources that it quite likely rests upon an actual historical incident in his lifetime.

Why the episode found a home in the Fourth Gospel and did so in this particular location have long been matters of discussion. There is no doubt that in chapter 7 and the remainder of chapter 8 Jesus is under judgment

---

[26] Actually the authorities are wrong on this score as well, since according to 2 Kgs 14:25 the prophet Jonah, son of Amittai, came from Gath-hepher in Galilee but whether the gospel expects its readers to be conscious of this is questionable.

[27] Cf. Gail O'Day, "The Gospel of John," 624.

[28] In these reflections I am indebted once more to Gail O'Day, "The Gospel of John," 625–26.

[29] For a comprehensive discussion of these matters, see Andrew T. Lincoln, *St. John*, 524–27.

from the Jewish authorities in a way analogous to the situation of the woman. The accusation he makes in 8:15: "You judge by human standards; I judge no one" is a very apt comment on the incident as a whole. At the end of his teaching in this sequence Jesus will depart from the temple, himself under threat, like the woman, of being stoned by zealots for the law (8:59; cf. 10:31-33; 11:8). The episode, then, is not entirely incongruous in its present position in the Fourth Gospel, and, of course, its presence in the Latin Vulgate has ensured its canonical status in the Catholic tradition.

After the introductory setting of the scene (7:53–8:2), the episode falls into a sequence of three dramatic moments: (1) The scribes and Pharisees bring the woman before Jesus and lay their accusation: 8:3-6a; (2) exchange between Jesus and the accusers: 8:6b-9; and (3) exchange between Jesus and the woman: 8:10-11.

The notice at the end of John 7 (v. 53) that "each went home" makes little sense at the conclusion of the preceding sequence and so is best attached to the introductory setting of the scene with the woman in 8:1-2. Jesus himself goes out for the evening to the Mount of Olives and then returns at dawn to the temple, where he again begins to teach the people.[30]

For the scribes and Pharisees the main point is not to get the woman punished but to set a trap for Jesus (vv. 4-6a). She is simply a pawn in their scheme. Faced with her guilt, which is not in question in the scene (cf. v. 11c), Jesus must either resile from his characteristic policy of mercy toward sinners or else set himself in defiance of the prescriptions of the law.[31]

Jesus' gesture of stooping down and writing on the ground (v. 6b) is a wordless refusal to engage the issue as they present it.[32] What it was that he wrote has been the subject of fruitless speculation for centuries. Perhaps he was only doodling. There could be a hint, however, of a new "law," written from a lowly, humble posture in contrast to the Sinai dispensation written and promulgated from on high, which is presently bearing so heavily upon the woman. When the accusers in frustration press their suit (v. 7a), it is from this lowly posture that he "looks up" at them and puts his searing

---

[30] The first three verses are very close to a similar notice in Luke 21:37-38, which may indicate that the episode was first located there before being translated to its present position; cf. Andrew T. Lincoln, *St. John*, 527.

[31] Lev 20:10; Deut 22:22-24. It is not certain that the Mosaic penalties for adultery were carried out in New Testament times. Some see one side of the dilemma facing Jesus to be that of giving offense to the Roman authorities if he agrees to the woman's condemnation, since the Romans reserved the decision about capital punishment to themselves; cf. 18:31.

[32] Cf. Gail O'Day, "The Gospel of John," 629.

proposition (v. 7bc): "Let anyone among you who is without sin be the first to throw a stone at her."[33] Jesus does not confront the law directly. He just points out that the only person who could have a right to condemn another is one who has never sinned. If, as occurs (v. 9a), the eldest is the first to leave, presumably that is because he has had a longer space of life in which to accumulate sin.

This way the punitive legal prescription simply falls away. Jesus has a better way of dealing with sin than condemnation and punishment. He does not deny or condone sin. (The episode does seem to presuppose that the woman is in fact guilty—though glaringly absent from the scene is her male accomplice.) His entire concern is to rescue the woman from her terrible plight and set her free for a new direction of life: "Go and from now on sin no more" (v. 11c).

A subtle point about the episode is that Jesus never actually looks at the woman while she is the subject of accusation. His bending down and writing may be a ploy to avoid this. It is only when her accusers have melted away that he looks up and speaks to her as one free from accusation—from them and, above all, from him (vv. 10-11a). He, who is without sin (cf. 2 Cor 5:21), and hence the only one actually credentialed to judge and condemn her from "on high," has actually gone down on the ground before her to restore her dignity and self-esteem—making of the scene a parable of his whole saving work, just as later when he kneels to wash his disciples' feet (13:3-11).

The "orphaned" status of this story in the textual tradition until it found a home in some Western manuscripts of the Fourth Gospel probably reflects early Christian uneasiness with Jesus' apparent leniency in a case of sexual misconduct. So much more prone is the religious instinct to condemn and punish rather than to rescue and set on the path to life. And often, of course, the most paralyzing accusations are those that we inflict upon ourselves. In any case, we can only be immensely grateful that this precious gem did find a place in the Christian tradition. As Raymond Brown has stated:

> Its succinct expression of the mercy of Jesus is as delicate as anything in Luke; its portrayal of Jesus as the serene judge has all the majesty that we would expect of John.[34]

---

[33] Deut 17:7 prescribes that the witnesses to a capital offense should be the first to raise their hand to execute the sentence.

[34] Raymond E. Brown, *John I–XII*, 336.

Jesus in Jerusalem at the Feast of Tabernacles (2): 8:12-59

The second part of the Tabernacles sequence begins with a splendid claim by Jesus to be the "Light of the world" (v. 12a). The claim takes us back to the opening words of the Prologue where we read "in him (the Word) was light and the light was the life of human beings" (1:4), a light that shines in a darkness that is not able to extinguish it. We noted in that context that the coming of the Son into the world as "light" (v. 9) was the evangelist's way of seeing God's original act of creation ("Let there be light!" [Gen 1:2]) being realized in Christ—so that in every act and word of Christ as told in the gospel that creative contest between light and darkness proceeds.

Now, in further conflict with the authorities and in a setting where the illumination of the temple throughout the feast led to its being described as the "light of the world," Jesus stakes his claim to be the world's true Light. He insists that the person who follows him (in discipleship) will not "walk" (= live) in darkness but "will have the light of life" (v. 12b), that is, the light that leads to the gaining of (eternal) life (cf. 1:4).

Following this introductory claim, the sequence unfolds in five stages, the last three of which cohere to some extent around the topic of descent from Abraham.

1. Jesus' True Testimony: 8:13-20

2. Jesus' True Origins, Destination, and Identity: 8:21-30

3. Freedom through the Truth: 8:31-38

4. True and False Paternity: 8:39-47

5. Jesus, Greater than Abraham: 8:48-59

These five passages are like patches of differing colors sewn together to make a single quilt. It is difficult to trace a coherent argument across them and hardly worth trying to do so. What, in fact, lends a measure of unity to the sequence is the mounting hostility and, in the latter part, as I have noted, the motif of descent from Abraham. The recurring themes of judgment and condemnation remind us that, in an anticipation of a trial scene at the time of his arrest, Jesus is on trial here before the world represented by the Jewish authorities (characterized first as "the Pharisees," then and for the most part as "the Jews" or simply "they").[35] Yet, again and again, Jesus insists that, in

---

[35] As Francis J. Moloney observes, "Throughout chs. 7–8 'the Jews' and the Pharisees are the same group" (*John*, 273).

attempting to judge him, the world is putting itself on trial and setting itself up for condemnation. Keeping this forensic feature of the narrative in mind will make it more understandable if not more attractive. If we are to gain anything from this off-putting sequence, such profit will probably come about more from concentrating on the words of Jesus as stand-alone statements rather than as responses in an interaction that is making any progress in mutual understanding.

1. *Jesus' True Testimony: 8:13-20*

The Pharisees counter Jesus' claim to be the Light (v. 12) by pointing out (v. 13) that since he is testifying on his own behalf his testimony is not authentic (literally, "true"[36]). On a human level the objection has force. In the legal systems of ordered human society it is a commonplace that the personal testimony of an individual needs to be validated by the evidence of others. But Jesus cannot submit to such requirements or tests.[37] He comes from the heavenly world of the Father, a world to which he is returning and concerning which he alone can bear witness in regard to what he has seen and heard (3:31-32). Since no one else can provide such evidence, there can be no witness beyond his own self-revelation (v. 14).[38] They, on the other hand, being ignorant of such matters and judging him on purely human terms (literally, "according to the flesh" [v. 15a]), refuse to accept his witness, thereby demonstrating their captivity to a hostile world of unbelief.[39]

In contrast to them, Jesus insists (v. 15b) that he judges no one. Then, in what appears to be instant self-contradiction, he states that if he *does* exercise judgment his judgment is valid because behind it stands the One who sent him, namely, the Father (v. 16). So completely unified is he with the Father that whatever judgment he makes is simply that of the Father—so that in a strictly personal sense he both judges and does not judge at the same time. Moreover, even on the legal terms on which they place such weight ("in your law" [v. 17]), this combined judgment of Jesus himself and of the Father is valid: it fulfills the prescription of the law that two witnesses are required to sustain a charge (vv. 17-18; cf. Num 35:30; Deut 17:6).

---

[36] The Greek word *alēthēs* has the sense here of "valid"; cf. Francis J. Moloney, *John*, 266.

[37] "When the light shines in the darkness it cannot prove itself to be light except by shining" (Lesslie Newbigin, *The Light Has Come: An Exposition of the Fourth Gospel* [Grand Rapids, MI: Wm. B. Eerdmans, 1983], 103).

[38] Cf. Rudolf Schnackenburg, *St. John*, 2:192.

[39] Cf. Andrew T. Lincoln, *St. John*, 266.

The adversaries respond, "Where is your father?" (v. 19a), apparently wanting him to produce his human father in order to provide at least some measure of testimony beyond himself.[40] For Jesus such misunderstanding simply shows that they do not know the Father (v. 19bc). The argument is circular and seems to be going nowhere. The crux of the matter—now and throughout the continuing exchange—is that human beings cannot submit the revelation of the divine to purely human criteria of judgment. Confronted with the Light, they can only accept the conversion it requires or else withdraw back into the darkness, drawing down judgment upon themselves (3:16-21). In this sense Jesus does not have to exercise judgment (v. 15b); judgment takes place simply through his coming into the world as its Light.

Appropriately Jesus is pronouncing "these words" (v. 20a) in the temple,[41] the role of which he is replacing as life-giving Light of the world. The darkness would love to extinguish the Light by laying hands upon him (v. 20b). It fails to do so because "his hour," the moment appointed by the Father for the final confrontation, has not yet arrived (v. 20c).

2. *Jesus' True Origins, Destination, and Identity: 8:21-30*

The issue of Jesus' origin and destiny continues in a fresh contest to establish his identity. Jesus again asserts that he is "going away" to where his adversaries, for all their efforts to seek him out, will not be able to follow. The consequence will be that they will "die in their sin" (v. 21). This fate (repeated in v. 24) will stem from their failure to respond with faith to his appearance and his witness. Central to the discussion at this point is a firm distinction between two spheres of existence: one "above," from which Jesus has come and to which he will return, and one "below," the level upon which his adversaries are operating (v. 23). Faith is the only means of bridging the gap between these two spheres.[42] While remaining physically in the world "below," believers see the human flesh of Jesus transparent to the sphere from which he has come (1:1-2) and in which he continues to dwell with the Father (1:18, 51). Through faith they are "born again"/"born from above," as Jesus explained to Nicodemus (3:3-7), and so become "children of God" (1:12-13), sharers already in the divine eternal life. Failure to believe, on

---

[40] Cf. Andrew T. Lincoln, *St. John*, 267.

[41] The specific location, "in the treasury," likely refers to the court where large receptacles for offerings to the temple stood; cf. C. K. Barrett, *John*, 340.

[42] Cf. Francis J. Moloney, *John*, 271.

the other hand—the essence of "sin" in the Fourth Gospel[43]—entails separation from this source of life and ensures that physical death will mean eternal death ("you will die in your sin[s]").[44]

The adversaries interpret his talk of "going away" as an intention to commit suicide (v. 22). The misunderstanding shows the gulf between the two levels of understanding, which through lack of faith cannot be bridged. Ironically, Jesus will lay down his life (10:18)—and do so at their hand. But this laying down will not be suicide but a sacrificial giving up of his "flesh for the life of the world" (6:51).

Jesus stresses (v. 23) the difference between the two spheres from which, respectively, he and his adversaries come: they are "from below," he is "from above"; they are "from this world," he is "not from this world." In itself "the world" is the world that God loved so much as to send the beloved Son for its salvation (3:16). But, precisely as the object of divine love, the world must be freed from its prevailing darkness and sin, and elevated to share the life (the "eternal life") of the sphere from which Jesus has come. Insisting upon the necessity of grasping the bridge between the two "worlds" that his appearance represents, Jesus repeats (v. 24) his warning more strongly: "Unless you believe that I am (*egō eimi*), you will die in your sins" (v. 24).

The adversaries are obviously baffled by "I am" (*egō eimi*). Their reaction, "*Who* are you?" (v. 25a), seems to show them stumbling at the missing predicate.[45] They have failed to understand, as the gospel expects believers to understand, that the mysterious expression without predicate alludes to the formula of divine revelation occurring over and over in (Second) Isaiah, as, for example, in 43:10:

> You are my witnesses, says the LORD . . .
> so that you may know and believe me
> and understand that *I am he.*

Or even more relevantly in the present context, Isaiah 43:25:

> *I am He, I am He*
> who blots out your transgressions for my own sake,
> and I will not remember your sins.[46]

---

[43] Cf. Raymond E. Brown: "In Johannine thought there is only one radical sin of which man's [*sic*] many sins (plural in v. 24) are but reflections. This radical sin is to refuse to believe in Jesus and thus to refuse life itself" (*John I–XII*, 350).

[44] Cf. Andrew T. Lincoln, *St. John*, 267.

[45] Gail O'Day, "The Gospel of John," 634.

[46] Cf. also Isa 41:4; 45:8 (LXX), 19 (LXX), 22 (LXX); 46:4, 9 (LXX); 48:12; 51:12.

Jesus, whom John pointed out as the Lamb of God who takes away the sin of the world (1:29), is here presenting himself in this divine role. He bears God's name ("I am"; cf. Exod 3:14-16) not in a static sense but in the function of a divine reaching out to an alienated world in reconciliation. If his present adversaries cannot grasp this saving revelation they stand in peril of consigning themselves to eternal loss along with the rest of the unbelieving world.

Instead of explaining the mysterious title, Jesus utters a word of frustration: "Why do I bother to speak to you at all!" (v. 25b).[47] He goes on to distinguish what he could offer on his own account (v. 26a)[48] from what he has directly from the Father (v. 26b). On his own account he has much to say and much judgment of his own to make, but he forbears to do so in the interests of communicating what he has heard from the One who sent him— the One who is "true" (*alēthēs*) in the Johannine sense of being utterly trustworthy and faithful. Again, however (v. 27), he has left the crowd completely behind. They do not recognize that the One who sent him is in fact the God whom he calls "Father."

In a climactic statement (v. 28a) Jesus goes on to specify the moment that will be the high point of revelation: "When you have lifted up the Son of Man, then you will know that I am" (*egō eimi*). As in 3:14 and later in 12:32-34, the "lifting up" refers to his being lifted up in crucifixion. A difference is that, whereas the other two expressions are passive, here Jesus unambiguously indicates his opponents as the active agents of his execution. But how will this outward triumph on their part constitute in any sense a revelation of his true identity? Surely, it will appear as nothing but his ultimate defeat. Behind, however, the horrible outward details of the execution, faith will discern in its free embrace by Jesus the supreme moment of revelation: the manifestation of the divine essence ("I am") as nothing else than love, sacrificial love reaching out to the world in life-giving reconciliation (3:16). That is why Jesus can conclude (vv. 28b-29) by insisting on his absolute unity with the One who sent him: he is in no sense an independent agent, acting alone; everything he says and does—above all the embrace of the cross—is in accord with the will of the Father, whose saving name ("I am") he bears before the world.

---

[47] The translation of v. 25b is much disputed, especially the sense of the Greek expression *tēn archēn*. Aside from an expression of frustration (cf. Francis J. Moloney, *John*, 271), the statement could respond more directly to the question in v. 25a in the sense of "(I am) what I have been telling you from the beginning"; cf. C. K. Barrett, *John*, 343; thorough discussion in Raymond E. Brown, *John I–XII*, 347–48.

[48] Taking the Greek verb *echō* in the sense of "I can"; cf. C. K. Barrett, *John*, 343.

Jesus is placing before his hearers here a choice and even an appeal. "Do you want to be on the side of those who bring judgment upon themselves by encompassing my death, or will you join those who in faith will discern in that death the true, life-giving revelation of God?"[49] As if to highlight this latter positive possibility, the narrative, somewhat surprisingly, informs us that many believed in Jesus at this point (v. 30). And, for all its polemical tone and content, the controversy contains some of the gospel's most sublime christological statements. Without the revelatory "I am" statements (vv. 24, 28) our understanding of John's theology of the cross would be much impoverished.

3. *Freedom through the Truth: 8:31-38*

At this point we enter upon a sequence of unparalleled ferocity between Jesus and representatives of Judaism. On a superficial reading it constitutes a true "text of terror" in terms of Christian attitudes to Jews and Judaism. It is doubtful whether elements from it should ever feature in public liturgical readings. Scarcely any section of the gospel reflects so clearly the bitterness of the separation of the Johannine community from mainstream Judaism of its day. As such the sequence has a role to play in understanding that separation in terms of historical inquiry. It has little of edification and much of danger when read, without nuance or explanation, as Scripture today.

Paradoxically in view of where it will end, the sequence opens on a positive note. "To the Jews who had believed in him" (v. 31a),[50] Jesus utters words of both warning and promise. Initial belief is not enough. To be "truly" his disciples it is necessary to remain (*menein*) in his word: that is, to have ongoing exposure to the revelation of God uniquely communicated by him (cf. esp. 17:3).[51] Through this revelation, they will know the truth—that is, know God as Jesus reveals God to be—and such knowledge of the truth will set them free (vv. 31b-32).

---

[49] This is to take the statement in v. 28a as still holding out a promise of salvation to the adversaries; cf. Rudolf Schnackenburg, *St. John*, 2:202–3; Gail O'Day, "The Gospel of John," 635; Francis J. Moloney, *John*, 271–72.

[50] This reference has caused much debate—especially in view of the highly negative turn taken by the narrative in vv. 31-47. The reference would seem to be to Jews who have given Jesus a partial hearing but are yet to really "remain" or "dwell" (*menein*) in his word if they are to escape the accusations shortly to be leveled; cf. Francis J. Moloney, *John* 275, 277.

[51] Cf. Francis J. Moloney, *John*, 275; Gail O'Day, "The Gospel of John," 637.

The last phrase has become a slogan in appeals for freedom, whether in a social or ecclesiastical context. As Raymond Brown pointed out many years ago,[52] such usage, while understandable, has moved a long way from the theological sense it has in the present context and in Johannine thought more generally. The nature of the freedom that Jesus has in mind becomes clear as the dialogue/debate moves on. "The Jews" vigorously object to any suggestion of their "becoming" free: as "seed of Abraham" they are already free and have never been the slaves of anyone (v. 33). On a political level, of course, the protest is unfounded. Many times in their history, beginning with the situation in Egypt from which they were delivered at the time of the Exodus and right up to occupation under Rome at the time of the gospel, the Jewish nation found itself in a situation of political subjection akin to slavery. More likely the thought is running on a spiritual level. As descendants of Isaac, the son of the free wife of Abraham, in distinction from Ishmael, the son of his slave girl Hagar (Gen 16:15; 21:9-21; cf. Gal 4:21-31), the Jews thought of themselves, schooled by the Torah, as enjoying a degree of freedom from vices and evil inclinations prevalent in other nations.[53] Jesus contests this claim (vv. 34-38). Freedom cannot be assumed simply on the basis of ethnic descent. It is shown by behavior. Those who commit sin cannot claim to be free; on the contrary, they are slaves to sin (v. 34).

In something of a parable-like parenthesis (vv. 35-36), Jesus treats of the contrast in a household between the situation of a slave and that of a son. In view of the claim to be seed of Abraham just made by "the Jews" (v. 33), what may be in mind is the contrast between Abraham's sons, Ishmael and Isaac. Whereas the free son Isaac remains in the household, Ishmael, the son of the slave girl is driven out so that he will have no part in the inheritance (Gen 21:8-14).[54] Applying this to the present situation, Jesus insists (v. 36) that if "the Jews" want to be free, the only way they can obtain this is to allow him, the free Son, to set them free. Through their believing in his revelation of the truth as just explained (vv. 31b-32) they would share his state of "remaining" forever, that is, of enjoying—as "children of God" (1:12)—the divine eternal life.

The necessity of being set free, with its implication that they are presently in a situation of slavery, is precisely what "the Jews" are contesting (v. 33). To counter this, Jesus points (v. 37) to the evidence: seed of Abraham though they be, their slavery to sin is shown by their seeking to kill him, an

---

[52] Raymond E. Brown, *John I–XII*, 355.

[53] Cf. C. K. Barrett, *John*, 345.

[54] Cf. C. K. Barrett, *John*, 346.

intent amply displayed already on several occasions (5:18; 7:1, 25, 30, 44-45; 8:20). Whereas (v. 38) he speaks out of what he has "seen" in his existence with the Father (1:1, 18)—that is, out of the Father's will to communicate eternal life to human beings (3:16)—they, in their attempts to kill him, are doing what they have learned from (their) father. Though not explicit at this point, it seems necessary to understand that by "father" here Jesus already has in mind the devil. Their determination to slay the Son of God raises the question whose children they really are. Jesus leaves the answer unstated at this point. The terrible answer will shortly emerge as the argument proceeds (cf. v. 44).[55]

4. *True and False Paternity: 8:39-47*

"The Jews" respond to Jesus' cryptic allusion to their "father" by repeating their insistence that Abraham is their father (v. 39a; cf. vv. 33, 37). For Jesus the true criterion of paternity is conduct, not ethnic descent.[56] The continuing intent on their part to kill him—one who has done nothing but speak to them the life-giving revelation ("truth" [v. 40b] from God—shows how different their behavior is to that of Abraham, refuting their claim to be his "children" (vv. 39b-40). They are in fact doing the works of another father (literally, "your father" [v. 41a]).

Once again (cf. v. 38b) Jesus does not at this point name this "father," but the insinuation of alternative parentage and the drift of the argument is sufficient to draw from "the Jews" a protest and claim that raises the stakes very considerably: "We are not illegitimate children;[57] we have one father, God" (v. 41b). Descent from Abraham has fallen away. Divine paternity is now at stake.[58]

---

[55] Cf. Francis J. Moloney, *John*, 278. The possessive pronouns "my" and "your" before "father" in each case are not found in the best manuscripts. This makes it possible to avoid hearing a reference to the devil here by reading the verb *poiete* as an imperative and so hearing an exhortation—to do the works of the Father (that is, God [NRSV, NAB; cf. Raymond E. Brown, *John I–XII*, 356; Gail O'Day, "The Gospel of John," 639]; or Abraham [Andrew T. Lincoln, *St. John*, 271]). The general run of thought and the virtually identical parallel in v. 41, where the indicative is clear, argue for the indicative and at least an implied reference to the devil; cf. C. K. Barrett, *John*, 346–47; Ugo Schnelle, *Johannes*, 176.

[56] Cf. C. K. Barrett, *John*, 347.

[57] Lit., "We have not been born as a result of fornication"—as implied in Jesus' talk of a separate "father."

[58] The claim reflects the Jewish sense of uniquely enjoying the privilege of being (metaphorically) sons and daughters (or children) of God; see the discussion of 1:12-13 above.

Jesus takes them at their word (vv. 42). If they truly had God as their father, they would love him (Jesus), for he has "come out" from God and is present now before them[59] not on his own account but entirely as one sent by the Father.[60] They do not understand what he is saying (literally, "my speech" [*lalia*]) because they cannot truly "hear" his word (*logos*).[61] The distinction between the two Greek words is crucial: what Jesus is now "saying" is an outward expression of the deeper reality that he truly is: the revelatory Word of God (1:1). It is because "the Jews" stumble at the more surface level that his deepest communication makes no impression (v. 43).

Divine fatherhood excluded, Jesus brings out into the open the accusation he has been driving at for some time: their "father" is the devil. The murderous intent they have upon his person shows them to be offspring of the one who was a murderer and a liar from the beginning (v. 44). First mentioned here in the gospel, the devil will feature as Jesus' principal antagonist in the closing chapters. Where God is the giver of life and has sent the Son into the world solely to promote that cause, the devil is the very antithesis: life-destroyer.[62] Where Jesus is the embodiment of divine truth, revealing God as God really is ("I am"), the devil is "the father of deceit" (conventionally: "the father of lies"). The reason that the adversaries do not believe Jesus is not because they can convict him of sin—they cannot (v. 46a). It is because, having derived their inclinations from their "father," they are resistant to truth and so cannot believe in Jesus, who speaks nothing but truth (vv. 45-46).[63] Only those who are from God—that is, those "born of God" (1:12), "born from above" (3:3, 7)—really hear God's words (v. 47). The adversaries (literally, "you") do not hear them because they are not born of God. While the accusation of parentage from the opposed direction is not restated, it clearly remains hanging in the air.

Attributing failure to see the truth to demonic manipulation was not uncommon or particularly remarkable in the wider milieu of the gospel. One

---

[59] The language (Greek: *exēlthon*) clearly refers to the incarnation and embodiment of the divine presence in the world.

[60] "True love for God would manifest itself in love for the one who has come as God's uniquely qualified representative" (Andrew T. Lincoln, *St. John*, 272).

[61] C. K. Barrett, *John*, 348.

[62] Cf. the story of the Fall as presented in the book of Wisdom: "God created us for incorruption, and made us in the image of his own eternity, but through the devil's envy death entered the world, and those who belong to his company experience it" (Wis 2:23-24).

[63] This seems to be the basic logic of vv. 45-46, though the "propositions" of the argument do not flow in the order that a modern reader might expect; see Francis J. Moloney, *John*, 280–81.

only has to look at the Dead Sea Scrolls to see examples of intra-Jewish debate of similar ferocity and vituperation. One should also not forget Jesus' words to Peter in the Synoptic tradition, "Get behind me, Satan" (Matt 16:23; Mark 8:33), nor Paul's characterization of rival Jewish Christian missionaries as "ministers of Satan," deceitfully disguising themselves as ministers of righteousness (2 Cor 11:13-15).[64]

That said, the offensiveness of the polemic to contemporary sensitivity and in particular its capacity to be interpreted in a downright anti-Semitic direction remains.[65] I really wonder whether passages such as John 8:39-47 should be included in Christian lectionaries and regularly read out in public. Certainly, it is highly irresponsible and gravely unethical if their public reading is not accompanied by a clear reminder that such polemic on the lips of Jesus in no sense has Judaism or Jews as such in view but reflects what was basically an intra-Jewish debate conducted in the language and literary form of its time.[66]

Reflection. With these interpretive caveats firmly in mind, even this text may have something to say to us on a more personal spiritual level. For anyone seeking to make progress in the spiritual life there will always be a contest between the vision of God revealed by Jesus and the distortions and false images suggested by what in the Ignatian spiritual tradition is dubbed the "bad spirit" but which can also be attributed to the prejudices, fears, and resentments that linger deep in the human psyche and distance us from God. The contest between the "truth" revealed by Jesus—the truth about God and the truth about ourselves—is constantly at odds with forces that seek to mask it and prevent us from attaining the "more abundant" life that it holds out. We may not want to think of Satan as our "father" nor embrace any of the angelology (demonology) that is part of the worldview of the Fourth Gospel. But we would be foolish to take lightly the struggle for light, life, and truth within the soul.

5. *Jesus, Greater than Abraham: 8:48-59*

Reacting strongly to Jesus' attribution to them of demonic rather than divine paternity (vv. 44, 47), the adversaries attempt to pay back Jesus in his own coin by accusing him (v. 48) of being a Samaritan and of being himself

---

[64] For a fuller survey of this wider context, see Andrew T. Lincoln, *St. John*, 272–74.

[65] On this, see the powerful reflections of Gail O'Day, "The Gospel of John," 647–51.

[66] Cf. Francis J. Moloney, *John*, 282.

possessed (literally, "having a demon").[67] Jesus ignores the "Samaritan" jibe and denies the charge of possession (v. 49). He brushes off their dishonoring (*atimazein*) him by pointing out that he has no need to be concerned with his own honor (literally, "glory" [*doxa*]) because, just as he honors the Father, so the Father will see to his glory in a final judgment (v. 50). The riposte plays upon the interplay between "honor" (*timē*) and "glory" (*doxa*). At one level it is simply a matter of reputation. At a deeper level, to be richly developed in the closing chapters of the gospel, the Father will see to Jesus' glorification at the time of his exaltation (upon the cross) and return to the divine realm from which he has come (17:1, 5). This will be the moment of judgment (= condemnation) for all who have "dishonored" him during his earthly life.

Mention of divine judgment (*krinein*) leads to a solemn, albeit cryptic, pronouncement: "Amen, amen, I say to you, whoever keeps my word will never see death" (v. 51). The central function of the revelation that Jesus has come to impart is to communicate (eternal) life to those who hear and keep the word in which that revelation is contained.[68] They will "not see death"— not in the sense that they will never die physically, but in the sense that they will not experience the death of the soul that renders physical death eternal death (cf. 11:25-26). Freed from the death-dealing deceit of Satan (v. 44), believers have already passed from death to (eternal) life (5:24).

Jesus' claim to dispose over death and life provokes the adversaries simply to renew (v. 52a) their charge that Jesus must be "mad" (literally, "have a demon"). In a characteristic misunderstanding they presume Jesus is speaking of present human life and physical death. They point (vv. 52b-53) to outstanding figures from the biblical record—Abraham and the prophets—who have died. Who does Jesus think he is (literally, "who are you making yourself out to be?" [v. 53c]) in claiming that those who keep his word will not "taste death"? Is he "greater" than "our father Abraham" and the prophets, all of whom have died?

The notion of being "greater than . . . Abraham" recalls a similar exclamation from the Samaritan woman ("Are you greater than our father Jacob?" [4:12]). It opens up for Jesus a seam of argument that will lead

---

[67] The "Samaritan" jibe reflects the poor relationship between Jews and Samaritans mentioned earlier in the gospel (4:9c); it is tantamount to branding Jesus an apostate and outside the community of Israel. The accusation of being possessed, while it could be a riposte to Jesus' accusation of their demonic parentage, probably amounts to little more than "You are mad"; cf. Raymond E. Brown, *John I–XII*, 358.

[68] Francis J. Moloney, *John*, 283.

directly to a majestic conclusion (v. 58). Jesus leaves that aside for a moment (vv. 54-55) to defend himself once more against the charge of making himself out to be someone extraordinary (cf. 5:18; 10:33; 19:7). He is not glorifying himself. The One who glorifies him—that is, accredits him for his life-giving mission to the world—is the One whom they claim to be their God.[69] They may make this claim, but in contrast to Jesus, who does really know this God, their claim does not rest upon knowledge (v. 55a). Driving home the point, Jesus repeats (v. 55b) by implication his earlier (cf. v. 44) bitter accusation involving the adversaries in the deceit characteristic of their real "father," the devil: if he were to deny his knowledge of God, he would be what they are: a deceiver (*pseustēs*).

"The Jews" had reintroduced (v. 52b) the figure of Abraham and his mortality as a key argument in their case against Jesus. Returning now to "Father Abraham," Jesus skillfully turns (v. 56) the tables on them, making the patriarch a witness in his, rather than their, cause.[70] They had asked incredulously whether he thought he was greater than "our father Abraham" (v. 53a). Jesus, appealing to a Jewish tradition according to which Abraham during his lifetime was given a vision of the future, specifically the messianic age,[71] claims that (far from regarding him as a rival or disowning him) Abraham "rejoiced" to see his day.[72]

Once more the adversaries exclaim in disbelief (v. 57). They interpret Jesus' claim in a crassly physical sense, that is, in terms of his human lifetime. Moreover, they turn his words around to make it a matter of his seeing Abraham, rather than vice versa. For Jesus to have seen Abraham he would have to have been alive at the same time as the patriarch, which is nonsense, seeing that he is certainly not more than fifty years old.[73]

But all this appeal to Abraham and the question about whether Jesus is "greater" than he, has only served to prepare the way for one of the most exalted christological claims in the entire gospel. With the solemn formula

---

[69] The best textual reading actually records direct speech: "Who you say, "He is our God." The direct speech implies Jesus' contention that the God they claim as their own is not the God of Jesus (the Father) but the god who is, according to his accusation in v. 44, the devil; cf. Francis J. Moloney, *John*, 386.

[70] Cf. Andrew T. Lincoln, *St. John*, 276; Gail O'Day, "The Gospel of John," 646.

[71] See C. K. Barrett, *John*, 351–52; Gail O'Day, "The Gospel of John," 646, for details.

[72] The basis for the tradition seems to rest upon the biblical text, Gen 17:7, where Abraham's laughter at the prospect of having a son in his advanced age was taken by the rabbis in the sense, not of skepticism, but of joy.

[73] The number gives no indication as to Jesus' actual age. A common view saw fifty as more or less the term of a man's working life; cf. Francis J. Moloney, *John*, 286.

("Amen, amen ") Jesus declares (v. 58), "Before Abraham was, I AM." However exalted, Abraham, like all human beings, had to come into being (Greek: *genesthai*) and then live for a set span of years. Jesus, as the Prologue made clear from the start (1:1), has shared and will share forever the eternal being of God. As earlier in the sequence (vv. 24, 28), along with preexistence, "I AM" connotes bearing and revealing to the world the life-giving name of God.[74] As Raymond Brown has said, "No clearer implication of divinity is found in the Gospel tradition."[75]

With this majestic claim the debate comes to an end. The adversaries have no answer other than to pick up stones to inflict upon Jesus the biblically prescribed penalty for blasphemy (v. 59a; cf. Lev. 24:16). They enact in this way the murderous intent that he had accused them of all along, justifying his accusation. Jesus, however, hides himself and departs from the temple (v. 59b). The secret departure here at the end of Tabernacles corresponds to his equally secret arrival (7:10). Recalling Ezekiel's vision of a similar departure of the divine Presence (Shekinah; Ezek 10:18-19; 11:23), the Light that has shone for a time in the temple, eclipsing its light, has now gone out.

Reflection. It has been a long journey through this discourse at Tabernacles, and, as I said at the start, it contains many accusations in its polemical exchanges that are distasteful to readers today. I hope, however, to have shown that in amongst all the polemic are the "nuggets of (christological) gold" without which the Fourth Gospel would be something else. If we can concentrate on those and handle the polemic with understanding and sensitivity, then even these chapters can have something to say for our time.

The Light of the World Heals the Man Born Blind: 9:1-41

With this episode, which occupies the whole of chapter 9, we arrive at one of the most appealing sections in the Fourth Gospel. We move from the hostile and fruitless engagement between Jesus and the authorities in chapters 7–8 to an artfully constructed drama, where perhaps the most engaging character in the entire gospel goes on a journey of enlightenment to arrive

---

[74] Especially apposite is Isa 43:10, where YHWH's eternal being is contrasted with the temporal existence of purported rivals; cf. Andrew T. Lincoln, *St. John*, 276.

[75] Raymond E. Brown, *John I–XII* 367.

at mature faith in Jesus.[76] Although the tone and the outcome are very different, the story of the man born blind remains part of the long sequence centered upon the feast of Tabernacles.[77] At the feast Jesus has revealed himself publicly to be Light of the world (8:12). But the world, in the shape of the authorities, has refused to come to the Light and the Light, publicly at least, has "gone out" (8:59). In the face of that public refusal and departure of the Light, chapter 9 dramatizes one person's coming to the Light in faith and discipleship.

The symbolic narrative unfolds in eight scenes the claim of Jesus to be the Light of the world (8:12), employing the image of blindness as a symbol of unbelief and, correspondingly, the overcoming of blindness as an image of enlightenment and faith. Once again, too, we see the characteristic Johannine pattern where a human need (in this case, congenital blindness) is overcome miraculously by Jesus, followed by a discourse or dramatic development that unfolds the miracle as a sign pointing to a deeper revelation: that Jesus is indeed the life-giving Light of the world (1:4b).[78]

It is natural to focus upon the man born blind and his journey. But it is important to be aware from the start that two parties are on a journey in John 9. While the man born blind moves from physical blindness to physical sight and beyond this to spiritual enlightenment, another party—variously called "the Pharisees" and "the Jews" but basically consisting of the religious authorities—moves from physical sight to spiritual darkness and unbelief. A signal feature of the literary artistry of this drama is the way in which it juxtaposes these two journeys going in opposite directions, one ascending to the Light, one descending into darkness, like two cable cars working up and down a mountain. Unlike cable cars, however, it is precisely the interaction of the parties, becoming increasingly hostile as the drama proceeds, that provokes and stimulates the former blind man's growth—both as human being and as a person on a journey to faith. In any case, we cannot simply

---

[76] "We have seen in the closing verses of chapter 8 how the darkness seeks to destroy the light. Now we see, by contrast, the light destroying the darkness" (Lesslie Newbigin, *The Light Has Come*, 120).

[77] The entire Tabernacles sequence actually continues right through to 10:21, where a new feast, Dedication, takes over (vv. 22-39). Strictly speaking, Jesus' reflection upon the episode with the Man Born Blind (9:39-41) continues without a break into the "Good Shepherd" discourse in 10:1-18, and the sequence closes with a reference to the healing of the blind man in v. 21. While recognizing this unity across 9:1–10:21, it is convenient to take chapter 9 as a single whole; cf. Francis J. Moloney, *John*, 290; Andrew T. Lincoln, *St. John*, 280.

[78] The sequence has several features in common with the healing of the paralyzed man at the pool of Bethesda in chapter 5: most notably, the violation of the Sabbath (5:9-10; 9:14-16).

identify with the positive journey of the man and distance ourselves entirely from those who take the opposite direction. Doubtless, both journeys have some reflection in our lives.

The narrative in John 9 falls into a sequence of eight scenes, clearly distinguishable by the characters interacting in each:

1. Jesus and the Disciples: 9:1-5

2. Jesus and the Man Born Blind: 9:6-7

3. Man Born Blind Discusses His Cure with the Local People: 9:8-12

4. Man Born Blind Interrogated by the Pharisees: 9:13-17

5. "The Jews" Interrogate the Parents of the Man Born Blind: 9:18-23

6. The Pharisees Interrogate the Man Born Blind Again: 9:24-34

7. Jesus and the Man Born Blind: 9:35-38

8. Jesus and the Pharisees: 9:39-41

We can set it out schematically as follows:

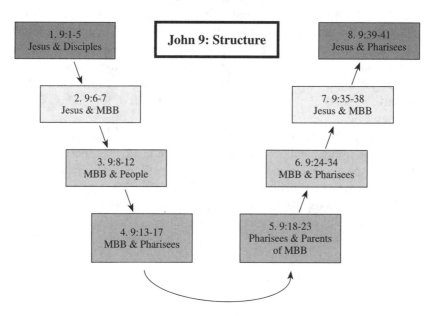

There is a certain symmetry here in that Jesus appears in the first and last scene (both involving a discussion about "sin") and also, in the second and second-last scene (in each case with the man born blind). In a way unparalleled in the gospel, Jesus is physically absent from the four central scenes of the drama—though he and his action (healing on the Sabbath) is the chief topic of discussion—or rather, of interrogation—throughout.

Scene 1: *Jesus and the Disciples: 9:1-5*

As Jesus walks along—presumably still in Jerusalem in the aftermath of the feast of Tabernacles—he sees a man described as blind from birth. Reflecting a conventional view that illness or physical disfigurement is a punishment for sin, the disciples rather coldly ask Jesus whether the congenital affliction was the consequence of his own or his parents' sin. We might well ask how the man could in any sense have sinned before being born.[79] Likewise, Ezekiel 18:20 rebuts the idea that guilt could be passed on down generations, not to mention the fact that the entire book of Job mounts a sustained challenge to the conventional idea that suffering and affliction must necessarily be interpreted as punishment for sin.

Jesus in no sense endorses any such view. In fact, he denies (v. 3a) that sin on the part of either the man or his parents has contributed to his being blind. Apart from this, he does not enter into a discussion of the mystery of human suffering either in general or in respect to the man. Instead, foreshadowing the development to follow, he points (v. 3b) to a positive consequence that will flow from this particular case: it will serve to reveal "the works of God." It will serve this purpose in the sense that what Jesus will perform for the man will model how all his works express and make effective the design of God to shine the saving light of life in the world's darkness.[80]

Jesus in fact pauses for a moment to reflect on this wider mission, employing a little parable or proverb for the purpose: "We must carry out the works of the One who sent me, while it is still day, since the night is coming when no one is able to work" (v. 4). The "day" is the time of Jesus' earthly life when like the sun he functions as the "light of the world" (v. 5). Before that "day" comes to an end and the darkness returns, he must carry out the "enlightening" mission of which his action in regard to the man born

---

[79] The possibility of prenatal sin to account for physical defect was discussed in Jewish circles; cf. C. K. Barrett, *John*, 356.

[80] We have to be careful not to press the Greek *hina-* clause in v. 3c, so as to convey too instrumental a sense of the divine intention: namely, that God willed that the man be born blind to serve a wider divine purpose. The Greek construction is open to expressing consequence as well as purpose.

blind will offer so striking an illustration. The statement explains why Jesus must take direct action in regard to the man, rather than, like the disciples, simply speculating about the cause of his affliction.[81]

Scene 2: *Jesus Heals the Man Born Blind: 9:6-7*

The miracle itself occupies a very short space in the wider story. Without any request from the man but impelled by his mission as just explained, Jesus proceeds to a very physical cure. Bending down to the earth, he makes mud with his spittle,[82] anoints the man's eyes with the mud (v. 6), and then sends him off to wash in the Pool of Siloam (v. 7a). This destination is significant. As noted earlier, during the feast of Tabernacles water was drawn daily from this pool and carried in procession to the temple, an acknowledgment of the pool's life-giving role for the population of Jerusalem. Even more significant is the popular etymology of the pool's name as meaning "sent" (v. 7b). What brings about the blind man's cure is not mere contact with the waters of the pool but the fact that he goes to wash there because he was "sent" by the One who has been himself sent from the Father on a life-giving mission to the world.[83] The washing away of mud from the man's eyes through the waters of Siloam ("Sent") leaving him able to see, becomes an outward pointer to the deeper spiritual enlightenment that he is about to undergo.

Scene 3: *The Man Born Blind Discusses His Cure with the Local People: 9:8-12*

We now learn that the man had (like Bartimaeus in the Synoptic tradition [Mark 10:46-52; Luke 18:35-43; cf. Matt 20:29-34]) been a beggar and hence a familiar sight in the locale where he sought alms. His cure inevitably becomes a matter of public discussion and divided assessment in the neighborhood (vv. 8-9b). Some say he is the former beggar, some that he only

---

[81] The first person plural ("We [*hēmas*] must carry out " [v. 4a]), which would appear to be the more original reading, hints at the future inclusion of the disciples in Jesus' mission; cf. C. K. Barrett, *John*, 357. Through their "works" the Light will continue to shine and give life to the world (cf. 14:12).

[82] Spittle was held to have medicinal properties in the ancient world. Jesus employs it in two similar cures in Mark's Gospel (7:31-37; 8:22-26 [also a blind person]) and comparable cures are recorded in nonbiblical literature; cf. C. K. Barrett, *John*, 358.

[83] Cf. Francis J. Moloney, *John*, 292.

looks like him. The man himself, displaying for the first time a characteristic honesty, bluntly replies: "I am he" (v. 9c).[84] Asked about how his eyes came to be opened (v. 10), he again responds with a plain recital of the facts of his cure by one, whom he simply refers to here, at the beginning of his journey of faith, as "the man called Jesus" (v. 11).

Scene 4: *The Man Born Blind Interrogated by the Pharisees: 9:13-17*

At this point there begins the first of three scenes of inquiry and inter-rogation by the religious authorities, described first as "Pharisees," later as "the Jews" (vv. 18-23). Why the people bring the formerly blind man to the authorities is not explained. It could be that, faced with an inexplicable oc-currence that seems to raise theological issues, they think it appropriate to bring the matter before "the experts." More likely, since, as we now learn (v. 14), the day on which Jesus performed the cure was in fact the Sabbath (cf. 5:10), some may already be concerned about an implied breach of the law. Making clay involved kneading, one of the thirty-nine categories of work forbidden on the Sabbath.[85] When the Pharisees, then, hear the man again tell how he has come to see, a theological dilemma confronts—and divides—them (v. 16): on the one hand, the man (Jesus) who performed all the actions involved in this cure cannot be "from God" since he does not observe the Sabbath; on the other hand, how can a sinner perform an act such as this requiring, surely, divine power? They thrust the question back upon the man (v. 17), who begins, as a result, his journey of knowledge of Jesus. Opting decidedly for the second side of the dilemma, the man responds that Jesus must be "a prophet," therefore someone definitely "from God" (cf. v. 16).

Scene 5: *"The Jews" Interrogate the Parents of the Man Born Blind: 9:18-23*

Still disturbed by the dilemma presented by the case, the authorities (now "the Jews") begin their endeavor to question and ultimately discredit the facts. Unable to believe that the man who now has his sight was really born blind, they summon the parents to check out the matter (v. 18). The tone of their questioning (v. 19) is already incredulous, if not subtly abusive

[84] In a Johannine context it is hard to hear this phrase without picking up its echoes of Jesus' own self-identification: 4:26; 6:20; 8:24, 28, 58; 18:5.
[85] See C. K. Barrett, *John*, 359–60; Gail O'Day, "The Gospel of John," 654.

("whom *you say* was born blind").[86] They seek from the parents the same explanation they had sought from their son (v. 19; cf. v. 15a): how does he now see? Like their son, the parents choose to remain with the facts, refusing to speculate on the "how": they know that the man is their son and that he was born blind; how he now is able to see or who opened his eyes, they do not know (v. 20-21ab). They seek to distance themselves from the entire matter, pointing out that their son is of age and can speak for himself (v. 21cd). The evangelist explains (vv. 22-23) their timidity as due to the fact that the authorities had decreed that anyone who confesses Jesus to be the Christ should be expelled from the synagogue.[87] In any case, the timidity of the parents serves as a foil to highlight by contrast the boldness that the man himself increasingly displays.[88]

Scene 6: *The Pharisees Interrogate the Man Born Blind again: 9:24-34*

The second and final interrogation of the man by the authorities is nothing less than a bullying attempt to get him to change his story. Demanding that he admit the truth (literally, "Give glory to God" [v. 24b]),[89] they insist upon the one thing that they claim to "know": that Jesus is a sinner (v. 24c); he must be, because he broke the Sabbath. Growing ever more confident, the man stands simply by what he knows and does not know.

---

[86] Cf. Francis J. Moloney, *John*, 293.

[87] At this point the later experience of the Johannine community has crept into the story, suggesting a cost—expulsion from the synagogue—that its members had to pay in their own day rather than a threat that was real at the time of Jesus. The man born blind is beginning to "model" the discipleship of this later time, while his parents illustrate would be disciples of Jesus who lack the courage to confront the cost. The expression "to be put out of the synagogue" (Greek: *aposynagōgos genesthai*) has played a significant role in the determination of the time and context in which the Fourth Gospel was written—notably through the seminal work of J. Louis Martyn, *History and Theology in the Fourth Gospel* (see p. 6, n. 10 above), who proposed that the term reflects the use of the *Benediction against Heretics*, introduced into the synagogue worship as a device to establish a more unified Jewish identity following the destruction of 70 CE. See further, C. K. Barrett, *John*, 361–62; Gail O'Day, "The Gospel of John," 657–58; Steven T. Katz, "Issues in the Separation of Judaism and Christianity after 70 C.E.: A Reconsideration, *Journal of Biblical Literature* 103/1 (March 1984): 43–76, esp. 71–76.

[88] Andrew T. Lincoln, *St. John*, 284.

[89] "Give glory to God" is a traditional formula for placing persons under an oath to speak the truth, as in Josh 7:19; cf. Jer 13:16. Ironically, the man will speak the truth and so give glory to God, whereas those who enjoin him to do so fail in both respects; see Gail O'Day, "The Gospel of John," 658–59.

Whether Jesus is a sinner is not ultimately for him to know or judge; what he does know is that he himself was blind and now can see (v. 25). Jesus has broken the Sabbath and done so with divine assistance. The theological dilemma remains.

Pathetically, the authorities make yet another attempt to get the man to explain how Jesus opened his eyes (v. 26). Perhaps a further recital of the process will convince him that a breach of the Sabbath was involved and consequently that Jesus must be a sinner. Boldly, the man refuses (v. 27ab). They didn't listen when he recited the facts before. Why do they want to hear it all again? Do they want to become his disciples (v. 27c)?

The question displays a mocking bravado. It also serves to introduce the theme of discipleship that now becomes a matter of contestation between the man and the authorities. Their insulting response actually states the truth: he is becoming a disciple of Jesus (v. 28ab), whereas they are disciples of Moses (v. 28c). The advantage of their discipleship, they claim, is that it is based upon what they clearly "know": that God spoke to Moses, whereas where this man is "from" neither they nor anyone else really knows (v. 29). A heavy irony is in play here. Moses, it is true, did have the unique privilege of speaking face-to-face with God, a conversation that took place when the divine presence (Shekinah) descended in a pillar of cloud upon the Tent of Meeting (Exod 33:7-11). But God did not have to descend to meet Jesus or converse with him. He is "from" God in the transcendent sense of having being "with God in the beginning" (1:1; 17:5). God may have spoken with Moses but Jesus is God's very Word (1:1), the divine presence "become flesh" on earth (1:14).[90] This is what the authorities cannot grasp, fixated as they are upon the Sabbath and an understanding of the law of Moses that is being placed under intolerable pressure by the facts staring them in the face. Discipleship of Moses will have to undergo a radical reassessment in order to cope with a discipleship involving a far deeper unity with the divine.[91]

Emboldened all the more, the man taunts his interrogators, playing upon their professed "ignorance" ("we do not know") of Jesus' origins and giving them a little lesson in theology along the way (vv. 30-33). What is really "amazing" is not so much the miracle as their continuing refusal to come to any "knowledge" of Jesus' origins despite the reality that they cannot deny: Jesus opened his eyes. God does not listen to sinners but only to those who are devout and do the divine will. It is unheard of that anyone has or ever could have without divine assistance opened the eyes of a person

---

[90] Cf. Gail O'Day, "The Gospel of John," 659.

[91] We recall Jesus' earlier claim: "If you believed Moses, you would believe me, for he wrote about me" (5:46).

blind from birth—because something akin to an act of creation is involved (v. 32). The only conclusion that can be drawn is that this man must be "from God"; otherwise he could have done nothing of the kind (v. 33).

We note that the man has not gone beyond his knowledge of the facts considered in the light of conventional Jewish theology. He is not making high christological claims in regard to Jesus. He is simply contesting the authorities' refusal to accept that Jesus must be "from God."

Refuted by the undeniable facts and the sound theological interpretation placed upon them by the man, the authorities can only fall back upon personal abuse and physical violence (v. 34). Who is he, daring to teach them— he who must be a sinner (literally, "wholly born in sins")[92] because of the affliction with which he was born? They are employing the age-old strategy of those whose claim to authority is crumbling under the weight of evidence: they resort to abuse, blind standing upon authority, and violence.[93]

Scene 7: *Jesus and the Man Born Blind: 9:35-38*

Jesus now reenters the story—to which of course he has been central all along, albeit physically absent. Learning of the man's expulsion, the One who will shortly identify himself as the Good Shepherd (10:11, 14) seeks him out and puts to him the question of faith that leads to discipleship: "Do you[94] believe in the Son of Man?"

We may wonder why belief is raised in respect to the title "Son of Man." A more general understanding of Johannine theology might suggest belief in Jesus as "Son of God" (cf. especially 3:18; 20:31).[95] Neither in John nor in the Synoptic tradition does "Son of Man" appear elsewhere as an object of belief. Some light on the use of the title here may be shed by the man's question, "And who is he, sir, that I may believe in him?"[96] In both the Synoptic and Johannine usage "Son of Man," while normally a self-designation of

---

[92] The plural "sins" may imply that not only the man but also his parents were sinners, and hence his congenital affliction (countered by Jesus in vv. 2-3).

[93] The expulsion of the man fulfills the threat mentioned in regard to his parents in v. 22.

[94] The personal pronoun "you" (singular) brings out the sense, "Do you, in contrast to those who expelled you, believe?"; cf. C. K. Barrett, *John*, 364.

[95] Some manuscripts do read "Son of God"—almost certainly a later attempt to substitute the more expected title; cf. Raymond E. Brown, *John I–XII*, 375; C. K. Barrett, *John*, 364.

[96] As C. K. Barrett points out (*John*, 364), the man's question can be understood in two ways: (1) the man has no understanding of what "Son of Man" might mean and seeks clarification; (2) the man understands the title but is asking about the identity of the one who bears it. The second view seems more appropriate (so C. K. Barrett; also Raymond E. Brown, *John I–XII*, 375). A similar ambiguity with reference to the title occurs in 12:34.

Jesus rather than a confession of faith, has an essential connection with judgment, stemming from its likely origins in the vision recorded in Daniel 7:13-14. Presumably, it is because judgment features so strongly in the present episode that belief in Jesus is proposed here under this title.[97] The disciples judged the man, attributing his blindness to sin (v. 2); the authorities have been judging Jesus all along and have just themselves judged (= "condemned") the man (v. 34), while he himself has been carefully assessing the status of Jesus in view of the gift of sight received. Jesus will soon (v. 39) claim that he has come into the world "for judgment," a fate which those now judging him will undergo. We are moving, in fact, to a perfect illustration of the Son's mission as outlined in 3:17-19:

> God did not send the Son into the world to condemn the world, but in order that the world might be saved through him. Those who believe in him are not condemned; but those who do not believe are condemned already, because they have not believed in the name of the only Son of God. And this is the judgment, that the light has come into the world, and people loved darkness rather than light because their deeds were evil.

As he stands upon the threshold of faith, the formerly blind man is coming to the Light, because the Light has come to him. Exposing his life to the Light, he is in this sense undergoing judgment here and now and finding salvation (cf. 5:24). The authorities, on the other hand, by refusing to come to the Light, are exposing themselves to judgment in the sense of "condemnation" (*krima* [v. 39]).[98] It is likely, then, that the overall context of judgment accounts for Jesus' posing the question of belief in terms of himself as "Son of Man."[99]

In response to the man's query about the identity of the Son of Man, Jesus makes a celebrated self-revelation akin to that made earlier to the Samaritan woman (4:26): (literally) "You have seen him and the one who is speaking with you is he" (v. 37). There is a wonderful implication in the use of the Greek perfect tense (*heōrakas*) in the first phrase: the man was able to see Jesus physically from the moment his eyes were opened, but ever since then—and prompted indeed by the questioning and hostility he has

---

[97] Cf. John Painter, *Quest for the Messiah*, 319–20.

[98] The Greek word stem *krisis/krinein* ranges in meaning over both the process of judging (in an impartial discerning of the truth) and a possible negative outcome of such discernment in the sense of "condemnation."

[99] Cf. George W. E. Nickelsburg, "Son of Man," in *Anchor Bible Dictionary*, ed. David Noel Freedman (New York: Doubleday, 1992), 6:137–50, esp. 146–47.

undergone—he has been on a journey of increasing spiritual vision, of which the opening of his physical eyes has been a symbol. He is now about to learn that his physical sight of the human Jesus amounts really to a sight of the Light of the world because Jesus is that Light made flesh, the revelation of the only Son of the God whom no human being can look upon and live (1:18). God, yes, spoke to Moses, as the authorities in their taunting had claimed (v. 29). But now "the one who is speaking with (him)," the Son of Man in whom he should believe, is the very revelation of God.[100]

The man enacts a confession of faith: "I believe" by prostrating himself before Jesus (v. 38).[101] The physical act indicates the depth of understanding to which he has now arrived. The Greek address "*Kyrie*," which in v. 36 probably meant little beyond a polite "Sir," now conveys the full meaning of "Lord," as in Thomas's confession before the risen Jesus: "My Lord and my God" (20:28).[102] In worshiping Jesus the formerly blind man is acknowledging in him the presence of God,[103] ironically fulfilling the injunction brusquely thrust upon him to "give glory to God" (v. 24).[104]

Scene 8: *Jesus and the Pharisees: 9:39-41*

A final dialogue between Jesus and the Pharisees sums up the meaning of the episode as it comes to an end.[105] Jesus brings the theme of "judgment" explicitly to the fore, stating that it is for this purpose—judgment— that he has come into the world (v. 39a). The further comment that this is "so that those who do not see may see and those who see may become blind" (v. 39b) is best taken in a consecutive rather than a final sense. It was not God's intention in sending the Son into the world that the world should experience judgment in the negative sense of condemnation. On the contrary, the divine intent from the start was to save the world by allowing human beings to anticipate and pass through judgment by coming to the Light (cf. 3:16-21). Unlike the man in his previous state of blindness, the Pharisees may be able to see in a physical sense. But they have rendered themselves "blind" in the

---

[100] Francis J. Moloney, *John*, 295–96.

[101] On the manuscript evidence a good case can be made for omitting vv. 38-39a, see C. K. Barrett, *John*, 365. The narrative is greatly impoverished without this response from the man and most recent commentators accept it as original; see Francis J. Moloney, *John*, 299.

[102] Cf. Andrew T. Lincoln, *St. John*, 287.

[103] Cf. Rudolf Schnackenburg, *St. John*, 2:254.

[104] Cf. Gail O'Day, "The Gospel of John," 661.

[105] C. K. Barrett, *John*, 365.

only sense that ultimately matters: the spiritual blindness that cuts them off from the saving light brought by Jesus. The blindness that now afflicts them is not divine punishment. It is a consequence of the attitude they have themselves chosen to adopt toward the Light come into their world.

Hearing Jesus' pronouncement and sensing that it may be all too applicable to themselves some Pharisees try to brush it off, exclaiming, "Surely, we are not blind?" (v. 40). The form of the exclamation expects the answer "No." And Jesus (v. 41a) at one level seems to agree: in a physical sense they are not blind. If they were simply blind in this sense (like the man born blind initially), they would not claim to be able to see and would not "have sin." Their sin "remains" (*menei* [v. 41b]) because they claim to see in a spiritual sense, when in fact in this sense they really are blind.

The disciples had raised the question of sin in their initial judgment about the man born blind. They had simply assumed that his affliction was due to sin; the only question was whether it was his sin or that of his parents. The Pharisees had judged Jesus a sinner because he broke the Sabbath, rendering themselves "blind" to the truly remarkable aspect of what he had done, which should have pointed—as it did for the blind man—to a wholly different assessment. Now they have placed themselves in a true situation of sin by refusing to accept the truth: the truth about Jesus and the truth about themselves. As long as they persist in this attitude, their "sin" in this fundamental sense will endure.

Reflection. The negative note on which the narrative ends is a reminder that there are two parties on journeys in the story: the positive journey of the man born blind to ever-growing faith; the negative descent on the part of the authorities ("Pharisees"/"Jews") into ever-deeper spiritual blindness and "sin." What makes the narrative distinctive is the way it brings out the contrast between these two parties in regard to the perception of reality. Continually questioned about Jesus, the man never goes beyond the evidence; he simply sticks to the facts and draws conclusions only as they are forced upon him. His journey into ever-deeper faith and understanding of Jesus is a journey into reality in every sense of the word.

The adversaries, on the other hand, who are realizing that they are losing their grip on the situation, resort more and more to denial. Their stratagem of summoning and browbeating the man's parents backfires badly. In the end, they can only resort to unfounded accusations, personal abuse, and appeals simply to their authority and status. Even in purely human terms their incapacity to perceive and accept reality is painfully exposed. On a more spiritual level, they refuse to come to the Light lest their deeds be exposed (3:19-20). They who judged the blind man as a sinner end up, despite their protests (v. 40), blind themselves and encased in sin.

What ultimately emerges, then, is a sense that faith, far from being a flight into unreality and make-believe, actually entails a heightened capacity to see and accept the truth: the truth about oneself (including a sober recognition of one's own proneness to self-deception and selfishness), the truth about the world, and the truth about God's outreach to the world in the person of the Son to draw human beings out of selfishness and delusion to the freedom of divine eternal life.

The Good Shepherd: 10:1-21

In the first half of John 10 Jesus presents himself as the Good Shepherd—from ancient times one of the most cherished christological titles in the Christian tradition. While this title and its associated images represent a change from the "light/blindness" motifs in the preceding chapter, we are still within the ambit of the feast of Tabernacles. In fact, the discourse that Jesus gives in 10:1-21, contrasting himself as the good shepherd with others who break in and ravage the flock, is really a reflection upon the preceding episode.[106] Where the authorities have browbeaten, abused, and eventually cast out the man born blind, Jesus has sought out this "lost sheep" and brought him into the community of faith.

The "shepherd" image, whether applied to God or to human rulers, has an important prehistory in the Scriptures of Israel that the present sequence reflects and develops in many ways. The outstanding passage in this respect is Ezekiel 34. Addressing the neglect and abuse of the people by rulers who, on the model of David, were meant to be their "shepherds," YHWH describes himself as the "Shepherd" who will gather, heal, and feed the scattered flock and set up a true Davidic shepherd who will rule with integrity and justice. (Before studying the discourse in John 10:1-21, it would be helpful to read Ezekiel 34 in its entirety.)

For all its undoubted appeal, Jesus' description of himself as "Good Shepherd" (vv. 11, 14) is simply the most familiar of a kaleidoscope of motifs in 10:1-21. All flow from the basic image of a Palestinian sheepfold where sheep are kept secure during the night before being called and led out by their shepherd to pasture. It is important not to allow the idea of Jesus as

---

[106] Cf. the comment from some of the authorities at the end (v. 21), explicitly referring to Jesus opening the eyes of the blind man.

Good Shepherd so to swamp the discourse as to prevent the remaining images from having their say.

The first section of the passage, vv. 1-5, introduces the basic image of the sheepfold (Greek: *aulē*).[107] A bridge statement (v. 6) then leads into two christological applications of the image, where Jesus first identifies himself as the "Gate" of the sheepfold (vv. 7-10) and then as the "Good Shepherd" of the sheep (vv. 11-18). A final section records the divided response of the audience to the discourse (vv. 19-21). In v. 6 the initial image is described as a *paroimia*. This Greek word can mean "parable" but, reflecting the Hebrew term *mashal* that lies behind it, *paroimia* can have a wider sense, including not only a developed story (as in our usual understanding of parable) but also a simple illustration or metaphor, or even a riddle or puzzle. The flexible meaning of the term goes along with how the basic image evolves in the present context. The opening section (vv. 1-5) does not so much offer an image of a sheepfold in a static sense but a description of what happens in practice each morning when shepherds arrive at the sheepfold to call out their sheep for pasture. They come to the gate, the gatekeeper lets them in, they call out to their sheep, and these, recognizing the voice of their shepherd, follow him out of the sheepfold. This is not exactly a parable in the sense of a developed story with a final punchline (as in the Synoptic parables). It is more an illustration taken from everyday life that provides an "image field" that the subsequent christological applications exploit in various ways.[108] We should be aware from the start that the applications do so quite freely. They do not follow the developing line in strict logic or consistency. For example, the basic image might lead us to expect that Jesus would be the shepherd who comes through the gate, but in the first application, vv. 7-11, he identifies himself with the gate itself. This inconsistency can be a bit disconcerting to our logical minds. What we have is, as I said before, a rich kaleidoscope, rather than a strict logical pattern.

The Image of the "Sheepfold": 10:1-6

Central to the opening image of the sheepfold (vv. 1-5) is a basic contrast between two different modes of entry into the sheepfold and the way the sheep react to each. Using the solemn, "Amen, amen," introduction, Jesus begins with the negative (v. 1): the one who does not enter through

---

[107] The term here probably refers to an enclosed courtyard attached to a house where sheep are kept secure during the night; cf. C. K. Barrett, *John*, 368.

[108] Cf. Francis J. Moloney, *John*, 303.

the gate of the sheepfold but gets in some other way—presumably climbing up over the wall—is a thief and robber.[109] The one, on the contrary, who approaches to enter through the gate of the sheepfold is the (genuine) shepherd of the sheep; for him the gatekeeper will open the gate (vv. 2-3a). So much for mode of entry. Now (vv. 3b-5) the image focuses upon the reaction of the sheep.[110] The sheep are alert to the voice of their own shepherd (v. 3b); he calls each of his own by name (v. 3c) and leads them out of the sheepfold (v. 3d). When he has brought out all his own sheep, he goes before them and they follow him because they know his voice.[111] In conclusion (v. 5), the image returns to the negative side where it had begun (v. 1): the sheep will not respond to the call of a stranger; they flee from him at his appearance because they do not recognize the sound of his voice. The two motifs, then, that have been central to the developing image are, in the first place, entrance through the gate and, second, recognition of the voice. Both will feature in the christological application to follow.[112]

Jesus, "the Gate": 10:7-10

Whereas we might have expected Jesus, in this application of the image, to have identified himself with the (rightful) shepherd who enters *through* the gate, in contrast to those who violently climb over the wall, he in fact identifies himself with the Gate itself, literally, "the Gate of the sheep" (v. 7). The identification suggests that there is no other way to the sheep save through him. This idea is not pursued, however, and we move instead to a negative contrast with "all who have come before (him), who are characterized as "thieves and robbers," to whom "the sheep have not listened" (v. 8).

---

[109] "Robber" (Greek: *leistēs*) has the sense of violence as well as theft. It was also used to describe bandits and armed rebels, notably Barabbas (John 18:40).

[110] It is not necessary to recognize a separate parable beginning at 3b. We have simply the development of the fluid image.

[111] The adjective *idia* ("his own") appearing before "sheep" in both v. 3c and v. 4a might suggest that the sheepfold contains sheep belonging to several flocks, each with their own shepherd, in which case the shepherd would be calling out his own sheep by name from the wider flock; so, C. K. Barrett, *John*, 369; Rudolf Schnackenburg, *St. John*, 2:282. In v. 5, however, the "other" or "alien" seems to refer not to another shepherd (who presumably would enter through the gate) but to the one who enters violently, as stated in v. 1; cf. Raymond E. Brown, *John I–XII*, 385.

[112] It is possible, in allegorical fashion, to start making identifications of the characters—the shepherd as Jesus and the intruders as the authorities—within the context of the initial parable (vv. 1-5). A more dramatic sense prevails if the applications begin with Jesus' solemn identification of himself as the "Gate" in v. 7 and continue with "Good Shepherd" in v. 11.

The sweeping indictment hardly embraces all the leaders and prophets of Israel before Jesus. On the Fourth Gospel's own rating elsewhere, figures such as Abraham, Jacob, Moses, and David in no way appear in such a light. More likely in mind are rulers such as Herod, high priests, and other religious figures closer to the time of Jesus and the gospel. In the view of the Johannine community, rather than acting as shepherds, they have plundered and ravaged the community of Israel ("the sheep").

When Jesus identifies himself a second time as "the Gate" (v. 9) the image moves in a new direction. The sheepfold is a place of protection for the sheep at night. At nightfall they must enter it through the gate in order to be safe (literally, "to be saved"). By the same token, at dawn they must go out through the gate in order to find pasture, the sustenance they need for life. As the means of entry and exit for the sheep, the gate is in this way both life-protecting and life-sustaining. This is the sense of "the gate" that Jesus applies to himself. It is through constant interaction with him in prayer and other practices of the spiritual life that believers find sustenance and life in the full Johannine sense. Where the thief comes only to steal and kill and destroy (v. 10a), Jesus has come that they may have life and have it in abundance (v. 10b).

This last claim goes to the heart of the Fourth Gospel's theology. The "abundance" in view is not merely quantitative. The mission of the Son is to communicate to the world a qualitatively enhanced life: life that, beyond mere mortal existence, is a participation, as "children of God," in God's own eternal being (1:12; 11:52; 20:17; 1 John 3:1-2, 10; 5:2).[113] Jesus is the "Gate" through which all must come and go in order to find and sustain life in this full sense.

Jesus, the "Good Shepherd": 10:11-18

Finally, we arrive at the image for which the passage is most celebrated: Jesus' presentation of himself as the "Good Shepherd" (v. 11). The Greek adjective *kalos*, conventionally translated in this context as "good," has a fairly wide range of meaning. Basically it refers to the attractiveness or admirable quality of a person or thing—either because of outward physical quality ("beautiful," "handsome") or because of usefulness or nobility. The context makes clear that it is the last sense that is operative here: Jesus is the "good shepherd" *par excellence* because he is prepared to give his life

---

[113] Cf. Rudolf Schnackenburg, *St. John*, 2:293; C. H. Dodd, *Interpretation*, 149.

for the sheep.[114] Later (vv. 14-15) he will point to a further aspect in which this "goodness" consists: that of mutual knowledge between shepherd and sheep. But the dominant quality, to which he will return at the end of the section (vv. 17-18), is that of being prepared to give his life in order to preserve the life of the sheep.

Once again, within the same cluster of images, there is a negative contrast (vv. 12-13). Over against the noble shepherd who is prepared to give his life for his sheep is set the idea of the hireling (*misthōtos*). The hireling has no sense of ownership in regard to the sheep. Motivated only by payment, rather than by any intrinsic concern for the sheep, he abandons them when a wolf appears, with the result that they are ravaged and scattered. The evangelist probably had Jewish leaders in mind in this negative depiction. But there is no need for us to pursue the allegory in this negative direction. It is best to let the negative contrast (which falls away from now on) simply serve to highlight the qualities of the Good Shepherd: Jesus' self-sacrificing action in regard to his flock stems from an all-encompassing love. To be a member of that flock is to know oneself included among those for whom Jesus is willing to die.[115]

The second basis upon which Jesus rests his claim to be the Good Shepherd (v. 14a) is that of mutual knowledge. He knows his sheep and they know him with a knowledge reflective of the knowledge existing between Father and Son. Beyond mere intellectual recognition, "knowledge" here has its biblical overtones of mutual love and interpersonal experience. In this sense the motif of reciprocal knowledge (vv. 14b-15ab) does not really introduce a new criterion for the "goodness" of the shepherd. There is continuity between the reciprocal knowledge and love between the Father and Jesus, and the knowledge and love of Jesus for his sheep that induces him to lay down his life for them (v. 15c).

If we set aside for a moment the rather intrusive comment about "other sheep" in v. 16, we can trace the development of this theme in the remaining sentences (vv. 17-18). The phrase "For this reason" at the beginning of v. 17 does not mean that the Father loves Jesus because of his preparedness to lay down his life. On the contrary, it is because Jesus is utterly enveloped in the Father's prior love for him and for the world (3:16) that he has become the instrument of that love in laying down his life. And, precisely because it is

---

[114] Besides the biblical background (Ezekiel 34), also present may be the Greco-Roman motif of a "noble death," in which a freely chosen death represents a victory over one's enemies; cf. Andrew T. Lincoln, *St. John*, 299.

[115] Cf. Gail O'Day, "The Gospel of John," 672–73.

a matter of love, Jesus insists that his laying down of his life (v. 17b), and his resumption of it in resurrection (v. 17c), is an exercise of freedom.[116] Love is at once supremely free and supremely attuned to the desires and wishes of another (the beloved). So Jesus, going to his death, is both utterly free and utterly obedient to the Father. The event itself (crucifixion) and the events leading up to it will involve the machinations of many human players (Judas, the chief priests, the high priest, the Roman governor), manipulated in various degrees by Satan. They will inflict upon Jesus a most brutal and violent death. What he is insisting upon here is what will also be clear during the events themselves: the powerlessness of all these figures to take any action against him ("no one takes [my life] from me" [v. 18a]; cf. 18:4-11; 19:10-11) had he not freely chosen to surrender himself in love and obedience to the Father. Readers of the gospel are being prepared here for the way in which they are to view the events of the passion: not as the brutal execution of a helpless captive but as the enactment in love of the divine shepherding role, pledged to Israel and now extended to the world as a whole:

> For thus says the Lord GOD . . . As shepherds seek out their flocks when they are among their scattered sheep, so I will seek out my sheep. . . . I will bring them out from the peoples and gather them from the countries, and will bring them into their own land. . . . I will feed them with good pasture. . . . I myself will be the shepherd of my sheep . . . says the Lord GOD. (Ezek 34:11-15)

The extension of this divine pledge beyond Israel lies behind the reference in v. 16 to "other sheep not of this fold" that are to be brought into the flock. The "other sheep" are Gentiles who will be aggregated to the original flock of Israel when Jesus, "lifted up from the earth" (in crucifixion) draws all (people of all nations) to himself (12:32). The result will be the constitution of "one flock, one Shepherd" (v. 16e).[117] Believers from the Gentile world, ourselves included, can therefore think of themselves as sought out, gathered, and brought into the life-giving fold (the community of believers) by the Shepherd who enacts the divine outreach of love to the world (3:16).[118]

---

[116] The sense of purpose in v. 17b ("I lay down my life in order to take it up again") does not have to be pressed. It is, again, an expression of freedom, as developed further in v. 18: just as Jesus can dispose over his own death, so he can dispose over his resurrection.

[117] An alternative reading, well-attested in the manuscript tradition, goes, "they shall become (*genēsontai*) one flock, one Shepherd," giving the sense of Jesus bringing about unity. The reading goes better with "one flock," not so well with the following "one Shepherd."

[118] "The Gentile mission is itself an activity of Christ, just as his ministry in Palestine was" (C. K. Barrett, *John*, 376).

A Divided Response: 10:19-21

Once again (cf. 9:16) Jesus' words evoke a divided response from "the Jews" (v. 19). While the majority conclude that he is possessed and mad,[119] and hence undeserving of a hearing (v. 20), others are more circumspect (v. 21): his words are not those of a possessed person, since such a one could not open the eyes of a blind man. Here, as in the case of the blind man, we have a group prepared to recall and point to evidence. The dogmatic view that leads many to reject Jesus' words flies in the face of the reality that has been before their eyes. Jesus has not only claimed to be the promised Shepherd of Israel (Ezek 34) but his claim also rests on evidence.

---

[119] Lit., "he has a demon and is mad." Since madness was attributed to demonic possession the two charges really amount to the same thing; cf. Raymond E. Brown, *John I–XII*, 387; C. K. Barrett, *John*, 377.

Dedication:
Jesus, Consecrated and Sent into the World:
10:22-42

After the long sequence (7:1–10:21) for which the feast of Tabernacles provided a background, a final scene of Jesus' ministry in Jerusalem is set within the feast of Dedication (Hanukkah). This feast was of comparatively recent institution at the time of Jesus. It commemorated the rededication of the temple and reconsecration of its altar in 165 BCE following the successful Maccabean revolt against the regime of the Seleucid Greek ruler Antiochus IV Epiphanes. As told in 1 Maccabees 4:41-59, the Jewish leader Judas Maccabeus, having repulsed the Antiochean army, went up to Jerusalem, rebuilt the altar, reinstituted correct worship, and, together with all the people, determined that on each anniversary of the date (the twenty-fifth day of the month Chislev) a weeklong feast should be held to commemorate the joyful event. Dedication thus falls at the beginning of winter in December, some two months after Tabernacles—though in some continuity with the joyful harvest feast.

As the fourth and last of the feasts that form the background to Jesus' ministry in John 5–10 (Sabbath, Passover, Tabernacles), Dedication does not contribute much to the details of this short sequence, save in one central point appearing in v. 36. As the temple and its altar were reconsecrated to serve as the locus of God's presence and worship in Israel, Jesus speaks of himself as "consecrated" and sent into the world for a similar purpose.

After an indication of the setting (vv. 22-23), the sequence consists of two altercations between Jesus and "the Jews" (10:24-30, 32-38). The exchanges are separated by an attempt to stone Jesus (v. 31) and brought to a close by a similar hostile reaction (v. 39). The chapter ends with the withdrawal of Jesus across the Jordan (v. 40), where he receives a more positive response from those who note how the witness of John the Baptist in his regard has proved true (vv. 41-42).

Contest at the Feast of Dedication: 10:22-39

Is Jesus the Messiah? 10:22-30

The setting of the sequence in the temple in the portico of Solomon (vv. 22-23) is plausible in view of the onset of winter at the time of Dedication. Situated on the east side of the temple and facing inward, the portico was shielded from the cold winds that blew from the east at this time of the year. The setting in the portico of the ruler (King Solomon) who had built the prototype of the present temple also prepares the way for Jesus' self-presentation as the One whom the Father has sent to replace the function of the temple in the world (cf. 2:13-22).

As Jesus walks up and down in this location, "the Jews" surround him and, with a tone of exasperation, demand that he settle the "messianic question" once and for all (v. 24).[1] This issue has run through Jesus' contest with the authorities at the feast of Tabernacles (7:25-31, 40-43; cf. 9:35). It has been heightened by the strongly messianic overtones in his claim (10:11, 14) to be the (Davidic) Good Shepherd foretold in Ezekiel (34:23). Right from the start (cf. 1:20-21) the authorities have never budged from their purely conventional understanding of the messianic role—a role that Jesus eluded when the crowds that he had fed miraculously sought to make him king (6:15). While the gospel does present Jesus as Messiah (20:30), it makes abundantly clear that the title and role as applied to him far outstrips conventional understanding. Hence his continuing refusal to answer their demand "plainly."

Jesus meets the attempt to pin him down with the retort that he has in fact given them a response to the question but has been met by unbelief (v. 25a). They would have an answer if only they were prepared to regard with faith the "works" which he does "in the Father's name" (v. 25b). His works—principally, though not exclusively, the miracles he performs in relief of human need—attest his messianic status. To those who view them

---

[1] The encircling has a hostile note to it. The curious Greek phrase in v. 24b is usually translated, "How long will you keep us in suspense?" (NRSV, NIV) but is best rendered in a more negative tone: "How much longer will you go on annoying us?" Cf. Gail O'Day, "The Gospel of John," 676; Andrew T. Lincoln, *St. John*, 304.

with faith they point to the unique relationship he enjoys with the Father, a relationship transcending messianic status beyond all expectation.

Jesus attributes (v. 26) the lack of faith on the part of his interrogators to the fact that they do not belong to his "sheep." This leads into a sustained reflection (vv. 27-28) on all the benefits accruing to those who do belong to his flock. The reflection reprises and develops much of the pastoral imagery of the preceding sequence (10:3, 4, 14, 16). Those who truly are Jesus' sheep respond to his voice; he knows them and they follow him; he gives them eternal life, which means that they will not suffer eternal loss since no one can snatch them out of his hand. The reason that no one can alienate them from him is that they are the gift to him from the Father and the Father is greater than any other force or agency (v. 29).

The discourse is attractive for what it positively says in regard to those who do believe. As a response to the interrogators it sounds simplistic and smug. It also confronts us once more with the idea that failure to believe is something for which human beings are responsible and yet at the same time is the result of the mysterious choice and working of God. For the author and the original audience of the gospel this was simply the way in which they came to terms with the failure of the bulk of Israel to share their belief in the crucified Messiah. For us the holding together of human free choice and divine determination in this way is more problematic. At the same time, we should be careful to note what is not said: there is no suggestion that God has rejected those who have chosen not to believe. Their choice also remains contained within the divine will, which the gospel consistently presents as directed to the saving, rather than the rejection, of human beings (3:16-17). Human choice, whether positive or negative in regard to the revelation of Jesus, remains enclosed in divine mystery.

Finally, we cannot simply pass over the simple yet profound statement that concludes the discourse: "I and the Father are one" (v. 30). In the immediate context this pronouncement simply asserts the complete unity of Father and Son in warding off any attempt to ravage the believing "flock." It is a particular instance of the more general sense of the unity of Father and Son in the Son's saving mission. From the earliest generations, however, the statement has rung in the ears of Christian interpreters in a more profound sense, one that has to do with the being rather than the action of God. "Father and Son are united in the work of salvation because they are united in their being."[2] In this extended understanding, the statement becomes one of the

---

[2] Andrew T. Lincoln, *St. John*, 306.

most striking expressions of the gospel's Christology. Needless to say, it has played a significant role in the development of the classic doctrine of the Trinity.[3]

Jesus' Oneness with the Father: 10:32-39

In the face of a renewed threat to stone him (cf. 8:59), Jesus points out (v. 31) that he has displayed to them many "good works from the Father" and asks for which of them they are attempting to inflict on him this penalty (v. 32). The adjective "good" (*kalos*) in the phrase "good works from the Father" has the sense of works beneficial for others.[4] Jesus is pointing out that all his activity—more particularly his miracles—have been directed to the benefit of his people. They have been "from the Father" in the sense that, in the total union that he has with the Father, they are expressive of the Father's will for the salvation of Israel. The leaders, then, if only they could interpret them rightly, should be grateful for his works, rather than seeking to do away with him.

Not surprisingly, this response makes no impression on the adversaries. Refusing to be drawn into the naming of any "work," they go straight to the real issue: blasphemy (v. 33). They are preparing to stone Jesus because, though a man, he has been making himself out to be God. That is blasphemy, for which the penalty is death by stoning.[5]

Once again, then, it is Jesus' relationship with the Father that is the point at issue. To refute the charge of blasphemy Jesus makes (vv. 34-38) one of the oddest appeals to Scripture in the New Testament as a whole.[6] Psalm 82 contains the sentence:

> I said, "You are gods, children of the Most High, all of you;
> nevertheless, you shall die like mortals,
> and fall like any prince. (Ps 82:6-7)

[3] Cf. Raymond E. Brown, *John I–XII*, 403.

[4] On the range of meaning of the Greek adjective *kalos* see above pp. 172–73.

[5] Though it may be the clear implication of the Johannine text, "making oneself equal to God" (also 5:18) does not correspond exactly to the crime of blasphemy as set out in Lev 24:10-16, for which death by stoning is the prescribed penalty; nor does it reflect the understanding of the offense in later Jewish legislation. The charge reflects controversies over Jesus' status between Jews and Christians around the time of the gospel's composition; see C. K. Barrett, *John*, 383–84.

[6] In what follows I am much indebted to the interpretation of Andrew T. Lincoln, *St. John*, 307–8.

In the original psalm the "gods" in question would appear to be the gods of foreign nations who have failed to see to the exercise of justice and allowed oppression to prevail. Later Jewish tradition saw an intra-Israel address here, directed either to judges who failed to discharge their duties or to the Exodus generation as a whole: they were addressed by God at the time of the giving of the law at Sinai but forfeited the immortality that its acceptance held out through their worship of the golden calf (Exodus 32). As used by Jesus in his rebuttal of the charge of blasphemy, however, the first words quoted from the psalm, "I said, 'You are gods,' " are taken completely out of context and pressed into service in an *a fortiori* logic ("light and heavy" [Hebrew: *qal wahomer*]). For the purpose of the argument the only salient elements are God's address ("I said") and the content of that address ("You are gods"). The logic then runs (vv. 35-36): if "your law" (that is, Scripture, to which you appeal and which cannot be set aside) dubs "gods" those addressed by God's word ("I said"), then how can you denounce as blasphemy the claim to be Son of God on the part of One whom the Father has "consecrated" (*hagiasen*) and sent into the world? If a quasi-divine epithet can be applied to those addressed by God's word (at Sinai), how much more can a truly divine epithet be appropriated by One who was not only addressed by God in an act of consecration for mission but in fact represents the Word incarnate addressed by God to the world (1:14)?

The fact that mention of "consecration" stands before that of "sending" into the world implies the preexistence of the Son. It evokes the opening phrases of the gospel: "In the beginning was the Word and the Word was with God and the Word was God" (1:1). Jesus' refusal to state simply "Yes, I am the Messiah" (cf. v. 24) is now fully understandable. In view of his origins and the nature of his mission, the title "Son of God" (v. 36c) is far more appropriate. Jesus has not "made himself out to be God" (v. 33d). He enjoys divine status by virtue of his eternal filial relationship and union with the Father.

The motif of "consecration" (cf. 17:17, 19) has the sense of being set apart for God's purpose."[7] Vessels and sacred implements used for the worship of God in the temple were "set apart" from those used for all other purposes in this way—as liturgical vessels (patens and chalices) continue to be so regarded today. The application of the motif to Jesus communicates the sense of his being solemnly enjoined by the Father to undertake the mission of bringing life to the world. Beyond this, the wider context of the

---

[7] C. K. Barrett, *John*, 385.

feast of Dedication inevitably confirms the impression of Jesus as the replacement not only of the temple (as the seat of divine presence) but also of its altar as the locus from now on of worship.[8] As he explained to the Samaritan woman, what the Father now requires is "worship in Spirit and truth" (4:21-26).

In conclusion (vv. 37-38), Jesus once more points to the evidence of his "works," as objects of faith. If his adversaries will not believe him (that is, his words), look at what he is doing and see if his works do not point unmistakably to his union with the Father—a union expressed now in terms of mutual indwelling ("that the Father is in me and I am in the Father"; cf. later 14:10-11; 17:21). The double expression of knowing ("that you may come to know and continue to know") communicates the sense that faith involves an initial perception of the revelation of God in Jesus that is simply the beginning of a lifelong calling to plumb ever more deeply the mysterious union of Father and Son.[9] We are back with his earlier claim, "Amen, amen, I tell you, the Son can do nothing on his own, but only what he sees the Father doing; for whatever the Father does, the Son does likewise" (5:19).

Jesus' exalted claim to unity with the Father once again (v. 39a; cf. v. 30) leads "the Jews" to seek to stone him, but he manages to "depart from their hand" (v. 39b). His destiny is following a divine program that they are powerless to control. When the "hour" arrives to surrender himself into human hands, that will be entirely an expression of his own freedom (10:18; 18:4-12). Meanwhile, just as his "sheep" are secure within the hand of the Father, so also is he.[10]

Jesus Withdraws across the Jordan: 10:40-42

Jesus' escape from the authorities brings to a close the long witness in Jerusalem that had begun when he "went up to the feast (Tabernacles)" (7:10). Before he made that journey we were told that "he did not wish to go about in Judea because the Jews were looking for an opportunity to kill him" (7:1). The reaction to his witness during the months stretching from Tabernacles to Dedication has borne out the truth of that observation. Judea is indeed a locale of deadly risk for him. Such a consideration will be an important background to the decision he will shortly make (11:7) to return to Judea in order to raise his friend Lazarus from the dead. In the meantime

[8] Cf. Andrew T. Lincoln, *St. John*, 309.
[9] Cf. C. K. Barrett, *John*, 386; Rudolf Schnackenburg, *St. John*, 2:313.
[10] Cf. Andrew T. Lincoln, *St. John*, 310.

(vv. 40-42) he withdraws, not back to Galilee, but to the east of the Jordan, the locale where John had carried out his baptizing ministry[11] and where he will be for the time being secure.

The sequence as a whole ends (vv. 41-42) on a positive note that closes off the witness of John. "Many" come to Jesus in this place where John had been baptizing. They remark that, whereas John had "done no sign"—in accord with his disclaimer of being the Messiah (1:20, 24; 3:28)—all that he said about Jesus (1:26-27, 29-34, 36)—had proved true. This leads many to come to faith in Jesus there. These concluding sentences tell us that John has fulfilled his role in the schema of salvation. Having deflected any messianic interest from himself and freely owning his lesser status, he has successfully performed his role of witness (1:6-8, 15), drawing people to faith in Jesus. He has, as he foresaw (3:30), become less and less while Jesus has become more and more. In the spirit of these gracious words, the selfless Baptist now departs from the narrative of the gospel.

---

[11] In 1:28, John is said to have been baptizing at "Bethany across the Jordan." This Bethany, never successfully identified, must be a different Bethany from the Bethany, a village on the outskirts of Jerusalem, which, as the home of Lazarus and Martha and Mary, will feature prominently in the following episode (John 11:1); cf. C. K. Barrett, *John*, 175.

The Gathering Conflict: 11:1–12:11

The Raising of Lazarus: 11:1-54

The raising of Lazarus from the dead is the last and greatest of the signs worked by Jesus in the Fourth Gospel. It is also the one that has most grasped Christian imagination down the centuries. It taps into and addresses the most basic human concern: how to bear the end of life, how to live with the prospect of death—both our own death and that of those we love.

In the structure of the gospel, this last sign brings to a climax and concludes the public ministry of Jesus. It also functions as a bridge to the second half of the narrative. What begins as a kindness to a family that Jesus loves soon becomes a notorious public event that renders the authorities in Jerusalem hostile to Jesus beyond endurance. The raising of Lazarus is the "last straw" that sets irrevocably in motion the moves to bring about his arrest, condemnation, and execution. Going to Judea to give life to the one he loves will in the end cost Jesus his own life. As we shall see, the sequence in John 11 functions in this way as a microcosm of the entire action of the gospel.

The raising of Lazarus is the first part of a series of scenes in which this friend of Jesus is central:

1. The Raising of Lazarus: 11:1-54

2. The Approach of Passover: 11:55-57

3. The Anointing at Bethany: 12:1-8

4. The Plot against Lazarus: 12:9-11

1. *The Raising of Lazarus: 11:1-54*

Like the healing of the Man Born Blind in John 9, the raising of Lazarus features a series of scenes in an extended drama. Setting it somewhat apart from the earlier signs is the variation of the pattern whereby a sign (miracle) is followed by a discourse or dialogue that brings out the deeper, symbolic meaning. In this case the miracle (the physical raising of Lazarus) comes at the end. The theological and the dramatic climax do not coincide. The dramatic miracle at the end functions as a sign confirming the truth of Jesus' earlier claim, in dialogue with Lazarus' sister Martha, to be "the resurrection and the life" (v. 25).

The sequence as a whole falls into eight scenes:

Scene 1:   The situation: Jesus receives the message that Lazarus, his friend, is ill; his reaction: 11:1-6

Scene 2:   The discussion and decision about going to Judea: 11:7-16

Scene 3:   Jesus arrives in Bethany; the situation there: 11:17-19

Scene 4:   Jesus and Martha: 11:20-27

Scene 5:   Jesus and Mary: 11:28-32

Scene 6:   The raising of Lazarus: 11:33-44

    6a: Jesus' emotional reaction to the general grief: 11:33-37

    6b: Jesus arrives at the tomb: 11:38-40

    6c: Jesus' thanksgiving prayer to the Father: 11:41-42

    6d: Jesus summons Lazarus out of the tomb: 11:43-44

Scene 7:   Reaction to the raising: faith and report: 11:45-46

Scene 8:   The plot of the Sanhedrin against Jesus: 11:47-54

Before considering the sequence in detail, it will be helpful to recall certain geographical considerations that have been building up as the gospel proceeds. At the close of his ministry in Jerusalem, in the face of yet another attempt to arrest him (10:39), Jesus has withdrawn to the east across the Jordan (10:40). This trans-Jordan region provides a safe haven for him in contrast to Judea, and in particular Jerusalem, which are places of mortal danger. This geographical background is crucial to the drama of the narrative.

Scene 1: *The situation: Jesus receives the message that Lazarus, his friend, is ill; his reaction: 11:1-6*

This opening scene introduces the main characters in the story, Lazarus and his two sisters Mary and Martha, who live in the village of Bethany on the outskirts of Jerusalem.[1] From the start (v. 1) we are informed of the essential fact from which the entire drama will spring: Lazarus is ill—gravely ill, as will soon appear. We are also (v. 2) informed that Mary is the one who anointed Jesus with ointment and wiped his feet with her hair. Curious though it may be, this anticipatory notice of a later incident (12:1-8) serves to tie the event about to be told—the death and raising of Lazarus—to the death of Jesus, since Mary's anointing is later explicitly interpreted as a preparation for burial (12:7).[2] It also indicates that the members of this family reciprocated Jesus' love for them. What Jesus will do for Lazarus takes place in a context of mutual love and affection displayed in table fellowship.

The sisters' message to Jesus contains in fact the first indication of his love: "Lord, he whom you love is ill" (v. 3). They do not mention Lazarus by name. He is going to be totally passive throughout. His role in the drama is simply to be the object of Jesus' self-sacrificing love.

Jesus responds (v. 4) to the news of Lazarus's illness with a pronouncement: "This illness does not lead to death" (v. 4b), which, on the surface at least, will prove untrue. This illness *will* lead to death: Lazarus will shortly die and, through going to Judea to raise him, Jesus will set in motion events leading to his own death. In neither case, however, will the illness lead *ultimately* to death: Lazarus will be brought back to ordinary human life and Jesus will rise to a new order of existence.

But the conquest of death is not tied solely to the resurrection. In his death upon the cross Jesus will most transparently reveal the nature of God. In this sense the cross will be the supreme moment of both his and his Father's "glorification." That is why Jesus adds (v. 4cd) that Lazarus's illness, even though it will lead to his death, will also be for "the glory of God" and his own glorification.[3] Since the death of Jesus is ultimately for the life of the world (6:51), the illness of Lazarus, which remotely brings it about, is not a sickness leading to death but something ordered to the life-giving glory of God.

The scene ends with two statements (vv. 5-6) that seem to stand in flat contradiction. The evangelist stresses (v. 5) the love that Jesus has for Martha and her sister and Lazarus. Such love, we might expect, would impel Jesus to leave immediately for Judea to attend to his ailing friend. On the contrary,

---

[1] Taken in isolation, this opening sentence corresponds rather well to the situation presupposed in Luke 10:38-42. The Lukan story, of course, makes no mention of a brother, Lazarus, and leaves unnamed the village where the episode occurred.

[2] Cf. Gail O'Day, "The Gospel of John," 685–86.

[3] The title "Son of God" occurs in the gospel particularly in contexts where Jesus presents himself as one with the Father in giving life (3:16-18; 5:19-29; 10:36; 11:25-27; 20:31).

we are told, "When, therefore, he heard that Lazarus was ill, he stayed two days longer in the place where he was" (v. 6). Jesus loves . . . yet Jesus stays. How is this an exercise of love? In effect, as will become apparent, Jesus lets Lazarus die. Later, the first thing each sister will do on meeting Jesus is to voice this inconsistency: "Lord, if you had been here, my brother would not have died" (vv. 21, 32). Something very central to the whole episode is being held before us here: the seeming incompatibility between (God's) love and (God's) letting people die.[4] We note also that, according to v. 5, the love of Jesus is directed as much to the sisters (who are mentioned first) as to Lazarus. This is an important early signal that the narrative will address human grief for death as much as Lazarus's death in itself.[5]

Scene 2: *The discussion and decision about going to Judea: 11:7-16*

When in due course Jesus puts before the disciples his plan to go to Judea (v. 7), their response (v. 8) highlights the danger. During his recent appearance in Jerusalem he narrowly escaped death by stoning (8:59; 10:31). A fresh visit will surely meet with similar hostility.

Jesus addresses their hesitation with a parable (vv. 9-10).[6] The parable presupposes awareness of the Jewish way of reckoning time in Jesus' day and also a distinctive understanding of light. The day was reckoned as the time from sunrise to sunset and divided into twelve hours. The day, then, was strictly the space of time during which one could see. What gave the ability to see was the light of the sun, which created light "in" the eye. Absence of light (from the sun) without meant an absence of light within. Not to "have the light" (cf. 12:35-36) meant failure to see.

---

[4] This is sharply to take issue with Raymond E. Brown, *John I–XII*, 423, who regards v. 5 as merely an unnecessary gloss.

[5] The delay of Jesus coheres with his initial brushing off of his mother's implied request at Cana (2:4) and his refusal to go up to the feast of Tabernacles at the urging of his brothers (7:6). Human agenda does not control the Johannine Jesus. The two-day delay also allows for the four days during which, according to the narrative (v. 39), Lazarus will have been in his tomb when Jesus finally arrives.

[6] The parable consists of a rhetorical question followed by two balanced sentences, each consisting of three clauses, standing in antithetical parallelism:

Are there not twelve hours in the day?
If any one walks in the day, [A]
he does not stumble, [B]
because he sees the light of this world. [C]
But if he walks in the night, [A']
he stumbles, [B']
because the light is not in him. [C']

The parable has more than one layer of meaning. At the most basic level the point would be that since Jesus' final hour has not yet come he—and the disciples—can walk in safety without fear of harm from his adversaries; they can go to Judea and attend to Lazarus as if walking in the safety of the day, lit up by the "light of the world," that is, the sun. At the same time, we recall Jesus' comment when responding to the disciples' question about the man born blind: "We must work the works of him who sent me, while it is day; night comes, when no one can work. As long as I am in the world, I am the light of the world" (9:4-5). In light of this comment the present parable suggests the idea of a limit upon Jesus' activity: he must go and give life to Lazarus now because the time is coming (the darkness) when such activity will no longer be possible. Both ideas—opportunity and limit—can in fact be held together: because it is still "day," Jesus *can* go in safety to Lazarus and he must go *now* since time is running out.

The sense of Jesus himself as the "Light of the world" is, of course, pervasive in the gospel (1:4; 8:12; 9:5; 12:46). Within this christological understanding the clause "because the light is not in him" (v. 10c) must refer to the lack of inner light within a disciple who no longer walks with Jesus. The parable then becomes an exhortation to the disciples not to be afraid to go with Jesus to Judea. Since they will be with the Light, they will always be walking by day no matter how threatening the night of opposition. If they choose not to walk with him, no matter how secure they may feel in their "safe territory," they will be choosing the darkness and, in that darkness, may "stumble."[7]

After this exhortation, Jesus renews (vv. 11-15) his proposal of going to Judea. "Our friend[8] Lazarus has fallen asleep and I am going to wake him" (v. 11). "Sleep" was a common metaphor for death in the early Christian community (1 Thess 4:13-14; 1 Cor 15:6, 18, 20, 51; Matt 13:24; Mark 5:39; Luke 8:52). As sleep is a condition from which one wakes refreshed and renewed, for believers death is only a temporary absence before one "wakes" in resurrection. In the present context Jesus' talk of "sleep" probably goes beyond the Christian metaphor. It is not simply a matter of Lazarus "waking" at the general resurrection. Jesus is going to anticipate that event by "waking" him here and now.

The ambiguity attached to "sleep" leads the disciples into a classic instance of misunderstanding. They think Jesus is speaking about ordinary

---

[7] The thought is close then to that of 12:35: "The light is with you for a little longer. Walk while you have the light, so that the darkness may not overtake you. If you walk in the darkness, you do not know where you are going."

[8] This is the third expression of Jesus' love for Lazarus.

sleep and seize upon the information with relief: if Lazarus is sleeping, received wisdom suggests he will recover (v. 12: literally, "he will be saved"); the risky plan of going to Judea can safely be shelved. But this is a blind alley (v. 13). Jesus is speaking of the "sleep" of death; "waking" Lazarus means resurrection. Ironically, though, the disciples' mistaken assumption, "he will recover," speaks the truth. Lazarus will be saved, but only because Jesus is going to Judea to raise him.

Faced with the disciples' misunderstanding, Jesus brushes aside the euphemism of "sleep," declaring bluntly: "Lazarus is dead" (v. 14). Addressed as it is to the problem of death in the community of believers, the story makes no attempt to evade or conceal the harsh fact of death. Lazarus is dead—as believers have died and will die. Whatever remedy Jesus brings to death confronts the reality head on. There is no denial of death, no message of pious, glib comfort here.

Provocatively, Jesus states (v. 15) that he is "glad" he was not there. This is because—as both sisters will later point out (vv. 21, 32)—his presence would have prevented Lazarus from dying. He is glad he was not there because the death of Lazarus will present the disciples with a chance to come to deeper faith.[9] The reality of death is both the supreme challenge to faith and the greatest spur for its exercise. Of the disciples and their faith we in fact hear no more. It is Martha—and through her the subsequent Christian believer—whom Jesus will challenge to work through this death to a deeper level of faith.

The deliberation ends (v. 16) with a resigned acceptance by Thomas of Jesus' proposal. His pessimistic appraisal of the likely outcome is of a piece with his character in the rest of the gospel (cf. 14:5; 20:24-29; 21:2).[10] Thomas is the realist who understands that to follow Jesus means risking death. His comment underlines once again the fact that Jesus is putting his own life in danger by going to Judea.

Scene 3: *Jesus arrives in Bethany; the situation there: 11:17-19*

The scene now shifts to the neighborhood of Bethany. From what follows it appears that, on arriving at the village, Jesus does not go directly to the house of Martha and Mary, nor to the tomb of Lazarus. His "finding" that Lazarus had already been four days in the tomb must presuppose some

---

[9] Cf. Rudolf Schnackenburg, *St. John*, 2:327.

[10] In the Synoptic Gospels, Thomas simply appears among the list of the Twelve. In the Fourth Gospel he has a distinct narrative role.

message received on the way. In contemporary belief the soul of the deceased hovered about the corpse for some time after death. By the fourth day, however, the features of the deceased were no longer recognizable. This was taken to be a sign that the soul had definitively left the corpse and irreversible corruption set in.[11] If Lazarus is four days dead, the miracle required to raise him will be a stupendous one indeed. At the same time, precisely because he has been subject to corruption as well as death, Lazarus can represent all who undergo the normal processes of death and physical decay. His raising will not be simply an exceptional case of temporary respite from death but a symbol, a pledge of something offered to all.

The proximity of Bethany to Jerusalem (v. 18) means that "many of the Jews" become participants in the action as well (v. 19). These Jews have come for the purpose of consoling Martha and Mary for the loss of their brother. It could be, then, that we should not attach to them the hostile rating that normally attaches to the phrase "the Jews" in the gospel. In this scene "Jews" could simply refer to inhabitants of Jerusalem or Judea. In the long run, however, matters are not so simple. The presence of these visitors will ensure that what might have been kept within the family, so to speak—the raising of Lazarus—becomes a matter of public notoriety, in a locale (Judea) where such notoriety is mortally dangerous for Jesus. Though some "Jews" come to a certain measure of faith after witnessing the raising (v. 45), others will inform the authorities, a report that will lead directly to the plan to arrest and do away with him. Ultimately, then, the presence of "the Jews" here is not positive.[12]

Scene 4: *Jesus and Martha: 11:20-27*

In Jesus' meeting and dialogue with Martha—the first of two contrasting scenes involving Lazarus's sisters—we arrive at the theological high point of the drama. On hearing that Jesus had arrived, Martha goes (v. 20) immediately to meet him, while her sister Mary remains in the house, adopting the posture of the grieving that will characterize her throughout the episode (vv. 31, 33).[13] On meeting Jesus, Martha voices what is clearly a word of remonstrance: "Lord, if you had been here, my brother would not have died" (v. 21). There is a sense of disappointment with Jesus—a disappointment

---

[11] Cf. Rudolf Bultmann, *Gospel of John*, 401, n. 8; Raymond E. Brown, *John I–XII*, 424.

[12] Cf. Francis J. Moloney, *John*, 337–38.

[13] The varying reactions of the two sisters correspond to the characterization of each emerging from Luke 10:38-42: more active Martha, more passive Mary.

all the more poignant for the reader who knows that the delay of Jesus has been deliberate. But implicit in her disappointment is also a note of faith. If he had been here, he could have prevented Lazarus from dying. Her faith is at least such as to believe that the presence of Jesus has the power to rescue from grave illness (cf. the faith of the royal official: 4:46-54).

And Martha shows some openness to further possibilities in that she goes on (v. 22) to express confidence that "even now" God will grant whatever Jesus asks from him.[14] What is it that she dares to hope Jesus might ask from God? With Lazarus four days dead and buried, surely only his raising could be in view. Yet her responses later in the dialogue (vv. 24, 27) and above all her eventual reluctance to open the tomb (v. 39) argue strongly that she does not envisage such a remedy at all.

Assessing the level of Martha's faith is a critical problem throughout this section. The evangelist is either being inconsistent or—more likely—deliberately elusive and vague. He has Martha express the human reaction to bereavement that all, and particularly believers, share: a keen sense of powerlessness and the absence of God ("Lord, if you had been here"). At the same time the evangelist has Martha express, not a specific hope (that her brother be raised), but an open-ended, generalized confidence that God can and will do something more.

Jesus' initial response, "Your brother will rise again" (v. 23), is itself ambiguous. In a further instance of misunderstanding, Martha takes his assurance as a word of comfort, reflecting popular religious belief in the general resurrection at the last day. But Jesus' words foretell what is about to happen not on the last day but here and now in this present time and place. At the same time, by making Jesus appear to give consolation in terms of the conventional Jewish eschatology and having Martha give even more explicit utterance (v. 24) to that same hope, the evangelist sharpens a contrast central to his purpose: the contrast between the standard future eschatology shared by Jews and Christians alike and the present or realized eschatology proclaimed in the word of revelation that now follows.

Brushing aside that future hope and the somewhat lame consolation that it offers, Jesus dramatically announces to Martha (vv. 25-26) the presence here and now of resurrection and life. He does so in the form of an "I am" statement followed by a couplet which enlarges upon its implications for believers.

---

[14] Her sister Mary will later (v. 32) voice the same complaint, but without a similar addition of hope.

I am the resurrection and the life (v. 25b):

[A] The one who believes in me, even if they die, they will live.

[B] And whoever lives and believes in me will never die. (v. 26ab)

The "I am" statement is of the predicative form familiar from other Johannine contexts where a climactic point of revelation has been reached. These statements proclaim not so much what Jesus is in himself. The predicate—in this case "resurrection and life"—refers to what he has to give or communicate to the world. In a context simply of hope for the distant prospect of resurrection on the last day, Jesus claims to be personally the communicator of resurrection life, not just in the future, but here and now.

This revelation completely outstrips the horizons of the conversation up to this point where only the death of Lazarus and his rising at the last day had been in view. What Jesus announces here is something of universal significance—a gift for the entire human race, of which the raising of Lazarus when it comes will be a sign and symbol. What Jesus will be for Lazarus he can be for all who die. What he can be for the grieving Martha, he can be for all who grieve. The simple miracle story is at this point becoming a revelatory discourse with significance for all.

The couplet unfolds this wider meaning. The first line (v. 25c), "The one who believes in me, even if they die, they will live,"[15] announces that if a person believes in Jesus that person's physical death cannot annul life as death normally does. There is a present gift of eternal life that transcends death and carries on beyond it. Jesus and Martha, and indeed the whole company in this scene, are confronting the fact of death, the death of one person, Lazarus. Outwardly, the immediate remedy would seem to be to restore Lazarus to life here and now—and this Jesus will shortly do. But Jesus is inviting Martha to move beyond this immediate problem to contemplate a deeper truth. If Lazarus is restored simply to this life, he will live for a time and then die again; it will be a marvel but not a lasting remedy. Jesus uses this present predicament to draw Martha, and all who share both her grief and her faith, to a vision where death is conquered, not by a return to present mortal life, but by the gift of an "eternal life" which perdures even through death. Lazarus's death—and shortly his raising—will be a symbol of this vastly wider truth.

---

[15] In the interests of inclusive language I have adapted the masculine singular usage of the original Greek.

The second line of the couplet (v. 26) basically repeats the same statement about the believer, but this time the starting point is not death but life. We can translate it somewhat more freely so as to read, "And everyone who lives believing in me shall not die for ever." "Lives" here refers to ordinary human life.[16] Those who are alive and whose lives are essentially determined by faith in Jesus do not face the prospect of death in an ultimate sense. Though their physical mortality remains, though they will in fact actually die, their faith ensures that they are living here and now the life of eternity; in this sense they "shall not die for ever."

So, pausing to look over the couplet as a whole, we can recognize that the concepts of death and life are both being used in two senses: an ordinary, physical sense and a spiritual, eternal sense. The two senses do not run simply in parallel but one (the ordinary) functions as a symbol of the other. The pronouncements Jesus makes about death, life, and faith prepare the way for understanding the restoration of Lazarus to ordinary physical life as a symbol of the eternal life that Jesus, as "resurrection and life," communicates to all believers here and now.

The claim Jesus makes here stands in parallel to a similar claim in the discourse following his healing of the paralyzed man at the pool:

> Amen, amen I say to you,
> the one who hears my word and believes him who sent me, has eternal life;
> that one does not come into judgment, but has passed from death to life.
> (John 5:24)

In this earlier sign Jesus had claimed to be "ever at work" as his Father is at work, sustaining creation (v. 17). He is not merely the agent of eschatological judgment in the sense of conventional messianic expectation. Believers already "have" eternal life within their grasp. He does not take away physical death; he lets believers die, as he let Lazarus die. But he communicates to believers before they die an "eternal life" transcending death.

Following his self-revelation, Jesus (v. 26c) questions Martha as to whether she believes "this," that is, his claim to be "resurrection and life." Martha says, "Yes," but fills out her response with a confession of Jesus' status in terms of three stock titles: "Christ" (Messiah); "Son of God"; "the One who is coming into the world" (v. 27).

---

[16] So, Rudolf Bultmann, *John*, 403; C. K. Barrett, *John*, 396; Rudolf Schnackenburg, *St. John*, 2:331, 515, rather than to eternal life or the life of faith in strict agreement with the "will live" of the preceding sentence (so, C. H. Dodd, *Interpretation*, 365; Raymond E. Brown, *John I–XII*, 434; Andrew T. Lincoln, *St. John*, 324). The latter interpretation has problems with "believes" since logically it should precede "lives" taken in this sense.

What is the level of Martha's faith at this point? The first two titles reappear in the climactic statement of purpose found at the end of the gospel: "These are written that you may believe that Jesus is the Christ, the Son of God, and that believing you may have life in his name" (20:31). The eternal Word, as "true Light," was described as "coming into the world" in the Prologue (1:9). These parallels suggest that coming to faith in Jesus in terms of these titles achieves the gospel's aim. The titles "Messiah," "Son of God" would then bear full christological weight and Martha's use of them reveals a faith fully responsive to the exalted revelation of Jesus.[17]

Matters, however, are not so simple. The first two titles can be understood in a "purely messianic" sense, that is, as expressing simply conventional messianic expectation. We find this for "Son of God" early in the gospel when Nathanael, having confessed Jesus in these terms (1:49), is told that his faith journey must go further: "greater things than this you shall see" (1:50-51). The third title, "He who is coming into the world," corresponds to the crowd's confession of Jesus at the close of the multiplication of the loaves (6:14). This, again, is not an adequate expression of faith. It remains possible, then, that Martha is confessing Jesus within categories that are still simply messianic. Though proceeding in her faith journey, she has not yet grasped the full meaning of Jesus' revelation.[18] In any case, the conversation breaks off, with no further clarification from Jesus. The action is now to be carried forward by the parallel exchange between Jesus and Mary.

Scene 5: *Jesus and Mary: 11:28-32*

Up till this point, Mary has remained within the house, locked in grief (v. 20b), surrounded, presumably, by "the Jews" who had come to offer consolation.[19] Hearing from her sister the news that Jesus has arrived and is

---

[17] So, most recent scholars: see, e.g., Rudolf Bultmann, *John*, 404, n. 5; Rudolf Schnackenburg, *St. John*, 2:332; C. K. Barrett, *John*, 396–97; Andrew T. Lincoln, *St. John*, 324; Gail O'Day, "The Gospel of John," 689; Sandra M. Schneiders, "Death in the Community of Eternal Life: History, Theology and Spirituality in John 11," *Interpretation* 41 (1987): 44–56, see 53.

[18] Supporting this view is Martha's subsequent hesitation about opening the tomb (v. 39), causing Jesus to remind her to keep on believing in order to see the glory of God. If Martha's faith is perfect at this early point, the actual sign (the raising) becomes, at least for her, a superfluous anticlimax. For this view, see Raymond E. Brown, *John I–XII*, 434; Dorothy A. Lee, *Symbolic Narratives*, 205–6; and especially Francis J. Moloney, *John*, 327–29, 339.

[19] Their presence may account for the fact that Martha speaks her message about Jesus' arrival "quietly." Mary will have to escape from their concern if she is to share her sister's experience of speaking privately with Jesus.

calling for her (v. 28), she rises swiftly and takes her grief to Jesus (v. 29), who, as we are told in something of an afterthought (v. 30), has stopped short of entering the house. The reason he has done so is perhaps because he is aware that it is full of "the Jews" who have come to console the sisters. It is not that they are hostile at this point. But one gains the impression that they dog Mary's tracks (v. 31) and somehow contain her in her grief.[20] In effect, their following of her to where Jesus is, and subsequently to the tomb, ensures that the final act will be a public one, with all the dangers that entails for Jesus.

Mary's encounter with Jesus is a poor, truncated piece compared with Martha's.[21] Seemingly enveloped in her grief, she falls at Jesus' feet in an extremity of emotion, echoing her sister's remonstration, "Lord, if you had been here, my brother would not have died" (v. 32c). Like Martha, she has sufficient faith to know that his presence would have made a difference but not enough to share her sister's more open-ended hope (v. 22). Her function in the story appears to be simply to highlight the sense of loss and disappointment at Jesus' absence already expressed by Martha (v. 21). This serves the evangelist's intention to address human grief at death as much as death itself.[22]

Scene 6: *The Raising of Lazarus: 11:33-44*

The encounters with both sisters concluded, the action now moves toward the dramatic climax. Before the actual raising of Lazarus, however, the evangelist pauses to dwell at some length upon the emotions of those taking part, most notably those of Jesus himself.

a) *Jesus' emotional reaction to the general grief: 11:33-37*. Before the raising of Lazarus (vv. 33-38a) there are no less than four descriptions of Jesus' emotional reaction. The opening sentence states that Jesus is "greatly disturbed in spirit" (*embrimēsato tōi pneumati*, v. 33b) and "troubled himself" (*etaraxen heauton*, v. 33d). Later, we are told that he wept (*edakrysen*,

---

[20] They want to comfort Mary, not realizing that she is going to the only One who can bring real comfort in the face of death; cf. Ugo Schnelle, *Johannes*, 214.

[21] Cf. Raymond E. Brown, *John I–XII*, 435; Rudolf Schnackenburg, *St. John*, 2:333. Francis J. Moloney, *John*, 330, 340, contests this view: for him Mary is "the character in the story reflecting true faith" (330), even if then she succumbs (v. 33a) and joins "the Jews" in their mourning, provoking Jesus' anger (v. 33b). This view of Mary seems inconsistent and over subtle.

[22] Cf. Andrew T. Lincoln, *St. John*, 326.

v. 35). Finally, Jesus is "greatly disturbed within himself" as he comes to the tomb (*embrimōmenos en heautōi*, v. 38a). In addition, we are told, "the Jews" see in these expressions of feeling an indication of Jesus' love for Lazarus (vv. 36-37). The evangelist seems to be underlining something important here.

While the prominence of the motif is clear, it is not easy to determine the nature of the emotions attributed to Jesus, nor how we are to understand their cause. That grief was an element seems clear from the statement that Jesus wept (v. 35). With the remaining three expressions the situation is more complex. The Greek verb *embrimasthai* means to make a sound in an outward show of anger, such as to snort. Here, the evangelist appears to restrict the sense to an interior movement by adding the phrase "in spirit" in the first case and "within himself" in the second. Nonetheless, usage of the verb elsewhere in the Bible (LXX Dan 11:30; Mark 1:43//Matt 9:30 [Jesus' stern charge to the leper he has cured]; Mark 14:5) suggests in both cases a reference to anger.[23] The remaining expression, "troubled himself," refers to a less defined but profound emotional disturbance. It occurs again in 12:27 and 13:21 to express Jesus' reaction at the prospect of death and betrayal. Putting all this together, we can conclude that the evangelist is at pains to convey that Jesus undergoes a deep emotional stirring, involving both grief and a strong surge of anger.

But what occasions Jesus' anger at this point? The statement in v. 33 implies that it was the sight of Mary's grief and that of the Jews who were with her that provokes Jesus' emotional reaction. This has suggested to many interpreters that what is making Jesus angry is the intrusion of "the Jews" into the scene,[24] and especially the lack of faith which their profound grief seems to show.[25] They simply grieve over the dead, with no flicker of hope such as Martha has displayed (v. 22).[26] Moreover, the final expression of Jesus' anger (v. 38) seems to follow further skeptical remarks of the Jews (vv. 36-37).

---

[23] Cf. the thorough discussion of C. K. Barrett, *John*, 399–400; Raymond E. Brown, *John I–XII*, 425–26; also Gail O'Day, "The Gospel of John," 690; Andrew T. Lincoln, *St. John*, 326.

[24] So, Gail O'Day, "The Gospel of John," 690.

[25] Rudolf Bultmann, *Gospel of John*, 406; Rudolf Schnackenburg, *St. John*, 2:336. Francis J. Moloney, *John*, 331, understands Jesus to be weeping in frustration and anger because Mary, lapsing from her initial faith, has joined "the Jews" in their excessive grief and unbelief.

[26] The Greek verb *klaiein* can express demonstrative outward wailing. In the Synoptic account of the raising of Jairus's daughter, Jesus rebukes and expels from the scene the professional mourners and wailers (Matt 13:23-25; Mark 5:38-40; Luke 8:52-53).

But accounting for Jesus' anger along these lines is hard to square with the fact that Jesus himself weeps and hence seems to share the general grief. A clue lies perhaps in the second expression of emotion in v. 33: "troubled himself." This same term recurs in 12:27, where Jesus, sensing (through the arrival of "the Greeks" [vv. 20-23]) that his hour of glorification has come, cries out, "Father, save me from this hour." This is only a moment of hesitation, because he goes on to add, "No, for this purpose I have come to this hour. Father, glorify thy name" (vv. 27-28a). Nonetheless, the cry does represent a shrinking from the prospect of death, something that parallels his agony in the garden in the Synoptic passion accounts (cf. also Heb 5:7-8). A third reference to being "troubled" occurs, as already mentioned, when Jesus announces that one of the Twelve is to betray him (13:21). All this suggests that his being troubled in the present passage (11:33) has something to do with the prospect of his death.[27] How, then, is it associated with the other emotions—anger and grief—in a coherent explanation of Jesus' feelings as he approaches Lazarus's tomb?

It may be best to understand Jesus' inner turmoil as arising out of being torn between two conflicting emotions. His weeping (v. 35) as he takes up the invitation to come and see the tomb shows a genuine empathy with those who weep for Lazarus.[28] Jesus, then, weeps at their grief. But that same grief intensifies the pressure upon him to restore Lazarus to life. At the same time he also knows that performing such a miracle will inevitably set in motion forces leading to his death. He is torn, then, between love for his friend and sympathy for the bereaved, on the one hand, and an all too human shrinking from death, on the other. His extremity of emotion stems from the impossible situation in which he is now placed.[29]

By depicting the emotions of Jesus so powerfully the evangelist underlines above all the cost to Jesus of the action he is about to perform. This continues the theme central to the episode from the start: that Jesus is placing his own life in mortal danger by journeying to Judea to help Lazarus and the sisters. We now learn how personal and bitter will be the cost to Jesus. He will give life to the one he loves by taking steps that he clearly foresees will cost his own life. This is what the elaborate descriptions of his emotions

---

[27] Cf. C. K. Barrett, *John*, 399; Andrew T. Lincoln, *St. John*, 334.

[28] By using a different Greek word (*dakruein*, as opposed to *klaiein*) for Jesus' reaction, the evangelist carefully distinguishes his response from the more strident grief of Mary and the Jews.

[29] "Jesus perceives that the presence and grief of the sisters and of the Jews are almost forcing a miracle upon him" (C. K. Barrett, *John*, 399).

convey as, following an invitation, "Come and see" (v. 34b),[30] he makes his way to the tomb.

The divided reactions of "the Jews" (vv. 36-37) underline the conflict in Jesus himself. On the one hand, they—correctly—perceive his tears to be a sign of his love for Lazarus. On the other hand, some of them, echoing the sisters' complaints (vv. 21, 32), point out the incompatibility between his love and his failure to take action when action might have had some success: could not he who opened the eyes of the blind man have kept this man from dying? In view of what Jesus is about to do the remark is highly ironical; it also heightens the drama. Yes, Jesus did fail to keep this man from dying, failed to work the (lesser) miracle of healing, which all knew he could effect. But this was only to leave the way open for a stupendous miracle beyond their power to imagine. Love has indeed let the loved one die—but only to effect, in the midst of grief, a far more mighty work.

b) *Jesus arrives at the tomb: 11:38-40.* As Jesus approaches the tomb (v. 38), a cave sealed with a large stone,[31] the evangelist again reminds us that he does so in a state of deep emotion. Whatever his feelings, Jesus' command to take away the stone (v. 39a) is firm and direct, indicating a decision clearly made. Martha's hesitation (v. 39b) conveys a sense of horror at the prospect of opening the tomb. Not only will there be an odor,[32] but, as we have already seen, it was commonly held that by the fourth day after death corruption would have set in to such an extent as to render the features of the deceased unrecognizable. It was not her brother that Martha was going to see. She has not grasped the meaning of the earlier word of revelation (vv. 25-26): that Jesus *is* "the resurrection and the life," who will display this truth symbolically by raising her brother from the dead.

Jesus' reassurance, "Did I not tell you that if you believed, you would see the glory of God?" (v. 40) is at first sight odd; nowhere has he made a

---

[30] The invitation is, of course, phrased in exactly the same terms as that which he had himself issued to two disciples at the beginning of his ministry (1:39).

[31] The use of caves, both natural and artificial, for burial was common Jewish practice. A horizontal or vertical shaft was cut to give access to the cave, which was sealed after burial with a large boulder. Lazarus's emergence from the tomb is more easily imagined on the supposition of horizontal access—such as also seems to be the presupposition in regard to the tomb of Jesus (cf. 20:1-12).

[32] "The spices with which the Jewish people normally prepared a body for burial were sufficient only to allay the odor of decomposition until burial. . . . By the fourth day these spices would have had no effect on a decomposing body" (B. H. Henneberry, "The Raising of Lazarus (John 11:1-44): an evaluation of the hypothesis that a written tradition lies behind the narrative" (PhD thesis, Catholic University of Louvain, 1983)], 181).

promise to Martha in such terms. His words do recall his statement to the disciples that Lazarus's illness was for the glory of God (v. 4) and also his subsequent remark that it would provide them with an opportunity to believe (v. 15). Here, his words seem intended to uncover the true implications of the act he is about to perform. All the bystanders, those who believe and those who do not, will witness the raising of Lazarus. They will in this sense see the miracle. But only those whose seeing is accompanied by faith will penetrate beneath the miracle to see it as a true Johannine "sign": the disclosure of the presence and life-giving power ("glory") of God.

c) *Jesus' thanksgiving prayer to the Father: 11:41-42.* The prayer Jesus offers before the open tomb (vv. 41-42) is not a petition but an act of communion with the Father, which the bystanders are allowed to "overhear." The prayer recalls that Jesus' whole life has been nothing but a projection in the world of the eternal communion between Father and Son (1:1, 18), while his ministry in all its aspects has simply been an expression of the Father's will to give life to the world (3:16-17; 4:34; 6:38; 10:10b, 18; 14:31; 15:10; 17:2; 19:30).[33] Jesus prays, then, not for power to work the miracle, but for the faith of the bystanders: that they will grasp through and beyond the miracle some sense of his unceasing communion with the Father (1:18).

d) *Jesus summons Lazarus out of the tomb: 11:43-44.* With Jesus' union with the Father attested through his prayer, the way is now clear for the rather matter-of-fact description of the raising (vv. 43-44). As if waking his friend from sleep, Jesus cries out with a loud voice, "Lazarus, come forth!" The authoritative command, resounding throughout the realm of death, recalls an earlier prophecy concerning the hour "when the dead will hear the voice of the Son of God and live" (5:25), "when all who are in the tombs will hear his voice and come forth" (5:28-29). In heeding the Son's cry and coming forth, Lazarus anticipates all who will rise at the general resurrection. Alongside this future reference, however, his present coming back to life signifies the power of Jesus to be for believers here and now "the resurrection and the life" (v. 25).[34]

The evangelist dwells at some length upon the appearance of Lazarus as he emerges from the tomb (v. 44). The wrappings of death still envelop

---

[33] "It is because he is one with God that he prays and because he prays he is one with God" (Rudolf Schnackenburg, *St. John*, 2:339, citing W. Lütgert).

[34] "What is crucial is that Jesus has given (physical) life as a sign of his power to give eternal life on this earth (realized eschatology) and as a promise that on the last day he will raise the dead (final eschatology)" (Raymond E. Brown, *John I–XII*, 437).

him. Totally passive, his hands and feet bound in bandages, his face wrapped with a napkin (*soudarion*), he cannot be fully restored to human life until he is unbound and let go free.

There is one other place in the gospel where the wrappings of death feature strongly. This is the scene where Peter and the Beloved Disciple come to the empty tomb of Jesus (20:3-10). Looking into the tomb from the outside the disciple sees the linen cloths (*othonia*) lying there (v. 5). But when he goes into the tomb he sees something more, already seen by Peter (vv. 6-7): the napkin (*soudarion*) which had been on Jesus' head, not lying with the cloths, but rolled up in a place by itself. Straightaway, we are told, "he saw and he believed" (v. 8). What he saw constituted for him a sign of resurrection. The neatly folded, separately placed napkin convinced him that here was no evidence of grave robbery but instead an active, majestic resumption of life. Jesus, who had laid down his life of his own accord, had exercised a similar power to take it up again (10:18).[35]

Taken together, these two instances of resurrection, where in each case so much is made of the apparel of the grave, make clear that the evangelist wants us to see both a comparison and a contrast.[36] The napkin (*soudarion*) is the link. Lazarus is totally passive in his raising, summoned by the command of Jesus, needing to be loosed from the bonds of death, including the *soudarion* covering his face. How different the active rising of Jesus, who removes the cloth from his face, neatly folds it, and sets it aside. In this way, the raising of Lazarus functions as both anticipation and foil for the resurrection of Jesus.

Scene 7: *Reaction to the raising: faith and report: 11:45-46*

Most miracle stories end with an indication of the reaction on the part of the bystanders or crowd. This one is no exception. Paralleling an earlier reaction to the grief of Jesus (v. 37), the bystanders' response goes in two directions. Positively (v. 45), "many of the Jews . . . who had come with Mary" believe in Jesus on the basis of what they had seen. That is, they show the kind of faith that follows signs, a faith regarded as inadequate elsewhere in the gospel (2:23-25; 4:48; 6:26).

Alongside this positive reaction, there is a negative and, in the end, fatal response (v. 46). Some of the Jews go off and tell the Pharisees what

---

[35] For this see my study, "The Faith of the Beloved Disciple and the Community in John 20," *Journal for the Study of the New Testament* 23 (1985): 83–97.

[36] Cf. Gail O'Day, "The Gospel of John," 692; Andrew T. Lincoln, *St. John*, 329.

Jesus has done. In this they are perhaps more naive than malevolent. Presumably they do not deny the fact of the miracle: that Lazarus has been brought to life. But for them it is simply a fact, the political consequences of which are more significant than any deeper meaning.

Scene 8: *The plot of the Sanhedrin against Jesus: 11:47-54*

The plot that follows the raising of Lazarus (vv. 47-53) sets in motion the chain of events that will lead to Jesus' death. It also brings out the fuller meaning of that death. The authorities fear that the signs Jesus is working, culminating in this most spectacular one, will evoke belief in him as Messiah and allegiance to his cause on an ever-wider scale. Then the whole people will come under threat from Rome (v. 48). Giving voice to this apprehension for the safety of the whole nation, the high priest, Caiaphas,[37] makes a pragmatic observation: it is better that one man should die for the people, so that the whole nation might not perish (v. 50). The evangelist is quick (v. 51) to point out the irony contained in this advice. Here is the chief authority of the nation, while actively seeking to bring about Jesus' death, also spelling out in the same words the true meaning of that death. Jesus will not die because he has been made out to be a pretender to the throne of David. Nor will he die simply because he gave life to an individual, Lazarus. He is to die in order to give life ("eternal life") to a whole people and, in a wider view still, so that all the "children of God" might be gathered into one (v. 52).

The gathering in of the scattered "children of God" recalls the motif of the eschatological gathering of the Jewish Diaspora living among the nations (cf. Isa 43:5-7; 49:9-26; 60:1-22). But within the "children of God" the evangelist undoubtedly includes here believers from the Gentile world as well. As Jesus later prophesies (12:32), when he is "lifted up" (in death) he will draw all people to himself. For this reason the sign upon his cross must be written not only in Hebrew but also in the languages— Latin and Greek—which will make it symbolically readable to the whole world (19:20). Lazarus, whom Jesus calls to life at the cost of his own life upon the cross, becomes a type or representative of each member of a worldwide community of believers drawn into unity from the nations of the world. Through belief "in his name" they have been given "the power to become

---

[37] The gospel describes him as "High Priest that year." According to Jewish law high priests were appointed for life but the Romans appointed and deposed them with such frequency as to make the tenure seem annual. The sense is probably "High Priest that very memorable year"; cf. C. K. Barrett, *John*, 406; Francis J. Moloney, *John*, 343.

children of God" (1:12), sharing God's own "eternal life" and reflecting in their "oneness" the divine communion of love (14:21, 23; 15:9-11).

The high priest's advice is heeded. The authorities plot Jesus' death (v. 53). Attempts on his life had been made on several occasions before. But they were spontaneous reactions to his claims. The threat now comes from a formal deliberation of the highest authorities. In the face of this threat, Jesus withdraws from Jerusalem and its environs to the safety of the desert region to the east around Ephraim and remains there with his disciples (v. 54). The evangelist is once again underlining that in coming to Judea to raise Lazarus Jesus had put his own life at risk. More than risk, in fact, he has brought upon himself what amounts to a formal sentence of death.[38]

2. *The Approach of Passover: 11:55-57*

A small bridge passage intervenes to inform us of the approach of yet another feast: Passover. At the opening of the gospel John the Baptist had pointed out Jesus as "the Lamb of God who takes away the sin of the world" (1:29; cf. 1:36). At the approach of an earlier Passover Jesus had made his first visit to Jerusalem, cleansed the temple, and spoken of the destruction of the "temple" that is his body (2:13-25). At a later Passover he had multiplied the loaves and fishes and spoken of a "bread of life" that would be his "flesh given for the life of the world" (6:51). Now a third, climactic Passover looms as the background for the "hour" when, as Paschal Lamb, Jesus will gain life for the world by taking away its sin.

Jerusalem in fact is swollen in population by many who had come up to "purify themselves" in preparation for the feast (v. 55b). Ironically, the purification they are seeking belongs to the past. It will be replaced by the more efficacious purification that Jesus will effect by dying at Passover as the Lamb of God. Nonetheless, these pilgrims want to see Jesus and discuss among themselves whether he will come up for the feast (v. 56). The formulation of the question[39] suggests a belief that this is unlikely since, as we are told (v. 57), the chief priests and the Pharisees had given instructions that anyone who knew his whereabouts should inform them so that they could stone him to death. In this we have a further reminder that the threat to Jesus' life in Jerusalem and Judea is public and very real.

---

[38] Andrew T. Lincoln, *St. John*, 331.

[39] The formulation in the Greek suggests the meaning, "He will not come, will he?"; cf. C. K. Barrett, *John*, 410.

3. *The Anointing at Bethany: 12:1-8*

To underline the role of Lazarus as representative of all for whom Jesus is going to die, the evangelist has his story continue somewhat beyond the actual raising. Six days before the fateful Passover Jesus is again in Bethany, at a dinner hosted by the family of Lazarus. In a rather heavy-handed way the evangelist twice mentions the presence of Lazarus, "whom Jesus had raised from the dead" (vv. 1, 2). True to the pattern that emerges also from the parallel scene in Luke 10:38-42, Martha takes the active part, serving at table, while Mary performs a service of loving devotion to Jesus: she anoints his feet with costly ointment and wipes them with her hair (v. 3).[40]

In view of Jesus' own inexorable movement toward death, Mary's loving service is totally appropriate. Jesus has given life to her brother at what will soon be the cost of his own life. By anointing his feet with costly ointment (so costly that its aroma fills the whole room),[41] Mary shows both that she appreciates the cost and that she is ready to offer something costly in return. The mercenary protest of Judas (vv. 4-5) that Jesus instantly rebuts (vv. 7-8) highlights the extravagance of her action and its appropriateness at this time.[42] Judas's concern for the poor is hypocritical and false, since, as we are told (v. 6), he actually helped himself to the contents of the common purse. Reacting to his protest, Jesus does not undermine concern for the poor but points out that such a concern can be exercised at any time, whereas Mary has recognized that the moment for responding physically to his act of love is unique and will not return.[43] As the first beneficiary of Jesus' costly death, Lazarus is present to see and ponder it all, once more standing in for all who receive the gift of life from Jesus.

---

[40] The Johannine account of this incident coheres with the quasi parallel that Luke places much earlier in the ministry of Jesus (Luke 7:36-50) in that, like Mary, the unnamed woman in that episode anoints Jesus' feet and wipes them with her hair. It agrees with the Matthean (26:6-13) and Markan (14:3-9) accounts in locating the episode at the beginning of the passion narrative and in the protest about "waste."

[41] The beautiful aroma contrasts with the foul odor of death that Martha feared would emanate from Lazarus's tomb (11:39). "Through Mary's act, the stench of death that once lingered over his household has been replaced by the fragrance of love and devotion" (Gail O'Day, "The Gospel of John," 701).

[42] Since a denarius amounted to a day's wages, on Judas's estimate, the value of the ointment (three hundred denarii) amounted to a year's earnings.

[43] The Greek of v. 7 is notoriously difficult to translate; for a thorough review of the possibilities, see C. K. Barrett, *John*, 413–14. The best sense of the highly elliptical sentence appears to be: "Let her alone; she has been (unknowingly until now) keeping it for the day of my burial"; cf. Raymond E. Brown, *John I–XII*, 449.

4. *The Plot against Lazarus: 12:9-11*

Lazarus's role in the story is not quite over. A short bridge passage informs us that great crowds of the Jews came out to Bethany, not only on account of Jesus but also to see Lazarus, whom he had raised from the dead (v. 9). In this they exhibit the kind of curiosity in the marvelous that the evangelist tends to downgrade. More seriously, their interest in Lazarus moves the authorities to resolve to put him to death as well, since his restoration is leading "many of the Jews" to go away and believe in Jesus (v. 11). As personal living testimony to Jesus' power to give life, he too falls foul of the authorities' murderous designs, foreshadowing the hostility that the later community of believers will also in due course attract (15:18-21; 16:2-4). So in this further respect Lazarus becomes a type for subsequent believers. Life is not given—or received—without cost. The forces of death cannot tolerate the living witnesses of life. In this sense Thomas in his pessimism (v. 16) accurately discerned the outcome.

Reflection. Immediately preceding the passion, the Lazarus sequence in the Fourth Gospel powerfully enacts the truth that Jesus gives life at the cost of his own life. Our analysis of John 11 has shown how again and again the evangelist reminds us that Jesus puts his own life at mortal risk when he goes to Judea at the sisters' request. All comes to a climax in the scene before the tomb where we find Jesus torn between two powerful emotions: the love which impels him to work the sign and the shrinking from the prospect of his own death, an outcome which he knows the raising of Lazarus will bring on. Nothing could underline so clearly the cost to Jesus that communicating life incurs. Nothing could bring out so forcefully the love that impels the gift.

In this sense the narrative leading up to the raising of Lazarus stands as a microcosm of the entire action of the gospel. In order to give life to a friend at the point of death Jesus left his "safe country"—beyond the Jordan—to enter a territory (Judea) of mortal danger. In the sweep of the gospel as a whole, the Word, who is "with God" (1:1, 2), "(ever) in the bosom of the Father" (1:18), leaves that "safe country" to come to a world which "God so loves" (3:16), but which is at the point of death because it has turned away from the source of life. Though he comes to "his own," he enters a sphere of mortal danger because his own will know him not (1:10-11).

Within this wider view, Lazarus is a character with whom anyone who reads the gospel can identify. "I" am Lazarus—in the sense that Jesus left his "safe country" to enter this world, placing his life in mortal danger in order to save me from death, to communicate, at the cost of his own life, eternal life to me. I am the "friend" of Jesus—he or she whom he loved. For me Jesus has wept. Before my tomb, so to speak, he has wrestled with the cost of life-giving love. It is to call me forth into life, to strip from me the bands of death that Jesus has come into the world and given his life. So I am to read the forthcoming account of the passion and death of Jesus with intimate personal involvement, knowing that Jesus is undergoing all this insult and suffering for love of me and to give life to me.

Beyond this identification with Lazarus, in the figures of his grieving sisters, Martha and Mary, the evangelist addresses the human situation of all who grieve at the prospect or actuality of death. We have noted how strongly the evangelist underlines the motif of Jesus' delay in setting out for Bethany. Jesus loves and yet, as both sisters point out (vv. 21, 32), Jesus lets die. The Lord of life is not there when he is desperately needed. How can this absence be reconciled with love?

By so highlighting this conflict between love and letting die, the gospel accepts and legitimates the keen sense of God's absence felt by all believers who confront the fact of death. The stark reality is not avoided. We recall Jesus' bald assertion: "Lazarus is dead" (v. 14). No attempt here to smother the brutal fact with pious sentiments of a conventional kind. On the contrary, the reality is accepted, the sense of God's absence acknowledged, and an invitation given to set out with Martha on a journey of faith, a journey which proceeds from and accompanies as long as is necessary the full process of grief.

Normally present in human grieving—and not unconnected with the sense of God's absence—is an element of anger. As we have seen, anger features among the complex of Jesus' feelings as he goes to Lazarus's tomb. Jesus is angry before the fact of death—angry at Lazarus's death and the general grief it has caused, but angry too because giving life to his friend means confronting the prospect of death for himself. In its own way the Lazarus story gives permission for anger to be recognized, owned, and expressed as an inescapable part of grief, not at all inconsistent with faith. On the contrary working through anger—as Jesus appears to work through his anger in this episode—is part of the deepening of faith that confrontation with death requires.

Finally, Jesus weeps (v. 35). Jesus does not wail and mourn as do Mary and "the Jews" in their slender faith. The evangelist is careful to choose a different word. But Jesus weeps with and for the grieving family. In his weeping the divine weeps with the human, showing again the full compatibility between faith and genuine human sorrow.

Jesus, it is true, does in the end give back Lazarus to his grieving sisters. Christians reading the story in the context of recent bereavement will perhaps sense keenly that what Jesus did for Martha and Mary he has not done for them. But the miracle restores Lazarus simply to mortal human existence; he will die again. The lasting remedy to death occurs within a vision of faith that has come to see, beyond ordinary life and death, a life transcending these boundaries—seeing the raising of Lazarus not as a temporary remedy to the grieving of this particular family, but as a symbol of the eternal life communicated by Jesus to all.

The Lazarus narrative was undoubtedly framed for the Johannine community as it faced the increasing phenomenon of death in its own ranks. How could death have a place in what was supposed to be "the community of eternal life"?[44] How could Jesus somehow be present, be "remaining" with the community, if members continued to die. It was presumably such painful questionings as these that led the community or its leading theologian to the distinction between "natural" and "eternal" life which runs through the entire narrative, becoming explicit in 11:25-26.

What the story of Lazarus provided for the first readers of the Fourth Gospel it continues to do for succeeding generations. Medical science and technology may prolong life. It may help people elude the grasp of death in many situations hitherto seen as fatal. But against all death lodges its undeniable claim. The same progress of science has helped us to see death as a natural process. But the primitive emotions aroused by death—the prospect of our own mortality, grief, and dismay at the demise of others—remain just as strong. God lets us die and lets our loved ones die. Death, especially death that comes suddenly, prematurely, wantonly, remains the aspect of human existence that most challenges the existence, sovereignty, and goodness of God.

The story of Lazarus, with its full acceptance of human death and grieving, with its realism about the cost of giving life, with its invitation to enter upon a deeper journey of faith, speaks as powerfully to the present as it did to the past. God is neither indifferent to the distress death brings nor unsympathetic to our struggles of faith. More than anything else in the gospel, Jesus' demeanor in John 11 expresses divine involvement in human grief and suffering. In the person of the Son, God becomes vulnerable, physically and psychologically, to death. At its deepest level the story of Lazarus invites us to believe in God as the One who gives life in death and

---

[44] The phrase is taken from the title of Sandra M. Schneiders' perceptive study of John 11: "Death in the Community of Eternal Life," (see p. 193, n. 17 above).

out of death. To every believer, confronted like Martha with mortality, Jesus addresses his words: "Did I not tell you that if you would believe you would see the glory of God?" (11:40). Each of us has a perfect right, indeed an invitation, to write ourselves and our world into the script —to be, each one of us, Lazarus, whom Jesus loved and for whom he gave his life.

The Approach of the "Hour": 12:12-50

What the gospel refers to as the "hour" of Jesus—the revelation of glory as he is lifted up on the cross—is fast approaching. The approach of the hour is closely linked, as we have seen, with the raising of Lazarus since it is this sign that has triggered the formal decision of the authorities to move definitively against Jesus. In fact, references to Lazarus are so woven into the subsequent episodes in Jerusalem that the sequence comprising 11:1–12:36 really makes up a single narrative block. For the sake of convenience, however, I see a new section beginning with the entry of Jesus into Jerusalem and continuing to the end of chapter 12.

The material then flows in a sequence of scenes as follows:

1. Jesus' Entry into Jerusalem: 12:12-16

2. The Reaction of the Crowd and the Pharisees: 12:17-19

3. The Coming of the Greeks: The "Hour" of the Son of Man: 12:20-36

4. Concluding Reflections upon Jesus' Witness to Israel: 12:37-50

1. Jesus' Entry into Jerusalem: 12:12-16

In parallel with its three Synoptic counterparts, the Fourth Gospel describes a triumphal entry of Jesus into Jerusalem at the beginning of what is to be the last week of his life. In contrast to the Synoptic accounts Jesus does not go on to cleanse the temple; he has done that at a first Passover visit to Jerusalem at the beginning of his ministry (2:13-22). Moreover, whereas the Synoptic accounts have Jesus make preparations for his entry—specifically giving instructions for the procuring of a colt for him to ride—in the Fourth Gospel he gets hold of a colt himself and then rides upon it in deliberate reaction, it would seem, to the triumphal welcome he receives from the pilgrims who have come up for the feast. Hearing of his approach they go out to meet him with palm branches and shouts of acclamation. The carrying of palm branches was a traditional feature of public expressions of triumph and joy, especially for the welcome of a ruler, as when Simon Maccabaeus took possession of Jerusalem (1 Macc 13:51) and the purification of the temple by Judas Maccabaeus (2 Macc 10:7).[1] The evangelist reinforces the sense of a royal and hence messianic entry by adding to the acclamation, "Hosanna! Blessed is the one who comes in the name of the Lord,"[2] the title "the King of Israel."[3]

The welcome and the acclamation echo the attempt on the part of the Galilean crowd, miraculously fed at an earlier Passover, to make Jesus their king (6:14-15). As on that occasion (when he withdrew to the mountain by himself), Jesus takes evasive action. He transforms the nature of the entry by finding a colt and sitting upon it (vv. 14-15), thereby turning his entry into Jerusalem into a fulfillment of a prophecy from Zechariah (9:9):

Do not be afraid, daughter of Zion.
Look, your king is coming,
sitting on a donkey's colt!

The fulfillment of this prophecy confirms that Jesus is a king—as he will later acknowledge before Pilate—but a king, the nature of whose rule differs sharply from that of contemporary rulers who rule by fear and impressive display of power.[4] His choice of a humble mount signals, as Zechariah indicates, a kingship that attracts rather than imposes allegiance (cf. 12:32). It is for this reason that the quotation begins with "Do not fear" rather than "Rejoice greatly" as in the original of Zech 9:9. "Do not fear" is a standard

---

[1] The mention of palm branches is peculiar to the Fourth Gospel; it is John, therefore, who has given the church "Palm Sunday."

[2] The expression "Hosanna" (lit., "Please (Lord), save us") is taken from Psalm 118 (LXX 117):25. The blessing, taken from the following verse and originally pronounced over pilgrims, "coming in the name of the Lord" to Jerusalem, is used here in a messianic sense to "the One who is to come"; cf. John 6:14; 11:27.

[3] The Greek connective *kai* appearing before the title (though not in all manuscripts) conveys the sense of the "Coming One" as "the King of Israel," that is, as the Messiah; cf. C. K. Barrett, *John*, 418. "King of Israel" appears elsewhere in the gospel at Nathanael's confession in 1:49. Outsiders (Pilate) and the hostile authorities employ "King of the Jews" (18:33, 39; 19:3, 19; cf. 19:14).

[4] "Jesus is not the king of Israel expected by the crowd but the Messiah promised by Zechariah" (Francis J. Moloney, *John*, 351).

formula of reassurance in biblical accounts of human encounters with the divine. It occurs in another prophetic text, Zephaniah 3:14-17, which has several verbal links with the quoted Zechariah text and which the evangelist may intend the biblically literate reader to call to mind as well:

> Sing aloud, O daughter of Zion; . . .
> The king of Israel, the LORD, is in your midst; . . .
> On that day it shall be said to Jerusalem:
> Do not fear, O Zion;
> . . . The LORD, your God, is in your midst.

Prefaced by the phrase "Do not fear" and with the remaining likely allusions to this passage from Zephaniah, the Zechariah text as quoted holds together the sense of divine presence and human approachability characteristic of the gospel's depiction of Jesus.[5]

As in the case of Jesus' action in the temple (2:22), the evangelist steps in to explain that the disciples did not understand the meaning of what was transpiring at this point but remembered it with understanding "after he was glorified" (v. 16). They did recognize that the crowd was acclaiming Jesus as Messiah. What they understood only in the light of his "glorification" (passion, death, and resurrection) was the meaning of his completing his entry riding upon a colt. Experience of his glorification led them to "remember" this gesture and see it as the fulfillment of the text from Zechariah. They could then understand it as a corrective to the messianic reception he was receiving from the crowd, a revelation of the true nature of God's rulership in Israel. Later (14:26) Jesus will tell the disciples that a key role of the Paraclete Spirit will be to assist such enlightened "remembering" on the part of the disciples.

2. Reaction of the Crowd and the Pharisees: 12:17-19

The account of the entry concludes with the reactions of various parties to the event (vv. 17-19). In this respect the evangelist could hardly have created a more confusing report had he set out to do so. In the way of retrospective explanations that are a feature of the gospel, he appears to want to offer a belated explanation as to why the pilgrims in Jerusalem for Passover went out to meet Jesus as stated in v. 12. The reason is that they had heard about the "sign" of his raising Lazarus from the dead. When this crowd joined those who had accompanied Jesus from Bethany, they added their

---

[5] Cf. Gail O'Day, "The Gospel of John," 707–8.

testimony to those who had actually witnessed the sign.[6] The evangelist's explanation may not be helpful in regard to sorting out the crowds, but his intention is clear: to stress again that the raising of Lazarus lies behind the acclamation of Jesus as messianic king and the increase of his popularity among the populace at large.

This popular enthusiasm leads to heightened concern on the part of the authorities (v. 19). In desperation "the Pharisees" admit their impotence, remarking, "You see the world has gone after him!" (v. 19c). The observation is replete with irony at more than one level. Despite the measures taken, the foreboding expressed by Caiaphas (11:50-52) is proving to be prophetically true. The enthusiastic crowds show that the "world" is indeed "going after" Jesus—albeit not with an understanding of his kingship that he approves. As the arrival of "the Greeks" in the very next scene will show, Jesus is indeed beginning to draw people to himself as "Savior of the world" (3:16-17; 4:42).[7] The designs of the authorities to bring Jesus and his cause to an end are slipping through their fingers. In the currents swirling about him a divine project is at work that will not be deflected or gainsaid.

*Reflection.*The celebration of Palm Sunday in the tradition of the church holds both the acclamation and the redefinition of Jesus' kingship together. The faithful enact the celebratory procession, hailing Jesus as King but later go on to hear the correct orientation of that kingship in the reading of the passion. The continuing allusions to the raising of Lazarus remind us that Jesus' kingship is at the service of a costly giving of life. As the Son of God sent into the world Jesus reclaims the divine kingship over Israel and the world—a kingship that exists solely to rescue the world from the darkness of sin and draw it into the light of life.

3. The Coming of the Greeks:
The "Hour" of the Son of Man: 12:20-36

At this point several themes of Johannine theology come together in great concentration. Jesus has made a messianic entry into Jerusalem amid high popular enthusiasm. While the crowds are wild with excitement, his adversaries are wringing their hands in despair. There is a sense of a gathering crisis. Up till now we have often been told that Jesus' "hour"—the mo-

---

[6] Reading the better attested temporal conjunction *hote* rather than the conjunction *hoti* introducing a clause in indirect speech.

[7] Cf. Gail O'Day, "The Gospel of John," 708.

ment of his glorification in death—has not yet arrived.[8] Now, the arrival of some "Greeks" indicates the imminence of the hour. In a series of exchanges with the crowd Jesus wrestles with the prospect of his death and explores its meaning at unparalleled theological depth.

After the sentences describing the approach of "the Greeks" (12:20-22), the exchanges between Jesus and the crowd fall into three main sections: the necessity for Jesus' death (vv. 23-26); Jesus' interior struggle at the prospect of his death (vv. 27-30); the consequences of that death and urgency of appropriate human response in view of its imminence (vv. 31-36a). The sequence concludes with Jesus' withdrawal and concealment (v. 36b).

The Approach of the Greeks: 12:20-22

The approach of the Greeks who "want to see Jesus" is one of those scenes in the Fourth Gospel that seem to go nowhere. We don't know whether the Greeks ever got to meet Jesus—though the implication is that they did not. His own response to the news of their arrival (v. 23) seems to go off on a tangent. For the evangelist, however, it is their approach that is all-important. The actual time for Jesus' word to reach people outside the Jewish world (Gentiles) lies beyond his death and resurrection.[9] This is why the approach of representatives of that non-Jewish world triggers the response in Jesus that it does. As he explains later (v. 32), it will be when he is "lifted up from the earth"—in crucifixion and death—that he will draw all (people) to himself. If these representatives of the Gentile world are already being drawn to him and want to see him, this is a sure indication that the moment of his death—his "hour"—is at hand. Hence his reaction to their arrival in the way described (v. 23).

These Gentiles have come up to Jerusalem to "worship" at the feast, that is, the Passover. Throughout the gospel several feasts have been the backdrop for Jesus' witness in a way that shows him to be the replacement of Jewish institutions. While these "Greeks," have come up to worship in the temple along with the mass of other Passover pilgrims, their interest in Jesus marks them out as forerunners of all from the Gentile world who, after

---

[8] Cf. 2:4; 4:21, 23; 7:30; 8:20.

[9] Virtually all interpreters of the gospel take these "Greeks" to be non-Jews ("Gentiles") who had converted to the faith of Israel either as proselytes (that is, full converts) or "God-fearers" (the Lukan term to describe people from the Gentile world who embraced the faith but not the ritual practice of Judaism). C. H. Dodd puts it well: "These Greeks are the vanguard of mankind coming to Christ" (*Interpretation*, 371).

his death and resurrection, will come to "worship" not in the Jerusalem temple but in the One (Jesus) who replaces that temple as the locus of God's presence on earth. Their worship will be that "worship in spirit and truth" about which Jesus spoke to the Samaritan woman (4:20-24).

Desirous of "seeing" Jesus, these "Greeks" approach the disciple of Jesus who most obviously has a Greek name: Philip, from Bethsaida in Galilee (v. 21). Philip takes their request to Andrew, the other disciple with a Greek name, and together they inform Jesus. This rather charming "mediated" approach to Jesus via his (presumably) Greek-speaking "minders" echoes the attraction and call of the original (Jewish) disciples at the beginning of the gospel.[10] The parallel forges a connection between the call of the original Jewish disciples and the future discipleship of believers from the Gentile world. As Jesus invited the original (Jewish) disciples to "come and see" (1:39), so these Gentiles, in their desire to "see" Jesus foreshadow a discipleship to come when the life-giving benefits of his death and exaltation become available to a wider world of faith.

The Son of Man Must Die: 12:23-26

As noted above, Jesus does not respond directly to the request of the Greeks to see him. Instead, for the reason implied in v. 32, the approach of these Gentiles, triggers off a pronouncement that "the hour has come for the Son of Man to be glorified" (v. 23). Twice before, Jesus has escaped attempts to murder him because his hour has not yet come (7:30; 8:20). For the same reason he was initially reluctant to respond to his mother's observation about the lack of wine at the Cana wedding (2:4). Now the "hour" has come for the revelation of his "glory" in his obedient death upon the cross. His death is the moment ("hour") of supreme revelation of his glory because it is the occasion when his perfect unity with the Father will be most clearly displayed, when he will most transparently reveal the essence of God to be self-sacrificing love (1 John 4:7, 16).

Meanwhile (vv. 23-26) a little excursus establishes the necessity for this glorification to come about through death. While Jesus' death is primarily in view, the reasoning, beginning with a "seed" image (v. 24), is couched in

---

[10] Andrew, the first named disciple, recruits his brother, Simon Peter (1:39-42). The next day Jesus himself calls Philip (v. 42), who in turn recruits Nathanael (vv. 45-46). In both references to Philip (1:44 and 12:21) he is described as being "from Bethsaida in Galilee," reinforcing the parallel. The mediating role of Andrew and Philip here could reflect a tradition that these two played a role in the Gentile mission; cf. Rudolf Schnackenburg, *St. John*, 2:382.

general terms and in the end (vv. 25-26) becomes something of an exhortation addressed to all would-be disciples. Jesus' dying becomes a paradigm of the principle that true life ("eternal life") is gained through self-sacrificial love.[11]

"Seed" and "sowing" imagery (v. 24) is prominent in the Synoptic parables (Mark 4:3-8, 26-29, 31-32; Matthew 13:3-9, 24-30, 31-32) and Paul uses it to explain the nature of the risen body (1 Cor 15:36-38). Here in the Fourth Gospel the "seed" image projects a contrast between remaining "alone" (a single grain) and "bearing much fruit" in the sense of multiplying. The seed can only be productive beyond itself if it falls into the ground, germinates, and in this sense "dies." Applied in allegorical mode to Jesus, the image explains why he, a single individual, must die in order to bear multiple "fruit" in the shape of a worldwide community of life and love.[12]

The series of axioms that follows (vv. 25-26) is also widespread in the Synoptic tradition (Mark 8: 35//Matt 16:25//Luke 9:24; Matt 10:39//Luke 17:33 [= "Q"]). Where that tradition speaks in terms of "saving" or "losing" one's life, the Fourth Gospel speaks of "loving" or "hating" one's life in order to save it for eternal life. To "hate" one's life does not mean despising oneself or one's life as having no value. (In fact, a good deal of spirituality is concerned with accepting one's life as it has been and is likely to remain.) It means living one's present life with an attitude that goes beyond mere self-preservation at all costs (= "loving" one's life). It means being ready to sacrifice one's life (in the Semitic idiom of the gospel, to "hate" it) in the interests of a vision that has gone beyond the horizons of this life to embrace the self-sacrificing life of God. Andrew Lincoln has put this very well:

> In this teaching on discipleship, to save, find or gain one's life is to attempt to live one's life as though one owned it and it is an enterprise doomed to failure because life is a gift from God, who can also take it away. On the other hand, to lose one's life is to renounce the attempt to secure life for oneself and, instead, to spend it in the service of God and others. Those who lose their lives in this way find that they receive those lives back from God.[13]

"Loving" or "hating" one's life in this sense is not something one does alone. The believer adopts this way of life in intimate association with Jesus ("serving" and "following" him), so that where he is, in humiliation and

---

[11] Cf. Andrew T. Lincoln, *St. John*, 350.

[12] Cf. Andrew T. Lincoln, *St. John*, 349; cf. C. H. Dodd: "Without the 'death' of the seed no crop; without the death of Christ, no worldwide gathering of mankind" (*Interpretation*, 372).

[13] Andrew T. Lincoln, *St. John*, 350.

then in glory, there his disciple also will be (v. 26ab; cf. also 14:3; 17:24).[14] Intimate association with Jesus in this way will then lead to the disciple's sharing in the "honor" and glory Jesus receives from the Father on the basis of his obedience and sacrificial love (v. 26c).

Jesus Confronts His Death: 12:27-30

We arrive now at a moment of unique revelation in the gospel. Jesus, who for the most part seems to stride through the narrative like a god on earth, here confesses to disturbance of soul,[15] shrinking in a very human way before the prospect of death. The momentary deliberation, "What shall I say? Father, save me from this hour?"[16] (v. 27a), corresponds to the Gethsemane scene in the Synoptic tradition (cf. esp. Mark 14:36; Matt 26:38-39; Luke 22:41) and the echo of that scene in the Letter to the Hebrews:

> In the days of his flesh, Jesus offered up prayers and supplications, with loud cries and tears, to the one who was able to save him from death, and he was heard because of his reverent submission. (Heb 5:7)

In the Johannine account the moment of hesitation is instantly corrected. Jesus does not pray for rescue.[17] The reason he has "come to this hour" is that the Father's name be glorified, that God's true nature be revealed through the sacrificial love of his death on the cross (v. 27d). Hence the prayer that comes from Jesus' lips is, "Father, glorify your name" (v. 28a)—that is, "Let the process of death in which this revelation will be given go ahead." There is, then, no lingering in hesitation before death as in the Synoptic accounts of the "Agony" (especially Mark and Matthew). But the inclusion of this tradition, with its portrayal of Jesus at his most human, is precious testimony to the Fourth Gospel's sense of the cost to Jesus of his love-inspired contest

---

[14] Cf. the words of Ittai the Gittite to King David, when the king, leaving Jerusalem in the face of the revolt of his son Absalom, urged Ittai to go home to his own people and received the wonderful reply: "As the LORD lives, and as my lord the king lives, wherever my lord the king may be, whether for death or for life, there also will your servant be" (2 Sam 15:21).

[15] The language echoes Ps 42 (LXX 41):6-7, 12.

[16] It is possible to translate the second phrase either as a question (as here) or as a statement, in which case it becomes a real prayer—though one instantly reconsidered. The opening question ("What shall I say?") favors taking the second phrase as part of the question; cf. C. K. Barrett, *John*, 426.

[17] Francis J. Moloney's interpretation of this sentence ("Jesus asks the Father to bring him safely through this hour" [*John*, 353]) seems to force both the sense of "save" and the following preposition "from" (Greek *ek*).

with the powers of sin and darkness.[18] As we have seen, a similar sense of cost emerges from the descriptions of his personal struggle before raising his friend Lazarus.[19] Though otherwise Jesus seems so much in control, the divine love that his entire mission serves is no less a costly love in the Fourth Gospel than in other strands of the New Testament tradition (cf. esp. Rom 8:31-32).

Uniquely in this gospel Jesus' prayer to the Father ("Glorify your name") receives a response. A voice from heaven declares: "I have glorified it, and I will glorify it again" (v. 28b). In the Synoptic tradition, at the transfiguration, a Voice from the cloud confirms Jesus' identity as divine Son and the Father's "pleasure" in him as he begins his journey to Jerusalem to suffer and die (Matt 17:5; Mark 9:7; Luke 9:35). So here the Father's voice confirms that the passion, which Jesus is now directly confronting, will be the moment of his "glorification."[20] The signs (miracles) that Jesus has performed already en route to his "hour" have been anticipations of this revelation of glory (cf. especially 2:11; also 11:40). The supreme revelation is shortly to be given on the cross. That is why the Voice can speak in two tenses: "I have glorified (my Name) and will glorify it."[21]

The crowd, which has been the silent audience to Jesus' revelation since his entry into Jerusalem (cf. vv. 17-18), divides in its reaction to the Voice. Some understand it as thunder, some as an address from an angel. To take it as yet another instance of the Johannine "misunderstanding" motif,[22] is hard to square with Jesus' subsequent remark (v. 30) that the sound was given not for his sake but for "your" sake.[23] Why, knowing that the crowd had failed to understand, would Jesus draw attention to an ineffectual divine communication of this kind? In the biblical tradition thunder is a widespread signal of the presence of God, and angels regularly feature as instruments of divine communication. Both interpretations on the part of the crowd could

---

[18] Cf. Rudolf Schnackenburg, "Even in John the cross has not lost its human darkness" (*St John*, 2:387).

[19] In view of this, I take issue with Gail O'Day who maintains that "an 'agony' scene would make no sense in this gospel" ("The Gospel of John," 712).

[20] Cf. Dorothy A. Lee, *Transfiguration* (New York: Continuum, 2004), 108.

[21] Cf. C. K. Barrett, *John*, 425–26; Andrew T. Lincoln, *St. John*, 351–52. Some interpreters relate the "I have glorified" to the whole compass of Jesus' earthly ministry, up to and including his death, while the future reference refers to the aftermath of that event, especially the drawing of all to himself; cf. Gail O'Day, "The Gospel of John," 712. In John 13:31-32 and 17:1-5, the "moments" of glorification seem to be "collapsed" into a continuum.

[22] So, Francis J. Moloney, *John*, 354.

[23] A difficulty seen by C. K. Barrett, *John*, 426.

signal an awareness that a theophany had taken place, that they were hearing some divine ratification of Jesus' prayer, albeit without full understanding.[24] Rather than an assurance for Jesus, the divine response would then be a sign prompting the crowd to respond with faith to the revelation being given (cf. 11:42).[25]

Jesus' Death as Judgment upon the World: The Urgency of Response: 12:31-36

In a further revelatory dialogue with the crowd Jesus continues to reflect upon his imminent death. The world that "has known him not" (1:10, 11) may be judging and condemning him to death. In that very act it is bringing "judgment" (*krisis* = "condemnation") upon itself and its ruler (Satan) will be "driven out" (v. 31). The presupposition here is that up till this point the human world has been held in the grip of Satan alienated from its Creator.[26] The obedient death of Jesus will break that grip as Satan is condemned and human beings set free for another allegiance, a life-giving allegiance to Jesus as "light" of the world. This allegiance, this "drawing of all" to himself, will come about when Jesus is "lifted up from the earth" (v. 32), a "lifting up" which, as the evangelist in a typical afterthought notes (v. 33), will occur when he suffers death by crucifixion. For those who view it with faith, this mode of execution will be the supreme revelation of God as love.[27] Hence its power to bring about a new allegiance, a "kingdom not of this world" (18:36; cf. 12:19), its rule based not on force or oppression but on the attraction of love.

The crowd rightly understands that the language of "lifting up from the earth" refers to execution (cf. v. 33). This creates for them a problem. Their acclamation at Jesus' entry into Jerusalem showed that they believe Jesus to be the Messiah. Yet their understanding of messiahship has no room for a Messiah who is to suffer and die, let alone suffer death by crucifixion. On

---

[24] I am indebted here to Gail O'Day, "The Gospel of John," 712.

[25] As in the concluding injunction, "Listen to him!" in the Synoptic transfiguration accounts: (Mark 9:7 and parallels).

[26] Cf. Satan's claim in the temptation accounts in Matthew and Luke to be able to deliver to Jesus the allegiance of all the kingdoms of the world and their glory (Matt 4:8-9; Luke 4:5-6).

[27] As in 3:14 and 8:28, the gospel plays upon the ambiguity in "lifting up," whereby it signifies both the physical lifting up involved in execution by crucifixion and the exaltation of Jesus in divine glory. Though human beings will physically "lift up" Jesus upon the cross, in so doing they will be unwitting agents of the Father's exaltation and glorification of Jesus.

the contrary, they have heard "from the law that the Messiah is to remain for ever" (v. 34a).[28] Hence, taking up Jesus' characteristic way of referring to himself as "Son of Man" (cf. v. 23) and seemingly identifying this with "Messiah," they exclaim, "Who is this Son of Man?" (v. 34bc), meaning "What kind of Messiah is this?" Not for the first time in the gospel (7:26-27, 40-42), being locked into a conventional understanding of messiahship inhibits further growth of faith.[29]

Jesus does not address the issue directly but responds with both a warning and an appeal (vv. 35-37). The warning resumes the "light/darkness" duality pervasive in the gospel (3:19-21; 8:12; 9:5; 11:9-10), with particular echoes of the opening verses of the Prologue (1:4-9). Precisely because he will "not remain for ever" Jesus urges his audience to "walk (in faith)" in the "little while" that "the light" is still among them—the Light that is himself (8:12; 9:5).[30] Now that the hour of judgment has come (v. 31), the light that he has personally shone during his ministry is about to be extinguished. Outside the community of faith, the world in which the light has shone for a time will lapse back into the "darkness" of sin and death. If they do not wish to be "captured" by that darkness (cf. 1:5a), not knowing where they are going (cf. 1 John 2:8-11), they must put their faith in the Light while it is still shining (v. 36ab). Exposure to the light, while searching, will not bring condemnation but an experience of salvation that places believers on the "other side" of judgment (3:17-20; 5:24), rendering them "sons (and daughters) of light" (v. 36c).[31]

Having made this appeal, Jesus departs and conceals himself (v. 36d). The language conveys the sense of a light being extinguished—in fact, the extinguishing of the Light. While there will be a further appeal from Jesus at the end of the chapter (12:44-50), it will be more in the nature of a reflection spoken out loud than a direct address to the crowd. Jesus' witness to the wider world has come to an end. The Light no longer shines in the darkness (1:5). From now on, until his very public trial and execution, Jesus will be alone with his disciples (13:1–17:26).

---

[28] "From the law" probably refers to the messianic witness of Scripture (OT) in general. A more specific reference could be the Davidic oracle alluded to in Ps 89 (LXX 88):36-37.

[29] Cf. C. K. Barrett, *John*, 428; Gail O'Day, "The Gospel of John," 713.

[30] Andrew T. Lincoln, *St. John*, 353.

[31] For this expression, uniquely here in John, see Luke 16:8; 1 Thess 5.5 (also Eph 5:8). The expression is a regular self-designation of the Qumran community as reflected especially in the War Scroll: 1QM 1:1, 3, 9, 11, 13, 14; 13:10, 16; 14:17; cf. also: 1QS 2:16; 3:13, 24-25; 4Q280 f2:1; 11Q13 2:8, 22.

4. Concluding Reflections upon Jesus' Witness to Israel: 12:37-50

With Jesus removed from the public scene, the evangelist offers a concluding reflection upon his ministry. To be more precise, what is offered is a theological reflection upon the failure of that ministry in regard to "his own," that is, his own Jewish people. In this sense the conclusion is really a response to the question as to why the statement in the Prologue, "he came unto his own and his own did not receive him" (1:11), has proved true.[32] The conclusion comes in two parts: first (vv. 37-43), the evangelist offers a scripturally based reflection on that failure; then (vv. 44-50) we hear a final appeal and lament from Jesus himself. To the understanding of the conclusion Gail O'Day has very helpfully brought an analogy from the theater: at the end of v. 36 the curtain has come down on the ministry of Jesus; the "playwright" (evangelist) emerges onto the stage and comments directly to the audience (readers) on what has taken place (vv. 37-43); then, with the stage empty and dark, the voice of Jesus is heard from the wings, making a final commentary on the drama (vv. 44-50).[33]

The analogy is helpful but it must be admitted that, compared with the rest of the gospel, this conclusion to the public life probably has little interest for the contemporary reader. The first section rather restrictively reflects concerns of the Johannine community in its own day; the second offers a summary of the main themes of the gospel but nothing that is really new.

The People's Failure to Believe: 12:37-43

It is difficult for us as contemporary readers of the gospel to appreciate how deep a trauma the failure of the bulk of Jewish people to accept Jesus as Messiah inflicted upon the early New Testament communities. The gospel wrestles with this issue from both the strictly theological side (divine intention and action) and that of human response—creating a tension between divine and human responsibility that is hard for us to grapple with today.

The reflection opens (v. 37) with a bald statement of the issue: despite all the "signs" Jesus had worked in their sight, the people had not come to faith in him. This negative response could lead to Jesus' entire ministry being construed as a failure on the part of the Father who sent him. To counter such a view the evangelist cites two texts from the prophet Isaiah (Isa 53:1 in v. 38; Isa 6:9-10 in v. 40). The first, from early in the Fourth Servant Song

---

[32] Cf. Francis J. Moloney, *John*, 368.
[33] Gail O'Day, "The Gospel of John," 718.

(Isa 52:13–53:12), sees the failure of Jesus' message to "get through" fore-shadowed in the prophet's own experience and therefore incorporated into the sweep of the divine plan of salvation. The second attributes the failure to a divine action of "blinding" and "hardening" that rendered such belief in fact "impossible" (v. 39).[34] We encounter here once again the standard biblical recourse to divine predestination to explain painful or difficult events or situations that we would more naturally attribute to failure on the human side alone. The explanation is doubly difficult in this instance since what is being proposed is not just divine foresight but divine causality in bringing about the failure to believe. Moreover, in contrast to Paul's recourse to the same motif in Romans 9-11, there is no explicit suggestion here that such a "hardening" may be a temporary measure, brought in for a salvific purpose (the conversion of the Gentiles) and ultimately to be reversed (Rom 11:25-26). Nonetheless, the evangelist may intend us to hear a glimmer of hope in that direction in the final positive phrase of the text "and I would heal them."

A typical Johannine afterthought (v. 41) attributes the prescience of the Isaiah texts to the fact that, like Abraham according to 8:56-68, the prophet "saw" the glory of Christ. The allusion would seem to be to the prophet's vision of divine glory as described earlier in Isaiah 6 (vv. 1-5): since Christ as preexistent Logos shared the glory of God (1:1, 14; 17:5), all visions of God's glory were also visions of the glory of Christ.[35]

This reprising of the motif of "glory" (*doxa*) prepares the way for a final reflection upon unbelief that turns now from divine action and intent to focus upon human response (vv. 42-43). The evangelist notes that "many of the leaders" (of the Jewish community) believed in Jesus but did not express their inner conviction in outward profession for fear of expulsion from the synagogue on the part of the Pharisees. The explanation clearly reflects the situation of the evangelist's own time rather than that of Jesus, when the successors of the Pharisees were in the ascendant and called the shots as far as social inclusion or exclusion was concerned. A faith based merely on "signs" was inadequate to sustain the demands of real disciple-ship, the "hating one's life" in order to "find" it in companionship with Jesus (12:25-26).

---

[34] This text from Isaiah appears widely across the New Testament tradition to deal with the problem of Jewish failure to believe in Jesus: Mark 4:17-18 (parallels: Matt 13:14-15; Luke 8:10); Acts 28:26-27; Rom 11:8. In quoting Isa 6:9-10 here the Fourth Gospel eliminates the references to "hearing" in the original in order, characteristically, to place all emphasis upon the motifs of "seeing" and "knowing"; cf. Gail O'Day, "The Gospel of John," 716–17.

[35] Cf. Andrew T. Lincoln, *St. John*, 358.

An ambiguity latent in the Greek word *doxa*—"glory"/"reputation" enables the evangelist to offer a final comment upon this inadequate belief (v. 43). These half-believers loved "the glory" (*doxa*) of human beings rather than the glory of God. The explanation conjures up the whole vision of the gospel. The entire mission of Christ represents an invasion of divine glory into the human sphere in order to hold out to human beings the prospect of sharing in life "from above" which is the "eternal life" of God. True faith opens itself up to this divine reality and the transformation it requires. Lack of faith or inadequate faith fails to be open to this divine dimension and remains on the purely "horizontal" level of human affairs where the values of power and prestige, honor and shame prevail and are inevitably oppressive. Enclosed within this limited world, unbelief is unable to live life here and now with the enrichment that comes from the divinely expansive offer of life.[36]

A Last Appeal from Jesus: 12:44-50

Jesus has already withdrawn from public view (v. 36). Though couched as a dramatic appeal ("Jesus cried out" [v. 44]), this concluding passage does not really advance the action or develop the theology of the gospel. Detached from time, space, and audience, it offers a resume of major themes in a way that corresponds to and forms something of an inclusion with the Prologue.[37] It begins (vv. 44-45) and ends (vv. 49-50) with Jesus insisting upon his unity with the Father, as he has done throughout the narrative. To believe in him is to believe in the One who sent him; to see him is to see the One who sent him—that is, to see the "unseeable" God (cf. 1:18; 14:9). He has come into the world as its "light" (v. 46; cf. 8:12), so that the one who believes in him does not remain in the "darkness" of sin and death that otherwise prevails therein.

The central sentences of the passage (vv. 47-48) take up the theme of "judgment," "the dark, reverse side of God's eschatological act of love and redemption."[38] As stated so clearly in 3:16-21, Jesus insists that he has come to "save" rather than judge (= "condemn") the world. He has come to save the world by speaking to it the words of life. But if those words are simply heard and not "kept," his word (*logos*), instead of giving life, becomes itself an instrument of condemnation. Here again we meet the Johannine sense

---

[36] Cf. Francis J. Moloney, *John*, 364–65.

[37] Cf. Andrew T. Lincoln, *St. John*, 361; Gail O'Day, "The Gospel of John," 717.

[38] Rudolf Schnackenburg, *St. John*, 1:401.

that human beings determine their judgment, both present and to come, by the attitude they adopt—acceptance or rejection—to Jesus as the revelation of God. To believe in and see him is to believe in and see God (vv. 44-45), and through this vision come to share, here and now, the divine "eternal life" (v. 50).

This résumé of the major themes of the Prologue closes off the account of Jesus' public witness to "the world," represented by "his own," that is, his own people, "the Jews." From now on he will have no dealings with the world until representatives of its rulers come in the darkness of night with swords, clubs, and lanterns to arrest him. "His own" are now restricted to the chosen band of disciples whom, in the intimacy of a shared meal, he will address at length, preparing them for their future mission to the world in extension of his own mission from the Father.

THE "HOUR" OF GLORIFICATION:
THE DISCIPLES' FUTURE MISSION:
13:1–21:25

The Last Supper: 13:1–17:26

Introduction to John 13–17

At the beginning of John 13 we move across a major division into what is generally regarded as the second half of the gospel: from the "Book of Signs" that anticipate the glorification of Jesus to the "Book of Glory" in which that glorification is arrived at and described. As we have seen, the culminating "sign," the raising of Lazarus, has triggered the hostility that will prove fatal to Jesus (11:1-54), while the arrival of the Greeks has indicated the imminence of the "hour" of glorification (12:20-36).

The transition to the "Book of Glory" is not, then, sudden or unprepared for. What is new is a change of audience. Up till this point Jesus has basically addressed "his own" in the sense of his own people, the Jews (1:11a). They have been the representatives of "the world" that God has so loved and sent the Son to save (3:16-17). For the most part, as we have been reminded over and over (2:23-24; 6:66; 12:37-43), they have either rejected his witness outright or responded with a far from adequate faith. As foreseen in the Prologue, "He came to what was his own, and his own people did not accept him" (1:11). From this point on, "his own" will be restricted to the band of disciples that have remained with him. Aside from interaction with those who arrest and put him on trial, they, not the outside world, will be his audience.

The change of audience also introduces a marked change of tone. The sharpness and polemic that has largely colored Jesus' discourse with "the Jews" gives way to an intrafamilial intimacy in the closed context of a farewell meal (chapters 13–17). There is a "horizontal" intimacy between Jesus and his chosen disciples. There is also and more fundamentally a "vertical" intimacy between Jesus and the Father, an intimacy into which the disciples are being drawn as God's "children," "born, not of blood or of the will of the flesh or of the will of man, but of God" (1:13). Jesus' sharing with the disciples the intimacy of his relationship with the Father lends the material in John 13–17 a sublimity of tone and content unparalleled in the biblical tradition.

The sequence set in the context of the final supper breaks down into three main units:

1. The Footwashing and Following Dialogue: 13:1-30

2. Jesus' Farewell Discourse: 13:31–16:33[1]

3. Jesus' Prayer to the Father: 17:1-26

The long discourse (13:31–16:33) itself falls into three sections: (A) an initial discourse (13:31–14:31) terminated by Jesus' command to rise and depart (14:31); (B) a central bloc (15:1–16:4a), where Jesus, through the image of the vine, first urges the disciples to "abide in his love" (15:1-17) and then warns them about the hatred and persecution they will incur from the world (15:18–16:4a); and (C) a second version of the initial discourse, in somewhat more negative tone (16:4b-33). If we allow the discourse proper to be broken up into these three elements, then the entire sequence at the Supper falls into five major blocks of roughly similar lengths, which can be set out as in the chart appearing on page 227. We can note that, according to this structure, the centerpiece of the whole is Jesus' instruction to "abide" in his love based upon the image of himself as "the true Vine" (with the experience of divine and human love within the community being matched by the contrary experience of hatred and persecution from "the world"). The second and fourth elements relate to each other as the two parallel versions of the discourse proper, while the two outer sections (the footwashing and Jesus' prayer to the Father) each in its own way, begin and conclude the entire sequence. I am not suggesting that these divisions are in any sense watertight compartments or silos: themes and motifs appear and reappear across them quite freely. I put forward this structure as an aid to getting some purchase upon this large block within the gospel.

---

[1] Some interpreters (e.g., Francis J. Moloney, *John*, 371; Gail O'Day, "The Gospel of John," 731) link 13:31-38 with the footwashing and its aftermath, beginning the discourse at 14:1. In my view the departure of Judas on his errand creates the new atmosphere for the discourse, suggesting that it is better to associate vv. 31-38 with what follows than with what precedes; so, Raymond E. Brown, *John XIII–XXI*, 608–9; C. K. Barrett, *John*, 449; Andrew T. Lincoln, *St. John*, 386.

Structure of John 13–17

```
                    ┌─────────────────────────────────┐
                    │  Discourse B: 15:1-16:4a:        │
                    │                                  │
                    │  "Abide in my Love": 15:1-17//   │
                    │  The World's Hatred: 15:18–16:4a │
                    └─────────────────────────────────┘


     ┌──────────────────┐              ┌──────────────────┐
     │  Discourse A:     │              │  Discourse C:    │
     │  13:31–14:31      │              │  16:4b-33        │
     └──────────────────┘              └──────────────────┘


┌──────────────────────┐              ┌──────────────────────┐
│  Footwashing &        │              │  Jesus' Prayer to    │
│  Following Dialogue:   │              │  the Father:         │
│  13:1-30              │              │  17:1-26             │
└──────────────────────┘              └──────────────────────┘
```

The entire scene takes place at an evening meal just before the Passover—though, in contrast to the Synoptic tradition, Jesus is not celebrating the Passover meal with his disciples.[2] In the Johannine chronology Jesus dies on the day before Passover ("Passover Preparation Day" [19:14, 31, 42]) just as the Passover lambs were being slain in the temple in preparation for the celebration of the Passover meal the following evening. Theologically, it is more important for John that Jesus dies as the Passover Lamb than that the meal be a Passover meal. This may also explain the absence of a eucharistic institution narrative from the gospel's account of the Supper. If the eucharistic institution tradition was strictly tied to the celebration of the Supper as a Passover meal, then its inclusion would have "disturbed" the Johannine chronology. It is relocated, then, to the earlier Passover context of John 6, where other rich overtones, notably connection with the gift of the manna and the life-giving Word of Jesus come into play—though the link to Jesus' death, so central to the Synoptic accounts and Paul (1 Cor 11:26), is not entirely absent (6:51c).

---

[2] In relation to days of the week the Synoptic and Johannine chronologies cohere: Jesus dies on the Friday, remains buried on Saturday, and appears as risen Lord on Sunday. The difference is that the Passover is located one day earlier (Thursday evening to Friday evening) in the Synoptic tradition, making the Supper a Passover meal. In John the Passover, falling on Saturday, coincides with the celebration of the Sabbath, which would explain why "that sabbath was a day of great solemnity" (19:31). See the helpful chronological chart set out by Gail O'Day, "The Gospel of John," 704–5.

1. The Footwashing and Following Dialogue: 13:1-30

We now enter upon the heart of the Fourth Gospel. In the symbolic action of washing his disciples' feet Jesus points to his coming death on Calvary as the supreme revelation of God as love. The solemnity communicated by the long Greek sentences with which the account of the supper begins is masked in more recent English translations. Breaking down the overladen Greek clauses into separate sentences makes for clarity and ease of reading. At the same time it frustrates the effect of the original which in two great sentences (vv. 1, 2-5) sweeps from Jesus' eternal origins with the Father to the concrete act—in human terms a servile act—of washing other people's feet. To catch the extraordinary revelation of God—"God at our feet"—in this gesture it is important to know that the first main statement ("he rose from supper") comes at the end of a string of participial phrases setting this action within wider cosmic conflict between God and Satan. The Fourth Gospel's presentation of God is nowhere more incarnational than in this scene.

The Footwashing: 13:1-5

The long opening sentence (v. 1) really serves as an introduction to the Supper sequence as a whole. It reminds us of the imminence of Passover, the festival in which Jesus will die as Passover Lamb (19:36). It tells of his "knowledge" that the hour had finally arrived for his passing from this world to the Father and presents that passing as the climactic expression of the love that has prompted his mission from the start. Jesus loves "his own" in the world "to the end" (*eis telos*) both in the qualitative sense of having loved them to the uttermost and also in the sense of loving them to the "end" of his life when he will expire with the words "It is accomplished" on his lips (19:30).[3]

In another sense that will not be the end of his love since "his own" will continue after his death not only in the immediate disciples with whom he is now supping but in those who will later become "his own" through their witness and word (17:20). We touch here upon the two main themes of the entire discourse to follow: (1) the departure of Jesus and the situation of the disciples in the following time; and (2) the readying of the disciples for that time—particularly in the sense that their mutual love for one another will have to fill the void of palpable love created by the physical absence of

---

[3] Cf. Raymond E. Brown, *John XIII–XXI*, 550.

Jesus. He is physically departing "from this world," but the divine love with which he has "so loved the world" will not cease in the world but continue in the love of "his own" in and for the world.

Against this supreme expression of divine love runs the counter current of demonic hostility that will bring Jesus to his death (v. 2). The devil has already induced one of Jesus' own companions here at table, Judas the son of Simon Iscariot, to betray him,[4] thereby solving the authorities' problem of getting their hands on Jesus quietly. Jesus has hinted at this prospect of treachery before (6:70). Now it will penetrate the intimacy of the shared meal as one of the Twelve becomes Satan's tool to bring Jesus down. Nonetheless, in a supreme display of divine love, Judas the betrayer will have his feet washed along with the others.

That guests at a dinner should have their feet washed was a customary expression of hospitality at the time—though normally it would take place before the meal began rather than in the course of it, as seems to be the case here.[5] Usually, too, it was a service provided by servants or slaves rather than by the host. Here, it is undertaken not only by the host but by One conscious of his divine origins and destination ("that he had come from God and was going to God"), and that what he was about to do was in every respect an enactment of his mission from the Father ("that the Father had given all things into his hands"). The direct movement from this solemn reminder of Jesus' origins and mission (v. 3) to the concrete actions of the footwashing (vv. 4-5) sets in stark juxtaposition divine status, on the one hand, and the human at its most humble and lowly, on the other. Rising from the table, Jesus departs from the privileged position of those who are being served. Laying aside his outer garment, he leaves himself dressed like a slave in a loincloth, save for a towel with which he girds himself for the work. Unassisted, he procures water, pours it into a basin, and begins to wash the feet of his disciples, ending by drying them with the towel wrapped around his waist.

There is no parallel in extant ancient literature for a person of superior status voluntarily washing the feet of someone of inferior status.[6] The whole

---

[4] One variant in the awkward Greek original of this sentence could convey the sense of the devil putting it into his own heart (i.e., deciding) that Judas should betray Jesus; so C. K. Barrett, *John*, 439; Francis J. Moloney, *John*, 378. In favor of the more usually adopted sense of the devil putting it into Judas's heart, see Raymond E. Brown, *John XIII–XXI*, 550.

[5] That is, reading the Greek present participle *ginomenou* rather than the aorist variant *genomenou*, which would suggest that the supper was already over; see C. K. Barrett, *John*, 439.

[6] Cf. Andrew T. Lincoln, *St John*, 367.

force of the episode is undercut unless its singular assault on the social categories of the time is noted.[7] Blending humble service and loving intimacy, it is a perfect enactment in Johannine terms of the opening stanza of the hymn quoted by Paul in his letter to the Philippians:

> Though he was in the form of God,
> [Christ] did not regard equality with God
> as something to be exploited,
> but emptied himself,
> taking the form of a slave. (Phil 2:6-7)[8]

Both Paul and John are at one in portraying divinity expressed in lowliness and humble service.

The Dialogue with Peter: 13:6-11

Peter reacts with astonishment and resistance when Jesus approaches to wash his feet: "Lord, are you going to wash my feet?" (v. 6). Jesus' reply (v. 7) to the effect that, while Peter may not understand now, he will understand later, coheres with similar statements in 2:22 (cleansing of the temple) and 12:16 (entry into Jerusalem on an ass): the full meaning of what he is doing now will only become apparent in the light of his death and resurrection. The footwashing and the cross will mutually illuminate each other as the supreme revelation of divine love expressed as service.

Instead of asking what it is he does not understand, Peter simply persists in his refusal (v. 8a). He cannot accept the reversal of values—the lord performing the service of a slave—that the footwashing implies.[9] Jesus, however, insists (v. 8b) that if Peter does not allow him to wash his feet, he will have no "share" (Greek *meros*) with him. This last phrase can be understood in two ways. With the footwashing seen as anticipating Jesus' salvific death on the cross, the meaning could be that Peter, like all human beings, needs to undergo the "cleansing" from sin achieved by the "Lamb of God, who takes away the sin of the world" (1:29; cf. 20:23). "Share" on this understanding would have the sense of a share in the eternal life won for

---

[7] That Jewish, as distinct from Gentile, slaves could not be required to wash their master's feet (cf. C. K. Barrett, *John*, 440) only serves to bring out the singularity of Jesus' action.

[8] Cf. Andrew T. Lincoln, *St. John*, 367.

[9] "To accept his service means . . . readiness to accept the disintegration of all the standards which the world uses to judge what is great and divine" (Rudolf Bultmann, *Gospel of John*, 471).

human beings by Jesus' suffering and death.[10] While such an understanding can hardly be ruled out, the intimacy of the occasion and the distinctive word "share" suggest a broader sense of fellowship with Jesus: that is, an appropriation of the values expressed in the footwashing in order to share the mission that will culminate in the divine "service" of the cross.[11] Allowing Jesus to wash his feet means for Peter the kind of involvement expressed earlier in the gospel:

> Whoever serves me must follow me, and where I am, there will my servant be also. Whoever serves me, the Father will honor. (John 12:26)

Still uncomprehending, Peter now (v. 9) goes to the opposite extreme, insisting that Jesus should wash not only his feet but his hands and head as well.[12] Jesus dismisses the suggestion with an image from everyday life (v. 10a): in the course of a day a person who has bathed has no need to bathe all over again; only the sandaled feet, in contact with the dusty and dirty streets, may need to be washed again. The disciples have already been made clean (= "bathed") by means of the word that they have continually heard from Jesus (cf. 15:3: "You have already been cleansed by the word that I have spoken to you"). What they need in addition is to appropriate the values, expressed in the footwashing. This will equip them to understand the "service" of Jesus on the cross and to embody his self-sacrificial love in their ongoing life in community and mission. Since—with one exception (v. 10b)—they are all clean there is no need for Peter or the others to submit to further cleansing beyond the washing of their feet.[13]

---

[10] Cf. C. K. Barrett, *John*, 441; Raymond E. Brown, *John XIII–XXI*, 568; Francis J. Moloney, *John*, 375. Though the community behind the Fourth Gospel was presumably familiar with baptism as a Christian rite of initiation, an allusion to the sacrament is hardly to the fore in the footwashing episode—and, as Brown points out, interpretation of Jesus' action along these lines has minimal support in the early Christian tradition.

[11] Cf. Andrew T. Lincoln, *St. John*, 367–68. As will appear later, this interpretation makes for a more integrated interpretation of 13:1-20 as a whole.

[12] His response is reminiscent of the similarly misguided suggestion of the Samaritan woman in 4:15.

[13] There is a major textual issue in v. 10a. The interpretation I have adopted (with considerable indebtedness to Andrew T. Lincoln [*St. John*, 363–64, 369–71]) rests on favoring the "longer reading," with most standard translations (NRSV, NIV, NAB, etc). A shorter reading, omitting the phrase "except for the feet" (Greek: *ei mē tous podas*), appears in some early manuscripts, and is adopted by most commentators on the basis that the inclusion of the phrase, in some conflict with Jesus' statement in v. 8b, renders the footwashing comparatively less important. The short reading, however, wrongly conflates the meaning of two Greek verbs— *louein* (= "bathe" [the entire body]) and *niptein* (= "wash" [a part of the body])—that are

The "exception" of course is Judas. Jesus does not "out" him at this point but simply leaves the enigmatic exception hanging in the air. The evangelist, ever eager to underline Jesus' full knowledge of the situation (cf. 13:1, 3), unnecessarily yet characteristically adds an explanatory comment to this effect (v. 11). We are reminded of the hostile counter current running against the expression of divine love. Judas has his feet washed but remains unmoved.

The Footwashing as Example of Love: 13:12-17

The scene that follows (vv. 12-17) may appear something of a letdown after the moving portrayal of Jesus on his hands and knees washing his disciples' feet. It seems to drain life out of that sublime act by interpreting it simply as a moral lesson for imitation. For this reason it has often been regarded as a later addition in the interests of ethical exhortation rather than theological understanding.[14]

Closer inspection shows it to be continuous with the footwashing that has just occurred. After resuming his outer clothing and place at table, Jesus begins to educate the disciples on the meaning of what he has done (v. 12). Imitation presupposes understanding. Jesus has to ensure that the disciples see the full symbolic meaning of his action and not remain, like Peter, fixated upon the concrete act alone. The sequence of statements in vv. 13-16 is somewhat out of kilter with the logic being developed, which seems to run as follows. The disciples call Jesus "Teacher" and "Lord" and rightly so, for that is what he is (v. 13). Yet (an implied rather than expressed premise), despite this exalted status, he has performed the humble, loving service of washing feet. Since a slave is not greater than his master, nor one who is sent (literally, "apostle") greater than the one who sends (v. 16),[15] they (the disciples) ought to be prepared to act as he has done: to wash each other's feet (v. 14).

While this injunction has been understood literally—and indeed in some Christian traditions acted out liturgically (at the celebration of the

---

otherwise invariably distinct. It is easier to explain the omission of the phrase on the basis of its apparent conflict with the final statement of being "clean all over" (v. 10c), rather than to explain its addition, which is usually done on the basis of strongly "baptismal" interpretation of "washing" in the text (sometimes with the statement about washing the feet seen as referring to the sacrament of penance). See further, Bruce M. Metzger, *Textual Commentary*, 240.

[14] Cf. Raymond E. Brown, *John XIII–XXI*, 462; Rudolf Schnackenburg, *St. John*, 3:23.

[15] Cf. Matt 10:24-25; Luke 6:40.

Lord's Supper on Holy Thursday)—the whole intent of Jesus is to instruct the disciples on the symbolic meaning of his act. He describes it (v. 15) as an "example" (Greek *hypodeigma*), that is, as something to be imitated not primarily or solely in literal terms but in any expression of the principle it enshrines: the radical reversal of social status and advantage in such display of self-sacrificing love. The footwashing anticipates Jesus' death upon the cross as a supreme divine expression of such love. It serves as an "example," which the disciples will be "blessed" to follow (v. 17) when they display similar self-sacrificial love in mutual service—even, in times of persecution, to the point of laying down their lives for one another, as he will lay down his life for them (15:13; cf. 1 John 3:16).[16]

Understanding the footwashing symbolically in this way holds together both the "soteriological" aspect that is particularly conspicuous in vv. 2-11 and the "exemplary" aspect more pronounced in vv. 12-17, thus preserving unity across the sequence.[17] It also prepares the way for a major theme of the entire discourse to follow (13:31–17:26): that the disciples' love for one another must, in the coming time of his physical absence, become the palpable replacement of the love they have received from him in extension of the love that he continuously receives from the Father.

The "beatitude" pronounced in v. 17 upon those who understand the meaning of Jesus' action and reproduce it in their lives reminds him once again of the presence of one whom it does not include (vv. 18-19). He has chosen them with full knowledge of their weaknesses as well as their qualities (v. 18b). This knowledge includes awareness that one of them will, through betrayal, fulfill a prophetic statement in one of the Psalms (v. 18cd): "The one who ate my bread has lifted his heel against me" (Ps 41[LXX 40]:10).[18] Jesus mentions (v. 19) this now before it happens, so that when it does, they may believe "that I am" (*hoti egō eimi*).

Appeal to this particular psalm underlines the sense of betrayal, not by an enemy, but by a member of his intimate band.[19] Beyond this is also the

---

[16] R. Alan Culpepper, "The Johannine *Hypodeigma*: A Reading of John 13," *Semeia* 53 (1991): 133–52, points to the sense of "exemplary death" that attends the word *hypodeigma* in Hellenistic Jewish texts; cf. also Francis J. Moloney, *John*, 376.

[17] Cf. Andrew T. Lincoln, *St. John*, 375–76.

[18] To turn away and lift one's heel against a person is a notable gesture of insult and contempt in Mediterranean culture; cf. Raymond E. Brown, *John XIII–XXI*, 554; Andrew T. Lincoln, *St. John*, 373.

[19] Cf. Gail O'Day, "The Gospel of John," 726. There is also perhaps an implicit hint in the reference to "eating my bread" that Judas has partaken in the eucharistic bread, the institution of which is not otherwise described in the account of the Last Supper. It is possible that the

sense that Jesus chose Judas with full prescience of his betrayal precisely so that the psalm verse would be fulfilled. The Psalms, traditionally attributed to David, were regarded as prophecies providing the "script" for the Messiah, David's son. When, in light of Jesus' explanation here, the disciples come to see this psalm fulfilled in the betrayal, passion, and death, those terrible events, rather than weakening their faith, will actually confirm it.[20] They will come to believe that he is the One of whom the Psalmist (David) spoke, that is, the Messiah—but, as the full resonance of the formula "I am" (*egō eimi*) suggests (cf. 8:24, 28), not merely the Messiah of conventional expectation but the unique revelation of the unseen God (cf. Isa 43:10).

The exhortation ends (v. 20) with a solemn (cf. "Amen, Amen") statement to the effect that the person who "receives" (presumably by faith) the witness of those (the disciples) whom Jesus sends, receives Jesus, and, beyond Jesus, the Father.[21] What prompts the inclusion of this (at first sight irrelevant) assertion is probably the sense of revelation of God contained in the "I am" claim just voiced. Jesus, who is the revelation of the Father, has chosen the disciples present at the Supper to be instruments through whom that revelation will continue after he has returned to the Father. They will be effective witnesses to that revelation when they understand how the footwashing discloses its meaning and when they reproduce in their love for each other the sacrificial love of Jesus that it embodies (v. 17). Yes, they are weak and frail—and one of them is about to be disclosed as a traitor. Yet it is they whom he has chosen, with full foreknowledge and intent, to be his witnesses before the world.[22]

The Traitor Revealed: 13:21-30

From the beginning of the Supper we have been aware of the presence of treachery in the person of Judas, one of the Twelve (v. 2). Jesus has hinted darkly of this presence to his disciples (vv. 10, 18-19). Now (v. 21), with strong emotion ("troubled in spirit") and deliberation ("Amen, Amen, I say to you"), he brings it out into the open: "One of you will betray me."

---

explicitly eucharistic section of the Bread of Life discourse, 6:51-58, originally stood in this context, with which it seems to have notable association: the verb *trōgein* appears four times in 6:54 and 56, and elsewhere only in this quotation in 13:18; the scriptural text as quoted by John has changed the plural "loaves" of the LXX to the singular "loaf" (*arton*); and shortly after 6:51-58 follows the first allusion to the betrayal in the gospel: 6:70-71; cf. Raymond E. Brown, *John XIII–XXI*, 571; C. K. Barrett, *John*, 445; Francis J. Moloney, *John*, 381.

[20] Cf. C. K. Barrett, *John*, 444.

[21] There is a parallel in Matt 10:40.

[22] Cf. Francis J. Moloney, *John*, 380.

Jesus' strength of feeling recalls his emotion prior to the raising of Lazarus (11:33; also 12:27). Here, it seems to be an expression of anguish and frustrated love. He has washed the disciples' feet in symbolic anticipation of laying down his life for them. Yet one of the chosen band gathered here remains not only untouched by the gesture but fixed in his determination to be the instrument of the force (Satan) ranged against him. Impotent to bring about conversion, divine love is at its most vulnerable here and yet is not withdrawn. Judas, along with the others, will be loved "to the end" (cf. v. 1).

Rather than being seated at table, those present at the supper are reclining, resting on their left arm. Reclining in this way immediately on Jesus' right is a disciple previously unmentioned but destined to be a leading character in the events of Jesus' death and risen life. Never named, he is simply described as "the disciple whom Jesus loved" (v. 23). Jesus loves all the disciples (13:1) but this disciple enjoys a special intimacy signaled here by physical closeness described literally as "lying in Jesus' bosom (*kolpos*)." The description recalls the end of the Prologue where the Son is said to be "ever turned towards the bosom (*kolpos*) of the Father" (1:18). In other words, the disciple whom Jesus loves is said here to be in the same relationship with Jesus as Jesus is, eternally, with the Father. The chain of intimacy so established[23] is of great significance for subsequent generations of believers. As will appear later on, the Beloved Disciple (as we may call him) is their representative in the saving events of Jesus' death and resurrection soon to unfold: through his witness they participate in these events, sharing in the chain of intimacy with the divine symbolized by his position in the "bosom" of Jesus.

Amidst the general consternation evoked by Jesus' pronouncement (v. 22), Peter, characteristically, takes the initiative. Reclining too distant from Jesus to put the question himself, he motions to the disciple to take advantage of his closeness to Jesus to find out the identity of the betrayer (v. 24).[24] This the disciple, leaning back against Jesus' chest (*stēthos*), proceeds to do (v. 25).

---

[23] The intimacy is unfortunately masked by leading English translations, which, perhaps fearful of any homoerotic overtones raised by translating "bosom" literally, make do with pallid generalizations: "reclining next to him" (NRSV, NIV); "reclining at Jesus' side" (NAB), so undermining the link with 1:18. Not so the KJV: "leaning on Jesus' bosom"!

[24] The verb *neuein*, translated "motions" (with NRSV), indicates nonverbal communication. On the likely arrangement of the disciples at the meal, see Raymond E. Brown, *John XIII–XXI*, 574.

Jesus does not give a direct answer but instead makes a symbolic gesture, preceded by an explanation, which should reveal to the disciple the identity of the traitor (v. 26). To take a morsel (*psōmion*), dip it into sauce, and hand it to a guest is a Middle Eastern gesture of honor and affection.[25] When Jesus takes the morsel[26] and hands it to Judas Iscariot with an accompanying explanation, that should have revealed, at least to the disciple, the identity of the traitor in their midst. Oddly, he takes no preventative action. His role in the narrative is primarily that of witness (cf. 19:35)—to be the one through whose reliable testimony subsequent generations gain access to what is taking place.[27]

The outreach of love enacted in the gift of the morsel is rebuffed. Judas remains unmoved. After—we should probably say, despite—his taking the morsel "Satan enters into him" (v. 27a), making him entirely the instrument of the powers of darkness. Frustrated in this final appeal, Jesus can only tell him to quickly go about his treacherous design (v. 27b). Once again, we come face-to-face with the curious blend of human freedom and divine control pervasive in the gospel. Judas has freely chosen his role—why, we do not know.[28] He has become the tool of Satan, yet his plan as such to encompass Jesus' death is held within a wider divine purpose to rescue human beings from Satan's grip. It is to progress that saving purpose that Jesus instructs Judas to go quickly about his errand.

The remaining disciples do not understand what is going on (v. 28). Two interpretations of Jesus' words are suggested. Since Judas holds the common purse, perhaps he is being instructed to buy necessities for the celebration of the feast or else to have something to give to the poor (particularly appropriate at the festival time [v. 29]). Though wrong, the interpretations explain the disciples' inaction in regard to Judas. The first serves to keep the Passover context in mind, while the second reminds us of Judas' self-serving protest at the loving action of Mary in anointing Jesus' feet (12:4-6).

Taking the morsel (v. 30a), Judas leaves the supper. His departure marks the beginning of "night" (v. 30b)—not only in a physical sense but, within the Johannine symbolism, the darkness of unbelief and hostility to God. The

---

[25] Ibid., 578.

[26] The reference to "taking" the morsel is textually uncertain, possibly reflecting an addition to the original under the influence of the tradition recording the eucharistic gestures of Jesus.

[27] Cf. Andrew T. Lincoln, *St. John*, 381.

[28] There are hints that the Fourth Gospel is aware that avarice played its part (as explicitly in Matt 26:14-16): Judas keeps the common purse (13:29a); he protests at the waste of the ointment Mary uses to anoint Jesus' feet (12:4-6).

"Light" (Jesus) has shone in the darkness. The darkness has not overcome it (1:5). But the shining of the Light is now restricted to the Supper where Jesus is alone with his remaining disciples. Outside, there is only darkness, of which Judas is now completely a part.

2. Jesus' Farewell Discourse: 13:31–16:33

The long discourse that Jesus speaks to his remaining disciples in the course of the Supper, for all its high theological moments, is not easy to get a handle on as a whole. It is rambling and repetitive, and contains internal contradictions. At one point (14:31) Jesus announces that the company is to depart and be on its way, only to resume the discourse much as before.[29] Elaborate theories of displacements and sources have been evolved to explain the composite and disparate nature of the discourse.[30] It is not my intention to go into such historical explanations here but rather to take the discourse as a continuous whole and attempt to find a pathway through it.

Before entering into the discourse, it will help to be aware that it falls into a literary genre well-known from other parts of the Bible: that of the "Farewell Discourse." In such a discourse a significant leader or teacher gives instruction to disciples just prior to death. The revered figure looks beyond his or her own death to the future awaiting the disciples, foreseeing the troubles and temptations that will inevitably arise, and offering appropriate warning and encouragement. The heightened emotional tone stemming from the imminence of death makes the discourse an effective means of reviewing and consolidating key concerns of the author, in this case the evangelist. The entire book of Deuteronomy is a farewell discourse pronounced by Moses before he dies on the threshold of the Promised Land. An outstanding New Testament example is Paul's address to the elders of Ephesus in Acts 20:18-35.

The device of a Farewell Discourse means that the instruction Jesus gives operates on two time levels. The discourse transports the reader back to the setting of the Supper at the close of Jesus' earthly life. But what is principally in view is the situation of the disciples after his departure to the Father. He speaks of "going away" and "returning" in a little while. At the time level of the Supper, "going away" refers to the departure from the present life he is about to undergo in dying on the cross; three days later he

---

[29] An older view that we are to understand Jesus as speaking the latter part of the discourse (15:1–17:26) on the way to Gethsemane is now largely discredited.

[30] For a survey see Raymond E. Brown, *John XIII–XXI*, 583–97.

will "return" to the disciples when he appears to them as risen Lord. On a broader level when Jesus speaks of "going away" he means his departure in the more lasting sense of his postresurrection ascension to the Father (20:17), from which time the disciples will be bereft of his physical presence. Corresponding to departure in this sense, there is to some degree, as in the Synoptic tradition, the sense of a "return" on his part at the end of time. More prominent, however, is a sense of Jesus' "return" in the form of his abiding presence as living Lord within the community of believers.[31] The device of the Farewell Address enables them to be assured that all they are experiencing and enduring in the time of his physical absence has been foreseen by Jesus and provided for by the Father, especially through the gift of "another Comforter," the Paraclete Spirit (14:16). As we read the various sections of the discourse we have to be aware that it oscillates between the two time levels, making Jesus' more imminent departure and return (in death and resurrection) a foreshadowing and indeed a paradigm of his more fundamental departure and return spanning the time of the church.[32]

Discourse A: *Jesus Is Going to Depart (1): 13:31–14:31*

The opening section of the discourse, 13:31-38, introduces two main themes that will run through the sequence as whole: (1) the departure of Jesus in the time to come; (2) the mutual love that members of the community must show toward one another in strict continuity with the love they have received from Jesus. The main body, 14:1-31, displays a changing pattern of interwoven themes, all revolving around the theme of Jesus' departure. It is not easily divided, though there appear to be transition points at vv. 15 and 25 just before a reference to the Paraclete Spirit in each case. Accordingly, I shall treat the material in four blocks: 13:31-38; 14:1-14; 14:15-24; 14:25-31, with headings indicating more minor divisions within them.

Introduction: Jesus Is Going Away: 13:31-38

The Coming "Glorification" of the Son: 13:31-33. One senses a palpable sigh of relief following the departure of Judas into the "night" (v. 31a; cf. v. 30). Jesus is now alone with disciples who, for all their weakness—soon to be exposed—are, in intention at least, basically loyal and devoted. The

---

[31] The discourse holds together both the future and present ("realized") aspects of Jesus' "return" in a way characteristic of the eschatology of the Fourth Gospel; cf. C. K. Barrett, *John*, 455.

[32] Cf. Andrew T. Lincoln, *St. John* 385–86.

traitor's departure initiates the process of bringing Jesus to his death. That is why the "glorification" of the Son of Man—the revelation to be given in his death and resurrection—is now underway.

Instead of a simple statement to this effect, however, we have in vv. 31-32 no less than five assertions of the mutual glorification of Father and Son in which past, present, and future are combined in an overloaded and confusing way.[33] We have to keep in mind that "glorify" in the biblical tradition basically has to do with the revelation of the unseen God. The glory of God was revealed in the Exodus events, especially when Israel stood before Mount Sinai. Now it will be shown in the death of the Son upon the cross. While this glorification is being brought about by the forces of darkness, to which Judas is now aligned, it is also the work of the Father who through the obedience of the Son will make the revelation of divine love most patent when Jesus gives up "his flesh for the life of the world" (6:51). That is why the glorification is mutual between Father and Son. Already set in motion through the departure of Judas, "glorification" can be spoken of as a single process embracing past, present, and future, not to be fully eclipsed until the Son returns to the glory that he shared with the Father "before the foundation of the world" (17:24). It is all rather complex but I think we can grasp what Jesus is saying here so long as we hold onto the central point that "glory"/"glorify" has essentially to do with the revelation of God in the person and fate of Jesus.

After this solemn beginning, addressing the disciples as "little children," Jesus announces (v. 33) that he will be with them only a little while longer because he is "going away" to where they are unable to follow. The address "little children" accentuates the intimacy of the gathering now that the one alien element, Judas, has left. The intimacy renders the prospect of Jesus' being with them only for a "little while" and then "going away" all the more dismaying. Like children bereft of their parents, the disciples will seek him, but, as he said to "the Jews" (7:33; 8:21-24) and now is telling them, where he is going they cannot follow. More immediately, Jesus is "going away" to his death; more ultimately, he is returning to the Father.[34] In both senses the disciples cannot follow and will feel his absence keenly. The discourse addresses this sense of loss and the new arrangements that will be in place to meet it.

---

[33] Finding five references to "glorification" means regarding as original the opening phrase of v. 32 ("If God is glorified in him"); it is wanting in some manuscripts; cf. Andrew T. Lincoln, *St. John*, 381.

[34] C. K. Barrett, *John*, 451.

The New Commandment: 13:34-35. It would be more natural if Peter's plaintive questions about where Jesus is going (vv. 36, 37) followed on immediately. Instead and somewhat intrusively Jesus speaks of giving the disciples a "new commandment" of love (vv. 34-35). In a wider perspective the commandment is not intrusive. It introduces a second and complementary major theme. The loss of love the disciples will experience through the absence of Jesus' physical presence is to be compensated for by the mutual love that they are to have for one another. He has already given them an exemplary paradigm of such love when he washed their feet. If they follow this example, they will be loving one another with the same self-sacrificial love with which he has loved them, and in this way remedying any felt lack of love that his departure may cause.

The commandment is "new" not so much in the sense of adding any ethical content to the commandment of love already in place (Lev 19:18; cf. Mark 12:29-31 and parallels). It is new in the sense of being required in the new situation following Jesus' departure to the Father. It is through the witness of the disciples' mutual love, even to the point of laying down their lives for one another, that those outside the community (literally, "all") will recognize them as disciples of the One who supremely laid down his life for others (v. 35).[35] The disciples' love for one another will be the tangible sign of their "remaining" in Jesus' love and in the mutual love of Father and Son that lies behind his entire mission (15:10).[36] In the physical absence of Jesus their fidelity to this new commandment will signal the continuation of that divine love and mission in the world.[37]

Peter Cannot Follow Now: 13:36-38. If we think of the love required by the new commandment as a love that may involve laying down one's life, the commandment may not be as foreign to Peter's problems with Jesus "going away" (vv. 36-38) as appears at first sight. Peter wants to know where Jesus is going—presumably, like "the Jews" mentioned earlier (7:35-36), thinking of some physical destination. Jesus does not indicate any destination but simply repeats that where he is going Peter is unable to follow him presently but one day will do so. "Follow" here has its biblical sense of discipleship. Peter is at present unable to follow not simply because Jesus is going to his death but because, as will soon become apparent, he lacks the required courage and generosity. A time will come when he will have those qualities (cf.

---

[35] Cf. Francis J. Moloney, *John*, 386.
[36] Cf. Gail O'Day, "The Gospel of John," 732–33.
[37] Cf. Andrew T. Lincoln, *St. John*, 388.

Jesus' prophecy in 21:18-19). But for the present in this respect he is wanting. A further protestation on his part (v. 37) that he is ready to "lay down
(his) life for (Jesus)" ironically echoes the description of the Good Shepherd
(10:11, 15, 17-18). Jesus takes up his words (v. 38) and then solemnly
("Amen, Amen") prophesies the coming failure on Peter's part that makes
them sound so hollow: before the cock crows he will have denied Jesus three
times.

Peter's failure will not be of the same order as the treachery of Judas.
Yet its revelation strongly communicates the sense of the disciples' frailty
and inability to grasp what is really at stake now that Jesus' "hour" has arrived. They are not yet ready for the high demands of discipleship (12:25-26).
Jesus has foreseen their weakness and coming infidelity but they remain
"his own" whom he unconditionally loves (v. 34). Later readers of the gospel
will take comfort from the fact that their own failings in discipleship have
likewise been foreseen by Jesus and no more lessen his love for them than
was the case in regard to the original disciples. Peter will have a more glorious day (21:18-19), but that will require the strengthening gift of the Spirit.
For the present Jesus indicates his awareness of the disciples' lack of understanding and proceeds in the remainder of the discourse to address it.

The Benefits of Jesus' Departure: 14:1-14

Many "Dwelling Places": 14:1-3. The disciples have been told that one of
their number is a traitor and have seen him depart. Another has had his
protestations of courageous following crushed by Jesus' prophecy of his
denial. Jesus has spoken of his own "departure" in terms that are as ominous
as they are obscure. It is understandable, then, that he should continue with
words of reassurance ("Do not let your hearts be troubled" [v. 1a]). He
himself had displayed disturbance of heart at the prospect of death (12:27;
cf. also 11:33; 13:31), and then found reassurance and peace in his relationship with the Father (12:28). Now he enjoins[38] his disciples to have a similar
trust in God in the face of the powers of darkness. The addition of "trust in
me" alongside "trust in God" introduces the motif of complete unity between
himself and the Father that will undergird the following exhortation.[39]

The principal cause of the disciples' dismay is Jesus' talk of his own
"departure" (13:33, 36-37). He moves (vv. 2-4) to explain how that departure,

---

[38] The two occurrences of the Greek verb *pisteuete* in v. 1b may be either indicative or
imperative. It seems best to take both as commands; cf. C. K. Barrett, *John,* 456.

[39] Cf. Gail O'Day, "The Gospel of John," 740.

even though it will deprive them of his physical presence for some time, is ultimately for their benefit. There are "many dwelling places" in his Father's house and the purpose of his going is to "prepare" a place for them in that "house" (v. 2).[40] The separation will not be permanent because, after he has prepared a place, he will return and take them to himself, so that the tangible company with him that they have enjoyed up till now will be renewed there in that house of the Father (literally, "that where I am, there you may be also" [v. 3]).

The very frequent choice of this text as Gospel in funeral services goes along with a popular conception of "heaven" as a kind of celestial motel in which the faithful departed may find lodging for eternity. Understood in this way it has brought and continues to bring comfort to many bereaved. The understanding is not wrong but hardly does justice to the theological depth of Jesus' statement, which may bring even greater comfort when fully appreciated. The Greek word translated "dwelling place" (*monē*) is one of the cluster of terms in the gospel that richly exploit the sense of the divine "dwelling" or "remaining" (*menein*). The whole purpose of the Son's mission in the world is that human beings might share the status of "children of God" (1:12), living the (eternal) life that the Son himself has enjoyed eternally with the Father. The coming departure of Jesus—his death, resurrection, and ascension to the Father—will "prepare" dwelling places for the disciples in the sense that this sequence of events will render them worthy to dwell, as "children," in God's household, so that "where he is"—not just spatially, but by right and privilege—they also may be (v. 3c). The assurance, then, is not just about location in "heaven," however that may be conceived; it is an assurance of eternal life and communion with God.

Jesus does, it is true, speak of returning and taking the disciples to the place he has prepared. In this we confront the variety of levels on which his talk of "going away" and "returning" operates throughout the discourse. He will go away in his imminent death and return as risen Lord. He will go away more fundamentally in his postresurrection ascent to the Father and not return until his coming at the end of time before the general resurrection.

---

[40] The Greek sentence in the second half of v. 2 is textually variant and can be read in more than one sense; cf. C. K. Barrett, *John*, 457. It seems best, with the NRSV, to read it as a question: "If it were not so, would I have told you that I go to prepare a place for you?" While Jesus has not explicitly given such an assurance to the disciples (the chief difficulty pressed against the interpretation: so, C. K. Barrett; Francis J. Moloney, *John*, 397; Gail O'Day, "The Gospel of John," 741), it is perhaps implicit in statements about his "going away" (12:26; 13:33, 36-37); cf. Rudolf Bultmann, *Gospel of John* 601, n. 4; Andrew T. Lincoln, *St. John*, 389.

There is also a suggestion of Jesus returning to take to the heavenly home the individual Christian at his or her death.[41] The subtly shifting threads of Johannine eschatology find a place for these more futurist expressions alongside, as we shall see, an insistence that even during the time of his coming physical absence Jesus will remain present in a variety of modes to his disciples, and that he and the Father will come and set up their "dwelling" within them in a milieu of divine love (14:22-24). The "dwelling places" in the house of the Father are "many" in the sense of being able to accommodate not just the Son but also those who, through his saving work, have been rendered worthy of sharing his filial status. But arrival at that status is not postponed till after death. Death will mean the revelation of the household (the "Father's house") in which believers have been dwelling all along through their association with Jesus.

Jesus, the Way: 14:4-6. A throwaway line from Jesus ("And where I am going, you know the way" [v. 4]) provokes a protest from the ever-realistic Thomas (v. 5; cf. 11:16; 20:24): if they do not know where Jesus is going, how can they know the way? The exchange introduces the key term "way" (*hodos*) and sets up one of Jesus' most significant statements about himself in the gospel:

> I am the way (*hodos*), the truth (*alētheia*) and the life (*zōē*);
> no one comes to the Father except through me. (John 14:6)

As in similar "I am" statements, the predicative terms in each case express not so much something about Jesus in himself but an aspect of the benefit he brings to the world. Moreover, the second and third terms in the present sequence are subordinate to and explicative of the first ("way"), which is primary. Jesus is the way to the Father because in him is to be found the revelation of the true reality of God ("truth"), which, when appropriated through faith, communicates a share in the divine "(eternal) life." [42] In describing himself as "way" Jesus is appropriating a characteristic self-description of divine Wisdom in the Jewish biblical tradition (Prov 4:11; 8:32; 23:19; Wis 10:17-18). He is also setting himself over against the claim of the Torah to offer the essential "way" or path to life (cf. esp. Ps 119:1, 14, 27, 32, 33, 128; Sir Prol 1, 10; 15:1; 19:20; 21:11; 34:8; 39:8).[43]

---

[41] Cf. Robert Kysar, *Maverick Gospel*, 120–21.

[42] Cf. Gail O'Day: "Jesus is the 'way' because he is the access point to God's promise of life" ("The Gospel of John," 743).

[43] Andrew T. Lincoln, *St. John*, 390.

It is in this context that the "exclusivity" of the claim in the second half of the text ("No one comes to the Father except through me") is best understood. The Wisdom tradition of Israel and the Torah in which it is expressed are themselves paths to life only as they point to and find their fulfillment in him. Life comes through true knowledge of God, and the cardinal tenet of this gospel from the beginning (1:18) has been that God is revealed in the human flesh of Jesus. The gospel does not exclude thereby all knowledge of God apart from Jesus but insists that he remains the touchstone or canon of any such revelation. His pattern of life, his teaching, his actions, the causes he embraced and for which he suffered—above all, the self-sacrificial love that brought him inevitably to his death—in all of these the nature of the unseen God is truly disclosed (cf. 1:18). At a time in Christianity when religious pathways to God other than Christian are being recognized more positively than in previous eras, it is important to read the christological claims of the Fourth Gospel for what they are asserting positively (even if couched in negative terms as in v. 6c) rather than for what they may appear to be excluding.[44]

Knowing the Father: 14:7-11. This positive sense comes to the fore when, speaking now to all the disciples, Jesus insists (v. 7a): "If you have come to know me, you will know my Father also."[45] The knowledge of him that they have acquired from the beginning of their discipleship, following the invitation "Come and see" (1:39), has all along been knowledge of the Father also (as in the promise to Nathanael: "You will see heaven opened" [1:51]). Now,[46] however, with Jesus' glorification underway (13:31), that promise is being fulfilled ever more intensely. So much so that Jesus can say, "You have already seen him" (v. 7b).

This emphatic statement is too much for Philip. Unable to grasp that the "seeing" of which Jesus is speaking refers more to intimate knowledge than physical sight, he protests with more than a hint of exasperation: "Lord, show us the Father, and that will be enough for us" (v. 8). The protest echoes the plea of Moses: "Show me your glory" (Exod 33:18) and, as often ob-

---

[44] On this see the extended discussion of Gail O'Day, "The Gospel of John," 743–45.

[45] An alternative textual tradition preserves this statement as a reproach ("If you had known me, you would have known my Father also"; cf. KJV) rather than a promise. The latter is better attested and better suited to the context; cf. C. K. Barrett, *John*, 458–59; Francis J. Moloney, *John*, 395, 398–99.

[46] Translating *ap'arti* as "now" (as in 13:19) rather than "henceforth"; cf. Rudolf Schnackenburg, *St. John*, 3:68, who points out that v. 7b represents something of a correction and clarification of the first part of the verse.

served, articulates the age-old longing of humankind for genuine spiritual experience.[47] For Jesus, however, it shows ignorance of himself as much as of the Father (v. 9b). Failure to recognize Jesus as the revelation of the Father despite the length of time that they have been with him is tantamount to failure to have truly "seen" him. It drives a wedge between the Father and himself, whereas between them there is perfect unity.

The language of mutual indwelling (Jesus being "in" the Father and the Father "in" him) in the following sentences (vv. 10-11) expresses this unity.[48] It is a unity revealed in both the words and the works of Jesus. As the accredited "agent" of the Father, everything that he says comes from the Father and everything that he does (his miracles in particular) is an expression and revelation of the Father's power. That is why the disciples must accept (*pisteuete* [v. 11]) the perfect unity that exists between them. If they cannot accept Jesus' assertions (his "words") to this effect, then they should believe on the more tangible evidence of his "works," that is, the miracles they have seen him perform through a power that patently belongs to God alone.[49]

"Greater Works": 14:12-14. In something of a little excursus (vv. 12-14) Jesus goes beyond the "works" that he himself does to consider the works his disciples will perform in the time beyond his departure to the Father. He makes what at first sight is one of the most extraordinary claims in the gospel: those who believe in him at this time will not only do the works that he does but ones that are "even greater" (v. 12b). How on earth could mere disciples do "works" (miracles!) that are "greater" than those performed by the Johannine Jesus? The answer would seem to lie in the explanation with which the statement ends: "because I am going to the Father" (v. 12c). If we think of "works" not simply as miracles but more generally as acts whereby the power and nature of God are made known, then the "greater works" could refer to the widespread winning of converts that will occur after Jesus' ascent to the Father (17:20; 20:29) when, following his glorification, the Spirit will be poured out to empower the disciples' mission (7:39).[50]

---

[47] Cf. C. K. Barrett, *John*, 499; Francis J. Moloney, *John*, 399.

[48] Rudolf Schnackenburg, *St. John*, 3:69; Francis J. Moloney, *John*, 399.

[49] The implication here of a faith based on "signs" (miracles) is somewhat at odds with the insistence at times in the gospel of the inadequacy of such faith (2:23; 4:48, but cf. 2:11 and 20:30-31). There is nothing inadequate, however, about a faith that begins with miracles but penetrates through the purely miraculous to see them as "signs," pointing to the presence of God's power working through Jesus.

[50] Cf. C. K. Barrett, *John*, 460.

The connection between Jesus' ascent to the Father and the disciples' "greater works" may also have to do with the motif of petition or intercession appearing in the following sentences (vv. 13-14).[51] There seems to be a suggestion that Jesus' presence with the Father places him in an even better position to continue the saving works he has been performing throughout his earthly life. The difference is that now he will be doing them through the disciples. They will be his accredited representatives. Hence, when they make petitions *as such*—that is, "in his name" (vv. 13, 14)—they can be fully confident that he will hear them and carry them out ("I will do" [twice]).[52] The petitions in view are probably those to do with the mission— its extension and overcoming of difficulties—rather than prayers for various kinds of benefits in general (though these need not be excluded). This is suggested by the stated ultimate goal: that the Father may be glorified in the Son (v. 13b). In the time following his departure to the Father, though physically absent, Jesus will continue to display the presence and power of the Father through the works that believers do in his name. What is required above all on the human side is faith (cf. v. 12): faith that discerns the divine presence in the world and has full confidence in the willingness and capacity of the Father—and of the Son who is ever in his presence (1:18)—to respond.[53]

Within the Divine Communion of Love: 14:15-24. The theme of love rises to the surface once more (cf. 13:34-35). Loving Jesus means keeping his commandments (v. 15). In Johannine literature "commandment (*entolē*)" has a specific sense related to faith and love. The basic requirement is to believe in Jesus as the revelation of the Father and then to enter wholeheartedly into the divine communion of love to which faith is the gateway and of which love for the brothers and sisters is the leading expression (13:34).[54]

"Another Paraclete": 14:16-17. If this ambience of love prevails, in the coming time of Jesus' absence the disciples will not lack something that his presence has provided hitherto: guidance, comfort, and strength in the face

---

[51] Verse 14 basically repeats what is said in v. 13 and is wanting in some manuscripts. Since its omission from the tradition is more easily explained than its addition, it is best regarded as original.

[52] Cf. Andrew T. Lincoln, *St. John*, 393.

[53] Cf. the instruction on confident prayer in the Synoptic tradition: Mark 11:22-24//Matt 21:21-22; cf. Luke 11:9-10.

[54] "(Jesus') commandments are not simply moral precepts: they involve a whole way of life in loving union with him" (Raymond E. Brown *John XIII–XXI*, 638).

of the hostility that will surround them. This is because he will ask the Father to give them "another paraclete" (*paraklētos*) who will remain with them until the "end of the age" (v. 16). We meet here the first of five references to the Spirit as "Paraclete," a unique feature of the Supper discourse in John. The primary meaning of the Greek term *paraklētos* is "advocate," though not in a narrowly professional legal sense (as, e.g., "lawyer").[55] A paraclete is someone that you would want standing beside you when you are in a difficult situation—under accusation, at a loss for what to say, needing defense.[56] The paraclete would be a person of some standing in society whose intercession on your behalf before authorities would be telling, whose character reference for you effective. The sense "consoler" or "comforter" associated with the description of the Holy Spirit as "Paraclete" in the Christian tradition[57] is not, then, primary. It is a legitimate secondary meaning derived from the effects of having a paraclete stand by one in times of stress.

The description of Spirit as "*another* paraclete" implies that Jesus has functioned as paraclete for the disciples up till now. In the future situation of his absence the Spirit will take over this role. As Jesus has been on trial before the world throughout his ministry, so the disciples will be on trial as they take up the mission in his name. It is in view of this trial situation, especially, that the Spirit is portrayed as "Paraclete."

The Paraclete is also dubbed "the Spirit of truth" (v. 17a). This is because, in the situation of being on trial before the world, the Paraclete will assist the disciples to witness to the "truth," that is, to the revelation of God as God truly is. The world will not physically see the Spirit, since the Spirit is not physical, nor will it have the spiritual capacity to detect the presence of the Spirit in the disciples (v. 17b).[58] But the disciples will recognize the Spirit's presence both in their communal life (*par' hymin*) and in a mode of inner presence within the individual (*en hymin*).[59]

---

[55] On "Paraclete" in John's Gospel, see especially the excursus of Rudolf Schnackenburg, *St. John*, 3:138–54, esp. 138–44; Gail O'Day, " The Gospel of John," 774–78 (excursus: "The Paraclete"); more briefly, Andrew T. Lincoln, *St. John*, 393.

[56] The Johannine sense of the Spirit as Paraclete corresponds then to the role of the Spirit when believers are on trial in the Synoptic tradition: Matt 10:19-20; Mark 13:11; Luke 12:11-12.

[57] As especially in the beautiful Latin Sequence *Veni Sancte Spiritus* recited at Pentecost.

[58] Cf. C. K. Barrett, *John*, 639.

[59] Cf. Rudolf Schnackenburg, *St. John*, 3.75–76. The Greek of v. 17c reads literally: "you know him because he abides/remains with you and will be within you." The puzzling movement from the two present tenses to the future at the end seems to reflect again the oscillation in the discourse between the time of the Last Supper and that of the later community. For other explanations, see Francis J. Moloney, *John*, 406–7.

Reflection. How believers today recognize the presence of the Spirit within the community and the individual is a good question. Experience of the Spirit is not solely the prerogative of the charismatic movement. Equally valid and perhaps more widely pervasive are more subtle manifestations. In the Ignatian spiritual tradition the whole purpose of entering into a program of spiritual exercises and of attempting to live a life attuned to the will of God in freedom rests on the presupposition that the promptings and tugs of the Spirit are constantly operative in people's lives and can be detected through proper direction and discernment. Likewise, in a rather different and more ancient tradition, commending the practice of meditation (the recitation over and over of a single phrase [normally, "Maranatha"]), Laurence Freeman writes:

> What happens is that a whole set of forces, inter-connected in the unity of our spirit, is released in our centre and radiates outwards to our lives. . . . All these real and necessary dimensions, all these inter-dependent forces are signs and symbols of one unified force, the one unified reality. This is the power of the reality of the Spirit of God who dwells in our heart, in the final depth of our spirit.[60]

Paul, too, was indicating much the same thing when he wrote of the Spirit's interceding for us "with groans too deep for words" (Rom 8:26).

Not Orphans: 14:18-20. After indicating the Paraclete Spirit as continuing his own role, it is somewhat surprising to hear Jesus insisting (v. 18) that he will not leave the disciples "orphans"— children bereft of a parent. He himself is coming back to them. "In a little while" the world will see him no longer, but they will see him because he lives and (on that account) they will live (v. 19).[61] The oscillation between Jesus "going away" in death and his return in his resurrection, on the one hand, and his more longstanding "going away" before his end-time return, on the other, appears again. "On that day" (v. 20a) must in first instance refer to the day of resurrection, when after his departure in death, in the "little while" of three days, he will return as risen Lord. The world will not see him then but they will see him. They will take the risen life they see in him as a pledge and sign of the eternal life

---

[60] Laurence Freeman, *Light Within: Meditation as Pure Prayer* (London: Darton, Longman and Todd, 1986; repr. Norwich: Canterbury Press, 2008), 22.

[61] "Jesus' resurrection life gives life to believers (v. 19b), because it is the ultimate demonstration that Jesus is indeed 'the resurrection and the life' (see 11:25-26)" (Gail O'Day, "The Gospel of John," 748).

that they too are destined to share ("because I live and you will live" [v. 19c]). They will understand his resurrection as a sure sign of his intimate unity with the Father ("you will know that I am in the Father"[62]) and will know themselves as even more intimately united with him than before ("and that you are in me and I in you" [v. 20]). In this perspective any sense of being "orphaned" falls away.

Living within the Divine Communion of Love: 14:21-24. In the course of these very dense sentences the perspective has shifted away from Jesus' departure (in death) and return (in resurrection) to a sense of the disciples' union with him in the time after his ultimate departure to the Father. In the context of this union the thought returns again explicitly to love (v. 21). An earlier proposition about "loving (Jesus)" and "keeping (his) command-ments" (v. 15) is reversed: "The one who has my commandments and keeps them is the one who loves me" (v. 21a). The easy reversal shows that a strict sense of cause and effect is not in play. It is all a matter of living within the divine communion of love. To live a life of sacrificial love for the brothers and sisters is to live a life of love for Jesus, and to live such a life is to be enveloped by the love of the Father (v. 21b). The Father's love is not condi-tional upon human love: the whole thrust of the gospel has put the divine initiative beyond question (3:16). What the believer will have entered into is the "reciprocity of love that unites Father and Son" (1:18).[63] In this context of love, Jesus finally (v. 21c) pledges that the believer will have a sense of his personal love and presence ("I will love him/her and reveal myself to him/her"). Though Jesus will be physically absent in the time of the church, believers who are caught up in the divine communion of love will enjoy a deep, personal knowledge of him.[64]

Jesus' talk of "revealing" himself prompts a further question from one of the disciples present at the Supper: from a Judas, whom the evangelist hastens to describe as "not the Iscariot" (v. 22).[65] Why will Jesus reveal himself only to the disciples and not to the world? The question, reminiscent

---

[62] Taking the "in" expressions as indications of unity; see above on 14:10-11.

[63] Cf. C. K. Barrett, *John*, 465. By the same token, as Raymond E. Brown (*John XIII–XXI*, 641) notes, if one turns away from the Son, one forfeits God's love.

[64] Cf. Paul, who never "knew Christ according to the flesh," that is, in his human history (2 Cor 5:16), yet provides the New Testament's most personal sense of being loved by him: "the Son of God, who loved me and gave himself up for me" (Gal 2:20b).

[65] Regarding this Judas we have no certain information. He does not appear in the Matthean and Markan lists of the Twelve, though a "Judas of James" is mentioned at the end of the Lukan lists (Luke 6:16; Acts 1:13); cf. Rudolf Schnackenburg, *St. John*, 3:80–81.

of the complaint uttered by "his brothers" in 7:3-4, seems to stem from a lingering expectation of Jesus along the lines of conventional messiahship.[66] This Judas has failed to grasp that the time has passed for Jesus to try to convince "the world"—in the first place the Jewish authorities—about the true nature of his messianic mission (12:37-50). Ignoring the question in the terms in which it has been put (cf. 3:4-8; 4:12-14; 14:5-7), Jesus takes the interruption as a chance to speak even more deeply about the divine communion of love (v. 23). If anyone loves him and "keeps his word" (the sense is the same as "keeping his commandments" [vv. 15, 21][67]), the Father will love that person (cf. v. 21b), and jointly ("we") Father and Son will make their dwelling (*monē*) within the person.

This sense of a combined divine indwelling within the heart of individual believers is one of the most extraordinary statements in the entire gospel. Earlier in the discourse (14:2-3) Jesus had pledged that there were many "dwelling places" in his Father's house and that he was going away to prepare a place among them for his disciples. Now the thought is reversed with a sense of the divine "at-homeness" within the hearts of those prepared to enter the divine communion of love. In the Old Testament tradition God dwelt with Israel wandering in Sinai and came to rest in the temple at Jerusalem, leading to Solomon's exclamation at the time of its inauguration: "But will God indeed dwell on the earth?" (1 Kgs 8:27). Earlier in the gospel (2:19-21) Jesus had spoken of himself ("his body") as the new temple of divine indwelling. Now that indwelling is extended to the bodies of believers.

The pledge is future ("we will come and we will make a dwelling place") but within the elusive eschatology of the Fourth Gospel it does not seem necessary to view that divine dwelling as postponed to a future beyond the "in-between" time that is the primary focus of the discourse.[68] The assertion is part of Jesus' insistence that he will not leave the disciples "orphans" because he is "coming" to them (v. 18). We now know that the "coming" involves not only himself but the full divine communion of love that later Christian theology described as Trinity. The pledge recorded in

---

[66] Cf. Gail O'Day, "The Gospel of John," 748.

[67] Cf. C. K. Barrett, *John*, 141–42.

[68] So especially, Francis J. Moloney, *John*, 404–5, 408, on the grounds that referring the divine indwelling to the "in-between" time renders the presence of the Paraclete unnecessary or collapses the distinction between the Paraclete and Jesus. This seems to me to press the shifting eschatology of the gospel too rigorously. See further, Andrew T. Lincoln, *St. John*, 399–400.

Zechariah, "Sing and rejoice, O daughter Zion! For lo, I will come and dwell in your midst, says the LORD" (2:10), is to be fulfilled beyond all expectation.[69]

Judas's question does receive something of a response in the negative warning about not loving Jesus that concludes the sequence (v. 24). Not loving Jesus means not attending to his "words" (= "commands") and his words are not his alone but those of the Father who sent him. Since the world fails on all these accounts, there is no point in Jesus' continuing to manifest himself to it at this time. This does not mean, however, that following his "victory" over the forces of the hostile world arrayed against him (16:33) the disciples will not continue his mission in and to the world.

Peace, Not Anxiety, in the Face of Jesus' Departure: 14:25-31

The "Reminding" Role of the Paraclete Spirit: 14:25-26. In the sentences that conclude this first part of the discourse the pervasive theme of Jesus' departure comes to the fore again. All that he has been saying has been said while "remaining" (*menōn*) with them (v. 25) but that remaining is about to come to an end. Once more (v. 26; cf. vv. 15-17) he points to the gift of the Paraclete—now explicitly identified as "the Holy Spirit[70]—as the remedy for the vacuum his own absence will create. The Paraclete will take up his teaching role.[71] The Paraclete will do so not in the sense of adding new teaching in a quantitative way but by "reminding" the disciples of things Jesus had said in such a way as to bring out the significance for the new situation in which they will find themselves.[72] Already in the gospel the evangelist has pointed out instances where the disciples "remembered" an action of Jesus with deeper understanding in light of his glorification (2:12; 12:16). In a similar way a key role of the Paraclete Spirit will be to bridge the gap between the past of Jesus' historical life and the ongoing post-Easter life of the church. Though far beyond the purview of the evangelist, some

[69] Cf. Raymond E. Brown, "If the incarnation (and death) of the Son was an act of the Father's love for the world, the post-resurrectional indwelling is a special act of love for the Christian" (*John XIII–XXI*, 648).

[70] The masculine pronouns used of the Paraclete in the second half of v. 26 show that the evangelist has in mind a personal presence, not just a force; cf. Raymond E. Brown, *John XIII–XXI*, 650.

[71] The phrase "in my name" possibly has the sense "to complete my mission"; so, Raymond E. Brown, *John XIII–XXI*, 653. Here, the Father sends the Spirit as in Paul's formulation in Gal 4:6.

[72] Cf. Andrew T. Lincoln, *St. John*, 397.

foundation has been seen in this text for the teaching office of the church (magisterium). This would not be in the sense of adding to revelation but of drawing out from the original deposit of faith new depths of meaning in the light of fresh historical and social circumstances.[73]

The Gifts of Peace and Joy: 14:27-29. With Jesus about to depart, his bequest of peace (v. 27) is at one level simply the conventional Semitic expression of farewell: "*Shalōm*" ("Peace"). In the present context, however, it is far more. In the biblical tradition stretching behind the gospels, "peace" is a central aspect of the salvation promised in the messianic age (e.g., Isa 52:7; 54:10; 57:19; 60:17; Zech 8:12; 9:10). It is in the first place and fundamentally peace with God—something which Jesus is uniquely in a position to give in view of the reconciliation he can offer because of his death and bequest of the Spirit (20:21-23). This is a peace that the world is utterly incapable of giving. Worldly authority can from time to time bring about an absence of hostilities between human beings and human societies; it cannot erode the fundamental insecurity and anxiety at the root of human existence. The peace Jesus is leaving with the disciples extends God's grace and love deep into the human heart. That is why, in the face of his departure, he can repeat the injunction with which he began: "Do not let your hearts be troubled or afraid" (14:1).

Pressing further in this direction, Jesus maintains that the news of his going away should actually be a cause for rejoicing on the part of the disciples (v. 28). If they truly loved him, they would rejoice that he is going to the Father, the reason being that "the Father is greater than I" (v. 28d). The statement has raised issues from the earliest times.[74] First of all, Jesus does not deny that the disciples already have some love for him. A deeper love, however, would actually greet the news of his departure—even though it means his death—with joy. This is because what is involved is no ordinary departure but a death-defeating journey through death to the Father that will bring to them and to all subsequent believers a share in the divine eternal life. When Jesus gives as a reason for this the truth that the Father is "greater" than he himself, he is not making a statement about intra-trinitarian relationships in the sense developed in later Christian theology. What he says should be seen in the same light as his earlier statement that the disciples would do

---

[73] Cf. Pontifical Biblical Commission (Rome), *The Interpretation of the Bible in the Church* (Vatican City: Libreria Editrice Vaticana, 1993) III, B, pp. 93, 105.

[74] For a survey of patristic attempts to ward off an Arian interpretation, see Rudolf Schnackenburg, *St. John*, 3:85–86.

even "greater works" than he and do so for the same reason: namely, because of his ascent to the Father (14:12). Up till now his mission has been limited to a particular time and place by the constraints of his life as incarnate Son. His departure to the Father, and the victory over the forces of darkness that it entails, will allow the life-giving power of God to flow beneficially into the world without restriction. It is in this sense—and not "ontologically"— that the Father is "greater."[75] Jesus is giving this explanation of his "departure" now before it happens so that when it does, the disciples will not simply grieve over it as would be normal at the death of a beloved friend and master (v. 29). On the contrary, his departure in death, instead of weakening or destroying their faith, should actually confirm it ("that you may believe" [v. 29b; cf. 13:19]).

The Time for Talking Is Over: 14:30-31. Rather curiously in view of the rest of the discourse to follow (15:1–16:33), Jesus announces that he no longer has many things to say while remaining with the disciples (v. 30a). In fact, the command to rise up and leave at the end of the next verse (v. 31c) shows that we have arrived at the close of the discourse in an early version of the gospel. There is no point in straining to find a narrative unity across the two sections of the discourse as a whole.[76] The command to depart is a relic of an early stage that the evangelist has chosen to respect and leave in its place. A reason for so doing could be that he felt it was too closely tied to the immediately preceding sentences to omit. Jesus, in effect, says at the beginning of v. 30, "My time for talking is almost over." The reason is that action is at hand. The "ruler of this world" (Satan) is approaching in the shape of the arresting party led by Satan's tool, Judas Iscariot. That ruler has no real power over Jesus.[77] But Jesus intends to freely surrender himself into the hands of its current instruments. Why? "So that the world may know that I love the Father and act entirely according to his command." Hence the injunction ("Rise up") to bring on the confrontation.[78]

---

[75] The problem arises when the comparison in regard to "greatness" is taken simply in itself without reference to the clauses that precede it and to the "greater works" in 14:12. For a similar solution, to which this is much indebted, see Andrew T. Lincoln, *St. John*, 398.

[76] For attempts to do so, see C. K. Barrett, *John*, 469–70; for a recent attempt along narrative-critical lines, see Francis J. Moloney, *John*, 412.

[77] Andrew T. Lincoln, *St. John*, 398, aptly suggests that the Greek phrase at the end of v. 30 might well be compared with the modern idiom in which a person might say, "The police *have nothing on me.*"

[78] The syntax across the ending of v. 30 to the end of v. 31 is open to various construals. If a comma is read at the end of v. 30, then v. 31 follows on as a kind of elliptical statement

In light of the negative rating of "world" that has been dominant throughout the discourse, the expectation that the world might recognize Jesus' love for the Father comes as a surprise. For a moment we seem to have the more positive sense of "world" seen earlier in texts such as 3:16 and 4:42 (cf. also 17:23).[79] The world may be under the domination of Satan and that is the reason for its current hostility. But the whole purpose of Jesus' departure in all its aspects is precisely to break that grip and liberate the world for its true purpose, which is to share the eternal life of God. Those in the world who come to faith will see the crucifixion of Jesus, not as his conquest by the power of Satan but as a victorious display of divine love.

Discourse B: *Abide in Love/Prepare to be Hated: 15:1–16:4a*

Despite the summons to rise up and leave (14:31), Jesus resumes his discourse much as before. The section that follows (15:1–16:4a) is the centerpiece of the entire sequence at the Last Supper and features what is possibly the best-known and best-loved text from the entire address: Jesus' description of himself as the "True Vine" (15:1). In the sentences that follow (15:1-17), aspects of this image are unfolded in the interests of the disciples' "remaining" (*menein*) or "abiding" in love (15:1-17). All of which stands in stark contrast to the following warning about the hatred and persecution that the community will experience from "the world" (15:18–16:4a).

The theme of Jesus' departure and return that prevailed earlier in the discourse (14:1-31) now gives way to that of the mutual indwelling and love between Jesus and the disciples, on the one hand, and among themselves, on the other.[80] Though spoken to the disciples in the context of the Supper, the focus is clearly now upon the situation of the later church. It will be a time of experiencing both love and hatred: divine love, which must be reflected within the community; hatred and persecution from the world outside. The dualism that is such a feature of the gospel is very much to the fore here. But there is no suggestion that love is simply to be confined within the community. The love that disciples are summoned to display is an extension

---

where some phrase such as "but (I cooperate with his plan) in order that the world might know that I love" has to be understood before the statement of purpose; cf. C. K. Barrett, *John*, 469. If, as seems best to me, v. 31 is taken as a fresh sentence, then the purpose clause at the beginning of v. 31 states the interior reason for rising and being on the way: it is to surrender to the power of Satan in accord with the design of God; cf. also C. H. Dodd, *Interpretation*, 408–9; Gail O'Day, "The Gospel of John," 752–53.

[79] Cf. Rudolf Schnackenburg, *St. John*, 3:87; Francis J. Moloney, *John*, 414.

[80] Cf. C. H. Dodd, *Interpretation*, 410; C. K. Barrett, *John*, 470.

of the divine love with which God "so loved the world" (3:16) and which impelled the mission of the Son, not to condemn the world but to give it (eternal) life. The disciples' love is to be a further extension of that divine mission in and to the world.

1. Abide in Love: 15:1-17

The first section (vv. 1-17) falls into two parts. The first, vv. 1-11, plays out the image of the Vine at the service of the central command to "abide" in love.[81] The second, vv. 12-17, is bound together by the command, at the beginning (v. 12b) and end (v. 17), that the disciples should "love one another."[82]

The True Vine: 15:1-11. Jesus' description of himself as "the true Vine" (15:1) is the last of the series of "I am + predicate" statements that are features of the gospel's Christology, the predicate indicating some aspect of what Jesus has come to communicate to the world. As is certainly the case here, the predicate almost always draws upon a significant motif from the biblical tradition. In that tradition, vine or vineyard is a frequent image for Israel. Psalm 80 is an extended plea to God to restore the well-being of Israel depicted as a vine brought out of Egypt by God but now sadly ravaged by the nations (vv. 8-13). Particularly notable is the image of the well-loved vineyard of Isaiah's friend in Isa 5:1-7, which, despite the attention lavished upon it, yielded only wild grapes (cf. also Ezek 15:1-8; 17:1-10; 19:10-14). When Jesus describes himself here as "the *true* vine" (*hē ampelos hē alēthinē*) there is an implied contrast with Israel as the unfruitful or ravaged vine,[83] while he himself is the nucleus of a renewed Israel which will yield the "fruits" that God, the proprietor of the vineyard, seeks.

Within the developing image Jesus identifies his Father as the vine-grower (v. 1b).[84] Later (v. 5) the disciples will be identified as "the branches."

---

[81] The "vine" metaphor is not, then, the main feature in itself, but rather the vehicle to articulate the importance of abiding; cf. Francis J. Moloney, *John*, 417.

[82] The "vine" motif functions both as an image and as an allegory in an intertwined way that renders otiose any attempt to distinguish image element (vv. 1-6) from an application element (vv. 7-17); cf. Gail O'Day's critique of Raymond E. Brown in this regard, "The Gospel of John," 755–56.

[83] Cf. the Parable of the Wicked Tenants in the Synoptic tradition: Matt 21:33-44; Mark 12:1-11; Luke 20:9-18.

[84] The identification recalls Jesus' earlier statement that the "Father is greater than I" (14:28) in the sense that the Father is the source of his mission; cf. Gail O'Day, "The Gospel of John," 757.

While it might have been more logical to identify them as such here at the start, the text lingers within the image for a while (v. 2), describing two actions of the vinegrower. He cuts away (*hairein*) every branch that does not yield fruit and prunes (*kathairein*) each one that does. (The word play between the two expressions, lost in translation, is apparent in the transliteration from the Greek.) A somewhat obtrusive comment (v. 3) to the effect that the disciples ("you") are already "pruned" (*katharoi*) through the word that Jesus has spoken to them makes clear the implication that the disciples are the branches of the vine. It also suggests that their association with Jesus has been a "pruning" now underway for quite some time.[85]

In this sense the disciples are "clean" (an alternative meaning of *katharoi*). Their task from now on is to "remain" (*menein*) in Jesus so that this status may not only endure but also bear fruit (v. 4a). Exploiting (v. 4bc) the rich ambiguity of the Greek verb *menein* ("abide"/ "remain"), Jesus explains that just as a branch (of the vine) cannot bear fruit of itself, but only in so far as it remains attached to (literally, "in") the vine stem, so the disciples will fail to bear fruit if they move away from such mutual indwelling with himself.[86]

"Bearing fruit"—a recurrent theme throughout the passage (cf. also 4:36; 12:24)—probably refers to all the ways in which the love of Jesus, which ultimately derives of course from the Father (the "vinedresser" [v. 1b; cf. v. 9]), finds expression in the love members of the believing community display toward one another. Such acts of love derive from the "sap" of divine love coursing from the "Vine" stem to the branches, which are at last (v. 5) explicitly identified as the disciples ("you"). "Branches" (= disciples) that remain in close union with the vine (Jesus) produce much "fruit" in this sense. Since union is essential for producing fruit (literally, "without me you can do nothing" [v. 5c]), disciples that fail to remain in the vine are "cast out" (v. 6ab). Like dried-up branches, they are gathered up, cast into the fire, where they are burnt (v. 6cd).

It is all too easy for the religious imagination to see straightaway here a reference to the fires of hell, casting a very dark shadow across what is otherwise such a positive and attractive sequence. It is unlikely, however, that within the allegory that is being developed something so specific is

---

[85] The "word" that Jesus has spoken is probably to be understood to refer generally to the entire interaction between Jesus and the disciples over the course of his ministry; cf. C. K. Barrett, *John*, 474.

[86] The opening sentence of v. 4: "Remain in me, as I (remain) in you" is best taken as referring to mutual indwelling; cf. C. K. Barrett, *John*, 474. As we have seen, the language of "indwelling" is a characteristic Johannine expression of union.

meant.[87] It is the uselessness rather than the guilt of the severed branches that is being highlighted when the image of the vine is drawn out in this direction. Disciples who fail to maintain their union with Jesus become simply worthless. They should be expelled from the community with as little hesitation as a vinedresser would have in cutting off, gathering, and disposing by fire of withered and unfruitful branches.

Even so, the Johannine prescription for dealing with unproductive (in love) community members seems draconian—especially when compared, say, with the carefully calibrated process of dealing with recalcitrance outlined in Matthew 18:15-17. Once again, we have to reckon with the single-mindedness of the Johannine focus upon love as the sole fruit and requirement for life in the community. Love is the supreme test of union with the Lord. There is no place within the community for one who has severed ties with that sole source of love.

Within the basic image of "bearing fruit," the following sentences (vv. 7-8) revisit some earlier themes. If the disciples "remain" in Jesus and his "words" (*rhēmata*) remain in them, whatever they ask for will be granted them (v. 7; 14:14). Their union with Jesus will ensure that their prayer is so totally in accord with the divine will as to guarantee an unfailing response. Likewise, as the Father is "glorified"—that is, revealed and made present—through the work of the Son (13:31-32; 14:13; 17:1), so that same revelation continues in the ongoing "fruitfulness" of the disciples in their union with the Son.[88] Their lives of love will reveal them to be truly his disciples and in this sense continuers of his revelation of God as love.[89]

The sequence approaches a climax in a beautifully rounded couplet (vv. 9-11) that begins and ends with the Father's love for the Son (3:35; 5:20; 10:17; 17:24, 26). As the Son has lived and conducted his mission by "remaining"/"dwelling" continually within the divine love (cf. 1:18), so the disciples should "remain"/"dwell" within the extension of the divine love that they have experienced and will continue to experience from Jesus.[90] They will do so by "keeping his commandments," the essence of which is reproducing that love in their communal life. That will be to "remain"/"dwell" in his love as he "remains"/"dwells" continually in the love of the Father (1:18).

---

[87] Cf. Rudolf Schnackenburg, *St. John*, 3:100.

[88] Cf. C. K. Barrett, *John*, 475.

[89] "The Son is only intent on the glorification of the Father (cf. 13:31f; 14:13; 17:1) and, after his return to the Father, makes use of the disciples for this purpose" (cf. 17:10) (Rudolf Schnackenburg, *St. John*, 3:102).

[90] "The aorist *ēgapēsa* denotes the whole act of love lavished by Jesus upon his disciples and consummated in his death" (C. K. Barrett, *John*, 475).

No joy can be compared with the joy of discovering that one is very much loved by someone whom one longed to be loved by but did not dare hope that such might ever be the case. Such a thought seems to lie behind the final word of Jesus in this section (v. 11). He has "said these things" to the disciples in order that his joy may be in them and their joy complete. In other words, by sharing with them a sense of the love he receives from the Father, he is also communicating to and sharing with them a sense of the eternal joy he experiences through that reception of divine love. The ultimate goal of his saving mission then is joy: that human beings, through being drawn into the communion of love that is the godhead, may share in the joy prevailing in that communion of love. When they share to the full the "eternal life" of that communion, their joy will be "complete."

Love One Another: 15:12-17. While the image of the vine slips into the background, the basic theme of "remaining"/"abiding" in divine love continues as Jesus explains what this entails for the community. He has associated abiding in his love with keeping his commandments (15:10) and early in the discourse (13:34-35) had spoken of a "new commandment": that they should love one another as he had loved them. Now, in a section neatly bound together by restatements of the commandment at beginning (v. 12b) and end (v. 17), he makes more explicit the quality of love required if it is to be a true reflection of the love the disciples have received from him and ultimately from the Father. In the wider literary culture of the time there was much discussion of friendship and, more specifically, of what might be its most extreme expression.[91] Both that wider culture and Jesus, as portrayed here, are agreed that the supreme expression of love for a friend is to lay down one's life for the friend (v. 13).[92] What distinguishes Christian love is that it is modeled upon and is the extension of Jesus' self-sacrificial love for the disciples. Implicit behind the expression "as I have loved you" is the thought of the Good Shepherd who freely lays down his life for the sheep (10:11, 15, 17-18), the One who also forfeited the security of his own life by journeying to Judea to restore life to Lazarus, his "friend" (11:11; cf. vv. 3, 5, 35).[93] We recall too the "example" of self-sacrificial love that Jesus has

---

[91] For references in Greco-Roman literature see Rudolf Schnackenburg, *St. John*, 3:109–10.

[92] As C. K. Barrett, *John*, 476–77, astutely notes, Jesus is not saying here that love for friends is the highest form of love—superior, for example, to the love for enemies commended in the Synoptic tradition (Matt 5:43-48; Luke 6:27-35); love for enemies is not in view. What is being said is that there is nothing greater that you can do for your friends than to die for them.

[93] "Friend" (*philos*) has the particular sense in Greek of "one who is loved," which the English word "friend" does not quite capture; cf. Raymond E. Brown, *John XIII–XXI*, 664.

provided by washing the feet of the disciples as a foreshadowing of the death he will undergo to render them "cleansed" from sin. Abiding in love, then, means reproducing in their communal life the same self-sacrificial love that they, his friends, have received from him (cf. 1 John 3:16).

In something of a little excursus (vv. 14-15) Jesus expands for a moment upon the motif of the disciples as his friends, contrasting it with that of servants or slaves. Though he remains master (13:16; 15:20) and as such commands them (vv. 12, 14, 17), the relationship has moved into one of friendship. Whereas a master simply issues commands to a slave or servant without giving any explanation of the reason for the service to be performed, friends carry out the wishes of the loved one on the basis of intimacy and shared knowledge. Jesus has made known to the disciples all that he has heard from the Father (v. 15d). From the start he has involved them in the intimacy of his relationship with the Father and made them fully aware of his mission to give life to the world (3:16). As friends, then, they know that the self-sacrificial love that he is requiring of them in their relationships with one another is simply an extension of the divine love in which they now "abide."

Abiding in that love, however, is not a privilege to be enjoyed in a static kind of way. As the Father's love impelled Jesus on mission to the world, so Jesus has "chosen" the disciples as instruments for the extension of that mission. They have been selected and "appointed" to go out and "bear fruit" (v. 16). With this last phrase the image of the vine makes a brief reappearance. As before, "bearing fruit" means the flourishing of divine love in the community through intimate union with the Vine (Jesus). "Go out" adds the nuance of mission: the disciples are to embody love in the world so as to attract their fellow human beings to the Source of that love (cf. 12:32). The fruit is to "remain" (v. 16d) in the sense of continuing after Jesus' departure to the Father (3:16). During this time and on this mission the disciples can pray with the same confidence of being heard as Jesus does because they will be sharing his relationship with God (cf. 20:17).[94]

A repetition of the initial command, "Love one another" (v. 17), brings to a close the section that began with Jesus' identification of himself as the

---

The Fourth Gospel uses the two verbs *philein* and *agapan* without difference of meaning; cf. C. K. Barrett, *John*, 477; Gail O'Day, "The Gospel of John," 758.

[94] Gail O'Day, "The Gospel of John," 759. The formulation of the last clauses in v. 16 might suggest that the answering of the disciples' prayers was conditional on their "bearing fruit," which seems to reverse the expected logic. The logic cannot be pressed too hard. The sense seems to be that the continuance of the "fruit" (the disciples' successful mission) will attest to the fact that, because of their intimate union with Jesus, the Father has unfailingly heard the disciples' prayers—prayers by which the mission should always be accompanied (14:13-14; 15:7; 16:23-24, 26).

"true Vine" (15:1-17). The twin themes that have dominated it—abiding in divine love and loving one another as the fruit of that abiding—now recede. They will reappear in Jesus' concluding prayer (17:21, 23, 26).

2. Prepare to be Hated: 15:18–16:4a

From the love that the disciples experience from God and from one another, Jesus turns to the polar opposite: the hatred and persecution they can expect from the world. We move from one of the most sublimely positive passages in the gospel to one of the most negative and troubling. The "world" appears here in a most negative light.[95] Worse still, it soon becomes clear that the primary representatives of this hostile world in the passage are the Jewish leadership, significantly reinforcing the potentiality of the gospel to convey negative, if not anti-Semitic attitudes to Jews and Judaism.

We might well wish that the passage could be expurgated from the text. But it appears in our lectionaries and so requires interpretation. Moreover, it does have a place in the story in the sense of providing a necessary context for the community of love described in the first part of the chapter. Without it, that community might simply float in the air, so to speak, removed from all contact with its surroundings in a way that would deny the central truth of the gospel: that the Word became flesh in the world (1:14). The important thing is to understand the passage in its historical context, before seeking ways to handle it responsibly in church life and practice today. Most important is to understand the way "world" is being used in the passage and to avoid a simple identification with usage of the term today.

The passage breaks down into three main parts: (1) a long sequence (vv. 18-25) bound together by the motif of "hate" running through it; (2) another short assurance concerning the Paraclete (vv. 26-27); and (3) a more specific warning about persecution in the shape of expulsion from the synagogue (16:1-4a). The opening sequence itself falls into three sections, with vv. 18-19 indicating the hatred of the world, vv. 20-21 indicating how hatred will find expression in persecution, and vv. 22-25 insisting that the hatred of the world, being without grounds, is inexcusable.

Hatred from the World: 15:18-19. First, let us be clear about the way in which "world" (*kosmos*) is being used here. The Fourth Gospel uses *kosmos*

---

[95] For those of the Catholic tradition, the contrast with the approach to the world taken in the Second Vatican Council's Constitution *On the Church in the Modern World* (*Gaudium et Spes*) will be very stark.

in a range of meanings, some quite positive.[96] "World" can refer to the entire creation: all things, which were "made" through the Word (1:3) and which according to the account of creation (Gen 1:1-31), God saw to be good. More specifically, "world" can refer to the entirety of human beings. This is the world that God "so loved" and sent his Son so that it might not be lost but have eternal life (3:16). In essence this human world, too, is good but the gospel presupposes that, factually at least, the human world has fallen into the grip of forces—Satan, "the ruler of the world" (14:30)—alien to the Creator, which is why it needs to be saved. More negatively, "world" can refer to that part of humanity that has definitively said "No" to the saving mission of the Son and hence to the divine offer of life. The "world" in this last sense has made up its mind and simply responds to God's outreached hand (Christ) with unbelief and hatred, rather than faith and love.[97] Since it is to Israel that the Son's mission has in the first instance been directed, the primary representatives of this nay-saying world are those members of Israel (chiefly the leadership) who have rejected him and who, by the time of the writing of the gospel, have extended that rejection to the community of believers gathered in his name. As stated already in the Prologue,

> He was in the world, and the world came into being through him; yet the world did not know him. He came to what was his own, and his own people did not accept him. (John 1:10-11)

"World" in this thoroughly negative sense is not restricted to "the Jews." Pilate, as representative of the Roman *imperium*, has certainly aligned himself with it by the end of the passion.

The chief purpose of Jesus' warning is not simply to comfort the disciples by foreseeing the hatred that they will experience. The aim is to explain its cause and to encourage and embolden them as they take up his mission of proclaiming the Word in the face of such hatred.[98] If they experience hatred from the world—as indeed they will—this will simply be an extension of the hatred he himself has experienced and will experience to the end (v. 18). It is because of their union with himself that the world

---

[96] Cf. Sandra M. Schneiders, "The Word in the World," *Pacifica* 23 (2010): 247–66, esp. 256–57.

[97] Cf. David Rensberger: "It is the world as it has been structured by human will and rationality, but also and especially by human self-absorption and selfishness in opposition to God and to the good of other people. In short, it is human society as such, as it is organized and maintained for the good of some but to the harm of others and to the detriment of the love of God" (*Johannine Faith*, 146).

[98] Rudolf Schnackenburg, *St. John*, 3:114.

hates them. He has chosen them out of the world, so that they no longer belong to it but to him. That union, founded on self-sacrificial love, represents a direct challenge to all that the world holds dear and seeks to control; hence the hatred it displays (v. 19).[99]

Persecution from the World: 15:20-21. The hatred that the disciples will experience from the world will primarily display itself in persecution (vv. 20-21). On the principle that "a servant is not greater than his master,"[100] if representatives of the world have persecuted Jesus, they will persecute disciples who have taken up the mission in his name.[101] They will likewise be as unreceptive to the disciples' message (literally "word") as they have been to that of Jesus.[102] The ultimate reason for this negative response is their "ignorance" of the One who sent him, that is, the Father, the true nature of whom Jesus will reveal on the cross to be love. Since the "world" in this negative sense deals in hatred rather than love, it cannot respond in any other way to such revelation—whether by Jesus or by the disciples in his name—other than with hatred and persecution.

The World Has No Excuse: 15:22-25. This response is inexcusable and manifests the world's "sin" (vv. 22-24). If the Son had not come into the world, the world might have had some excuse for its failure. Since, on the contrary, he has come and, in word and deed, revealed the true nature of God, the world has no excuse and is locked in sin. "Sin" here has the meaning distinctive to it in Johannine literature: refusal to believe in and accept the Son as the One sent by the Father to be the definitive revelation of God ("the truth"). It is to "take away" sin in this fundamental sense that the Lamb

---

[99] Cf. Andrew T. Lincoln, *St. John*, 415; also David Rensberger: "The struggle of the Johannine community becomes a paradigm for the great struggle that results when God's will to redeem the world engages with the world's unwillingness to be redeemed" (*Johannine Faith*, 138).

[100] The implication that the disciples are "servants" (*douloi*) here is not at odds with Jesus' calling them "friends" rather than "servants" a few sentences earlier on (vv. 14-15). Jesus reaches for a fresh image to make the point that the disciples cannot expect to be treated any less roughly than he himself.

[101] The assertion reflects the fact that at some stage in its life the community responsible for the gospel experienced persecution from fellow Jews. There is some evidence for this in the New Testament and other early Christian literature. However, Christian readers must keep in mind that after Christianity became the majority religion in Europe and elsewhere, the situation was well and truly reversed.

[102] That is, understanding the final sentence of v. 20 as an unfulfilled condition and so as expressing a totally negative response—*pace* C. K. Barrett, *John*, 480; Gail O'Day, "The Gospel of John," 763, who see a reference to a twofold response, positive as well as negative.

of God has come into the world (1:29), offering human beings the chance to be drawn into a love relationship with God of unparalleled intimacy and grace (1:17-18). Particular sins, which the gospel does recognize (20:23), are simply a manifestation of sin in the sense of this underlying and fundamental refusal to respond in faith and love.[103]

In a rare explicit citation (cf. 12:38; 13:18; 17:12; 19:24, 36) Jesus appeals (v. 25) to Scripture to assure the disciples that the hatred directed to himself—and ultimately to the Father—is not something unexpected or unforeseen. It fulfills the words of Psalm 69:5, "They have hated me without cause,"[104] in the sense that Jesus has given no grounds to justify it—even if he has just explained what lies behind and prompts it.

The reference to this psalm as "their law"[105] shows, once again, that it is primarily the Jewish world that is in view: "his own" to which the Word came and by which, for the most part, he was "not known" (1:11). We cannot share the assumption that such refusal to accept was as perverse or as set in the face of clear evidence as the gospel here suggests. Nonetheless, there is perhaps a kernel of truth in the text that transcends its original context and reaches us across the years: love—unbounded, selfless, pure gift—is hard for human beings to handle and accept. It invites to relationship and hence to change and growth, beyond the limits of views and perceptions with which human beings have been comfortable hitherto. Sin at its most fundamental is perhaps a refusal to believe that one is lovable to God at all, that God could be so good as to love simply because that is the divine nature, without preexisting grounds or cause. We are not far here from what the English Benedictine theologian Sebastian Moore described as the essence of sin.

> God loves us. . . . And God's taste is excellent. Whatever other people may think of us, God thinks a lot of us, and he's right. *Sin* consists in disagreeing with God's estimate: in saying, "No, I'm really nothing to write home about." Sin is the failure to love ourselves as God loves us. Sin . . . makes nonsense out of the beauty of creation and knocks the life out of everything.[106]

Ultimately, it all repeats the pattern of the primeval sin in the Garden (Genesis 3), where the serpent contrived to bring the first pair down by distorting the

---

[103] Cf. Craig R. Koester, "The Death of Jesus," 146.

[104] The reference could also be to Ps 35 (LXX 34):19, but the citation of Psalm 69 elsewhere (2:17; 19:28) makes it more likely that this psalm is in view.

[105] As in 10:34, the Greek word *nomos* has reference here to scriptural books beyond the Pentateuch.

[106] Sebastian Moore and Anselm Hurt, *Before the Deluge* (London: Geoffrey Chapman, 1968), 53.

truth about God—portraying the prohibition concerning the fruit of one tree as a ploy by God to keep something back from the human pair, thereby eroding love, intimacy, and trust.

The Paraclete as Witness: 15:26-27. For a third time in the total discourse Jesus gives the disciples an assurance concerning the Paraclete Spirit.[107] Here, in the context of the world's hostility, the Paraclete's role is that of bearing witness concerning Jesus (v. 26). How and in what circumstances that witness is carried out in fact is not immediately clear. Some light may be shed on this when Jesus lays alongside the witness of the Spirit that of the disciples themselves, on the grounds that they "have been with (him) from the beginning" (v. 27). We are probably to understand the witness of the Paraclete and that of the disciples not as two parallel strains of witness but as a common witness in which the witness given by the disciples is the outward and visible sign of that provided by the Paraclete.[108] The context in view would seem to be that of situations where the disciples find themselves put on trial because of their faith in and allegiance to Jesus. In that situation, as stated explicitly in the Synoptic parallels, it will not be "you who speak, but the Spirit of your Father speaking through you" (Matt 10:20; // Mark 13:11; Luke 12:12). The fact that the disciples Jesus is addressing at the Supper have been with him "from the beginning" means that they are qualified to provide a witness to the truth reaching back to the earliest moments in which the incarnate Word displayed his glory (2:11). When they are put on trial before the world on this account, they can be confident that Jesus himself, through the presence of the Paraclete, continues in them his witness to the truth.

Expulsion from the Synagogue: 16:1-4a. Jesus rounds off this central section of the discourse with a warning about persecution in very concrete terms. The disciples will experience expulsion from the synagogue (v. 2a) and even the threat of death, proceeding from people who think that by killing them they will be performing an act of worship to God. Once again, as in similar references in 9:22 and 12:42, it is clear that the historical experience of the

---

[107] The Paraclete is stated (v. 26) to be sent by Jesus "from the Father" and "comes out from the Father." These statements were related in patristic times to the "processions" of the divine Persons within the Trinity. While valid in a wider interpretive sense, such theological elaboration goes beyond the original vision of the Fourth Gospel, which is more concerned to stress the continuity between the mission of the Paraclete and that of Jesus; cf. Rudolf Schnackenburg, *St. John*, 3:118.

[108] Cf. Rudolf Schnackenburg, *St. John*, 3:117–18; Gail O'Day, "The Gospel of John," 765.

Johannine community in a Jewish context is in view.[109] Again, too, the impulse for such persecution is attributed to ignorance of the true nature of God (8:19, 54) and specifically of Jesus as the unique revelation of the Father (1:18). It is hard to lift this text in any way out of its very concrete anchoring in early Christian experience. On a more general level, however, it may serve as a further reminder (cf. 13:35; 15:12-14; 1 John 3:16) that witness to Jesus before the world and adherence to the values he embodied may involve the sacrifice even of one's life; it may involve coming to an "hour" (16:2b) when witness (*martyria*) will really involve martyrdom, as Jesus has come to his hour.[110] This prospect, as Jesus acknowledges (16:1a), may be a stumbling block to faith. It is precisely to ward off such "scandal" that he is mentioning it now (*tauta lelalēka*, vv. 1a, 4a), so that if and when such an "hour" materializes they will remember his words and stand firm.

While set in its first century Jewish context, the prophecy attributed here to Jesus does indeed have in one respect an all too familiar contemporary reference. The rise of religious fundamentalism provides almost daily reports of people being killed or maimed by those who think that in so doing they are performing an act of worship to God. While such intolerance on religious grounds may at present be seen principally, though by no means entirely, in regions of the Islamic world, we cannot forget that Christianity has had its centuries of intolerance as well, the most notorious instance in Catholic Christianity being the Inquisition.[111]

Reflection upon the Hatred of the World. John 15:18–16:4a presents more of a challenge to contemporary interpretation than almost any other passage in the gospel. For believers who are experiencing persecution it may indeed have immediate and direct relevance and offer no small measure of comfort—though even then its stark dualism may lock those experiencing persecution or emerging from it into fixed attitudes toward the other and dogmatism in belief that render the slightest movement toward understanding, forgiveness, or reconciliation virtually impossible. We cannot remain so strictly within the Johannine purview as to forget that in the wider Christian tradition Jesus commanded love and prayer even for enemies and persecutors (Matt 5:43-47;

---

[109] Evidence for Jewish persecution of Christians to the extreme of inflicting death is hard to find. For some indications in early Christian literature (aside from Acts 6:8–8:1 [Stephen]; 23:12-15; cf. Gal 1:13; 1 Thess 2:14-16), see Rudolf Schnackenburg, *St. John*, 3:122; also Francis J. Moloney, *John*, 435.

[110] Cf. Andrew T. Lincoln, *St. John*, 413.

[111] As David Rensberger points out, "The condemnation of John 16:2 falls, as it has fallen for centuries, on Christian rather than on Jewish heads" (*Johannine Faith*, 139).

Luke 6:27-36). We should also note that the Johannine tradition, while warning of the hatred of the world, never suggests or implies in any degree that believers should respond in similar coin.[112] If it is in and through his self-sacrificial love that Jesus "has overcome" the world (16:33), his disciples can only hope to do so by following the same way.[113]

The key thing is to appreciate the specific and restricted sense in which the gospel is using the term "world" at this point and not draw simplistic "anti-world" messages from it in a way that runs counter to the incarnational thrust of the gospel as a whole. World-denying language can all too easily become life-denying language in a way that leads to an extreme asceticism and negative attitude to the body fundamentally at odds with the authentic Christian tradition.[114] In 17:15 Jesus makes clear that he is not asking the Father to take the disciples out of the world but to ensure that they do not "belong" to it in the sense of falling captive to its values and ideals.

In this latter sense the passage challenges the church to be fully present in the world while remaining, especially in its structures and procedures, distant from values, attitudes, aspirations, and expectations by which the power structures of the world achieve and maintain control of human life. Faced with hostility from the world, the church can all too readily withdraw into a sectarian posture, seeking security behind rigid walls of dogmatism in its own tenets and condemnation of everything else—a posture which the present passage, wrongly interpreted, can all too easily reinforce. By the same token the passage can usefully remind communities all too comfortable with the surrounding world that such is not the Christian way. A community living by the self-sacrificial love flowing from its union with the true Vine will necessarily threaten and experience hostility from the world in which it lives. The present passage makes clear that the experience of such hostility, while painful, is actually a guarantee of its conformity to the Lord, while the absence of such hostility to any degree should call for reflection and self-examination. In this wider perspective we can perhaps understand why the gospel placed alongside the sublime passage where Jesus counsels abiding in love a warning of the hatred and hostility of the world. Both are necessary instructions for the church in every age as it discerns, with the

---

[112] As, for example, in the movement behind the Dead Sea Scrolls, where the "Sons of Light" are bidden to "hate all the Sons of Darkness" (1QS [*Manual of Discipline*] 1:9-10), quoted in David Rensberger, *Johannine Faith*, 138.

[113] Cf. Gail O'Day, "The Gospel of John," 768.

[114] Cf. Gail O'Day, "The Gospel of John," 767.

assistance of the Paraclete Spirit, how to be the faithful extension in the world of God's incarnate love.[115]

Discourse C: *Jesus Is Going to Depart (2): 16:4b-33*

In the third part of the discourse at the Supper the theme of Jesus' departure and return becomes central once more, with again a measure of exchange between him and the disciples. As explained earlier, the similarities and parallels with the first part of the discourse (13:31–14:31), together with the command to depart in 14:31, have led many scholars to see John 16:4b-33 as a reworking of that discourse from a later period.[116] The more recent tendency is to interpret 16:4b-33 as part of a coherent, single whole, taking note of the tendency of the gospel to employ repetition as a literary device and to restate in new contexts what has been said before.[117]

That said, I think it has to be recognized that, whatever its origins, this second discourse does not quite sustain the theological heights of its earlier fellow. The sense of contrast and alienation from the world (as in 15:18–16:4a) remains strong. The role of the Paraclete Spirit is now not so much to strengthen and defend the faithful as to prosecute and convict the world (16:7-11). The main burden of Jesus' instruction is to stiffen the resolve of the disciples who are distressed at the prospect of his departure and to convince them that his departure to the Father is in fact in their best interest, since otherwise the Paraclete will not come.

The discourse as a whole is held together by the contrasting motifs of sorrow and joy that run through it. More for the sake of convenience than for any clear markers of division, it can be taken in three sections: (1) 16:4b-15: Jesus acknowledges the disciples' sorrow over his departure but explains why it is advantageous for them, since otherwise the Paraclete Spirit will not come; (2) 16:16-22: Jesus answers the disciples' puzzlement about the "little while" of which he is speaking with the aid of an image from childbirth; (3) 16:23-33: the motif of confident prayer reemerges and leads into further dialogue with the disciples.

---

[115] In these reflections I am particularly indebted to the concluding chapter in David Rensberger's study of Johannine sectarianism, "Sect, World, and Mission: Johannine Christianity Today," *Johannine Faith*, 135–54; also to Gail O'Day, "The Gospel of John," 766–68, who acknowledges debt to the same study.

[116] Raymond E. Brown, *John XIII–XXI*, 588–97, 710, sets out the parallels with characteristic thoroughness in a chart across pp. 589–91; see also Rudolf Schnackenburg, *St. John*, 3:123–24.

[117] Cf. Gail O'Day, "The Gospel of John," 770; Francis J. Moloney, *John*, 370–71, 439.

1. *Jesus' Departure No Cause for Sorrow: 16:4b-15*

As Jesus begins again to speak of his "departure" to the Father he explains (v. 4b) that he did not mention "these things"—that is, hostility and persecution—before because his presence with them rendered that unnecessary. Now, however, he has to address the grief and dismay that the prospect of his absence brings.

Better That Jesus Depart: 16:5-7. In this connection it is curious that he remarks that "none of you are asking me, 'Where are you going?'" (v. 5b) because in the earlier part of the discourse two of them, Peter (13:36) and Thomas (14:5), *had* asked him just that question. At one level, the discrepancy likely reflects two distinct versions of the same underlying tradition. On the other hand, we can note that Jesus is not pointing to the absence of questioning in the past (= "None of you has asked me") but to the present ("None of you *are asking* me").[118] In other words, the conversation has moved on. The disciples are no longer asking about where Jesus is going because they are still understanding his departure in terms of physical death and nothing more. Transfixed by grief at this prospect (v. 6), they have failed to grasp that his departure reaches beyond physical death to encompass a return to the Father from which great benefits will flow.[119]

Explaining these benefits is the chief theme of the sentences that follow (vv. 7-15). While spoken to the disciples at the Supper, the primary focus of Jesus' assurance rests upon the situation of the later church following his departure to the Father. That departure may be a source of grief for the disciples but it is a necessary condition for the coming of the Paraclete Spirit, whom Jesus will send to continue the comforting role his own physical presence has played up till now (v. 7). Free from the constraints that have bound the ministry of Jesus to a particular time and space, the comfort provided by the Paraclete will be available to later generations in new situations transcending such limitations. In this sense it is "advantageous" that Jesus "go away" to the Father.

The Forensic Role of the Paraclete: 16:8-11. Jesus expands upon the role of the Paraclete in a short passage (vv. 8-11) that is possibly the most difficult text in the entire discourse for readers today. The law-court ("forensic")

---

[118] Cf. C. K. Barrett, *John*, 485–86.

[119] Cf. Raymond E. Brown, *John XIII–XXI*, 710; Francis J. Moloney, *John*, 439. In some ways the evangelist (or final editor) of the gospel would have made things easier if Jesus had said, "None of you is asking, '*Why* are you going away?'"

context is to the fore again. But where before (15:26) the role of the Paraclete was that of acting as witness for the defense, now the role is that of prosecuting the divine case against the world. Jesus nominates three areas or grounds in terms of which the Paraclete pursues the prosecution: sin, righteousness, and judgment (v. 8), each elaborated in the verses that follow (vv. 9-11).[120] What emerges is a reversal of the trial situation in which Jesus has been placed throughout his ministry by the representatives of the world. It is a situation destined soon to culminate when he stands before the Roman governor. It is one also that believers will face following his departure to the Father. While the world is putting him—and subsequently them—on trial, leading to condemnation, in the divine perspective it is actually itself on trial and being "overcome" (v. 33).

In his ministry Jesus has been accused of being a sinner (9:24)—as have also those who have come to be his disciples (9:34 [Man Born Blind]). In the perspective of the gospel, sin is fundamentally the refusal to believe in the divine revelation ("truth") given by Jesus as Messiah and divine Son. The world's persistence in such refusal is the first count upon which the Paraclete Spirit shows that it, rather than Jesus, is open to conviction: "because they have refused to believe in me" (v. 9).[121]

"Righteousness" (v. 10) most properly refers to the legal status one enjoys after being acquitted of a charge. Jesus is on trial—as his followers will also be. Though he will suffer death, this will not be because he has been found unrighteous. If, having found "no case" against him (18:38b; 19:6b, 12), the Roman governor gives in and hands Jesus over to execution, it will not be on the grounds of justice ("righteousness") but through an all too human fear of losing "friendship" with Caesar (19:12). Jesus' personal "righteousness" will be vindicated because his death will actually be a "departure" to the loving embrace of the Father (v. 10b), something guaranteed by the fact that the disciples will, after a "little while" (16:16), no longer see him (cf. 20:17).

---

[120] The explanation in each case, beginning with the Greek conjunction *hoti*, is best understood in a causal sense: that is, as providing the reasons why the world is convicted; cf. Andrew T. Lincoln, *St. John*, 419–20.

[121] The Greek verb *elengchein* has the dual sense of (1)"bring to light," "expose"; (2) "convict someone of something." There has been much discussion as to which sense is applicable here: cf. C. K. Barrett, *John*, 486–88. "Convict" is applicable in the case of "sin" but seems less appropriate for the remaining two grounds, leading many to prefer "expose" (cf. Raymond E. Brown, *John XIII–XXI*, 705; Francis J. Moloney, *John*, 440, 445). It is both possible and preferable to hold both meanings together in the sense that exposure leads to conviction/condemnation; cf. Andrew T. Lincoln, *St. John*, 419–20.

Finally (v. 11), Jesus will, it is true, be "judged" (= "condemned") by the world and will die on that account. However, in the divine perspective, which the Paraclete makes known, "the ruler of this world" (Satan) in the very act of orchestrating Jesus' death will bring about his own condemnation; indeed, the process of his "casting out" (12:31) is already under way.[122]

How the Paraclete Spirit achieves this multiple prosecution of the world and makes it known to believers is not clear. A sequence such as this represents one of those areas where the Fourth Gospel brings back into the present the events of the final judgment which the Synoptic tradition in more literally apocalyptic mode assigns to the future (cf. especially the coming of the Son of Man as described in Mark 13:24-27; 14:62; and parallels).[123] Believers will frequently find themselves on trial before the world and at risk even of execution. Jesus pledges here that, at least in the forum of their individual and community consciousness, if not publicly to the world, the Paraclete Spirit will communicate to them a sense that it is not they but their judges and persecutors who are being convicted and condemned.

Paraclete as Future Revealer: 16:12-15. Following this very difficult passage, we seem to be back on more familiar ground in regard to the Paraclete in the sentences that follow, though the term itself does not actually occur. Jesus has many things to say to the disciples but they are unable to bear them now (v. 12). The sense of this seems to be that the experiences and situations in which believers of subsequent generations will find themselves are not something that the present disciples can properly envisage or imagine. On this account—because they cannot "bear" it—Jesus refrains from imparting to them the revelation appropriate for that new situation. But when "the Spirit of truth" comes he will at that time lead believers "in" ("into")[124] all truth (v. 13ab),[125] continuing thereby the revelation left incomplete by Jesus.[126]

---

[122] This is the sense of the Greek perfect *kekritai* at the end of v. 11.

[123] Cf. C. H. Dodd, *Interpretation*, 414; C. K. Barrett, *John*, 483; Gail O'Day, "The Gospel of John," 772–73; Andrew T. Lincoln, *St. John*, 420.

[124] The Greek preposition *en* ("in") is probably the preferred reading here but the sense of the variant *eis* ("into") should not be excluded; cf. Raymond E. Brown, *John XIII–XXI*, 707; C. K. Barrett, *John*, 489.

[125] The Greek word *hodēgein* is used in the LXX to translate the expression of God's guidance of the community or the psalmist in the right and safe way: Ps (LXX) 24:5; (LXX) 142:10; also (of Wisdom's guidance) Wis 9:11; 10:10; cf. C. K. Barrett, *John*, 489; Gail O'Day, "The Gospel of John," 773.

[126] Cf. Andrew T. Lincoln, *St. John*, 421.

To reinforce this point, the remaining sentences insist upon the absolute continuity of what the Paraclete Spirit will reveal with what the disciples have been receiving from Jesus. Pivotal is the Greek verb translated "declare" (*anangellein*) which appears no less than three times (vv. 13d, 14b, 15b). This verb has the sense, stemming from its usage in the Greek Old Testament, of "re-announcing what has been heard or announced before."[127] The Spirit will not be an independent agent, bringing fresh revelation in a quantitative sense.[128] Rather, the Spirit will speak from what he will hear[129]—presumably in the heavenly court. This will enable him to "declare to you the things to come," not in the sense of foretelling future events but in the sense of drawing out, in the new situations that will arise, fresh meaning in the events of Jesus' life (cf. 14:25-26).

The Spirit is no rival to Jesus (vv. 14-15): the Spirit in fact will "glorify" Jesus because everything he will reveal to the community will draw upon what Jesus himself has received from the Father, who has shared with him all that he has. In all these respects, believers of the future will be in no inferior position in regard to revelation than the original disciples: in fact, they will continually draw upon deeper reserves of revelation as the Paraclete Spirit leads them to an ever-deeper understanding of the meaning of Jesus' life for their times.[130]

Emerging from these convoluted sentences is the radically trinitarian theology of the Fourth Gospel—a sense of distinct divine persons held within an overall unity of being and operation. The Father expresses a life-giving Word to the world, a Word which the Son embodies and makes known in his human flesh; the Spirit, sent from Father and Son, continues the revelation of that Word to the community and the world in the post-Easter situation.[131] The ongoing teaching role of the church has a clear biblical foundation here.

---

[127] Cf. Raymond E. Brown, *John XIII–XXI*, 708; Gail O'Day, "The Gospel of John," 703.

[128] Rudolf Schnackenburg, *St. John*, 3:135.

[129] Reading the Greek verb in the future tense, *akousei*, rather than the variant in the present, *akouei* (as NRSV). The present is likely to be a correction introduced on dogmatic grounds; cf. Bruce M. Metzger, *Textual Commentary*, 247; C. K. Barrett, *John*, 489–90; Gail O'Day, "The Gospel of John," 773.

[130] Raymond Brown has put it well: "The declaration of things to come consists in interpreting in relation to each coming generation the contemporary significance of what Jesus has said and done. The best Christian preparation for what is coming to pass is not an exact foreknowledge of the future but a deep understanding of what Jesus means for one's own time" (*John XIII–XXI*, 716); cf. also Robert Kysar, *Maverick Gospel*, 131–32.

[131] Cf. Ugo Schnelle, *Johannes*, 273.

2. Sorrow Will Be Replaced by Joy: 16:16-24

The "Little While" of Jesus' Departure and Return: 16:16-19. The theme of sorrow at Jesus' departure comes to the fore once more in a rather labored exchange between him and the disciples. As we have noted several times already, the entire sequence at the Supper plays upon an ambiguity in regard to the "going away" and "return" of Jesus.[132] In the immediate setting of the Supper on the eve of his death, the first "little while" (*mikron*) that he mentions (v. 16a) must refer to the interval between the present hour and the time of arrest and death; the second "little while" (v. 16b) would then refer to the time between his death and his appearances as risen Lord "on the first day of the week" (Sunday: cf. 14:19). In and through this immediate setting, however, the conversation at the Supper addresses the time and concerns of the later church after Jesus' postresurrection return to the Father. The gospel, as we have seen, does in places (e.g., 5:25-29; 6:39-40, 54; 11:24) preserve the hope of Jesus' return "on the last day" as in the futurist eschatology of the Synoptic tradition. But the prospect of this return has begun to stretch out so indefinitely that it hardly makes sense to speak of this space of time as "a little while" and understand the promised "seeing" of Jesus as something destined to occur on this "last day."[133] The gospel seems to be suggesting that the joy the original disciples experienced on the day of Jesus' resurrection is something that should permeate the experience of all subsequent generations of believers (cf. 1 John 1: 4: "We are writing these things so that our joy may be complete").[134]

Jesus' words fail to reassure the disciples. They turn to a puzzled questioning among themselves about the two "little whiles" and Jesus' talk of "going to the Father" (vv. 17-18). His return to the Father, which as yet they do not fully understand, seems to be at odds with the prospect of seeing him again.[135]

Sorrow Will Turn to Joy: 16:20-22. Though aware of the disciples' puzzlement and desire to question him (v. 19; cf. 1:47-48; 2:24; 6:61, 64; 13:11), Jesus responds (vv. 20-22) not with an explanation but with a solemn affirmation ("Amen, Amen"). Believers will weep and mourn because it will

---

[132] In the present connection, C. K. Barrett speaks of a "studied ambiguity" (*John*, 491).

[133] So, Francis J. Moloney, *John*, 450, 451; Andrew T. Lincoln, *St. John*, 422–23; Ugo Schnelle, *Johannes*, 275–76.

[134] Cf. Rudolf Schnackenburg: "Not only Easter day but also the whole of the new age that begins with it is in mind here . . . the joy of the Johannine community . . . anticipates the eschaton" (*St. John*, 3:159); see also Gail O'Day, "The Gospel of John," 778.

[135] Cf. Raymond E. Brown, *John XIII–XXI*, 731.

be through dying that Jesus will go to the Father, while for the representatives of the world who bring it about, his death will be a source of self-satisfied, gloating joy. But, in a reversal reminiscent of the Beatitudes (Luke 6:21, 25), the disciples' grief (*lypē*) will be turned into joy (*chara*)—something that will be dramatically illustrated in Mary Magdalene (20:11-18) and the disciples themselves (20:20) on Easter Day.[136]

As elsewhere in the gospel (4:37-38; 5:19-20; 8:35; 10:1-5; 12:24), Jesus reinforces his assertion with an image from everyday life (v. 21). A woman, when her time ("hour") of giving birth has arrived, experiences distress (*lypē*) at the prospect of the pain that will be involved. When she has given birth, she no longer remembers the pain (*thlipsis*) because of her joy in having brought a fresh human life into the world. It is really for women who have gone through this experience to assess the aptness of the image.[137] However, it seems to offer an effective illustration of the transformation involved. We can set it out schematically as follows:

Before: Prospect of pain (*thlipsis*) ⟶ **grief** (*lypē*)

Birth   <new life>

After: **joy** (*chara*) ⟶ **forgetfulness** of pain.[138]

In a similar way (v. 22) the grief the disciples are presently experiencing at the prospect of Jesus' departure will be transformed into joy.[139] The cause of their joy is stated to be Jesus' seeing them, rather than their seeing him (as in vv. 16, 17). The difference is probably not to be pressed[140] but the formulation with Jesus as subject communicates the sense of divine initiative in the encounter. It also speaks to the situation of the later community of believers. They will not have a physical sight of the risen Lord but will know through their faith in the resurrection that they do live under his gaze and

---

[136] Gail O'Day, "The Gospel of John," 779; Andrew T. Lincoln, *St. John*, 423.

[137] Dorothy A. Lee, *Symbolic Narratives*, 211–12, discusses the image sympathetically.

[138] The language of the image raises echoes of Isa 26:17 and 66:7-14 (spoken of Jerusalem as in labor). "Hour," of course, is a Johannine designation for the moment of Jesus' passion and death, while the Greek word *thlipsis* often appears in the New Testament with regard to persecution (Matt 13:31; 24:9, 21, 24; Acts 11:19; Rom 5:3; 8:35; etc.) and with respect, in particular, to the trials expected to increase before the full dawning of the messianic age (Mark 13:19, 24; Rev. 7:14).

[139] Lit., "your heart will rejoice," a possible echo of Isa 66:14.

[140] Just as a medical practitioner might say to a patient in regard to a fresh appointment: "I'll see you in a month's time."

protection. The world will have trials in plenty in store for them over the years to come. But none will be able to take away the joy communicated by faith's vision of the One who in death and resurrection has "overcome the world" (v. 33).

No Further Need for Questions: 16:23-24. Moving beyond the image, Jesus does address to some extent the disciples' puzzled questioning about the "little whiles" of their not seeing and then seeing him by pointing (v. 23a) to a future ("on that day") when they will not feel the need to ask any questions.[141] Once again the issue arises as to when "that day" will be. To refer it to the last day in the fully future sense[142] would seem to place it too far beyond the purview not only of the present disciples but of post-Easter believers as well. The reference is obscure but the sense may be that the more believers appropriate the joy flowing from their faith in the risen Lord the more their questionings about his going and his return die away. In the oft-quoted remark of Rudolf Bultmann, "[I]t is the nature of joy that all questioning grows silent, and nothing needs explaining."[143]

With a further solemn affirmation ("Amen, Amen"), Jesus mentions (vv. 23b-24) another form of "asking" that will distinguish the time of eschatological joy: prayer to the Father in the firm confidence of being heard. This theme has appeared several times already in the total discourse (14:13-14; 15:7, 16). It now emerges strongly (cf. v. 26) in connection with the joy of which Jesus has been speaking. Although the disciples will not have the physical presence of Jesus in the time to come, their union with him will be so complete that their prayers to the Father will be as assured of response as his own prayer has been. The Father will respond to their prayer "in his name" in the sense of responding as though Jesus were the one making the prayer.[144] When the disciples (v. 25) begin to make their prayers in his name

---

[141] The Greek verb *erōtan* usually has the sense of "ask a question," though it can also mean to "ask for something," which is the sole meaning of the second "asking" verb, *aitein*, appearing here (v. 24). Though *erōtan* appears with the latter meaning occasionally in John (4:31, 40, 47; 12:21; 14:16; 16:26; 17:9), the first seems more appropriate here, rounding off the dialogue that began with the disciples asking questions among themselves; cf. C. K. Barrett, *John*, 494; Raymond E. Brown, *John XIII–XXI*, 722; Rudolf Schnackenburg, *St. John*, 3:159; Andrew T. Lincoln, *St. John* 424; Gail O'Day, "The Gospel of John," 780; against, Francis J. Moloney, *John*, 452.

[142] So, Francis J. Moloney, *John*, 452.

[143] Rudolf Bultmann, *Gospel of John*, 583; cf. Gail O'Day, "The Gospel of John," 780.

[144] That is, reading the phrase "in my name" after the verb "will give," which is the more difficult and hence more likely original reading in the manuscript tradition; cf. Raymond E. Brown, *John XIII–XXI*, 723; Rudolf Schnackenburg, *St. John*, 3:160; Francis J. Moloney, *John*, 450.

in this way and receive the desired response, they will experience a joy that enhances and completes the joy that they already have as a result of his resurrection (literally, "in order that your joy may be complete"). The joy will flow from the sense of intimacy with the Father that the hearing of their prayers will confirm. They will know that they are loved as Jesus is loved. Anyone who has experienced the hearing of prayer—whether in small things or great—knows something of the joy of which Jesus speaks at this point.[145]

3. *"I Have Overcome the World": 16:25-33*

Jesus begins to draw the discourse to a close with a reflection on the way he has spoken and points to a coming time when he will no longer petition the Father on behalf of the disciples because they will make their petitions directly, secure in the Father's love (vv. 25-28). This prompts a final response from the disciples (vv. 29-30), followed by a prophetic warning from Jesus that sweeps into a majestic conclusion to the discourse as a whole (vv. 31-33).

The Coming "Hour" of Direct Dealing with the Father: 16:25-28. In his reflection Jesus says (v. 25) he has been speaking "figuratively" (so, NIV; literally, "in figures of speech" [NRSV]). The Greek word *paroimia* has a wide range of meaning—parable, image, proverb, riddle. The most obvious reference would be to the image of the woman in labor in v. 21. The fact that Jesus speaks of "figures" (plural) suggests, however, a wider reference: namely, to the mysterious nature of his words throughout the Supper and indeed throughout his ministry as a whole. As he is "from above," his words are inevitably mysterious and obscure to those who have not as yet been "born from above" through the Spirit. We recall his words to Nicodemus to this effect (3:3-10). Since the disciples are not yet "born from above" and as yet lack the assistance of the Paraclete Spirit, they are struggling with his revelation of the Father and of "heavenly things" (*epourania* [3:12]) in general.

So much for the present. But "an hour" is coming when Jesus will no longer speak figuratively but will tell the disciples "plainly (*parrēsiai*) about the Father" (v. 25bc). "Hour" here indicates that the time in question is that

---

[145] It is possible, with Raymond E. Brown, *John XIII–XXI*, 728, to link vv. 23b-24 with what follows, down to v. 26, making petitionary prayer the subject throughout. However, that makes v. 25 something of an interruption, and the "not in riddles" theme of v. 25 is taken up later on (v. 29). We have to recognize a considerable interweaving of themes across 16:23-30.

of Jesus' death, resurrection, and ascension when he will be most transparently revelatory of the Father, not so much in words but in the whole "glorification" of God that these events will represent (13:31-32).[146] After that time and in light of these events the Paraclete Spirit will cause the disciples, now "born from above" (cf. 20:17), to "remember" the words of Jesus in such wise as to render them no longer "figurative" but "plain" (cf. 2:22; 12:16; 13:7). No more will there be any need for the disciples to ask Jesus questions (cf. v. 23).

Just as then there will be no need for the disciples to ask questions, so there will be no need for Jesus to place their petitions before the Father (v. 26).[147] Born "from above" as children of God (1:12; 20:17), they will enjoy a share in the intimacy and immediacy of access to the Father that hitherto has belonged to Jesus alone. "On that day" they will make their petitions in Jesus' name in a union and identity with him so close as to render separate prayer on his part unnecessary.

To bolster this confidence in direct prayer to the Father, Jesus assures (v. 27) the disciples once more of the Father's love for them (cf. 14:21, 23; cf. 15:9-11). The way this is formulated ("the Father himself loves you, because you have loved me and have believed that I came from God") could give the impression that the Father's love is conditional upon prior human love and faith in Jesus. This would be counter to the whole sense of divine initiative that runs through the gospel (cf., e.g., 3:16). Rather, the disciples have so intimate an involvement in the divine communion of love as to exclude any thought of Jesus having to come between them and the Father to make representation on their behalf. "The Father will love the disciples with the same love with which he has loved Jesus (17:23-26); and the Father, Jesus, and the disciples will be one (17:21-23)."[148] In effect, Jesus is including the Father within the relationship of friendship that he spoke of as existing between the disciples and himself (15:15).[149]

The disciples' faith may have been instrumental in drawing them into this circle of love. But focused on Jesus' origins—that he came from God—it

---

[146] Cf. Francis J. Moloney, *John*, 453.

[147] In this way, as v. 25 complements v. 23a, v. 26 (together with vv. 27-28) complements vv. 23b-24; cf. Gail O'Day, "The Gospel of John," 781.

[148] Raymond E. Brown, *John XIII–XXI*, 735.

[149] The use of the Greek verb *philein* for "love" here, where *agapan* is used of the Father's love in 14:21, 23, shows that there is no difference in meaning between the words in Johannine usage (cf. 21:15-17). *Philein* does communicate the sense that God and the disciples are "friends"; cf. Rudolf Schnackenburg, *St. John*, 3:163; Gail O'Day, "The Gospel of John," 781–82.

is still not adequate to the full scheme of salvation, including the "departure" from the world that has been the chief burden of his instruction throughout the Supper. To address this, Jesus concludes with a statement (v. 28) offering a perfectly balanced formulation of the full sweep of Johannine theology/ christology:

> I came from the Father and have come into the world;
> again, I am leaving the world and am going to the Father. (John 16:28)[150]

The couplet is spoken by Jesus in respect to his own personal mission. Since, however, the purpose of that mission has been to draw the world, currently in darkness, into the light and life of the divine communion of love (1:4-5), there is a sense in which every human person born into the world has "come from the Father" and is on a lifelong journey "to the Father." This is the essential "truth" about human life that the Son has come to communicate and witness to before the world.[151]

The Disciples' Inadequate Understanding of Jesus' Mission: 16:29-30. Granted the difficulties that the disciples will have with the actual process (arrest, trial, and execution) of Jesus' return to the Father, there is irony in the impetuous and rather patronizing outburst with which they now (vv. 29-30) commend Jesus for speaking "plainly" (*parrēsiai*), without any figure of speech. He may no longer be using a figure of speech—as in the image of the woman in labor (v. 21)—but that does not mean that they have understood the full range of his declaration about his mission in v. 28. The inadequacy of their faith is patent in the explanation they go on to give (v. 30). They believe that Jesus has come from God on the basis of his having no need to ask questions of people to know what they are thinking. Jesus had displayed this supernatural knowledge a few moments before (16:19) and at other times earlier in the gospel (1:48-49; 2:24-25; 4:19, 29). But it is hardly the most important grounds for faith in him. Moreover, their faith is still fastened upon his origins ("that you came from God"); they are still not "hearing" what he has been saying about his, now imminent, departure.

---

[150] The formulation has a chiastic structure: a ("from the Father"): b ("into the world"): b' ("leaving the world"): a' ("going to the Father"). Taking it as unified whole rests on reading the long text across the end of v. 27 and the beginning of v. 28, rather than a shorter version appearing in some Western manuscripts which omit the phrase "I came from the Father" at the beginning of v. 28. In favor of the long version (the majority view; also NIV, NRSV), see Raymond E. Brown, *John XIII–XXI*, 724–25.

[151] I owe this insight to my senior colleague Gerald O'Collins, SJ.

Warning and Conclusion: 16:31-33. Granted the inadequacy of the disciples' expression of faith, it is best to take Jesus' final response (v. 31) as a kind of ironic question ("So you believe now, do you?") rather than as an affirmation.[152] The time for adequate faith and understanding remains in the future. What lies immediately ahead (v. 32), and will, for all their protestations, show the inadequacy of the disciples' faith, is an "hour" of scattering and desertion as each of them returns "to his own (home)" (*eis ta idia*).[153] They are "his own," whom Jesus has loved "to the end" (13:1), his own sheep for whom he, as Good Shepherd, will lay down his life (10:11-12). Now they will themselves scatter and desert their Shepherd and leave him alone (*monos*).[154] Immediately, however, Jesus corrects that impression: he is not alone because his Father is with him. His isolation, right up to the moment of his death, is apparent: even in his death—in fact, supremely in his death—he remains ever "in the bosom of the Father" (1:18).[155]

The assertion of union with the Father prepares the way for the solemn note upon which the discourse ends (v. 33). The opening phrase "These things I have said to you" (v. 33a) gathers up the entire discourse. Its whole purpose has been that the disciples should have "peace" in their union with Jesus ("peace in me"). He has sought to counter their grief and dismay at the prospect of his departure. They will have "peace" if they grasp that his departure to the Father is to their advantage: that it will inaugurate an era of deeper understanding and knowledge through the presence and assistance of the "other Paraclete," the Spirit. They will have peace "in" him in so far as they preserve and live out the intimate union with him expressed in that simple phrase (15:1-11).

Over against their being "in" Jesus there remains their continuing existence "in the world" (v. 33b; 17:11, 15, 18). About this Jesus is quite realistic. Since though "in" the world the disciples are not "of" it (15:19: 17:14, 16),

---

[152] Grammatically, the form of the verb *pisteuete* is open to being read as either a question or an indicative statement.

[153] The language echoes that of Mark 14:27//Matt 26:31, where Jesus, on the way to Gethsemane, cites Zech 13:7 with reference to the desertion and scattering of the disciples.

[154] In the Johannine passion account the disciples are not actually said to desert Jesus at his arrest and one of them, the Beloved Disciple, follows Jesus to the foot of the cross. We seem to have here a remnant of an older tradition preserved in the Fourth Gospel but not totally harmonized with its wider narrative; cf. Raymond E. Brown, *John XIII–XXI*, 736–37.

[155] It is possible to see here a Johannine correction to the Markan presentation of Jesus' cry of dereliction on the cross: Mark 15:34; cf. C. K. Barrett, *John*, 498; against Gail O'Day, "The Gospel of John," 783. The two gospels are approaching the mystery of the death of God's Son from different angles. On a total theological view there is no contradiction between them.

they will experience affliction (*thlipsis*)—chiefly in the shape of the persecution from representatives of the world hostile to God. In the face of this, however, the disciples must be "of good cheer" (*tharseite*). Why? Because counter to appearances that may seem to prevail, Jesus has (already) "conquered the world" (v. 33c). In the hours to come he will shortly surrender himself into the powers of darkness, who will encompass his condemnation and death. So certain, however, is he that in this very act they are bringing about their own defeat he can pronounce even beforehand: "I have conquered" (*nenikēka*) the world."

Reflection. The blend of realism and triumph upon which the discourse comes to an end is the foundation of Christian hope. The closer believers adhere to Jesus and his values the less likely they are to be preserved from suffering the hostility of forces in the world opposed to God, to love, and to life.[156] Hope springs not from a perception that things are going to get better any time soon but rather from the conviction that the resurrection of Jesus shows that precisely in the defeats suffered for his love lies a victory that will have the final word.[157]

The dualism of the Fourth Gospel emerges strongly once more as Jesus' discourse draws to a close. He speaks of the defeat of the world itself—not just, as earlier (12:31; 14:30), of its prince (Satan). We must remember, however, that the disciples are to continue Jesus' mission to the world (cf. 17:20; 20:29). The world is still the world that the Father "so loved" as to send his only Son so that it may not perish but have eternal life (3:16). When, then, Jesus ends on the note of having "overcome the world," it is principally the world in the sense of the forces hostile to God and holding human beings in thrall that is in view. If the disciples simply withdrew from the world in a totally sectarian way and sought to have nothing to do with it as far as possible, then the world might leave them alone. It is when they are true to the divine mission of love to the world that they attract its hostility. Then they can know both the closeness of their unity with Jesus and their sharing, despite suffering, in his victory.[158]

---

[156] "Invariably it is those who show the world the possibility, and therefore the necessity, of living in love, living for others, without violence and without oppression, whom the world hates most passionately and exterminates most vigorously" (David Rensberger, *Johannine Faith*, 129; cf. also 99).

[157] Cf. Francis J. Moloney, *John*, 455.

[158] Cf. 1 John 5:4b: "And this is the victory that conquers the world, our faith."

3. Jesus' Prayer to the Father: 17:1-26

The Supper comes to a climactic end with an extended, reflective prayer addressed by Jesus to the Father.[159] This prayer, which the disciples are privileged to "overhear," has long been considered the high point of the Fourth Gospel.[160] Here, the gospel's sense of the intimacy between Father and Son is most readily laid bare, most strongly drawing us and inviting us to enter into its mystic vision. While located as the immediate prelude to his arrest, condemnation, and death, Jesus' reflections in the prayer transcend the limits of time and space even more intentionally than in the preceding discourse. The prayer takes us back to the vision of the Prologue with its sense of Jesus' eternal origins with the Father (1:1-2, 18). At the same time, he is already on the way to the Father, having crossed the threshold from time to eternity.[161]

While laying bare in this way the eternal relationship between Father and Son, the primary focus of Jesus in his prayer remains the future of the disciples and the later community of believers (the church) which they foreshadow and represent. While remaining in the world, as he is departing from it, they are to draw confidence from knowing that their life and mission in the world is continually accompanied by this intercessory prayer of Jesus. Again and again throughout the discourse he has urged them to address confident prayer to the Father in all the needs and difficulties they will encounter. Now he "models" such prayer and shows that, when they pray, his own intercession as the Father's beloved Son stands with and behind the prayers they offer.

The prayer has been variously divided by interpreters.[162] A convenient division proceeds along the lines of who or what is the primary focus of Jesus' attention in particular areas:

---

[159] There are ample precedents for "farewell discourses" to conclude with an extended prayer: most notably, the prayer of Moses in Deut 30:30–32:37; see further, Gail O'Day, "The Gospel of John," 787.

[160] Since the early Christian centuries the prayer has been referred to as Jesus' "(High) Priestly Prayer." The designation is appropriate in respect to the prayer's intercessory content. It tends to play down the connections between the prayer and the preceding discourse; it may also import cultic overtones that are not really present; cf. Gail O'Day, "The Gospel of John," 787.

[161] Raymond E. Brown, *John XIII–XXI*, 747.

[162] For a thorough discussion, see Raymond E. Brown, *John XIII–XXI*, 747–51; more concisely, Gail O'Day, "The Gospel of John," 788. The chief issue seems to be whether vv. 6-8 should be linked with vv. 1-5 or attached to vv. 9-19, or considered a separate unit. Also discussed is whether vv. 24-26 should be separated from vv. 20-26 (and even whether the break should be between vv. 24, 25).

1. Reflecting on His Mission, Jesus Prays for His Glorification: 17:1-5

2. Jesus Reflects upon His Disciples: 17:6-8

3. Jesus Prays for His Disciples, Who Are To Continue His Mission: 17:9-19

4. Jesus Prays for the Unity of Future Believers: 17:20-23

5. Concluding Personal Invocations to the Father: 17:24-26

1. *Reflecting on His Mission, Jesus Prays for His Glorification: 17:1-5*

The evangelist introduces Jesus' prayer with due solemnity (v. 1a). It rounds off the discourse ("Jesus spoke these things") and is preceded by a raising of his eyes to heaven—a conventional gesture of prayer (v. 17b; cf. 11:41b). Addressing the Father directly, Jesus announces that his "hour has come" (v. 17c). In view of this, he asks the Father to glorify him in order that the glorification may be mutual (v. 17d). As he now stands most imminently before the events that will lead to his death, he prays that they be set in motion to achieve this mutual glorification (cf. 13:31-32). His life is not something his adversaries are taking from him on their own accord. He is laying it down in free obedience to the mission received from the Father (10:18).

In virtue of this mission the Son has "authority" (*exousia*) over all human beings (literally, "all flesh")[163] (v. 2). As the sequence in 5:20-27 has made clear, this authority refers especially to the exercise of judgment. While judgment that could involve condemnation as well as destiny to resurrection and life, here, as in 3:16, it is entirely the latter that is in view.[164] The will of the Father from the start has been the rescue of human beings from the darkness of alienation from God that stifles life. Hence the goal of the "authority" that has been given to Jesus is that he should give "eternal life" to "all" (*pan*) whom the Father has given him.[165] As elsewhere in John, "eternal life," has the sense of human sharing in the life of God, the prerogative of those who have become through faith "children of God" (1:12; 12:52; cf. 20:17). In exercising his authority to bestow this status upon those who

---

[163] "Flesh" here has the sense of humanity as such (cf. 1:14), without negative implications.

[164] Cf. Rudolf Schnackenburg, *St. John*, 3:171; Gail O'Day, "The Gospel of John," 789.

[165] There is a sense of election in the phrase "all whom the Father has given," but not predestination; cf. Rudolf Schnackenburg, *St. John*, 3:171. Human beings remain free not to "come to the light" (ibid. 3:18-20).

receive him (1:13), Jesus will glorify the Father by bringing into being new children who honor him as such.[166]

In something of an aside (v. 3) Jesus offers what at first sight seems to be a definition of "eternal life" but is really more in the nature of a reminder of how such life is gained. Eternal life is knowing the "one, true God" and Jesus Christ whom God has sent. "Knowing" here is tantamount to believing.[167] Beyond intellectual knowledge it has the Semitic overtones of commitment to another person in relationship. The sense is not that one knows God, on the one hand, and Jesus, on the other, quite independently of each other. Rather, one appropriates the true revelation of God in and through the person and work of Jesus. To know God in this sense is to be drawn already into the "eternal life" of the divine communion of love, even if a "knowing as I am known" (1 Cor 13:12) remains in this life outstanding. The best commentary is given in 1 John 3:2:

> Beloved, we are God's children now; what we will be has not yet been revealed. What we do know is this: when he is revealed, we will be like him, for we will see him as he is.

After the clarification, Jesus returns to his prayer for glorification (vv. 4-5). He has glorified the Father on earth by completing the mission to the world that the Father had given him (v. 4). Though expressed in the past tense (*edoxasas*) this earthly glorification will climax as Jesus dies upon the cross. His reference to "having completed (*teleiōsas*)" the work the Father appointed him to do both foreshadows and includes the majestic "It is accomplished" (*tetelestai*) that will be his final word before giving up the spirit (19:30). Now, however, moving beyond the earthly perspective, Jesus asks (v. 5) to be glorified in the presence of God with the glory that he enjoyed with the Father before the creation of the world. We are back with the opening vision of the Prologue (1:1-2) and the echo of that in 6:62 ("What if you were to see the Son of Man ascending to where he was before?").

Jesus prays, then, to be restored to that pretemporal glory—but not in the sense of a flight from the world, reversing the incarnation.[168] The divine embrace of the world in self-sacrificial love (3:16) will remain a life-giving revelation through the witness of the disciples assisted by the Paraclete Spirit. It is to the disciples and their task in this respect that Jesus now directs his prayer.

---

[166] Cf. Raymond E. Brown, *John XIII–XXI*, 751.

[167] Cf. C. K. Barrett, *John*, 504.

[168] Cf. Gail O'Day, "The Gospel of John," 790: "To speak of Jesus' return to God and the glory that he had before creation does not negate the incarnation, but rather reinforces its scandal."

2. *Jesus Reflects upon His Disciples: 17:6-8*

In the context of his own return to the Father, Jesus devotes an extensive part of his prayer to the disciples whom he will be leaving in the world. In a somewhat repetitive and convoluted way—though in harmony with the overall solemnity of the prayer—he reviews (vv. 6-8) the preparation he has given them for this task. He has revealed God's "name" to those that the Father has given him "out of the world" (v. 6). The note of election that returns here does not have the intention of excluding some while including others but rather of communicating to the disciples—and the believers who will succeed them—a comforting sense of having been chosen by God and gifted to Jesus. As he sets about praying for them, Jesus is "reminding" the Father that they belong to him just as much as to himself. They are worthy of the Father's care because they have responded positively and appropriately to the revelation he has given them. In particular—as variously stated several times across vv. 7-8—they have acknowledged in faith that everything that Jesus has said and done has proceeded from the Father, reflecting the fundamental truth of his own origins with God and his being sent into the world by God.

These reflections to the disciples on the success of Jesus' ministry may seem overly optimistic in light of his prophecy of their coming failure at the close of the preceding discourse (16:32). His confidence in their mature faith and knowledge of his origins reflects more the situation of the later church than the time of the Supper.[169] The contrast is not so much with the disciples' historical weakness at the time of his passion but with the ongoing disbelief of the world. Jesus is making out a "case" for the disciples' worthiness and the worthiness of their successors in later generations to receive the protection of the Father.[170]

3. *Jesus Prays for the Disciples, Who Are To Continue his Mission: 17:9-19*

In Jesus' extended prayer for the disciples (vv. 9-19) several familiar themes recur. Prominent still is consciousness of their remaining in the (hostile) world while Jesus is leaving the world to return to the Father. When Jesus says (v. 9) that he is praying for the disciples and not for the world, this does not mean that the world no longer remains an object of divine concern. We have to hold a dualistic sense of separation from the world in suspense until it is balanced by the motif of mission to the world that will

---

[169] Cf. Raymond E. Brown, *John XIII–XXI*, 742.
[170] Cf. Rudolf Schnackenburg, *St. John*, 3:178.

emerge later (vv. 17-19; 20-22). For the time being the focus is exclusively upon the disciples in distinction from the world, particularly in their preciousness to Jesus himself and to the Father.

By way of introduction, Jesus states the grounds for the Father's hearing his prayer for the disciples (vv. 9b-11a). It is not that the Father needs to be persuaded. But, as before at the tomb of Lazarus (11:41-42), Jesus offers this "reminder" to the Father so that the listening disciples may have their sense of preciousness in the divine sight reconfirmed. As often in John, the logic is somewhat roundabout. Jesus reasons that, since the disciples are the Father's "gift" to him and since all he has he shares with the Father, so the disciples are also the Father's possession—and hence worthy objects of divine care.

What makes them particularly deserving of such care is the fact that he himself has "been glorified" in them (*dedoxasmai en autois* [v. 10b]). Usually in the gospel it is the Father who is glorified in Jesus: in the sense that in his human person ("flesh") the being and power of the unseen Father is disclosed (1:18). Here, Jesus appears to be saying that the disciples are so transformed by the formation he has given them that they will disclose *his* presence and identity when he is no longer physically in the world. When in their community life they love one another as he has loved them, all will know that they are his disciples (13:35).[171] In the new situation (v. 11a) when they will remain in the world as he goes to the Father,[172] they will "glorify" him before the world as he has glorified the Father throughout his earthly life and supremely at this "hour."

It is for their preservation in this crucial role, in the midst of a hostile world, that Jesus now (vv. 11b-19) prays on their behalf. The opening invocation, "holy Father," foreshadows his praying later for the disciples' "sanctification" (vv. 17-19). Holiness is the essential prerogative of God, as distinct from all creatures and all taint of evil. If human beings have any goodness it is entirely the creation and gift of God, the source of all holiness. Now, with Jesus' departure to the Father, the disciples stand in need of a new measure of protection in order to reflect in the world the holiness of the One who, through the work of Jesus, they can claim to be their "Father" (1:12; 20:17).

What Jesus asks for the disciples is summed up in the word "keep" (*tēreson*) which appears three times in this part of the prayer. "Keep" goes along with the sense of Jesus as Shepherd that seems to run not far below

---

[171] Cf. Gail O'Day, "The Gospel of John," 792.

[172] Since Jesus is speaking to the Father it makes more sense for him to say he is "coming" (to the Father) rather than, as so often when speaking to the disciples, saying he is "going away"; cf. C. K. Barrett, *John*, 507.

the surface. A key aspect of a shepherd's role is to keep the sheep under his care united; scattered or lost, they are vulnerable to theft or attack. So Jesus prays to the Father to "keep (the disciples) in the name" which he has given to Jesus "in order that they may be one as we are one" (v. 11b). As the bearer of God's name, Jesus has stamped the identity represented by the name on the disciples. He prays that they be preserved in the unity of that identity, so that their unity in love may reflect in the world the divine communion of love.

Keeping the disciples together in this sense is all the more necessary because of the new situation they face following Jesus' departure to the Father (vv. 12-13). Up till now, he (as Shepherd) has kept them together. Only one ("the son of perdition" [Judas][173]) has been lost—a loss that had, in any case, been foretold in the Scriptures (Ps 41:10; cf. John 13:18-19). Now, in view of his imminent departure to the Father, Jesus speaks these words while still in the world in order that the disciples may have his "joy (*chara*) fulfilled in them" (v. 13). As elsewhere in the gospel, the joy experienced by Jesus stems from his intimacy with the Father and the sense of being loved that goes with it. His own joy will be "fulfilled" (*peplērōmenēn*) in them when the disciples that he has "kept" in the Father's name share the same sense of intimacy and awareness of being loved by God.[174]

From this positive sense of the disciples' privilege, Jesus' thoughts— and prayer—turn, in a more negative vein, to their situation in the world (vv. 14-16). By giving them the Father's "word" (*logon*)—the word by which they have been "cleansed" (15:3)—Jesus has drawn them into the sphere of his "otherness" from the world and "at homeness" with God. They no longer belong to the world, as he does not belong to the world (v. 14cd, v. 16[175]). On this account they have incurred the world's hostility and its hatred to all that is intrinsically other than itself (cf. 15:19).[176]

The strongly dualistic note that reemerges here is tempered by a crucial qualification that Jesus immediately makes (v. 15). Though the disciples do not belong to the world, Jesus does not pray that they be taken out of the world. They are to remain in the world (cf. also v. 11). What is needed is

---

[173] "Son of perdition": a Semitic phrase (elsewhere only 2 Thess 2:3) meaning "one destined for perdition"; cf. C. K. Barrett, *John*, 508. Francis J. Moloney, *John*, 467, 470, seems to be isolated in seeing a reference to Satan rather than Judas.

[174] The Greek word "*plēroun*" has the sense of fill or top up so that the filling of something is complete.

[175] While v. 16 more or less simply repeats v. 14, the repetitious style of the prayer overall suggests its originality; cf. Rudolf Schnackenburg, *St. John*, 3:184.

[176] Cf. C. K. Barrett, *John*, 509.

that, in this existence in the world, they be "kept" from the Evil One.[177] Though Jesus has radically "overcome the world" (16:33), the malign influence of its ruler lingers, leaving the disciples vulnerable to attempts to savage the Shepherd's flock and reverse his victory. The community needs divine protection if it is to live out faithfully its identity and vocation in the world.[178]

In the culminating plea (vv. 17-19) in this part of the prayer Jesus asks the Father to "sanctify" the disciples "in the truth" (v. 17a). From the biblical background (cf. Jer 1:15 [Jeremiah]; Exod 28:41 [Aaron and his companions]), "sanctification" has the sense of being set apart for sacred work or duty.[179] Jesus' earlier identification of himself as "the One whom the Father has sanctified and sent into the world" (10:36) adds the note of being set apart specifically for mission. A person "sanctified" in this way is so indelibly and publicly marked out for mission as to be rendered incapable of being engaged in any other purpose. Jesus is, then, asking the Father to do for the disciples what God has already done for him: set them apart to continue in the world his witness to the truth (cf. 18:37).[180] An explanatory comment, "Your word is truth" (v. 17b), recalls the statement that the disciples have been "cleansed" by the word that Jesus has spoken to them (15:3). To be "sanctified in truth," then, means being preserved through the word of God from contamination by the standards of the world in the course of the mission in the world.

If, then, the disciples do not belong to the world, as Jesus does not belong to the world, this does not mean their removal from the world. On the contrary, they are "set apart" from the world and "sanctified" precisely so that they can be "sent back" into the world in continuance of the Son's mission (v. 18). Jesus is "sanctifying" himself (v. 19a) for the disciples (*hyper autōn*) in the sense of laying down his life—as Passover Lamb (1:29)—for their purification from sin (cf. 13:6-10).[181] He now prays (v. 19b) that, in their mission in the world, the sanctified status that he has gained for them be preserved so that they can truly fulfill their witness to the truth. The

---

[177] The Greek phrase *ek tou ponērou* could be read simply as "from evil." A personal reference to Satan as the personification of cosmic forces in the world opposed to God is suggested by a string of references in 1 John: 2:13-14; 3:12; 5:18-19; cf. Gail O'Day, "The Gospel of John," 793.

[178] Cf. Gail O'Day, "The Gospel of John," 793.

[179] Cf. C. K. Barrett, *John*, 501.

[180] Cf. Gail O'Day, "The Gospel of John," 793.

[181] A reference here to the Son's self-sacrificial death is guaranteed by the phrase *hyper hymōn*, the preposition *hyper* being almost invariably used in the Fourth Gospel with reference to dying for the sake of others (6:51; 10:11, 15; 11:50, 51, 52; 13:37, 38; 18:14); cf. Rudolf Schnackenburg, *St. John*, 3:187.

continuity emanating from this passage between the Son's mission to the world and that of the disciples is remarkable.

4. *Jesus Prays for the Unity of Future Believers: 17:20-23*

As his prayer moves to its final stage, Jesus prays explicitly for later generations: those who will believe in him through the "word" of the disciples (v. 20).[182] Though later generations are in view, the distinction between them and the historical disciples present in the room is not the main point. What is uppermost here is a sense of mission: that belief is something to be witnessed to and passed on to others who do not yet believe.[183] The distinction, then, is between those in any generation who are believers and those who may come to believe on the basis of their witness.[184] Jesus prays not only for the preservation and flourishing of believers in themselves but for their effectiveness as instruments for imparting the divine life to the wider world (cf. 20:29; 1 John 1:1-4). That is why his prayer reaches out to all generations, down to our own.

What will draw converts to the community of faith is the palpable witness of unity flourishing within it. That is the essential presupposition of Jesus' repeated prayer for unity in the following sentences (vv. 21-23).[185] The oneness for which Jesus prays is not something that the community can achieve by human effort alone, loving one another in a "horizontal" sense. It is a gift from above, a participation on the part of the community in the oneness existing between Father and Son. It is then, in a "vertical" sense, a participation in the divine communion of love, a communion and unity that is expressed, characteristically for John, in the language of "indwelling": "As you, Father, are in me and I am in you, may they also be in us" (v. 21bc; cf. 23a).[186]

---

[182] A stricter rendering of the Greek word order could suggest that Jesus prays for those who "believe through their (the disciples') word (of testimony) to me"; cf. C. K. Barrett, *John*, 512.

[183] Cf. Francis J. Moloney, *John*, 474–75.

[184] Cf. Gail O'Day, "The Gospel of John," 794.

[185] Verses 20-21 and vv. 22-23 consist of lengthy and closely parallel sequences in the Greek, each featuring a series of piled-up purpose clauses, expressing the content and the ultimate goal of Jesus' prayer: namely, that the world should believe; cf. Raymond E. Brown, *John XIII–XXI*, 769; Gail O'Day, "The Gospel of John," 794–95.

[186] "The community will experience oneness because they share in the mutuality and reciprocity of the Father/Son relationship (cf. 14:23; 15:8-10)" (Gail O'Day, "The Gospel of John," 795).

The "missionary" goal (v. 21c; cf. v. 23d) of this oneness is that the world may believe (v. 23: "may know")[187] that Jesus is the one sent by the Father (cf. 3:17; 5:24, 36; 7:28-29; 8:18-19; 12:45, 49). To fully grasp what Jesus is praying for here we have to draw on reserves of Johannine theology disclosed earlier in the gospel. At the close of his public ministry Jesus had declared: "I, when I am lifted up from the earth, will draw all people to myself" (12:32). The drawing power of what would otherwise be totally repellent—death on a cross—is the drawing power of love. When Jesus' death in this form is perceived, not as a hapless fate, but something freely embraced in a supreme expression of love (10:17-18), then it draws all to the revelation of God that it embodies.

That revelation is, again characteristically for John, expressed in terms of "glory" (*doxa*). When Jesus states (v. 22a) that he has given to believers the glory that the Father has given him, in order that they might be one as he and the Father are one, he means that he has imparted to them a quality of love reflective of the divine love. It is by discerning this love made palpable in the community that the world—or at least those drawn by grace—will come to know Jesus as the true revelation of God, the revelation of God as love (1 John 4:8). Beyond this still (v. 23d), the world will know that the Father loves believers as he loves Jesus.[188]

There could hardly be a higher or more daring statement of the privilege of the believing community than this: to know that they are loved by the Father with the same divine love as the Son is loved, that they are drawn into the depths of that divine intimacy, and that Jesus prays that they be "perfected" in that love (v. 23b).[189] When believers display such love before the world, they draw the world to the revelation of love displayed by Jesus and so to that "knowledge" of God from which flows "eternal life" (17:3).

Reflection. Jesus' prayer for unity in this text has understandably featured prominently in the ecumenical aspirations of the Christian churches. What the ecumenical movement has sought is corporate unity—the degree of unity

---

[187] Once again, we see "believing" and "knowing" in close parallel in Johannine thought; cf. Rudolf Bultmann, *Gospel of John*, 518. The parallelism rules out Brown's pessimistic view (*John XIII–XXI*, 778) that the "knowing" in v. 23 occasions the world's self-condemnation rather than its conversion.

[188] It is a testimony to the boldness of this statement that a variant in the Western textual tradition reads "that I (Jesus) should love them as you have loved me." The attribution to the Father is undoubtedly more original; cf. Raymond E. Brown, *John XIII–XXI*, 513.

[189] Lit., "that they might be perfected into one" (cf. Francis J. Moloney, *John*, 479). Elsewhere in the gospel (4:34; 5:36; 17:4; 19:28) this language of "perfection" is used of the completion of Jesus' own work in obedience to the Father.

aspired to depending upon on the ecclesiology of the various traditions. Such a sense of institutional unity was probably far removed from the purview of the community behind the Fourth Gospel.[190] Moreover, the historical disunity of the Christian church could be seen as rendering totally unrealistic the hope that unbelievers would be drawn to the true knowledge of God through the love manifested in the community. That may not, however, be the case on the more local level where communities can, at least from time to time, display the genuine attractiveness of divine love. What the Johannine text does insist upon is the sense that believers, in their communal as well as their individual life, are drawn into the divine communion of love and that in their attempts to reflect that love they have the prayer of Jesus firmly behind them. They can never give up on the quest that their institutional life be reflective of divine love. Nor can they so turn in upon themselves as to forget that the divine love that pulses in their veins is the same divine love that "so loved the world" as to give the "only Son" that the world might not perish but have eternal life (3:16). The Fourth Gospel may sharply separate the believing community from the world but it does so with a sense of "sanctification" for mission precisely to the world.

5. *Concluding Personal Invocations to the Father: 17:24-26*

Jesus brings his prayer to a close with a more general reflection upon his own mission and desire for the disciples. A repeated direct address to the Father (vv. 24, 25), along with the language of "wanting" (*thelō*) rather than "asking" (v. 24b), heightens the emotional tone and sense of intimacy. Since his will is always aligned with that of the Father (4:34; 5:30; 6:38), Jesus can simply state what he desires. Here, his desire is that those whom the Father has given him should be where he is (or will be) "in order that they might see the glory which you gave me because you loved me before the foundation of the world" (v. 24). These words echo once more the vision of the Prologue. Although the disciples have already glimpsed the glory of Jesus during his earthly life (2:11), the proper location of his glory is in his existence with the Father (1:1-2, 18) from which he came and to which he is now returning (16:28). The disciples will "see" his glory in this fullest sense when they themselves have joined him where he then will be, in the glory that pertains to him as the Father's beloved Son.

Earlier in the Supper Jesus had told the disciples that where he was going they could not then follow (13:33, 36). He had promised them that in

---

[190] The evidence of the Letters of John does indicate, however, that unity had become a problem for the community (1 John 2:7-11, 19; 3:11-24; 4:20-21; 2 John 4-11; 3 John 9-10).

due course he would return and take them to the "many dwelling places" in his Father's house (14:2-3). Now at the climax of his prayer he opens up once more that vision and that promise—though the way to it will involve sharing his suffering before sharing his glory (cf. 12:24-26; 21:18-19 [Peter]; also Rom 8:17-18).[191] It is an eschatological vision extending beyond the death of individual believers.[192] But, in the distinctive eschatology of the Fourth Gospel "seeing" Christ's glory can begin here and now before that final consummation (1:14; 2:11; 11:40). At the beginning of his ministry, Jesus had promised Nathanael that he would see "greater things: heaven opened and the angels of God ascending and descending upon the Son of Man" (1:51). That promised vision of "commerce" between heaven and earth, precisely as such, points to a vision of glory that begins in the human life of Jesus while remaining continuous with the glory that he shares with the Father from before the foundation of the world. In these final words of Jesus' prayer, the gospel seems to open up a vision where the barrier between this life and the next falls away. Once again, the First Letter of John provides the first and best commentary:

> Beloved, we are God's children now; what we will be has not yet been revealed. What we do know is this: when he is revealed, we will be like him, for we will see him as he is. (1 John 3:2)

And the conclusion of Paul's "Hymn to Love" is not far removed:

> For now we see in a mirror, dimly, but then we will see face to face. Now I know only in part; then I will know fully, even as I have been fully known. And now faith, hope, and love abide, these three; and the greatest of these is love. (1 Cor 13:12-13)[193]

Beyond Paul and John, we are dealing with a continuity of knowledge and experience of the divine to which mystics down the ages have added their testimony.

---

[191] Cf. C. K. Barrett, *John*, 514.

[192] Some recent interpreters (Gail O'Day, "The Gospel of John," 796; Andrew T. Lincoln, *St. John*, 439–40) insist that the eschatological destiny in view here is communal rather than concerned with the fate of individuals. The latter can hardly be excluded, however, in light especially of Jesus' words to Martha (11:25-26) where the dismay caused by the death of individual believers is clearly in view; cf. Raymond E. Brown, *John XIII–XXI*, 779–80; also *Introduction*, 240; Rudolf Schnackenburg, *St. John*, 3:195.

[193] Cf. Rudolf Bultmann: "The only thing that is clear is that an existence for the believers with the Revealer beyond death is requested, and thus promised. Death has become insignificant for them (11:25f); but not in the sense that they can ignore it because the earthly life is now complete and meaningful in itself; but because their life is not enclosed within the limits of temporal-historical existence" (*Gospel of John*, 520).

Jesus' final invocation (vv. 25-26) adds the adjective "righteous" (*dikaie*) to "Father." The epithet adds a closing element of solemnity but also, because of the forensic associations of "righteous" in the biblical tradition,[194] prepares the way for the sharp distinction that Jesus once again makes. The world—again understood in its most negative sense—has not "known God" (cf. 1:10) and in this sense has brought upon itself condemnation (3:18-20) and forfeiture of eternal life (17:3).[195] But the mission of the Son to make God known in the world—and so bring it eternal life—has not been a failure. The Word came to "his own" and his own (people) knew him not (1:11), but out of that people and out of those from other nations who would respond to their witness there has emerged a community reborn as children of God through faith (1:12), a "beachhead" of a renewed humanity destined to fulfill God's original design (3:16). These have truly "known" that Jesus has come from God (v. 25c), because he has "made known" God's "name"—that is, his essential nature—to them (v. 26a). Jesus will continue to do so (v. 26b)—presumably through the work of the Paraclete[196]—so that his mission to make God known in the world will continue.

While the prayer thus climaxes in a high concentration around the theme of "knowing/not knowing God," it reverts at the very end (v. 26cd) to the note of love. The purpose for which Jesus has striven to make God known is that the love with which the Father has loved the Son from all eternity may be "in them" and that he too may be "in them." The community, in its communion of love with the Godhead, is to be the locus of divine love in the world, as Jesus himself as incarnate Logos has been and will be until the end (19:30) the embodiment of the same divine love. Though now "departing" from the world, in the supreme expression of that love, he prays/ declares/promises that the community of believers will enjoy a palpable sense of his loving presence within them.[197]

---

[194] Such language is rare in John; when it occurs it is always in the context of judgment (5:30; 7:24; 16:8, 10); cf. Gail O'Day, "The Gospel of John," 796.

[195] The opening Greek conjunction *kai* after the invocation at the beginning of v. 25 may have a concessive sense: "though the world has not known you, *I* have known you and *these* (the disciples) have known."

[196] The fact that Paraclete is not mentioned in the Prayer does not mean that the role is not presumed; cf. C. K. Barrett, *John*, 515; Rudolf Schnackenburg, *St. John*, 3:197.

[197] Whether the Greek phrase *en autois* should be understood in the sense of "within (the hearts of) individual believers" or "among them" in a communal sense is not clear; probably both senses are meant; cf. C. K. Barrett, *John*, 515. The pledge of Jesus' ongoing presence recalls the similar promise in the mission charge that concludes Matthew's Gospel (28:20).

The Passion and Death of Jesus: 18:1–19:42

In its telling of Jesus' arrest, trials, execution, and burial, the Fourth Gospel parallels the Synoptic tradition more closely than anywhere else. That said, John's account retains its own highly distinctive character. It communicates, for example, so little sense of Jesus' actual suffering that some wonder whether the term "passion" is really applicable in the case of John.[1] The gospel does not deny the reality of Jesus' execution by crucifixion. It assumes the reader's knowledge of the appalling cruelty and suffering that such a death involved. What it does seek to portray—and does so very effectively—is the total freedom and control of events with which Jesus goes to his death.

The effect could be to present Jesus as an automaton, unfeeling and untouched by all that is being done to him. This could lend an air of unreality to the account in comparison, say, with the unrelieved starkness of Mark. What the Fourth Gospel is seeking to portray, however, is a freedom and control proceeding from a choice already long made to undergo all this in divine love for humankind. There is no hesitation, no shrinking on Jesus' part, from the "cup" set before him. A hint of that, corresponding to the Synoptic "Agony" tradition, occurred earlier (12:27-28). Now that is well in the past. Impelled by divine love to give himself up for the "life of the world" (6:51), Jesus actively orchestrates his own arrest (18:4-9; cf. 13:27).

The other distinctive feature of the Johannine account is a pervasive theme of judgment. As already noted, Jesus has in effect been on trial before "the world" (represented by "the Jews") virtually from the outset of his public life. This sense of being on trial is a major focus of his discourse at the final Supper, where the future trials of believers are also in view. It is

---

[1] Cf. Gail O'Day, "The Gospel of John," 799.

not surprising, then, that the Fourth Gospel should make the trial of Jesus preparatory to his execution the centerpiece of the passion story. The death of Jesus may be the dramatic climax, but the key theological issues are thrashed out between him and the representatives of the world as he stands before Pilate, the Roman governor (18:28–19:16a). In this lengthy scene the evangelist employs irony with consummate skill to show that, while Jesus may stand before the Roman judge with the shouts of his accusers ringing in his ears, it is they, not he, who are on trial and it is they, not he, who are overcome and condemned.

The passion story falls into five clearly discernible stages:

1. The Arrest of Jesus: 18:1-12

2. Jesus before the High Priest; Peter's Triple Denial: 18:13-27

3. Jesus on Trial before Pilate: 18:28–19:16a

4. The Crucifixion and Death of Jesus: 19:16b-37

5. The Burial of Jesus: 19:38-42.

The long central section describing the trial before Pilate appears in a carefully constructed pattern. I shall indicate this pattern when discussing the section in detail.

1. The Arrest of Jesus: 18:1-12

In his discourse at the Supper Jesus spelled out the meaning of his impending death. The opening phrase of the passion narrative proper ("After Jesus had spoken these words" [v. 1]) ensures that we keep this connection in mind. Outwardly, human hatred and violence will deprive Jesus of life. But we who remember his words know that his going to death is a supremely free expression of union with the Father and self-sacrificial love for humankind.

As in the Synoptic accounts, Jesus goes out from the supper room with his disciples to a wooded area ("a garden") east of Jerusalem, across the Kidron valley (v. 1).[2] Judas, the traitor, now returns to the story (vv. 2-3).

---

[2] The Johannine account does not mention a journey to the "the Mount of Olives" (Mark 14:26; Matt 26:30; Luke 22:39) or specify the place as "Gethsemane" (Mark 14:32; Matt 26:36). It does mention crossing what it describes literally as "the winter-flowing Kidron," a phrase which appears also in the description in 2 Sam 15:13-31 of David's flight from Jerusalem and ascent of the Mount of Olives (15:23) at the time of Absalom's rebellion. Mention

Aware that Jesus often gathered there with his disciples, he arrives, leading a cohort of soldiers and police from the chief priests and Pharisees, armed with lanterns and torches and weapons. "Cohort" translates the Greek word *speiran*, the use of which points to Roman involvement in the arrest.[3] Historically improbable, the involvement of Romans at this point conveys the sense of the whole world now arraigned against Jesus.[4] The arresting party comes in the darkness to apprehend the Light. Because they walk in the darkness and not in the Light (12:35; cf. 3:19; 8:12; 11:9-10) they need the artificial light of lamps and torches.[5] Thinking that force will be required, they carry weapons—though Jesus will yield himself to them in obedience to a divine script of which they know nothing.[6]

What follows is not so much an arrest as a confrontation in which Jesus takes the initiative and remains totally in control (vv. 4-9). The mention of his full consciousness of all that lies ahead of him (v. 4a)—mistreatment, suffering, and death—underlines once more the extremity of the love involved in the decision already made. He goes out of the garden (presumably a walled enclosure of some kind) and asks them who they are looking for—a first indication of his intent to take total responsibility upon himself, keeping his disciples safe and uninvolved.[7] Their reply, "Jesus, the Nazorean," has a pejorative ring about it, recalling Nathanael's first response to the human origins of Jesus (1:46).[8] The lowly designation sets up the contrast for Jesus' majestic declaration: "I am" (*egō eimi* [v. 5c]). At one level, this is a simple self-identification: "I am the one you are looking for." As readers of the gospel, however, we cannot fail to hear yet another echo of the divine name, "I am" (Deut 32:39 [LXX]; Isa 43:25; 51:12; 52:6 [LXX]; cf. John 8:24, 28, 58; also 4:26; 6:20). Confirming this is the reaction of the arresting troop, who immediately fall backward to the ground (v. 6).[9] The representatives of worldly power are rendered powerless in the presence of the divine Son.

---

of the stream may imply an allusion to this flight of David; cf. Andrew T. Lincoln, *St. John*, 442.

[3] *Speiran* denotes a Roman cohort of either 500 or 200 men.

[4] Cf. Rudolf Schnackenburg, *St. John*, 3:222–23; Gail O'Day, "The Gospel of John," 802; Andrew T. Lincoln, *St. John*, 443.

[5] Cf. Raymond E. Brown, *John XIII–XXI*, 813; Gail O'Day, "The Gospel of John," 802.

[6] Cf. Francis J. Moloney, *John*, 483.

[7] "When the wolves come the good shepherd does not flee, but goes forth to lay down his life so that the sheep may be safe" (Lesslie Newbigin, *The Light Has Come*, 239).

[8] Cf. Francis J. Moloney, *John*, 485.

[9] For a similar human response to a sudden encounter with the divine (theophany), cf. Ezek 1:28; Dan 10:9; Acts 9:3-4.

Meanwhile, in a typical Johannine afterthought, we are told (v. 5d) that Judas has been standing there with them. In contrast to the Synoptic accounts, there is no need for him to identify Jesus in the darkness; no place for the treacherous kiss (Matt 26:49-50; Mark 14:45; Luke 22:47); Jesus has identified himself. Irrevocably cut off from having any part with him (cf. 13:8), Judas is now simply "with them"—with the worldly powers that are being "overcome" in the very process now under way (16:33b).[10]

The display of divine presence has made clear where true power and authority rest. The way is now open for the action willed by God (Jesus' arrest) to proceed. Hence Jesus repeats his question and receives the same response (v. 7). There being no need for further self-identification, his concern turns to his disciples. He is the one they are looking for. Well, then, let these others go free (v. 8). Here, the Good Shepherd speaks—the shepherd prepared to lay down his life to save the lives of the sheep committed to his care. The disciples will escape with their lives, a symbol of the salvation that the Shepherd will win for all by laying down his own life (10:11, 17-18).[11] For Jesus (v. 9) this fulfills a statement he had made to the effect that he had not lost one of those whom the Father had entrusted to him (17:12).[12] The defection of Judas does not undercut the truth of the prophecy since he has long since aligned himself with the world rather than with Jesus (cf. 6:70-71). The escape of the disciples, then, far from being a desertion as in the Synoptic accounts (Matt 26:56; Mark 14:50; cf. Luke 22:54b), further illustrates not only the loving concern of Jesus for "his own" but also his prescience and control of all that is taking place.

A final incident (vv. 10-11) confirms this impression. Simon Peter, who has a sword by him, draws it and strikes out at the servant of the high priest, cutting off his ear.[13] Jesus rebukes Peter, telling him to sheathe his sword and protesting, "Am I not to drink the cup that the Father has given me?" (v. 11c). The rebuke is not so much about Peter's recourse to violence but to his doing something that may hinder the progress of the divine plan. As in the case of the footwashing (13:6-9), Peter is getting it all wrong. The

---

[10] On the Johannine presentation of Judas as an example of the human failure to embrace the divine gift of love and instead surrender to the pull of evil, see Gail O'Day, "The Gospel of John," 803–4.

[11] Cf. C. K. Barrett, *John*, 520–21.

[12] The "fulfillment" formula places Jesus' own words on a level with Scripture, as later in 18:32; cf. C. K. Barrett, *John*, 521.

[13] While all four gospels tell of this incident, only John identifies the injured servant as Malchus, possibly preserving a historical reminiscence; cf. Gail O'Day, "The Gospel of John," 803.

"cup" that lies ahead of Jesus is the Father's gift. Nothing must get in the way of his acceptance of it for the life of the world.[14]

With these words Jesus allows the Roman cohort, together with the captain and men of the Jewish guard, to lay hold of him and bind him (v. 12). From now on he is physically a captive in their hands. But the whole episode has brought out that any control they have over him is entirely conditional upon his freely chosen surrender. The world may appear at last to have him in its power. But even as its representatives lead him away they are following a script that will lead to the victory of divine love.

2. Jesus before the High Priest; Peter's Triple Denial: 18:13-27

All four gospels describe an arraignment of Jesus before the Jewish authorities presided over by the high priest. All four closely associate this interrogation of Jesus with a simultaneous interrogation of Peter on the part of servants of the household, in the course of which Peter three times denies any association with Jesus. While the process described in the Synoptic gospels approaches something in the nature of a formal trial, the Johannine account is more akin to an interrogation following arrest, with no semblance of formal legal process. In fact, the evangelist gives equal if not greater prominence to Peter's interrogation and denial by placing the interrogation of Jesus (vv. 19-24) between the first (vv. 15-18) and the final two denials (vv. 25-27). The interweaving heightens the contrast between Jesus' openness and Peter's dissembling to great dramatic effect.[15]

The evangelist can underplay Jesus' arraignment before the Jewish authorities because Jesus has been continually on trial before them throughout his public life.[16] In fact, the high priest has already passed sentence of death upon him, as we are reminded in the course of the account (18:14; cf. 11:50). It would be anticlimactic to describe a repetition of the process following Jesus' arrest. Hence the gospel's scaled-down presentation of the interrogation of Jesus between the two-part account of Peter's denial.[17]

---

[14] Jesus' description of what lies ahead of him as a "cup" seems to be a Johannine reflection of the Synoptic "Agony in the Garden" tradition, where Jesus at first prays to the Father to remove the cup from him and only accepts it after a struggle. The Fourth Gospel has brought forward this motif: 12:27-28.

[15] Mark (followed by Matthew) comes close to this by locating Peter in the courtyard of the high priest's house (14:54) before describing Jesus' interrogation (14:55-65) and then telling of Peter's denials all together (14:66-72).

[16] C. K. Barrett, *John*, 523–24.

[17] Andrew T. Lincoln, *St. John*, 449–50.

Jesus before Annas: 18:13-14

The account is actually quite confusing in regard to the priestly figure before whom Jesus is actually arraigned. We are told (v. 13a) that those who have taken Jesus captive lead him bound "first of all" to Annas. We are then informed (v. 13b) that Annas was the father-in-law of Caiaphas, who was the high priest that year, and reminded (v. 14) that it was Caiaphas who had advised the Jewish authorities that it was better to have one person die for the people (cf. 11:49-50). When the questioning of Jesus is described (vv. 19-23), following Peter's first denial (vv. 15-18), the one who conducts the interrogation is referred to as "the High Priest" (v. 19) and Jesus is at the end slapped for not answering appropriately "to the High Priest" (v. 22). Finally, Annas sends Jesus, still bound, to "Caiaphas the High Priest" (v. 24). We learn nothing of any process before Caiaphas—only (v. 28) that "they" took Jesus from Caiaphas's house to the headquarters of the Roman governor. We know from other historical sources that Annas not only held the office of high priest for nine years himself (9–15 CE) but that he was succeeded by his son-in-law, Caiaphas, and then five of his own sons. He thus retained influence for a great length of time, and it is well understandable that he could have been referred to as "the High Priest" long after he had personally been deprived of the office.[18] This would explain the evangelist's referring to him as "the High Priest" in the description of the interrogation of Jesus (vv. 19, 22), while also allowing for a subsequent designation of Caiaphas by the same title. It seems that the evangelist does want us to understand that Jesus was interrogated by a high priestly figure (Annas) but doesn't want this to be Caiaphas because Caiaphas has already not only put Jesus on trial—albeit *in absentia*—but also pronounced a verdict (11:49-50). He is content to remind us of the latter by pointing out the close relationship between Annas and Caiaphas (v. 13b). While the evangelist may have access to an independent historical tradition according to which Jesus was brought before Annas, we can also think of literary-theological motives for "airbrushing" Caiaphas out of the interrogation and substituting Annas, who was as good as high priest in any case.

---

[18] Cf. C. K. Barrett, *John*, 524. For a thorough discussion of the careers of the two high priestly figures, see Raymond E. Brown, *The Death of the Messiah: From Gethsemane to the Grave: A Commentary on the Passion Narratives of the Four Gospels*, 2 vols. (New York: Doubleday, 1994), 1:404–11.

Peter's First Denial: 18:15-18

Having set the scene for Jesus' interrogation in this somewhat confusing way, the evangelist now turns to do the same for Peter's simultaneous denial. Peter "follows" (*ēkolouthei*) Jesus into the high priest's quarters through the good offices of "the other disciple," who, we learn, was "known" to the high priest (vv. 15-16). Though the reference is left vague, this unnamed disciple is probably "the disciple whom Jesus loved" (Beloved Disciple).[19] As elsewhere in the gospel, this disciple pairs off with Peter in a way that puts him in a more advantageous position (cf. 13:23-24; 20:10; 21:1-14; cf. 20:2). Here, speaking to the gatekeeper, he facilitates Peter's access to where Jesus is being held. But, whereas that disciple will "follow" Jesus to the foot of the cross (19:25-27), Peter's "following" will stop short in triple denial, as Jesus foretold (13:36-38).

The gatekeeper, who turns out to be a woman (*paidiskē*), brings about Peter's first denial (v. 17). Without hostility but apparently simply doing her duty, she asks, "You're not also one of this man's disciples, are you?"[20] Her expectation of a negative response gives Peter the chance to make an immediate denial: "I am not" (*ouk eimi*), a stark contrast to the affirmations (*egō eimi*) that we have just heard from Jesus (18:5, 8).

Characteristically, the evangelist adds (v. 18) some further detail to this first denial. Against the cold of the night, the servants of the high priest have lit a charcoal fire (*anthrakia*). Peter stands there with them, warming himself. Having cut himself off from Jesus and his love through denial, he is seeking the artificial warmth provided by the servants of the world. We shall remember this detail when later, by another charcoal fire, the warmth of Jesus' love will prevail (21:9, 15-19).[21]

Jesus Interrogated and Struck: 18:19-24

When the narrative returns to the interrogation of Jesus (vv. 19-23), the high priest (Annas: see above) questions him about his disciples and his teaching (v. 19).[22] On both accounts Jesus refuses to be drawn (v. 20). The Good Shepherd who has already seen to the safety of his disciples (v. 8) will not incriminate them now. Nor will he enlarge upon his teaching. It is all

[19] For this identification (which is not universally accepted) cf. Raymond E. Brown, *John XIII–XXI*, 822; Andrew T. Lincoln, *St. John*, 449, 452–53.

[20] The question is in the form of a question expecting the answer "No" in Greek.

[21] Andrew T. Lincoln, *St. John*, 453.

[22] The two topics have little in common with the charges laid in the Synoptic parallels (Matt 26:59-61; Mark 14:56-59; cf. Luke 23:2-3, 5). The evangelist is pursuing a different agenda.

"out there" long since in the sense that he has spoken publicly "before the world" represented by the Jewish leadership ("the Jews") in the synagogue (cf. 6:59) and the temple (cf. 5:14; 7:14–8:59; 10:22-39), the public places of meeting. He has nothing more to add to it because the time for his personal witness to the world has come to an end (12:36-50). If they want to know what he has taught, they have only to ask those who heard him during his years of public witness (v. 21).[23]

The response earns Jesus a sharp blow (*hrapisma*) from one of the police standing by (v. 22) and a reprimand about answering the high priest in this way.[24] For the first time in the passion narrative, apart from being bound, Jesus suffers physical violence. Beyond the actual violence, the sense of insult is uppermost: in the reprimand and the blow struck presumably upon the face. Well might readers of the gospel tremble at this point as a human being strikes out in insult and correction against One whom we know to be the incarnate Son of God (1:1-2, 14, 18). Heaven does not fall in; creation is not destroyed. With calm, divine majesty Jesus simply asks his assailant either to point out where in his response he has done wrong or else to explain why, if has not spoken wrongly, he should be struck in this way. No response to his protest is forthcoming. The session ends with the sense that this is the only way that the leadership can deal with Jesus: in the face of his innocence and majesty they have no reasonable legal argument to offer; they simply descend to the violence and insult that has always been the way of worldly authority when under threat from innocence and truth.

Peter's Second and Third Denial: 18:25-27

Unable to get anywhere with Jesus, Annas sends him, still bound, to Caiaphas (v. 24). In the meantime Peter has himself been subject to interrogation, now from the group of servants with whom he has been standing warming himself by the fire. In a somewhat more threatening tone perhaps, they repeat (v. 25) the servant girl's question, eliciting his second denial: "I am not" (*ouk eimi*). Finally (v. 26), and still more threateningly, one of them, a relative of the one whose ear Peter had struck, claims to have seen him with Jesus in the garden, provoking his final denial (v. 27a). The immediate crowing of the cock (v. 27b) fulfills the prophecy that Jesus had

---

[23] Jesus' insistence on the public nature of his teaching suggests that "those who have heard" refers to the authorities rather than to the disciples; cf. Gail O'Day, "The Gospel of John," 809–10.

[24] Implied behind the reprimand may be a prescription in the Covenant Code: "You shall not speak ill of the rulers of your people" (Exod 22:27 [LXX 22:28]).

made (13:36-38). He has been betrayed by one of his close associates and now denied by another. Both developments he has foreseen and foretold. He may be led off now, bound, to his outward fate. But all that, even these poignant blows, remains within a freely chosen divine purpose unfolding and foreseen. And, while for the present Peter's repeated "I am not" contrasts so negatively with Jesus' "I am," it will not be a final word. By a later fire, another triple interrogation will elicit protestations of love that will reconcile and heal, and Jesus will point to a "following" on Peter's part in which he will not fail but, in a heroic death, glorify God (21:9-19).

3. Jesus on Trial before Pilate: 18:28–19:16a

The trial of Jesus before the Roman governor is the centerpiece of the passion story in the Fourth Gospel. The evangelist describes Jesus' arraignment before Pilate at far greater length than in the parallel accounts in the Synoptic Gospels and, with considerable literary artistry, casts the account in a drama of seven contrasting scenes to bring out a distinctive theological vision. The issue around which all revolves is the kingship of Jesus. Outwardly, the question is whether Jesus is "King of the Jews." Though this is the messianic role that the Jewish authorities try to pin upon Jesus in order to have him crucified, in his interaction with Pilate Jesus will address the issue and show that, yes, he is a king but of a totally different order and allegiance.

To bring out how this false accusation of kingship ironically witnesses to Jesus' true kingship, the evangelist makes the soldiers' mock portrayal and veneration of him as "King of the Jews" (19:1-3) the centerpiece (scene 4) of the seven-scene drama. The remaining six scenes, three on either side of this central scene, then unfold in a series of interactions alternating in respect to whether they take place outside or inside the governor's palace, the praetorium. The constant change of location has Pilate shuffling back and forth from one setting to another, an outward reflection of inner turmoil. He is caught between his own conviction of Jesus' innocence and the pressure from the Jewish authorities to proceed to crucifixion. We can set it out schematically as follows:[25]

---

[25] The sevenfold chiastic division has long been noted; see Raymond E. Brown, *John XIII–XXI*, 858–59; *Death of the Messiah*, 1:757-59; Francis J. Moloney, *John*, 493; Andrew T. Lincoln, *St. John*, 458. Rudolf Schnackenburg (*St. John*, 3:242) and Gail O'Day ("The Gospel of John," 813) place the division between the sixth and seventh scenes at the end of 19:12 rather than 19:11.

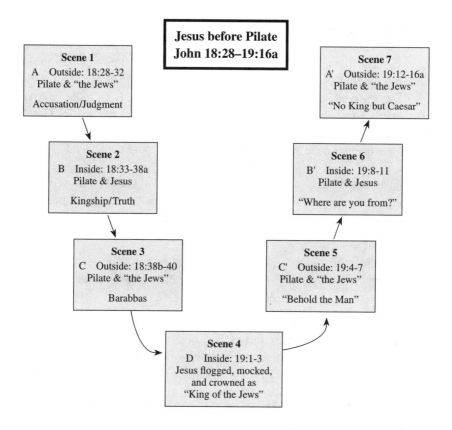

Jesus before Pilate
John 18:28–19:16a

Scene 1

A   Outside: 18:28-32
Pilate & "the Jews"

Accusation/Judgment

Scene 7

A'   Outside: 19:12-16a
Pilate & "the Jews"

"No King but Caesar"

Scene 2

B   Inside: 18:33-38a
Pilate & Jesus

Kingship/Truth

Scene 6

B'   Inside: 19:8-11
Pilate & Jesus

"Where are you from?"

Scene 3

C   Outside: 18:38b-40
Pilate & "the Jews"

Barabbas

Scene 5

C'   Outside: 19:4-7
Pilate & "the Jews"

"Behold the Man"

Scene 4

D   Inside: 19:1-3
Jesus flogged, mocked,
and crowned as
"King of the Jews"

The evangelist had a further reason for making the trial scene the centerpiece of the passion. As we have noted, from the beginning of his public ministry Jesus has been continually on trial before the world, represented by the Jewish authorities ["the Jews"]). Now he is on trial before the world in the wider sense represented by the Roman governor. What will emerge as the "trial" proceeds, however, is that it is the world, in both senses, that is on trial before his "witness to the truth" (18:37). In rejecting the One sent by God to "his own," the Jewish authorities forfeit the privilege, unique to Israel, of being "children of God" (1:12) and become simply one of the many nations subject to the worldly power of Caesar (19:15). In refusing to "come to the truth" Pilate fails to emerge from the darkness of unbelief and aligns himself with "the Jews" in their adherence to the world that is set against the life-giving revelation of the truth. Ironically, despite acting as the chief witness to Jesus' innocence, the judge in the case (Pilate) is the instrument of his own condemnation.[26]

The Roman trial is also one of the passages in the Fourth Gospel where the potential for anti-Jewish or anti-Semitic interpretation arises most strongly. Those who bring Jesus before the Roman governor and clamor for his death are consistently referred to throughout as "the Jews." The issue is particularly significant in that because the Johannine passion is read on Good Friday it is likely to be the one that becomes most anchored in the memory of those who attend the service on that day—many more than attend at other times. Personally, I believe the term "the Jews" should be expunged from all translations in public use and "the authorities" substituted in its place. Sermons and expositions need to educate people on the technical meaning of the phrase "the Jews" and the way in which the phrase functions in the Fourth Gospel.

Scene 1 (Outside): *Jesus Brought before Pilate and Accused: 18:28-32*

The Roman trial begins (v. 28) with the Jewish authorities bringing Jesus to the praetorium, the court of the Roman governor.[27] It is now dawn ("early") on the day of preparation for the Passover (19:14), which is to begin with the eating of the paschal lamb that evening. So as not to render themselves "unclean" and so unable to perform the ritual, the authorities are careful not to enter the residence of the Gentile governor.[28] While so scrupulous to safeguard their capacity to consume the paschal lamb of the old order, they are—ironically—bent on bringing about the death ("consuming" [cf. 2:17]) of the Lamb who truly takes away the sin of the world (1:29, 35; 19:31, 36).[29]

To accommodate their scruples Pilate goes out to speak to them, asking what charge they bring against "this man" (v. 29). With what appears to be plain insolence[30] they do not state any specific charge but simply insist that if

---

[26] Cf. Andrew T. Lincoln, *St. John*, 471–72;

[27] "Praetorium" is the technical term for the residence of a Roman provincial governor. The residence in view here is probably not the Antonia fortress in the vicinity of the temple but the palace of Herod; cf. C. K. Barrett, *John*, 531.

[28] Evidence that Jews at the time of Jesus considered themselves rendered unclean through entry into Gentile houses is slim; for a thorough discussion, see C. K. Barrett, *John*, 532–33. Whatever the historical situation, the evangelist's main concern is to bring out the irony.

[29] Cf. Raymond E. Brown, *John XIII–XXI*, 866; *Death of the Messiah*, 1:746; Rudolf Schnackenburg, *St. John*, 3:244; Andrew T. Lincoln, *St. John*, 460.

[30] "Impudence" (C. K. Barrett, *John*, 533); "petulance" (Rudolf Schnackenburg, *St. John*, 3:245).

he were not a malefactor, they would not be seeking to hand him over to Roman authority (v. 30). Behind the response would seem to be a concern to conceal the fact that the charge against Jesus is a purely religious one, an infringement of the law of Moses, which would not move Pilate to act against him. Hence the desire to portray him in general terms as a criminal dangerous to society on a variety of fronts. They do so, doubtless, in the hope that the governor, asking no further questions, will simply proceed to condemnation.

Pilate, however, exposes this ploy, telling them to take him and judge him themselves "according to your law" (v. 31a). This forces them to come clean on the fact that they are bent on securing Jesus' execution, something which they cannot achieve without the sanction of the governor since it is not lawful for them to put anyone to death (v. 31b). Whether historically the Jewish authorities, under Roman occupation, lacked the right to inflict capital punishment is a matter of dispute.[31] The evangelist simply assumes this to be the case and uses it to expose the murderous intent of Jesus' accusers and their need to arraign him on a political charge (messianic pretension as "King of the Jews") in order to secure his condemnation. As the evangelist notes (v. 32), this will ensure that Jesus undergoes the form of execution that the Romans were accustomed to inflict on political rebels—crucifixion—and so fulfill his prediction ("word") about the kind of death he would die when he spoke of being "lifted up from the earth" (12:31-32; cf. 3:14; 8:28). Once again, then (cf. 18:9, 27), we are reminded that, while pressing for his death, the authorities are following a divinely ordained script that includes their own condemnation.

Scene 2 (Inside): *Pilate and Jesus (1): 18:33-38a*

Determined to investigate the case himself, Pilate has Jesus brought inside the praetorium where he can interrogate him privately. His opening question, "Are you the King of the Jews?" (v. 33), shows he has seen through the ploy of Jesus' accusers. He knows that they are bringing him to trial on a political and hence capital charge. The Romans reserved to themselves the right to appoint client kings in their empire. To claim that title independently of Rome is tantamount to leading a rebellion.[32]

---

[31] Full discussion in C. K. Barrett, *John*, 53–35; also Andrew T. Lincoln, *St. John*, 460.

[32] Cf. Warren Carter, *John and Empire: Initial Explorations* (New York: T. & T. Clark, 2008), 302. "King of the Jews" appears in the passion narratives of the gospels (also Matt 2:2) only on the lips of non-Jews; Jews refer to the messianic king as "King of Israel" (John 1:49; 12:13; cf. Matt 27:42; Mark 15:32).

As so often in the gospel, Jesus reverses the interrogation (v. 34). He asks Pilate whether he is raising this issue of his own account or whether it is something others have suggested to him. In other words, Jesus is exposing the fact that the only reason the governor could have for raising this sensitive political charge is because the authorities are attempting to portray him as a "king" in order to secure his condemnation. Pilate's vigorous retort, "I'm not a Jew, am I? It is your own nation and your own chief priests who have handed you over to me" (v. 35a-c),[33] reinforces this impression: aside from their accusation he has no grounds for arraigning Jesus on such a charge. He concludes by simply asking Jesus to give account of himself: "What have you done?" (v. 35d). That is, Are you or are you not the messianic pretender ("King of the Jews") that they are making you out to be?

Jesus' response initiates the conversation about "kingship/kingdom" and "truth" that is the theological heart of the trial (vv. 36-38a). He does not answer directly the question as to whether he is a king. Instead, he speaks of his "regime" or "rule" (*basileia*) and first clarifies what it is not: it is not "from this world" (*ek tou kosmou toutou*). We have to understand this exclusion carefully. The Greek word *basileia* is not accurately translated by "kingdom" or "kingship" in English. If "regime" can be emptied of negative implications, it is perhaps the most accurate rendering, referring to the state of allegiance to God that it is Jesus' mission to institute in the world. Not being "from this world" does not mean having nothing to do with the world and belonging to a detached, purely spiritual realm. The reference, rather, is to origins.[34] The *basileia* does not originate in the world. It has come "from God," as Jesus has come from God. It can only be instituted by God, not by human beings—as in the failed attempt to make Jesus "king" following the miracle of the feeding (6:15). It represents an invasion of divine truth into the world "for the life of the world" (3:16; 6:51). As such, the *basileia* will necessarily challenge structures opposed to God and so have its effect in the world. But it will not engage the world on the world's terms.[35] Were it to do so, as Jesus goes on to point out, his "servants" would have fought to prevent his capture by "the Jews" (v. 36b). We recall the rebuke that one of those servants, Peter, earned when he did strike out with a weapon (18:10-11).

---

[33] "Nation" here probably refers not to the Jewish people as a whole but to its representative body, the Sanhedrin, which had already condemned Jesus (11:48-52). There is actually no "crowd" (*ochlos*) demanding Jesus' condemnation in the Johannine passion; the leaders alone play this role; cf. Rudolf Schnackenburg, *St. John*, 3:248; Gail O'Day, "The Gospel of John," 816.

[34] Cf. Gail O'Day, "The Gospel of John," 817.

[35] Cf. Rudolf Schnackenburg, *St. John*, 3:249; Andrew T. Lincoln, *St. John*, 462; Warren Carter, *John and Empire*, 303.

Unable to grasp Jesus' talk of a *basileia* that is not "from here" (v. 36d), Pilate remains fixated on the only idea of kingship that he can understand: "So you are a king, then" (v. 37a). In response, Jesus distances himself from the title ("You say I am a king" [v. 37b]) but does not reject it out of hand. As the wider context of the gospel has made clear, he is Israel's messianic king ("the King of Israel" [1:49; 11:27; 12:63; cf. 20:31), provided that title and role is understood in light of his mission from the Father. He provides this specification in a majestic summary (v. 37cd):

> For this I was born, and for this I came into the world:
> to testify to the truth.
> Everyone who belongs to the truth listens to my voice.

Here, the notion of "kingship," while not denied, is subordinated to Jesus' primary mission, which is that of being witness to "the truth":[36] that is, the revelation of God that exposes and strips away delusion and self-centeredness and draws human beings into the divine communion of love. The Son, who is ever "with God" (1:1-2, 18), became incarnate (literally, "was born"; 1:14) for this and entered the world for this:[37] that human beings, who are of the world, might share the (eternal) life of God (3:16).

Jesus concludes this statement of his mission with a remark that is for Pilate both an invitation and warning: "Everyone who is disposed to the truth listens to my voice" (v. 37e). "Disposed to the truth" translates a Greek phrase (*ho ōn ek tēs alētheias*) which has the sense of being open to the revelation of God that is entering the world "from above."[38] Such persons "hear the voice" of the One witnessing to the truth as the "sheep" in Jesus' earlier image (10:3, 16, 27) hear the voice of the (Good) Shepherd and follow.[39] Pilate, however, has a "tin ear" to such language. He demonstrates that he is not disposed to the truth by asking dismissively, "What is truth?" He then leaves (v. 38b) without waiting for an answer. The famous throw-away line simply evades Jesus' witness.[40]

---

[36] Cf. Andrew T. Lincoln, *St. John*, 463.

[37] The two expressions are virtually synonymous; cf. Raymond E. Brown, *John XIII–XXI*, 854; C. K. Barrett, *John*, 537.

[38] Cf. C. K. Barrett, *John*, 538.

[39] An echo of the "Good Shepherd" discourse is widely recognized here: cf. Raymond E. Brown, *John XIII–XXI*, 854; Rudolf Schnackenburg, *St. John*, 3:250; Gail O'Day, "The Gospel of John," 817.

[40] "Pilate's famous question … is meant to express … neither philosophical skepticism nor cold irony, and certainly not a serious search for truth; for the evangelist it is an avoidance and so a rejection of Jesus' witness" (Rudolf Schnackenburg, *St. John*, 3:251).

This first exchange between Pilate and Jesus has been interpreted in an abstract sense as representing the confrontation between the state and the revelation of divine truth in prophetic figures such as Jesus.[41] Such a view reads into the text philosophical issues of a later time.[42] It is, however, correct in acknowledging that the Fourth Gospel in no sense commends a withdrawal from the world into a purely "spiritual" sphere or sectarian stance. The "truth" upon which the gospel rests may not be "from this world" but the allegiance (*basileia*) that it demands inevitably has social and political consequences in the world.[43] The truth to which Jesus witnesses is the reality of God and of God's claim upon the world, which necessarily finds expression in love.[44] Such divine love, when embodied and lived out in human communities, will inevitably threaten and attract the hostility of social structures and regimes that retain their grip by fomenting fear, hatred, and resentment.

Scene 3 (Outside): *Pilate and the Jews: the Barabbas Stratagem: 18:38b-40*

Pilate has not responded adequately to Jesus' witness to the truth. But neither is he convinced that the prisoner brought before him is the dangerous rebel that "the Jews" are making him out to be. Returning outside to confront them, Pilate utters a first assertion of Jesus' innocence: he finds no grounds (literally, "cause") in the charge they are making (v. 38b). He then has recourse to a stratagem that may get him off the hook, relieving him from the pressure to condemn a prisoner of whose wrongdoing he is not convinced. He reminds "the Jews" of their custom that he should release to them a prisoner at the time of Passover.[45] Do they want him, then, to release "the King of the Jews" (v. 39b)? Granted that they have just brought Jesus before him for condemnation, the stratagem is hardly realistic. It is also strange that Pilate should refer to Jesus as "King of the Jews" when he has just expressed himself unconvinced that Jesus is guilty of the charge (sedition) that the title implies.

---

[41] So especially Rudolf Bultmann, *Gospel of John*, 652, 655–56.

[42] Cf. Raymond E. Brown, *John XIII–XXI*, 863–64.

[43] Cf. also Warren Carter, *John and Empire*, 303—though Carter has a different understanding of God's "truth," seeing it more in terms of God's faithfulness to commitment to save.

[44] David Rensberger, *Johannine Faith*, 117.

[45] Though mentioned in all four gospels, extrabiblical evidence for the existence of such a custom is minimal. See the comprehensive discussion of Raymond E. Brown, *Death of the Messiah*, 1:814–20.

Keeping the motif of kingship in the foreground, however, highlights the choice made by "the Jews" when they shout back, "Not this fellow but Barabbas" (v. 40ab)—especially when we learn, in a dramatically placed afterthought (v. 40c), that Barabbas was a bandit. In its primary sense the Greek term *lēistēs* has to do with robbery with an element of violence—though the term was also extended to cover guerilla leaders and rebels.[46] The only other place where it occurs in the gospel is as a negative foil to Jesus' image of himself as (Good) Shepherd (10:1, 8). In rejecting Jesus out of hand and choosing instead Barabbas so described, "the Jews" are rejecting their true Shepherd King and opting for the way of violence and rebellion that, ironically, they had attempted to pin on Jesus; they confirm that they are not sheep of his flock.[47] In sum, then, the episode reinforces the negative impression that the trial is creating in regard to "the Jews." While seeking the condemnation of Jesus they are placing themselves on trial and, in fact, allowing Pilate to expose their motivation and true allegiance.

Scene 4 (Inside): *Jesus Scourged, Mocked, and Hailed as "King of the Jews": 19:1-3.*

As noted above, this short scene is the centerpiece of the trial narrative in the Fourth Gospel. In Roman custom, flogging was a preliminary to death by crucifixion. It would normally be inflicted only after sentence of death had been passed. The same would apply to the soldiers' game of mocking a prisoner as "king." The Synoptic accounts of Mark and Matthew are more historically plausible, then, in placing the scourging and mockery of Jesus after his condemnation.[48] The Fourth Gospel departs from the more likely historical order in pursuit of a theological agenda of its own—or, rather, to bring out a theme that is latent in the Synoptic accounts but which John wishes to highlight strongly: Jesus' kingship.

Although often interpreted as such,[49] Pilate's having Jesus scourged (19:1) is hardly an attempt to placate the animosity of "the Jews" toward Jesus as it is to allow for his release. All along they have made it clear that nothing less than his death will satisfy.[50] In any case, it is highly unlikely that a prisoner would long survive so severe a punishment. As a customary preliminary to crucifixion, the scourging simply shows that Pilate is being

---

[46] Cf. BDAG, 594 (s.v.).

[47] Cf. Andrew T. Lincoln, *St. John*, 464.

[48] In Luke's account there is only a declaration of purpose by Pilate to have Jesus "chastised" (23:22) and no mention of mockery by the soldiers.

[49] Cf. Raymond E. Brown, *John XIII–XXI*, 886.

[50] Gail O'Day, "The Gospel of John," 818–19; Warren Carter, *John and Empire*, 305.

carried along against his better judgment in an inevitable slide toward Jesus' condemnation.

Within the praetorium the soldiers now act out their mock portrayal of Jesus as king (vv. 2-3). The crown of thorns they weave and place on Jesus' head is not so much an instrument of torture as an imitation of the radiant crowns worn by rulers in the Hellenistic world to signify divine status.[51] They clothe him in a robe that mimics the imperial purple. Finally, they approach him, hailing him, as if in allegiance, "King of Jews," only to suddenly strike him instead. On the surface level, it is just another instance of a cruel game played by soldiers upon one who is helplessly in their power. Ironically, however, they are proclaiming a deeper truth: that Jesus is truly a king. Yes, he is "King of the Jews"—though the leaders of that nation will not own it. Moreover, as non-Jews themselves, the soldiers represent the nations of the world ("the Greeks" [12:21]) whom Jesus will "draw" in allegiance to himself as king when "lifted up" upon the cross (12:32).

There is no reference in the Johannine account to the removal of the symbols of royal office (crown, robe) from Jesus. For the remainder of the trial and symbolically at least up till his death, the portrayal of him as king stands. He will die as the Shepherd King who, in contrast to the rulers of the world, lays down his own life that his flock may live (cf. 10:11, 15, 17). The scene here at the centerpiece of the trial admirably prepares the way for the Christian veneration of the cross on Good Friday, when believers approach their King, not to "receive him with blows," but with adoration and grateful love.

Scene 5 (Outside): *Pilate and the Jews ("Behold the Man"): 19:4-7*

Once again Pilate leaves the praetorium to confront "the Jews" (v. 4a). In a second declaration of Jesus' innocence (cf. 18:38b), he announces to them that he is bringing Jesus ("him") out to them "in order that you may know that I find in him no cause" (v. 4bc).[52] Had he found the case against Jesus proven, he would not be bringing him out but retaining him in the praetorium for eventual execution.[53]

---

[51] Cf. C. K. Barrett, *John*, 540.

[52] Some interpreters (e.g., Gail O'Day, "The Gospel of John," 819) see nothing genuine in Pilate's declarations of Jesus' innocence. Such a view is over-subtle and undercuts the drama of the narrative: the reader can still wonder at this point whether in fact Pilate will act according to his better judgment and release Jesus.

[53] This is the implication of the purpose clause beginning *hina* in v. 4c.

As Jesus emerges from the praetorium wearing the regal apparel (v. 5ab), Pilate does not, as we might expect, say, "Behold your King" (as later in 19:14-15), but "Behold the man!" (v. 5c). It is all as if to say, "Here is the fellow ('the man') you delivered up to me as falsely claiming to be your king and, yes, to show you how harmless and pitiful a claimant we regard him to be, we've decked him out as such, preparatory to his release." On another level, the designation "the man" likely alludes to the role of Jesus as "Son of Man," which in the Fourth Gospel, as we have seen, has particular reference to judgment.[54] Like Caiaphas in 11:50, Pilate would be stating more than he knows and actually presenting to the Jewish leadership the One who now and up to his eventual "lifting up" upon the cross is and will be their Judge. While "the world" in the person of Pilate and the Jewish authorities is tussling over the judgment (= condemnation) of Jesus, it is itself being brought before its Judge. When the authorities clamor in response, "Crucify him, crucify him" (v. 6a), they begin the process of his "lifting up" (cf. 12:23, 32). They are fulfilling Jesus' prophecy: "When you have lifted up the Son of Man then you will know that I am he" (8:28).

It is difficult, too, to avoid hearing in the phrase "the man" an allusion to the incarnation of the Word (1:14).[55] Jesus stands before the world as its judge in his simple humanity—portrayed as a king, yes, but as king that the world has wounded and struck. His incarnation and identification with all those who are persecuted and battered by the powers of the world has introduced a criterion of judgment unknown to the world. This is a judge who has truly "borne our infirmities" and been "wounded for our transgressions" (Isa 53:4, 5), One whose whole mission in the world has been to forestall any condemnation by offering himself as the Lamb who "takes away" its sin" (1:29).

In response to the calls for Jesus' crucifixion, Pilate attempts (v. 6b) to evade all responsibility, telling them to take him and crucify him themselves, since—his third declaration of Jesus' innocence—he still finds "no cause in him" (cf. 18:31; 19:4). The suggestion is unreal: the Jews did not have the legal power to carry out such an execution. Pilate is mocking them, calling attention to their impotence in this regard. His continuing resistance, though, makes them finally come clean about the real basis of their hostility to Jesus and why they want him dead (v. 7). The political pretext ("King of the Jews") gives way to the religious grounds on which he has given offense. They have

---

[54] An allusion to the "Son of Man" motif at this point is a matter of debate. In favor, see Francis J. Moloney, *John*, 495, 499 (and further references); Warren Carter, *John and Empire*, 305–6.

[55] Cf. C. K. Barrett, *John*, 541.

a law—the specific prohibition of blasphemy according to Leviticus 24:16 is in view—and according to that law he deserves to die because he has made himself out to be Son of God. In earlier passages of the gospel Jesus has indeed claimed to be God's Son (5:18: 10:33, 36; cf. 8:59). But he has not, as they assert, "made himself" out to be so. All along he has insisted that he is the Son whom the Father has consecrated and sent into the world (cf. 10:36). He acts only in accord with the will and design of the Father.

Scene 6 (Inside): *Pilate and Jesus ("Where are you from?"):*
19:8-11

Unmasking the real pretext upon which the authorities want Jesus condemned gives fresh impetus to the drama. The phrase "Son of God" strikes fear into Pilate: literally, "he feared all the more" (v. 8).[56] Up till now we have not been told in so many words that Pilate has felt fear but that is likely an implication of his breaking off the discussion about kingship with the throwaway question, "What is truth?"(v. 38a). It is also hard to understand his continual desire to release Jesus if he does not suspect that the prisoner brought before him represents more than a routine case of messianic pretense. "Son of God" suggests something supernatural, drawing Pilate well beyond his comfort zone. Hence the need to have a further conversation with the accused in private (v. 9a) and the opening question, "Where are you from?" (v. 9b).

Pilate's question airs, as we know, the fundamental question of Johannine Christology (cf. 1:1-4, 30; 7:27-28; 8:14; 9:29-30).[57] The question is not about Jesus' human origins but about whether he has some kind of origin in the suprahuman world that would underlie the claim to be "Son of God." Pilate in a sense is asking the right question, but Jesus refuses to answer (v. 9b). His silence matches his earlier refusal to enlarge upon his disciples and his teaching when arraigned before the high priest (18:20-21). Just as he has spoken openly to "the Jews" without effect and so closed off his witness to them, so he has already explained the nature of his "kingship" to Pilate and received a similar rebuff (18:38a); the time for revelation is over.[58]

---

[56] It is possible to understand the Greek phrase *mallon ephobēthē* simply as an intensive "he was greatly afraid" (so, C. K. Barrett, *John*, 542; Andrew T. Lincoln, *St. John*, 467; Gail O'Day, "The Gospel of John," 820). However, the comparative is the more natural reading and makes good sense along the lines explained; cf. Rudolf Schnackenburg, *St. John*, 3:260.

[57] Cf. Raymond E. Brown, *John XIII–XXI*, 892; Francis J. Moloney, *John*, 495.

[58] Cf. Francis J. Moloney, *John*, 496; Gail O'Day, "The Gospel of John," 821; Andrew T. Lincoln, *St. John*, 467.

Disturbed by Jesus' silence, Pilate resorts (v. 10) to bluster. He sharply reminds Jesus that he has the power (*exousia*) of life or death over him (literally, to set him free or to crucify him). Jesus breaks his silence to point out (v. 11) how relative and fragile Pilate's claimed authority actually is. He may have power over Jesus' physical life or death but has this only in virtue of its being "given to him from above (*anōthen*)." As in the conversation with Nicodemus (3:3), "from above" has a double meaning. On the purely human level, Pilate's authority is simply derivative: as he will soon be sharply reminded (v. 12), he holds it entirely at the behest of the ruler "above" him, namely, Caesar. On the deeper level, he holds it only in the sense of being the unwitting instrument of the divine design behind the life and mission of Jesus. In terms of who is free and who is necessarily under authority, it is Jesus, not Pilate, who wins hands down (cf. 10:17-18). Jesus may stand bound before Pilate, who, it is true, has the power either to release or condemn him. But the Roman governor cannot touch or take away the inner freedom of Jesus' love.[59]

The reference of Jesus' final observation: "Therefore the one who handed me over to you is guilty of a greater sin" (v. 11c) is not clear. In view of the singular ("one"), obvious candidates would be Judas or Caiaphas. Neither has, however, handed over Jesus precisely to Pilate (cf. 18:28). Most likely the reference is to the high priest as representing the Jewish leadership in general (cf. 18:35).[60] As members of God's own people, schooled by the law, they have had a better preparation for recognizing divine revelation than the Gentile. Their "sin," then, in refusing to do so in respect to Jesus is more culpable than that of Pilate.[61]

In making this comparison—his last word at the trial—Jesus has in fact exchanged roles with Pilate. He has assumed the role of judge, pronouncing with authority on who has the greater and who the lesser sin. In the persons of Pilate and the Jewish authorities, it is the world that is on trial here—before the One to whom the Father has given authority to execute judgment because he is (the) Son of Man (5:27).

---

[59] "Pilate, with all the power he thinks he has, is a secondary figure, only the man-in-between in a titanic battle between Jesus and the world" (Raymond E. Brown, *Death of the Messiah*, 1:842).

[60] Ibid.

[61] As noted all along, "sin" in the Fourth Gospel consists primarily—though not exclusively—in failure to acknowledge the revelation of God in Jesus; cf. Gail O'Day, "The Gospel of John," 821.

Scene 7 (Outside): *Pilate and "the Jews" ("No king but Caesar"): 19:12-16a*

The second exchange with Jesus has made Pilate all the more set on releasing him (v. 12a).[62] In a final scene,[63] he confronts "the Jews" with this intent, only to find them ready to play their trump card. Reverting to the more political charge against Jesus (v. 12b), they sharply remind Pilate whence his political authority actually derives: from Caesar. If he fails to act against one who is "making himself out to be a king," then he will show himself to be no friend of Caesar, since everyone who makes such a bid sets himself in opposition to Caesar.[64] This ramps up the pressure on Pilate to an intolerable degree. For all his claims to authority over life and death (cf. v. 10), he risks forfeiting the favor of the one (the emperor) from whom that worldly authority derives. Judge though he be, he is caught in the trap that has been laid for him. The choice before him now is not merely between Jesus and "the Jews" but between Jesus and Caesar.[65]

With matters coming to a head, Pilate brings Jesus outside once more (v. 13a) and sits[66] upon the seat of judgment.[67] The evangelist underlines the

---

[62] I take the phrase *ek toutou* at the beginning of v. 12 in a predominantly causal, rather than temporal, sense.

[63] Though the text does not explicitly say so, it seems that we are to understand at the end of v. 11 that Pilate has moved outside again to confront "the Jews." It is from this position that he "brings Jesus out" as stated in v. 13; cf. Raymond E. Brown, *Death of the Messiah*, 1:843.

[64] It is possible that "friend of Caesar" is a technical reference to a specific privilege bestowed upon those whose service of the emperor has won formal recognition; cf. Raymond E. Brown, *John XIII–XXI*, 879–80. In any case, both the emperor at the time of Jesus' public ministry (Tiberius) and the emperor at the time the gospel was likely to have been written (Domitian) displayed high sensitivity, with brutal consequences, to the slightest threat of disloyalty; cf. C. K. Barrett, *John*, 543–44.

[65] Andrew T. Lincoln, *St. John*, 469.

[66] The Greek verb *ekathisen*, translated intransitively as "sat," is equally open to a transitive meaning, rendering the sense that Pilate sat *Jesus* on the judgment seat. This would then constitute a further instance of Johannine irony, whereby Pilate, mocking "the Jews" by presenting Jesus as their judge as well as their king, would unwittingly (like Caiaphas in 11:49) be portraying the real truth of the situation: namely, that Jesus is Judge as well as King; so, Gail O'Day, "The Gospel of John," 822–23; Andrew T. Lincoln, *St. John*, 469–70. Raymond E. Brown, *Death of the Messiah*, 1:844–45 and 2:1388–93, rightly to my mind, points out that such an element of playacting runs counter to the solemnity with which the evangelist otherwise presents the situation (detailing place and time, etc.); cf. also Rudolf Schnackenburg, *St. John*, 3:263–54.

[67] The Greek word *bēma* refers both to a raised platform made of stone or wood and to the seat of judgment placed upon such a platform for the use of the judge when rendering judgment (cf. Rom 14:10; 2 Cor 5:10); see Raymond E. Brown, *Death of the Messiah*, 2:1388–89.

solemnity of the moment by specifying in some detail (v. 13b) the place ("The Stone Pavement" [*Lithostratos*], in Hebrew, "Gabbatha")[68] and time (Passover Eve, at the sixth hour). The time reference is particularly significant. On Passover Eve at this hour, the priests in the temple begin the slaughter of the lambs in preparation for the Passover meal to be taken that evening. When Pilate says to the chief priests, "Behold your king" (v. 14b), the pronouncement recalls the cry of John the Baptist, "Behold the Lamb of God" (1:29, 35). The King is the Lamb who takes away the world's sin.[69] At one level Pilate is mocking "the Jews," pointing to the pitiable figure that Jesus now presents as their king. At a deeper level, precisely in his wounded, pitiable state, Jesus is the king that Israel needs: a Shepherd King who is the instrument of human reconciliation with God. When, in a crescendo of rejection, they cry out, "Away, away (with him); crucify him" (v. 15a), Pilate again, in either genuine or, more likely, feigned surprise, exclaims, "Shall I crucify your king?" (v. 15b). This provokes from them at last the shocking cry: "We have no king but Caesar" (v. 15c).

The full force of this repudiation comes home in light of the solid biblical tradition of God as Israel's king.[70] Earlier in the gospel, the authorities had stoutly claimed the privilege of freedom under this sovereignty of God: they are no one's slaves (8:33). They are now forfeiting this unique privilege by taking on subservience to the emperor of Rome.[71] They are also, through this expression of foreign allegiance, abandoning any hopes for a messianic king, the hopes that prompted their interrogation of the Baptist early in the story (1:19-21; cf. 7:25-27, 40-42; 10:24). They are making a tragic turn away from God and the promises contained in the law to remain simply another vassal state of Rome.

Nonetheless, their expression of loyalty to Rome drives Pilate into a corner from which there is no easy escape. They have already warned him that to release Jesus would make him no "friend" of Caesar. By comparison

---

[68] "Stone Pavement" is a literal rendering of the Greek term *Lithostratos*. The identification of the location with a large paved area uncovered in the remains of the Antonia fortress in Jerusalem (now the *Ecce Homo* convent of the Sisters of Our Lady of Sion) is now largely rejected on the grounds that the pavement dates archaeologically from a later period. The Aramaic (not Hebrew) word "Gabbatha" is not a translation of *lithostratos* but probably means an elevated place or hill. For both terms and the possible location to which they are referring cf. Raymond E. Brown, *Death of the Messiah*, 1:845.

[69] Cf. Dorothy A. Lee, "Paschal Imagery in John," 24–25.

[70] The institution of human kingship in Israel was only grudgingly allowed by God (Judg 8:23; 1 Sam 8:7; cf. also Isa 26:13).

[71] Cf. Gail O'Day, "The Gospel of John," 823; Warren Carter, *John and Empire*, 309–10 (though with a very different interpretation of Pilate's motivation).

with their own protestation, it would make him appear less loyal than they—a risk Pilate can in no wise afford to run. He does not formally condemn Jesus but simply "hands him over to them to be crucified" (v. 16a). Since they cannot pursue this mode of execution without Roman involvement, we are presumably meant to understand that in fact Pilate ordered his soldiers to take the matter in hand. However, by describing his ultimate determination in this way the evangelist highlights the sense of grudging and unwilling surrender to *force majeure*.[72] Pilate has retained to the end his conviction of Jesus' innocence. He cannot sufficiently "come to the truth" in order to pursue what justice really requires. He has turned away from the Light and joined the adversaries of Jesus in the darkness of the world.[73] Judge though he be, sitting on the tribunal seat, he has joined the leading actors ("the Jews") in himself coming to judgment.[74]

4. The Crucifixion and Death of Jesus: 19:16b-37

While adhering to the basic storyline of the passion, the Fourth Gospel characteristically goes its own way in describing Jesus' death. Several of the details—the inscription upon the cross; the casting of lots for Jesus' clothes; the proffered drink of sour wine—are shared with the Synoptic accounts. But the Fourth Gospel handles them in its own way. Notably absent are the mockery of Jesus, the cry of dereliction, the darkening of the sun, the rending of the temple curtain, the reaction of the centurion. The reality of the brutal process of crucifixion is simply presumed. The evangelist has selected and shaped the tradition to portray Jesus dying with supreme dignity and freedom, a narrative illustration of his assertion: "I lay down my life in order to take it up again. No one takes it from me, but I lay it down of my own accord" (10:18). Having completed "to the end" (13:1) the work that the Father gave him to do, in love Jesus surrenders his life for the life of the world (3:16; 6:51).

---

[72] The Greek pronoun *autois*, then, retains a (probably intentional) ambiguity. It refers to the Jewish chief priests in the sense that Pilate surrenders to their desire; it refers also to the Roman soldiers who will now proceed to the execution (v. 16b). One recalls the similar involvement of both Jewish police and Roman troops in the arrest of Jesus (18:3).

[73] Cf. Rudolf Schnackenburg, *St. John*, 3:266-67.

[74] The Roman trial of Jesus began with the chief priests "handing over" (*paradidonai*) of him to Pilate because they did not have the power to put anyone to death (18:30-32). It ends, in inclusive mode, with his "handing" (*paradidonai*) Jesus "back" to them, having, against his better judgment, waived the prohibition against execution.

The account divides easily into five scenes:

1. The Crucifixion of Jesus under a Title Affixed to the Cross: 19:16b-22

2. The Division of Jesus' Garments: 19:23-24

3. The Bequest of Jesus' Mother to the Beloved Disciple: 19:25-27

4. The Death of Jesus: 19:28-30

5. The Piercing of Jesus' Side: 19:31-37

Attempts to find a formal pattern here seem rather forced.[75] However, the fivefold structure does make the bequest of Jesus' mother to the Beloved Disciple central, and, as we shall see, there are grounds, aside from the structure, for holding that the evangelist may have wanted to highlight the scene in this way.

Scene 1. *The Crucifixion of Jesus under a Title Affixed to the Cross: 19:16b-22*

Following Pilate's surrender, the soldiers take hold of Jesus (v. 16b).[76] However, as at his arrest in the garden, Jesus is not passive but fully in command. He shoulders the cross himself and goes out to the place of execution unassisted (v. 17). Laying down his life for the life of the world, in the freedom of love he strides to "the Place of the Skull, named in Hebrew 'Golgotha,' " where he is crucified (v. 18).

As in the Synoptic accounts, the evangelist does not expand or elaborate upon the appalling process involved but simply states the bare fact—along with the information (to be retrieved later [v. 32]) that "two others" were crucified there, with him in the middle. Moreover, while not denying the aspect of suffering and degradation, John is more intent on telling the "other side" of the story: a victory of divine love in which Jesus is exalted upon the cross to reign as King.

---

[75] So, e.g., Raymond E. Brown, who finds a chiastic structure, as in the Roman trial; see *John XIII–XXI*, 911–12; *Death of the Messiah*, 2:907–8.

[76] Although the form of execution demanded—crucifixion—could only be carried out by Roman soldiers (cf. v. 23: "the soldiers"), the "they" who take hold of Jesus are from the point of view of the syntax the same as those to whom Pilate surrendered him (v. 16a). The ambiguity continues the implication of the Jewish leaders in the death of Jesus.

In connection with this royal aspect the gospel exploits Pilate's fixing of a title upon Jesus' cross (v. 19).[77] "King of the Jews"—in the sense of a pretended rebel king—was the claim that the Jewish leaders had attributed to Jesus when bringing him before Pilate for condemnation (cf. 18:33). It is the charge upon which Jesus has been sentenced to suffer the form of execution reserved for rebels against the Roman state. Pilate publicly mocks "the Jews" by proclaiming to the world, in three languages (v. 20), that this crucified one is their king, despite their claim to have no king but Caesar (v. 15). When, understandably, they protest (v. 21), insisting that he should reframe the inscription so as to clarify that Jesus is their pretended rather than real king, Pilate refuses to budge: "What I have written, I have written" (v. 22).

In the face of their discomfort and with the irony characteristic of the gospel, Pilate thus affirms the truth that had been a matter of discussion between himself and Jesus (18:36-38): that he is a king, albeit not the king that a superficial reading of the title would suggest, but a King sent from the Father to institute in the world the reign (*basileia*) of truth.[78] Those drawn to the truth will see in the inscription a proclamation of true kingship, in which Jesus reigns from the cross, drawing to himself an allegiance of all who are on the side of truth (12:32). The multiple-language inscription announces the universal scope of that allegiance.[79]

Scene 2. *The Division of Jesus' Garments: 19:23-24*

Attention now turns to the Roman soldiers. An execution squad was entitled to the clothes of the condemned person. The Synoptic Gospels briefly record the division of Jesus' garments by lot in accordance with this custom (Mark 15:24b; Matt 27:35b; Luke 23:34b). The division by lot fulfills Psalm 22 (LXX 21):19:

> They divided my clothes (*ta himatia mou*) among themselves,
> and for my clothing (*ton himatismon mou*) they cast lots.

The Synoptic accounts almost certainly presume the fulfillment of the psalm but do not draw attention to this explicitly. The Fourth Gospel not only does

---

[77] We are not meant to understand that Pilate physically "wrote" the inscription himself, but that he was responsible for having it inscribed and placed upon the cross.

[78] "Jesus went to his death under a title unintentionally but profoundly true" (C. K. Barrett, *John*, 550).

[79] "Hebrew" (= Aramaic), the vernacular; Latin, the language of government; Greek, the language of trade and commerce; cf. Rudolf Schnackenburg, *St. John*, 3:272.

so (v. 24a) but finds in the parallel references to garments (*ta himatia* and *ton himatismon*) a basis for making a distinction between Jesus' outer garments (*himatia*) and his inner garment or tunic (*chitōn*).[80] Whereas the outer garments were easily divisible into four lots, one for each of the soldiers, the tunic was "seamless, woven in one piece from the top" (v. 23d). This led to the decision to cast lots for it rather than tearing it, fulfilling the prophecy contained in the psalm.

Symbolic interpretations of the undivided tunic have been many since earliest times, with two particularly prominent. On the basis of references in Josephus and Philo, the tunic has been related to the garment worn by the Jewish high priest, giving rise to the suggestion that Jesus is being portrayed here as priest.[81] But the high priestly garment is an outer rather than an undergarment as here in the case of Jesus.[82] More popular is the sense that the seamless and undivided robe represents the community of disciples for whose unity Jesus has prayed (17:11, 22-24).[83]

Within the penchant for double meaning characteristic of John it is well possible that the soldiers, while at one level going about their usual business in connection with the execution, are, despite themselves, symbolically signaling the inability of hostile forces to divide the community whose unity, like the weave of Jesus' garment, descends from above (v. 23e). A problem for this interpretation is that Jesus is actually deprived of his tunic.[84] However, the stripping stands in some continuity with his laying aside of his garments preparatory to washing the feet of his disciples (13:4), an action that foreshadows the cleansing (from sin) that he achieves for them in his passion and death. Memory of that gesture, where he actively lays aside his garments, could signal that, though Jesus is outwardly passive in this stripping, inwardly it is all an expression of his freely chosen embrace of death for the life of the world.

Regardless of symbolic meanings, the main focus lies upon the fulfillment of Scripture, which the evangelist is careful to point out. The seamlessness of the garment necessitates the casting of lots, an action that perfectly fulfills the words of the psalm. All, then, that is happening to Jesus—cruel

---

[80] In the original psalm the repetition of the reference to garments is simply a case of the parallelism of Hebrew poetry; cf. C. K. Barrett, *John*, 550.

[81] Cf. Raymond E. Brown, *John XIII–XXI*, 920–21.

[82] Cf. C. K. Barrett, *John*, 550.

[83] Cf. Raymond E. Brown, *John XIII–XXI*, 923; *Death of the Messiah*, 2:957–58; C. K. Barrett, *John*, 550, 552; (especially) Francis J. Moloney, *John*, 503.

[84] Cf. Rudolf Schnackenburg, *St. John*, 3:274; Gail O'Day, "The Gospel of John," 831; Andrew T. Lincoln, *St. John*, 475–76.

and shameful though it may be—is following a script long set out in the Scriptures with which Jesus is in perfect accord.

Scene 3. *The Bequest of Jesus' Mother to the Beloved Disciple: 19:25-27*

While the four soldiers divide Jesus' clothes, four other persons are also present by his cross: three women—the mother of Jesus, her "sister" Mary the wife of Clopas, and Mary Magdalene—and a fourth person, "the Disciple whom Jesus loved" (v. 25).[85] We have already met this disciple at the Supper, where he occupied a position of intimacy reclining on Jesus' breast (*kolpos* [13:23-25]). Later (19:35) it will emerge that he is the person upon whose witness the faith of the Johannine community rests (19:35; 21:24). He is, in fact, the representative or point of insertion into the events of Jesus' life for all subsequent believers. His intimacy with Jesus models the intimacy into which all believers are drawn, first with Jesus and then through him with the Father (cf. 1:18). Now a further aspect of that intimacy is to be disclosed.

First named as standing by the cross of Jesus is his mother.[86] We last heard of her as the first invited guest to the wedding at Cana (2:1). There, despite an initial rebuff from Jesus when she pointed out the lack of wine (2:3-4), her prompting of the waiters to do as he instructed them led to the provision of the "the best wine" (cf. 2:10). Appearing at the beginning and now at the climax of Jesus' public life, she clearly has a role within the narrative that, like that of the Beloved Disciple, is both personal and symbolic.[87]

As at Cana, Jesus addresses his mother as "Woman" (v. 26). As mentioned in regard to that occasion, the best explanation of this unusual address from a son to a mother is to see it as an allusion to the woman created as

---

[85] The syntax of the Greek sentence allows a reference to two, three, or four women; cf. Raymond E. Brown, *John XIII–XXI*, 904–5; C. K. Barrett, *John*, 551. Interpreters usually opt for four—particularly to balance the four soldiers (v. 23). The most natural reading of the Greek favors three: the mother of Jesus, his mother's "sister" Mary of Clopas, and Mary Magdalene. Since it is unlikely that Jesus' aunt would have borne the same name (Mary) as his mother, the description of Mary of Clopas as "sister" (*adelphē*) probably indicates a close relative rather than a sibling.

[86] Raymond E. Brown, *Death of the Messiah*, 2:1020, points out that her being first named suggests that she, rather than the disciple, is the primary focus of the episode.

[87] While this is widely recognized, there has been since patristic times a great variety of interpretation; see Raymond E. Brown, *John XIII–XXI*, 922–27; *Death of the Messiah*, 2:1020–26; Rudolf Schnackenburg, *St. John*, 3:278-82.

companion for the first man, Adam, whom he named "Eve, because she was the mother of all the living" (Gen 3:20). Jesus calls his mother "Woman" because she is the New Eve.[88] Whereas the former Eve was simply the mother of all human beings who come into existence, she is to be the mother of all those who through faith will be "born from above" into the "eternal life" of God. When Jesus instructs her to see in the disciple her "son" ("Behold, your son"),[89] he is instructing her to take as her children all those whom the disciple represents: the community of believers that is being born as the new family of God.[90]

When, correspondingly, Jesus instructs the disciple, "Behold, your Mother" (v. 27a), he is sealing the relationship from the other side, instructing the community to see his mother as their mother. He is sharing his divine Father with them (cf. 20:17). To complete the circle of familial relationship, he shares with them his human mother as well. The disciple, we are told (v. 27b), "from that hour took her into his own" (*eis ta idia*). Most current translations render the final phrase "into his (own) home" (e.g., KJV, NIV, NRSV, NAB, JB). The text is certainly open to this concrete sense whereby the disciple will make provision in his house and family for this woman now bereft of her Son. But the phrase *ta idia* has, as we have seen, a deeper resonance in the gospel. Referring initially to the people of God (1:11), it has come to stand for the intimate circle of believers whom Jesus has "loved unto the end" (13:1). It is, then, in the name of that community and as their representative that the disciple "from that hour" takes Jesus' mother into the family of believers to be their mother too.[91]

Scene 4. *The Death of Jesus: 19:28-30*

With the constitution of this new family as "his own" Jesus' mission in the world has been accomplished. "Knowing this" (cf. 13:1) he begins to bring his life to a close (v. 28). First, however, the accomplishment is to be demonstrated by a symbolic action fulfilling Scripture. All four gospels

---

[88] Cf. Raymond E. Brown, *John XIII–XXI*, 926. Brown seems to have moved away somewhat from this interpretation in *Death of the Messiah*, 2:1021, 1024, n. 98.

[89] Grammatically, "Behold" (*ide*) does not govern "your son," which is not in the accusative case. "Behold" is more in the nature of an exclamation, prefacing the solemn act of disposition.

[90] Cf. C. K. Barrett, *John*, 552; Gail O'Day, "The Gospel of John," 882. I am less persuaded that the mother of Jesus is being presented as a model disciple (so, Francis J. Moloney, *John*, 503–4; Andrew T. Lincoln, *St. John*, 477). The Fourth Gospel presents her as "over" the community of believers as "mother," rather than "with" them in discipleship.

[91] Cf. Rudolf Schnackenburg, *St. John*, 3:279.

record that on the cross Jesus was offered vinegar (*oxos*, sour wine) to drink.[92] For Luke (23:36) it is part of the soldiers' mockery; for Matthew (27:48) and Mark (15:36) it is a response to Jesus' cry of dereliction interpreted as a calling upon Elijah. In the Fourth Gospel, "in order that Scripture be fulfilled,"[93] Jesus directly initiates the offer of a drink by saying, "I thirst" (*dipsō*) (v. 28c). Immediately, the soldiers dip a sponge into a vessel of sour wine that happened to be at hand and putting it onto a branch of hyssop hold it to his lips (v. 29). [94]

To employ a branch of hyssop for this purpose is odd. Hyssop is a small shrub with flexible branches. It is suitable for sprinkling but not for conveying a sponge to the lips of a person raised above the ground.[95] Hyssop features in the Passover ritual set forth in Exodus 12:22 in that the blood of the paschal lamb is to be sprinkled upon the lintel and doorposts of houses with a branch of this plant. It is likely that the gospel's reference to the use of this (otherwise impractical) plant for the purpose of slaking Jesus' thirst is yet another presentation of him as Paschal Lamb (1:29, 36; 19:14, 36). His blood, shed on the cross on this Passover Eve, is working a deliverance recalling and also transcending the Exodus deliverance of old.[96]

Aside from this allusion, however, in what way does Jesus' declaration of thirst and drinking the sour wine explicitly fulfill Scripture (v. 28c)? No particular passage is cited. The text most likely in mind is Psalm 69 (LXX 68):22b: "For my thirst (*dipsa*) they gave me vinegar (*oxos*) to drink."[97] At the beginning of the passion, when Simon Peter had struck out with a sword to prevent his arrest, Jesus had rebuked him, saying, "Am I not to drink the cup that the Father has given me?" (18:11b). As he now approaches the moment of death, Jesus has indeed drained that bitter cup to the dregs.[98]

---

[92] The sour wine (*oxos*) was a diluted, vinegary wine drunk by soldiers and laborers; its presence at a scene of crucifixion would be normal; cf. Raymond E. Brown, *John XIII–XXI*, 909.

[93] The final clause (*hina teliōthēi*) is best understood in relation to what follows: "I thirst"; cf. C. K. Barrett, *John*, 553.

[94] "The world falsely attempts to assuage the thirst of the One who is himself the source of 'living water' (4:10, 13-14; 7:37-38)" (Gail O'Day, "The Gospel of John," 833).

[95] Far more practical for this purpose would be the "reed" (*kalamos*) mentioned in Matthew (27:48) and Mark (15:36).

[96] Cf. C. K. Barrett, *John*, 553; Raymond E. Brown, *John XIII–XXI*, 930; *Death of the Messiah*, 2:1076–77; Andrew T. Lincoln, *St. John*, 477–78; Dorothy A. Lee, "Paschal Imagery in John," 25.

[97] Cf. Rudolf Schnackenburg, *St. John*, 3:283.

[98] Cf. Rudolf Schnackenburg, *St. John*, 3:283, 284; Gail O'Day, "The Gospel of John," 832.

In light of the allusion to Psalm 69, the drink of sour (bitter) wine signals Jesus' complete fulfillment of the Father's will set out in Scripture.[99]

On this explanation it is understandable that Jesus, as soon as he has taken the sour wine, announces, "It is accomplished" (*tetelestai*), inclines his head, and hands over the spirit (*paredōken to pneuma*)" (v. 30). The sense of peaceful control right up to the end gives perfect expression to his earlier insistence: "No one takes (my life) from me, but I lay it down of my own accord" (10:18). His dying is a peaceful handing over of his life-spirit to the Father now that his work on earth has been accomplished.

Beyond this, the description of his expiry—literally, "he handed over the spirit"—is open to the interpretation that in his dying Jesus bestowed upon the community, symbolically present in the persons of his mother and the disciple, the gift of the (Holy) Spirit. Jesus, whom the Baptist pointed out as the One destined to "baptize with the Spirit" (1:33) and to "give the Spirit without measure" (3:34), does not simply yield up the spirit (as in Matt 27:50) but "hands over" (*paredoken*) the Spirit as a gift now that his glorification is underway (7:39).[100] In dying, Jesus has made available the Spirit to work the cleansing from sin foreshadowed when he washed his disciples' feet (13:3-10). In this way he has truly become the Lamb of God, who takes away the world's sin (1:29b). The gift of the Spirit which is symbolically anticipated here will become an actuality when later, as risen Lord, he communicates the Spirit to the disciples, empowering them to continue his reconciling mission to the world (20:22-23).

In laying down his life, Jesus has indeed loved his own "to the end (*eis telos*)" (13:2) and loved them in obedience to the God who so loved the world as to give up his only Son for its life (3:16). Though not stated here in so many words, the death of Jesus is the supreme expression of the truth that "God is love" (1 John 4:7, 16).

---

[99] Whereas the verb *plēroun* is elsewhere used with reference to the fulfillment of Scripture, here the gospel uses *teleioun*, the verb cognate with the repeated *tetelestai* (vv. 28, 30) to indicate the completion of Jesus' "work"; cf. C. K. Barrett, *John*, 553.

[100] Cf. Francis J. Moloney, *John*, 504–5; Raymond E. Brown, *Death of the Messiah*, 2:1082; Andrew T. Lincoln, *St. John*, 478. Understanding Jesus' expiry as the gift of the Spirit is sometimes rejected on the grounds that it renders otiose the risen Lord's imparting of the Spirit to the disciples on the day of his resurrection, 20:22-23 (so, e.g., C. K. Barrett, *John*, 554; Rudolf Schnackenburg, *St. John*, 3:285; Gail O'Day, "The Gospel of John," 833). This presses too rigid a time frame on the Johannine theology of Jesus' glorification. What occurs at the moment of Jesus' expiry is a symbolic anticipation that serves to link the later imparting of the Spirit with the saving effect of Jesus' death.

Scene 5. *The Piercing of Jesus' Side: 19:31-37*

Following Jesus' expiry upon the cross, the Fourth Gospel describes an aftermath without parallel in the Synoptic tradition and where, once again, the Jewish authorities are the instigators of the action taken (v. 31). The law of Moses prescribes that, to avoid pollution of the land (Deut 21:22-23), the bodies of executed criminals should not be left hanging after nightfall. The observance of this prohibition in the present case was particularly pressing in that the execution had taken place on the eve of the Sabbath—a Sabbath, moreover, of particular solemnity in that it coincided with Passover. Hence the request to Pilate to see to it that the usual means of bringing about the death of the crucified—breaking their legs—be acted upon so that the bodies could be removed before nightfall.[101]

With Pilate presumably having acceded to their request, the soldiers carry out the brutal procedure (v. 32). They break the legs of the two men crucified with Jesus, but when they come to him and find him already dead they do not break his legs (v. 33). Instead, one of the soldiers pierces his side with a lance, whereupon blood and water flow out (v. 34). The evangelist notes the presence of an eyewitness—a witness upon the truth of whose testimony the belief of the audience can safely rest (v. 35)[102]—and indicates a twofold fulfillment of Scripture in the events described (vv. 36-37).

By drawing attention to the presence of an eyewitness—presumably, the Beloved Disciple (cf. vv. 26-27)—the evangelist is signaling the unique significance of what has transpired.[103] At the most basic level, the spear thrust and the flow of blood and water puts beyond all doubt the fact of Jesus' death.[104] Much effort has been devoted to explaining from a medical point of view the physiological possibility of a flow of blood and water from the

---

[101] Breaking the legs was a standard way of hastening the death of the crucified, who might otherwise remain alive for some days; cf. C. K. Barrett, *John*, 555.

[102] The third and fourth clauses of v. 35 present some difficulty. It seems best to see the third (lit. "and that one [*ekeinos*] knows that he speaks the truth") as still referring to the disciple in a further affirmation of the reliability of his witness; cf. C. K. Barrett, *John*, 557–58. In regard to the verb in the final purpose clause, the textual tradition is divided upon whether an aorist (*pisteusēte*) or present (*pisteuēte*) is to be read (cf. 20:31). The latter, giving the sense of a continuation and deepening of faith already held rather than initial conversion, is to be preferred; cf. Raymond E. Brown, *John XIII–XXI*, 937.

[103] The only parallel is the statement about the disciple's witness at the conclusion of the gospel (21:24).

[104] 1 John 5:5 ("This is the one who came by water and blood, Jesus Christ, not with the water only but with the water and the blood") suggests that the physical reality of Jesus' death may have needed reinforcement in view of later docetic tendencies to deny it; cf. C. K. Barrett, *John*, 556; Gail O'Day, "The Gospel of John," 834.

body of a person treated as Jesus' body has been.[105] Such discussion would only be really useful if what the gospel was providing was a literal historical account, which is not the case.[106] On the contrary, the whole point of drawing attention to the presence and testimony of the eyewitness signals that we are to find here something out of the ordinary, something marvelous, to be understood in a symbolic rather than a literal sense.[107]

The best guide to an interpretation along these lines is to be found in the invitation cried out by Jesus at the Feast of Tabernacles earlier in the gospel:

> On the last day of the festival, the great day, while Jesus was standing there, he cried out, "Let anyone who is thirsty come to me, and let the one who believes in me drink. As the scripture has said, "Out of his heart shall flow rivers of living water." Now he said this about the Spirit, which believers in him were to receive; for as yet there was no Spirit, because Jesus was not yet glorified. (7:37-39)

We note here the references to "thirst" (cf. Jesus' thirst, 19:28), to believing (cf. 19:35), and especially to the flow of "living water" (cf. 19:34) subsequently interpreted as a reference to the Spirit, which believers will receive after Jesus had been "glorified" (cf. 19:30c). In light of these features common to 7:37-39 and the present passage it seems best to interpret the flow of water from Jesus' side immediately after his death as a symbol of the life-giving Spirit, communicated to believers as a consequence of the "glorification" now underway. It is presumably in reference to his death that blood is mentioned before water in the description of the flow from Jesus' side.[108] It is through the shedding of his blood in death that the Son of God has become the source of eternal life for all believers. In the person of the Beloved Disciple and with its faith based on his reliable witness, the future community of believers has access to this life-giving stream.[109]

---

[105] See Raymond E. Brown, *John XIII–XXI*, 946–47.

[106] Cf. Raymond E. Brown, *Death of the Messiah*, 2:1192–96.

[107] Ibid., 2:1179.

[108] Since patristic times, Christian tradition has found in the flow of blood and water a sacramental reference to Eucharist ("blood") and Baptism ("water"), respectively (cf. 3:5 [Baptism]; 6:53-56 [Eucharist]), an interpretation strongly defended by Francis J. Moloney, *John*, 505–6, 507. This venerable tradition is perhaps best regarded as a valid secondary meaning; cf. Raymond E. Brown, *John XIII–XXI*, 951–52; C. K. Barrett, *John*, 557; Rudolf Schnackenburg, *St. John*, 3:294; Gail O'Day, "The Gospel of John," 834.

[109] Cf. Raymond E. Brown, *John XIII–XXI*, 949–50; C. K. Barrett, *John*, 558; Gail O'Day, "The Gospel of John," 834; Andrew T. Lincoln, *St. John*, 479. "Blood (symbolizing his human life, given for the life of the world [cf. 6:51]) and water (symbolizing the Spirit) flow from

For a third and final time (cf. vv. 24, 28) the evangelist points out (vv. 36-37) that "these things" (the nonbreaking of Jesus' bones and the piercing of his side) took place to fulfill Scripture. The words cited—literally, "a bone of his shall not be broken"—do not correspond exactly to any text but are sufficiently close to the instructions regarding the paschal lamb in Exodus 12:46 and Numbers 9:12 to make an allusion to this ritual clear.[110] The fact that Jesus dies at the time when the lambs are being slain in the temple for the Passover ritual, along with the Baptist's indication of him as "the Lamb of God" at the beginning of the gospel (1:29), points in the same direction.[111] The fulfillment of Scripture contributes the sense that the death of Jesus, unlike that of the two crucified with him, has not ultimately been brought about by human agency but by his own free disposition in obedience to the Father (10:17-18).

The "other" Scripture text fulfilled is clearly part of Zechariah 12:10: "They shall look upon the one whom they have pierced" (v. 10).[112] But who, in the evangelist's mind, are "they" who "look upon" the one pierced? Clearly, in view of v. 35, the disciple is meant. But the plural reference must include also the soldier who has actually done the piercing and his fellows. The disciple, standing in for all believers, looks and sees the flow of blood and water as the fount of life. The soldiers who have carried out the execution as representatives of the world may see only defeat and judgment.[113] But the Zechariah text, fully stated, contains a hint of conversion. They have pierced him but, in view of the flow of blood and water that they witness, they may also experience the pouring out of "a spirit of compassion" that will lead them to "mourn for him, as one mourns for an only child, and weep

---

the New Temple to give life to the New Israel, the community gathered at the foot of the cross" (Sandra M. Schneiders, "The Resurrection (of the Body) in the Fourth Gospel: A Key to Johannine Spirituality," in *Life in Abundance*, ed. John R. Donahue, 168–98, see 179).

[110] "Jesus' body on the cross is both the New Paschal Lamb slain to give life and the New Temple from which that life pours forth," Sandra M. Schneiders, "Resurrection (of the Body)," 179.

[111] Also in view may be a statement about God's protection of the suffering righteous from Ps 34:20 (LXX 33:21): "He keeps all their bones; not one of them will be broken." This text would then have contributed the precise form of the verb (future passive, third person singular: *syntribēsetai*) to the text as quoted; cf. C. K. Barrett, *John*, 558; Andrew T. Lincoln, *St. John*, 481–82; Francis J. Moloney, *John*, 509.

[112] The Johannine text renders Zech 12:10 according to the Hebrew and alternative Greek translations of the Old Testament (Aquila and Symmachus). The LXX at this point goes in another direction; cf. C. K. Barrett, *John*, 558–59.

[113] Cf. Raymond E. Brown, *Death of the Messiah*, 2:1188.

bitterly over him, as one weeps over a firstborn" (Zech 12:10b-d). The full scriptural allusion may be sounding a more salvific note: the drawing of all to the Son when he is "lifted from the earth" (John 12:32).[114]

5. The Burial of Jesus: 19:38-42

The final act of the Johannine passion story is the burial of Jesus' body. In all four gospels the main agent in this is Joseph of Arimathea. Uniquely in the Fourth Gospel he is joined by another character, Nicodemus, whom we have met previously (3:1-10; 7:50-51). Both are represented as disciples, yet both have something of a shadow over their attachment to Jesus. Joseph is a disciple but "in secret, for fear of the Jews" (v. 38; cf. 12:42-43). Nicodemus, a Pharisee and a "leader of the Jews" (3:1), had come to Jesus secretly by night and had a conversation that tailed off inconclusively. Later, 7:50-51, he had earned the anger of his fellow Pharisees by reminding them that "our Law does not judge people without first giving them a hearing." While prepared to speak up for Jesus in this way, he does not give any indication of discipleship. Now, however, both men act the part of true disciples.

Joseph obtains permission from Pilate to remove the body of Jesus (v. 38). He is not, as in Mark 15:43 and Luke 23:50, described as a member of the (Jewish) council. Yet that he is a person of some prominence is implied by his approach to Pilate, who presumably assumes him to be acting on behalf of the Jewish authorities who had already obtained permission for the bodies to be removed (v. 31).

Nicodemus, who had come to Jesus by night, now plays his part while it is still day (v. 39). He brings a copious mixture of aromatic myrrh and aloes to enfold within the cloths he and Joseph bind around the body of Jesus according to the burial custom of the Jews (v. 40).[115] The measure—"about a hundred (Roman) pounds"—would amount to about 75 pounds or 34 kg in today's terms. As in the case of the abundance of the "best wine" at Cana (2:6) and Mary of Bethany's costly anointing (12:3), the extravagance is symbolic: Joseph and Nicodemus are lavishing on Jesus' body not only loving devotion but also a richness of expense more normally reserved for

---

[114] Cf. Rudolf Schnackenburg, *St. John*, 3:292–94.

[115] Myrrh (elsewhere in the NT only Matt 2:11) is a sweet-smelling resin used for embalming the dead. "Aloe" refers more generally to various kinds of scented wood. The mixture seems designed to overcome the odor of death. See further, C. K. Barrett, *John*, 559; Rudolf Schnackenburg, *John*, 3:297; Raymond E. Brown, *Death of the Messiah*, 2:1260–64.

royal burials.[116] As on the cross (19:19-22), so also in his burial Jesus reigns as king.[117]

The passion account had begun in a garden (18:1), and in a garden it ends (vv. 41-42). Pressed by the onset of the Sabbath, Joseph and Nicodemus have to make do with what is at hand. Near the place where Jesus had been crucified there was a garden and in the garden a new tomb in which no one had yet been laid. It is a temporary measure but, unbeknownst to them, a temporary resting place is all that will be needed. Moreover, whereas up till this point in the account of the burial reference had been made to "the body of Jesus" (vv. 38, 40), now in conclusion we are told simply: "There . . . they laid Jesus" (v. 42). The passion story ends, then, with the sense of Jesus asleep rather than dead. He has laid down his life. As king, he sleeps in his royal tomb, until he takes up again (10:18) the life he gave "for the life of the world" (6:51).

---

[116] As at the burial of King Herod the Great according to the report of Josephus; see Raymond E. Brown, *Death of the Messiah*, 2:1260.

[117] Cf. Andrew T. Lincoln, *St John*, 485–87; Raymond E. Brown, *Death of the Messiah*, 2:1260–61, 1268; Francis J. Moloney, *John*, 510–11.

The Risen Life of Jesus: 20:1–21:25

John's presentation of Jesus' risen life occupies the final two chapters of the gospel. John 20 describes scenes in Jerusalem; John 21 describes an extended appearance of Jesus by the lakeside in Galilee. In regard to the appearances of the risen Lord there are many points of contact with the Synoptic traditions, especially with that of Luke. However, as elsewhere, the Fourth Gospel goes its own distinctive way.

As we have seen, the gospel brings forward the time of Jesus' "glorification" to the "hour" of his death upon the cross. His being "lifted up" on the cross is, in fact, the vehicle of his return to the Father, having completed the mission entrusted to him (cf. "It is finished" [19:28, 30]). In view of this, his "return" to the disciples in a sequence of Easter appearances sits somewhat awkwardly within the theology of the gospel.[1] Nonetheless, while it is true that Jesus' work is accomplished upon the cross, that work is to be continued in the mission of the disciples (14:12; 17:20-21). Before they will be ready to begin it, they need to appropriate more deeply what Jesus has done and receive empowerment for mission by the Spirit. It is this continuing necessity on the part of the disciples—and of those who will later take up their mission—that the appearances of the risen Jesus address.[2]

Appearances of the Risen Jesus in Jerusalem: 20:1-31

The Jerusalem scenes contained in John 20 proceed in an orderly chronological sequence:

---

[1] On this see Rudolf Schnackenburg, *St. John*, 3:300–1; also Raymond E. Brown, *John XIII–XXI*, 1013–14.

[2] "[F]or John, the Easter event is also still part of the perfection of the love with which Jesus loved his own (13:1)" (Rudolf Schnackenburg, *St. John*, 3:301).

1. Easter Sunday Morning: The Disciples and Mary Magdalene at the Tomb: 20:1-18

2. Easter Sunday Evening: Jesus Appears to the Disciples (less Thomas): 20:19-23

3. Eight Days Later: Jesus Appears to the Disciples and Thomas: 20:24-29

4. A Preliminary Conclusion to the Gospel: 20:30-31

Scene 1. *Easter Sunday Morning:*
The Disciples and Mary Magdalene at the Tomb: 20:1-18

The first section (Sunday morning) divides into three scenes:

a) Mary Magdalene Discovers the Tomb Empty: 20:1-2

b) Peter and the Beloved Disciple Visit the Tomb: 20:3-10

c) Jesus Appears to Mary Magdalene: 20:11-18

a) *Mary Magdalene Discovers the Tomb Empty: 20:1-2.* All four gospels agree on one opening detail in their accounts of Jesus' risen life: that Mary Magdalene came to the tomb of Jesus on Easter Sunday morning and found it empty. In the Fourth Gospel she comes alone. This allows for a unique focus upon her— her grief, her loss, her wonderful rediscovery—unparalleled in the other accounts.[3] She comes early in the morning on the first day of the week while it is still dark (v. 1a). There is already a hint here of a new creation in which she, and other disciples, will pass from the "darkness" of unbelief to full Easter faith.[4] We are not told why she comes. It is not, as in the other accounts, to anoint Jesus' body; that service has already been performed (12:1-8). It seems that she comes to the last resting place of Jesus simply out of love to grieve his loss.[5]

---

[3] "Mary's depth of experience enables us to feel both the desolation at the beginning and later the overpowering joy of rediscovery and awakening" (Dorothy A. Lee, *Flesh and Glory*, 224).

[4] Cf. Rudolf Schnackenburg, *St. John*, 3:308; Francis J. Moloney, *John*, 518; Andrew T. Lincoln, *St. John*, 489.

[5] Cf. John 11:31, where "the Jews" think that Mary, sister of Lazarus, has gone to his tomb to weep there.

On arrival at the tomb Mary sees that the stone covering it has been removed (v. 1b).[6] She does not attempt to enter the tomb or even look inside. The stone's absence is enough to make clear that Jesus' body has been removed, either through grave robbery or hostile action on the part of the authorities. Already bereft of the living person of her Lord, she has now lost even his body. A strong sense of this loss rings through her plaintive report after she has run from the tomb to tell Simon Peter and the Beloved Disciple ("the other disciple, the one whom Jesus loved"):[7] "They have taken the Lord from the tomb and we do not know where they have put him" (v. 2).[8] Ironically, if only she and the other disciples knew, the "taking away" of Jesus' body involves not further human violence but a divine defeat of death.

b) *Peter and the Beloved Disciple Visit the Tomb: 20:3-10.* Luke's Gospel (24:12) records a brief, inconclusive visit of Peter to the tomb of Jesus following the women's report.[9] In the Fourth Gospel this tradition is notably enhanced, especially by the inclusion of the Beloved Disciple. Accompanied by this disciple, Peter "goes out" (v. 3) and makes for the tomb. The ensuing "race" shows both anxiety and deep residual love for the Master they have lost. The faster running of the disciple (vv. 4, 8) stems not from youth or superior athletic ability but from a greater degree of love. Arriving first at the tomb, the disciple does not enter but, bending down, peers into it and sees lying there the linen cloths (*othonia* [cf. 19:40]), in which the body of Jesus had been wrapped (v. 5). When Peter arrives, he does enter the tomb and sees the same linen cloths (v. 6). But he also sees something else: the veil (*soudarion*), which had been over Jesus' face, located not with the linen cloths but rolled up in a place by itself (v. 7).[10] Only after Peter has entered and seen all this does the disciple himself enter the tomb (v. 8a). Then, we are told simply and dramatically: "He saw and he believed" (v. 8b).

[6] The stone was not mentioned in the Johannine account of the burial. The gospel presumes knowledge of it from the common Christian tradition; cf. C. K. Barrett, *John*, 562.

[7] The full formulation here makes clear that the designations "the other disciple" (18:15-16; 20:3, 4, 8) and "the disciple whom Jesus loved" (13:23; 19:26; 21:7, 20) refer to the same person.

[8] The plural "we" communicates the sense that the loss is not just Mary's problem but that of the whole community of disciples, including especially Peter.

[9] Luke 24:12 is not entirely secure on textual grounds, being wanting in the Western manuscript tradition; cf. C. K. Barrett, *John*, 563.

[10] This is the accepted translation of the convoluted description of the face veil's separate location in the Greek; cf. Raymond E. Brown, *John XIII–XXI*, 986.

What was it that the disciple saw and what was it about what he saw that led him—in contrast to Peter, about whose faith nothing is said[11]—to believe? To grasp what the evangelist is driving at in the differing responses of the two disciples, it is important to note how the account brings out the distinction between what can be seen from outside the tomb looking in and what one can see upon actual entry into it. When the disciple enters and sees the separately placed *soudarion* as well as the cloths, the sight brings him to faith. The vital feature is the separate location and state of the *soudarion*.[12]

The significance of the *soudarion* emerges when we recall a detail from the raising of Lazarus: "The dead man came out, his hands and feet bound with bandages and his face wrapped with a cloth (*soudarion*). Jesus said to them, 'Unbind him, and let him go' " (11:44). In view of the role played by that event in precipitating the process leading to Jesus' own death, it is not unreasonable to see a parallelism between the death and raising of Lazarus, on the one hand, and the death and rising of Jesus, on the other. What the neatly folded and separately placed *soudarion* in Jesus' tomb indicates is that, whereas Lazarus was completely passive in his return to life, totally reliant upon the command of Jesus and needing others to remove the veil over his face, Jesus has actively raised himself. The neatly folded, separately placed veil is the culminating indication of a majestic reassumption of life. As the Good Shepherd had announced:

> No one takes it (my life) from me, but I lay it down of my own accord. I have power to lay it down, and I have power to take it up again. I have received this command from my Father. (10:18)

The parallel—and contrast—with the raising of Lazarus makes clear that it was the condition and the separate location of the face veil that sparked the disciple's faith. Here was not grave robbery or hostile activity. Here was a "sign" of the defeat of death, a divine reclaiming of life.[13]

The comment that follows as in v. 9, "for as yet they did not understand the scripture, that he must rise from the dead," might seem to undercut the

---

[11] Cf. C. K. Barrett, *John*, 563–64.

[12] Cf. Sandra M. Schneiders, "The Face Veil: A Johannine Sign (John 20:1-10)," *Biblical Theology Bulletin* 13/3 (July 1983): 94–97, esp. 95–96; Brendan Byrne, "The Beloved Disciple and the Community in John 20," *Journal for the Study of the New Testament* 23 (1985): 83–97, esp. 87.

[13] I have elaborated on this at greater length in my article "Beloved Disciple," esp. 87–89. The link with the Lazarus episode is widely recognized: see, e.g., Rudolf Schnackenburg, *St. John*, 3:311; Gail O'Day, "The Gospel of John," 841; Andrew T. Lincoln, *St. John*, 490; Dorothy A. Lee, *Flesh and Glory*, 221.

disciple's arrival at faith. It refers primarily to Peter and the remaining disciples, and in this sense highlights the disciple's superior disposition to faith.[14] None of the others had grasped the message of Scripture that the Messiah would rise from the dead.[15] Whereas Mary Magdalene, Peter, Thomas, and the other disciples will come to faith in the resurrection only after they have physically seen the risen Lord (20:11-20), the disciple believes on the basis of the "sign" constituted by the grave clothes; he has not needed to see Jesus. In this he foreshadows the faith of all subsequent generations of believers, upon whom Jesus pronounces a blessing immediately following his interaction with Thomas (20:29). Like him, they (we!) also do not "see" Jesus but believe on the basis of the "many signs" recorded in the gospel (20:30-31).[16]

c) *Jesus Appears to Mary Magdalene: 20:11-18.* Somewhat abruptly the focus reverts to Mary Magdalene, who—without explanation—is back at the empty tomb. In the scene that now unfolds—possibly the most poignant and heartwarming in the entire gospel—there is great emphasis upon her emotional state, specifically her weeping (vv. 11 [twice], 13, 15). Her experience in this scene will give perfect expression to Jesus' prophecy at the Last Supper:

> Amen, amen, I tell you, you will weep and mourn, but the world will rejoice; you will have pain, but your pain will turn into joy. (16:20)

Whereas previously Mary had simply reacted to the absence of the stone (v. 1), now, like the two disciples, she stoops down and looks inside the tomb (v. 11a). Instead of grave clothes, what she sees is a vision of two angels in white garments, sitting one at the head and one at the feet of where the body of Jesus had lain (v. 12). The presence of angels enclosing the space where Jesus' body had been points to a heavenly explanation of its emptiness: God has been at work. The angels do not offer any explanation (contrast Matt 28:5-6; Mark 16:6; Luke 24:5-7). The focus remains on Mary's emotional state, as they simply ask her why she is weeping (v. 13a). Her response echoes her earlier report to the disciples (v. 2b) but this time she speaks more

---

[14] The awkwardness of this explanation in the present text presumably stems from the evangelist's incorporation of the disciple into the wider Easter tradition as seen, e.g., in Luke 24:12; cf. Andrew T. Lincoln, *St. John*, 490–91.

[15] It is not clear whether Scripture in general or some particular text (e.g., Ps 16:10 or Hos 6:2) is meant.

[16] This is the main thesis of my article, "Beloved Disciple" (see n. 13 above); cf. also Francis J. Moloney, *John*, 521.

personally: "They have taken away my Lord, and I do not know where they have laid him" (v. 13).

Conversation with the angels ends as Mary turns back from looking into the tomb and sees Jesus standing there (v. 14ab). Absorption in her grief had prevented Mary from grasping the significance of the angels' presence. Now it prevents her from recognizing Jesus (v. 14; cf. 21:4-14).[17] He does not shock her immediately into recognition. Instead, like the angels, he asks (v. 15a), "Woman, why are you weeping? Whom are you looking for?" (cf. 1:38).[18] Thinking that the person standing before her is the gardener—the one responsible for the upkeep of the garden and its contents, including the tomb—Mary addresses him politely, "Sir" (*kyrie*), and asks if he is the one who has carried Jesus' body (literally, "him") away to tell her where he has placed him, so that she might come and remove him (v. 15). Having lost the living person of Jesus, Mary is desperate to find and in sense retain his body, unaware that that body stands before her in a glorious existence transcending the bounds of death.

When at last the risen One speaks her name (v. 16a), Mary recognizes his voice, as the sheep recognize the voice of the Good Shepherd (10:3-4, 14, 16, 27). Turning once more (cf. v. 14)[19] and reverting to her old way of addressing Jesus, she exclaims "*Rabbouni*" (v. 16bc), a Hebrew (actually Aramaic) form of address expressing both familiarity and endearment.[20] From Jesus' subsequent response (v. 17a), it seems too that she, who had been so desperate to find his dead body (vv. 13, 15) reaches out to grasp and hold on to his living physical person, now restored. The traditional understanding of his words, in art and translation ("*Noli me tangere*" [Vulgate]; "Touch me not" [KJV]), has cast a long shadow over the beautiful interaction unfolding here. Jesus is not forbidding Mary to touch him, as though his risen body was something that had to be preserved from human contact. The Greek expression *mē mou haptou* means "Do not hold on to me" rather than "Do not touch me."[21] Jesus is cautioning her against a bid on her part—expressed in the old address, "Rabbouni," and the attempt to hold on to him physically—to return simply to the relationship that she had enjoyed with

---

[17] Cf. Andrew T. Lincoln, *St. John*, 492.

[18] Cf. Gail O'Day, "The Gospel of John," 842.

[19] "She turns to him—an outward gesture, which at the same time expresses an opening up of her inner self and a believing openness to the risen Lord" (Rudolf Schnackenburg, *St. John*, 3:317).

[20] Gail O'Day, "The Gospel of John," 842.

[21] Cf. Raymond E. Brown, *John XIII–XXI*, 992; C. K. Barrett, *John*, 565.

him in the past.[22] She, and all the disciples, must let that go. She must allow him to complete the process of his glorification in a return to the Father, which will open up an entirely new relationship with him as promised at the Supper.

It is along these lines that we should understand the justification that Jesus gives for restraining Mary by saying, "For I have not yet ascended to the Father" (v. 17b). His death, resurrection, and ascension are all aspects of the one process of glorification. As explained at length at the Supper, when Jesus has returned to the Father, a new mode of presence, transcending the limits of space and time, will be established (14:1-4, 15-24, 28; 15:1-11; 16:4-15; 16:19-22). Until that is the case, Mary must not hinder the process by seeking to reinstate the old relationship. She must let him go to the Father so that the promised new way of being present may come about. This new presence will make available to subsequent generations, who unlike her have not walked with and touched Jesus in his prepassion life, an intimacy and a union equal to and indeed transcending that enjoyed by the original disciples. Mary's intense grief and her desperate search for his body have shown the depth of her love for him in the old way. All this serves as a foil, if you will, against which to measure the new mode in which love and discipleship are to continue, and indeed find "greater" possibilities through the gift of the Spirit (cf. 14:12).

Jesus, in fact, goes on to commission Mary (v. 17c) to be the messenger not only of his resurrection and ascent to the Father but of the implications of that ascent in the new situation. She is to bring "to my brothers (and sisters)" the wonderful announcement:

> I am ascending to my Father and your Father,
> to my God and your God. (20:17de)

Just before expiring on the cross, Jesus had shared his human mother with the Beloved Disciple—and, by extension, with all the subsequent generations of believers that the disciple represents (19:26-27). Now Jesus' ascent to the Father and sending of the Spirit will mean that he shares his divine Father with them as well, fulfilling the pledge aired in the Prologue:

> But to all who received him, who believed in his name, he gave power to become children of God, who were born, not of blood or of the will of the flesh or of the will of man, but of God. (1:12-13)

---

[22] Cf. Rudolf Bultmann, *Gospel of John*, 687; Francis J. Moloney, *John*, 526.

As Jesus' "brothers (and sisters)," believers are no longer "orphans" (14:18-21). Beyond discipleship, they enjoy the intimacy of his eternal relationship with the Father as members of the "family" of God (1:18).[23] This is the message that Mary in her privileged role (dubbed from the patristic period as "apostle to the apostles") brings (v. 18) to the remaining disciples.[24] The significance of her role in the gospel's account of Jesus' risen life cannot be overestimated.[25]

Scene 2. *Easter Sunday Evening: Jesus Appears to the Disciples: 20:19-23*

Without pressing the time framework too rigorously we are probably to understand that Jesus' ascension to the Father occurs between his appearance to Mary Magdalene and an evening appearance to the disciples on that same "first day of the week" (Easter Sunday).[26] The Jesus, then, who appears to the disciples is the already ascended Jesus, who, with his glorification (death, resurrection, ascension/return to the Father) complete, now sends the promised Spirit upon the disciples (cf. 7:38-39; 16:7).

The fact that the disciples sit behind closed doors "for fear of the Jews" (v. 19; cf. 7:13; 9:22; 19:38) suggests that Mary Magdalene's report has made little impact. The risen Lord meets them in their fearful, closed-in emotional state, just as he met Mary in her emotional state. The evangelist does not stop to explain how one who is sufficiently corporeal to show his wounds (and later invite Thomas to touch them) is sufficiently "immaterial" to pass through closed doors.[27] The risen Lord breaks through both the physical and emotional barrier just by standing in the midst and speaking, "Peace." On one level, this is simply the conventional Semitic greeting. On

---

[23] Jesus does not say, "to our Father," thereby preserving a qualitative difference between his divine sonship and that of believers. Nonetheless, it is not the difference that is stressed but the equivalence; cf. Rudolf Bultmann, *Gospel of John*, 689; Raymond E. Brown, *John XIII–XXI*, 1016, who draws attention to the similarity with Ruth's statement to Naomi, "Your people shall become my people and your God my God" (Ruth 1:16).

[24] The designation appears to go back to Hippolytus (ca. 170–235 CE); cf. Dorothy A. Lee, *Flesh and Glory*, 230.

[25] Cf. Gail O'Day, "The Gospel of John," 843; Dorothy A. Lee, *Flesh and Glory*, 226; Andrew T. Lincoln, *St. John*, 495.

[26] "(John) is fitting a theology of resurrection/ascension that by definition has no dimensions of time and space into a narrative that is necessarily sequential" (Raymond E. Brown, *John XIII–XXI*, 1014); cf. also Gail O'Day, "The Gospel of John," 843; Andrew T. Lincoln, *St. John*, 493.

[27] Cf. C. K. Barrett, *John*, 568.

a deeper level, it communicates the profound peace that Jesus had promised to give to the disciples, banishing fear stemming from the hostility of the world (14:27; 16:33). It is not merely a wish ("Peace be with you"); it is a declaration: "Peace is with you."[28]

While saying this greeting, Jesus shows the disciples his hands and his side (v. 20a). Beyond establishing that he who stands in their midst is truly the same person who had been crucified, the wounds signify the basis of the peace that he now imparts: a peace won through the victory over the world brought about by his death in self-sacrificial love. Likewise, the joy that now sweeps over the disciples (v. 20b) is not simply the joy at seeing a loved and lost one standing before them alive. The joy is, again, the joy promised at the Supper (16:20-24). They have wept and mourned while the world rejoiced (16:20). Now their sorrow has been turned into joy, a joy that no one will take away from them (16:22) because it is rooted in a victory over all that could threaten to destroy it. Significantly, the Lord continues in his risen life to bear the marks of the wounds inflicted upon him. As marked, for example, on the Easter candle, the wounds will display forever that the victorious divine love is a vulnerable love, imparting a peace and joy that the world cannot give.

A fresh impulse is given to the scene as Jesus repeats his assurance of peace (v. 21). The disciples are not simply to remain in their joy. No longer fearful, they must be readied to go out beyond the locked doors to continue in the world the mission that Jesus himself has received from the Father: "As the Father sent me, so I am now sending you" (v. 21b; cf. 13:20; 17:18).[29]

To activate this mission, Jesus breathes upon the disciples, saying, "Receive the Holy Spirit" (v. 22).[30] The Greek expression (*enephysēsen*) is the same employed for God's breathing life into the first human being in the Garden of Eden:

> Then the LORD God formed man from the dust of the ground, and breathed (*enephysēsen*) into his nostrils the breath of life; and the man became a living being. (Gen 2:7; cf. Ezek 37:9; Wis 15:11)

The implication is that what is taking place here is nothing less than the new creation or, rather, with strong echoes of the Prologue, the bringing of present

---

[28] Cf. Raymond E. Brown, *John XIII–XXI*, 1021.

[29] The two verbs of "sending" appearing here, *apostellein* and *pempein*, are used interchangeably throughout the gospel with reference both to the Father's sending of Jesus and his own missioning of the disciples; for references, see C. K. Barrett, *John*, 569.

[30] The close link between the statement of mission (v. 21b) and the sending of the Holy Spirit is shown by the participial phrase, "While saying this," at the beginning of v. 22.

creation into line with the original design of God, a design up till now thwarted by human sin. The disciples who receive the Spirit are, as Jesus promised Nicodemus (3:3-10), being reborn "from above" as "children of God" (1:12-13; 20:17). Engendered as God's children in this way and enlivened by the Spirit (cf. Ezek 37:1-15), they—and all those who receive and believe in their witness—will be the nucleus of a renewed people of God, the beachhead of the new creation in the world.[31] John the Baptist had pointed out Jesus as the One who would "baptize with the Spirit" (1:33). Now, following his glorification (7:38-39), Jesus fulfills this prophecy in full measure (cf. 3:34).[32]

Empowering the disciples with the Spirit in this way, Jesus specifies their mission as involving the "forgiving" and "retaining" of sins (v. 23). It is natural, especially for readers from the Catholic tradition, to think immediately here of the penitential discipline of the church, specifically the sacrament of reconciliation. While this is certainly not to be excluded, to confine the mission to the forgiveness of postbaptismal sins would be to adopt too narrow an understanding. We should recall what Jesus had said in regard to the Paraclete, "the Spirit of Truth" (15:26; 16:13), at the Supper.[33] The Spirit will lay bare both the goodness and evil of the world, proving it "wrong about sin, and righteousness and judgment" (16:8-11) when it fails to "come to the truth," fails to "come to the Light because its deeds are evil" (3:19-21). As bearers of the Spirit, the disciples are missioned to offer the world the reconciliation and eternal life won by the Son, whom the Father sent into the world not to condemn but so that the world might be saved through him (3:17). People who respond in faith, exposing their lives to the divine light and truth, find forgiveness of their sins and rebirth as members of the family of God. Those who refuse to believe and come to the light, bring down judgment upon themselves (3:18-19; 9:39-41; cf. 5:24-29). In this sense, their sins are "retained" (20:23b).

Through the gift of the Spirit, then, the risen Lord is empowering the community to declare both forgiveness and retention of sin. While such empowerment may in the first instance relate to admission (or nonadmission) of outsiders to the community in a missionary sense, there is no good reason to confine such forgiveness to sins committed before baptism or to the initial moment of belief. In its ongoing life the community will need both to cele-

---

[31] Cf. Sandra M. Schneiders, "Resurrection (of the Body)," 185.

[32] For a careful consideration of the appropriateness of describing this scene as the "Johannine Pentecost," see Rudolf Schnackenburg, *St. John*, 3:326–27.

[33] Here, I am much indebted to Francis J. Moloney, *John*, 533, 536.

brate and to draw upon the reconciliation won by the death of the Lamb (cf. 1 John 1:6-10).[34] In this sense the sacrament of reconciliation that has evolved in the Catholic tradition has a genuine scriptural foundation here.

Scene 3. *Eight Days Later:*
Jesus Appears to the Disciples and Thomas: 20:24-29

For many people the scene where the risen Jesus comes to meet Thomas in his refusal to believe, submits with divine courtesy to all his conditions, and elicits from him the supreme confession of faith is a favorite episode in the Fourth Gospel. Obtuse though he be, Thomas enjoys hero status for all for whom faith is something of a struggle. It is indeed one of the gospel's delightful paradoxes that its climactic statement of belief should be drawn out of disbelief and, if we recall earlier statements of this disciple, a pronounced tendency to the negative (11:16; 14:5).

The scene is introduced (v. 25) by the information that Thomas, "one of the Twelve" (cf. 6:67, 70, 71), was not with the disciples when Jesus came to them on the first day of the week. His response when told that they "had seen the Lord"[35] was an adamant refusal to believe unless a veritable cascade of conditions was met: seeing in Jesus' hands the mark of the nails, putting his finger into the marks, and his hand right into Jesus' side.[36] The other disciples had moved to belief and joy when Jesus showed them his hands and his side (v. 20). Thomas demands much more. Like Mary in her attempt to cling to the body of Jesus, he requires that the crucified One be present in full physical reality before he will believe the disciples' joyous report.[37]

---

[34] Some commentators, apparently concerned to steer interpretation of this passage away from forgiveness of postbaptismal sin in the Catholic sacramental sense, emphasize that for John "sin" is primarily unbelief, a theological failing, rather than a moral or behavioral transgression (cf. 15:22-24); so, e.g., Gail O'Day, "The Gospel of John," 847. This is true but not the whole picture. A key element or cause of unbelief in the Johannine sense is refusal to bring one's sins before the Light for exposure and remission (3:19-21; 8:21-24; cf. 1:29). The plural "sins" in v. 23 cannot simply be equated with "sin" in the distinctive Johannine sense. The classic discussion of this issue in regard to John 20:23, outstanding for its balance and fairness, remains that of Raymond E. Brown, *John XIII–XXI*, 1041–45; cf. C. K. Barrett, *John*, 571; Rudolf Schnackenburg, *St. John*, 3:326, 474; Andrew T. Lincoln, *St. John*, 499–500.

[35] The imperfect tense, *elegon*, in the Greek communicates the sense that the disciples had repeatedly tried to convince Thomas; cf. Raymond E. Brown, *John XIII–XXI*, 1025.

[36] The Greek expression (*ballein . . . eis*) communicates the sense of penetration.

[37] Cf. Francis J. Moloney, *John*, 537.

Eight days later, then—that is, on the same first day of the week (Sunday)—Jesus restages the earlier scene for the benefit of Thomas. Once more, despite the locked doors,[38] he comes among them, stands in their midst, and repeats his assurance of peace (v. 26). Turning to Thomas, he proceeds to meet, word for word, all the conditions laid down, ending with the exhortation, "Do not be unbelieving but believing" (v. 27).

We do not know whether Thomas goes ahead with the physical examination he had demanded. Jesus' words in verse 29 ("because you have seen me") suggest that, as in the case of the other disciples, sight was enough to bring him to faith. And not simply to faith in the resurrection but to elicit from Thomas the supreme christological confession in the gospel: "My Lord and my God" (v. 28). Thomas now shares the faith of Mary and the other disciples: like them he has seen "the Lord" (cf. vv. 18, 25). Beyond this he confesses that Jesus is "God." As readers of the gospel, we have known from the start (1:1, 18) that he bears this status. We have observed the struggle that he has had throughout his ministry—with the disciples but in particular with the Jewish authorities—to communicate that in his person and his "work" is disclosed the presence and power of the unseen God. Now we see a disciple who for a space has plumbed the depths of unbelief arrive and give fullest expression to this truth. Earlier Jesus had said to that same disciple (Thomas), "If you know me, you will know my Father also. From now on you do know him and have seen him" (14:7; cf. 5:23; 8:28). Thomas now knows that to have seen Jesus is indeed to have seen the Father (cf. 14:9).

Even if Thomas did not actually touch Jesus before his act of faith, his insistence upon the need to investigate the wounds so physically and deeply adds immeasurably to the significance of his confession when at last it is made. His movement from faithless insistence on proof to an unparalleled expression of faith brings out the sense of divinity streaming from the One who has been wounded unto death in such a way. As in the footwashing at the beginning of the Supper, God is revealed here not only as incarnate but as the One who gave himself up to the most degrading of deaths in self-sacrificial love for the world. Before Thomas and the group of the disciples gathered in the room stands an unambiguous depiction of the truth that God is love.

Moreover, in contrast, for example, to Luke 24:31, there is no statement about the departure or vanishing of the risen Lord. The Jesus who stands before the disciples as the embodiment of divine love is the One who has

---

[38] No mention now of the reason "for fear of the Jews" (v. 19): resurrection faith and joy has banished fear.

already returned to the glory that he had with the Father before the world was made (17:5). He will remain with the disciples and with the church that will derive from them in a new mode of presence through the Paraclete Spirit.

A final statement from Jesus (v. 29) opens up the perspective to that future. Jesus says to Thomas, "Because you have seen me, you have believed,"[39] and then adds, "Blessed are those who have not seen and yet have come to believe." In pronouncing this beatitude Jesus is not belittling Thomas. To do so would undercut the effect of his confession. But a distinction is being made between faith based upon sight of the risen Lord and faith that does not rest upon such sight but believes without seeing. The beatitude reaches out to and declares blessed believers of subsequent generations who, unlike Mary Magdalene, Thomas, and the other disciples who saw the risen Lord, have to believe simply on their—and the later church's—testimony, "We have seen the Lord" (v. 25; cf. v. 18). The beatitude is asserting that believers of such later generations (for whom the gospel is actually written: 20:30-31) are in no less advantageous a position than the original witnesses.[40] They can share the disciples' joy in the resurrection (v. 20b). There is even a hint of a greater blessedness accruing to them because a deeper, more creative faith is going to be drawn from their hearts.

If the coming to faith of later believers is different from that of Mary, Thomas, and the other disciples, it has a forerunner in the faith of the Beloved Disciple.[41] As we have seen, when this disciple entered the tomb of Jesus, the separately placed and folded face veil was sufficient to serve as a sign of the resurrection: "He saw and he believed" (v. 8b). True, his faith was based upon sight but it was sight simply of the grave clothes not sight of the risen Jesus.[42] In his coming to faith without seeing the risen Lord the disciple

---

[39] The statement can be read as a question ("Have you believed because you have seen me?" (NRSV; cf. also NAB; Andrew T. Lincoln, *St. John*, 503). To read it as a statement (NIV and most recent commentators) seems to give a better sense; see Raymond E. Brown, *John XIII–XXI*, 1027; C. K. Barrett, *John*, 573; Rudolf Schnackenburg, *St. John*, 3:334; Francis J. Moloney, *John*, 540; Gail O'Day, "The Gospel of John," 850.

[40] Cf. C. K. Barrett, *John*, 574; Rudolf Schnackenburg, *St. John*, 3:334–35.

[41] See my article, "The Faith of the Beloved Disciple and the Community" (p. 330, n. 13 above).

[42] We should note the pronoun in the first part of Jesus' statement to Thomas: "Because you have seen *me* you have believed." The distinction is not between seeing and believing on the one hand and not seeing and yet believing on the other. The point is whether one needs or does not need to have physical sight of *Jesus* in order to come to faith.

foreshadows and models the faith of the later community.[43] As in his presence at the foot of the cross and in his taking Jesus' mother to himself, in this respect too he stands in for believers of all later generations.

Scene 4. *A Preliminary Conclusion to the Gospel: 20:30-31*

> Now Jesus did many other signs in the presence of his disciples, which are not written in this book. But these are written so that you may come to believe that Jesus is the Messiah, the Son of God, and that through believing you may have life in his name. (20:30-31)

The Fourth Gospel consists of twenty-one chapters. But here at the end of chapter 20 we come across what looks very much like a conclusion to the entire work. It seems to signal that a "first edition" of the gospel ended here, with chapter 21 being added later and provided with a similar ending of its own (21:24-25). That may well have been the case for a short time— though for reasons that I shall mention in due course I believe that the material in John 21 is very much integral to the Johannine project as a whole.

The conclusion looks back and looks forward: back to all that it has recorded of Jesus' ministry up to and including his risen life, forward to the later generations of believers for whose benefit the record has been made.

The evangelist strengthens the impact of his account by stressing that what he has recorded is only a selection: he knows of "many other signs" that Jesus worked in the presence of his disciples that could have been included (v. 30). "Sign" (*sēmeion*), as we have seen, is the evangelist's preferred way of referring to Jesus' miracles. It is chosen because for John the miraculous aspect is not the proper place for faith to rest; for mature faith the marvelous functions as a sign pointing to a deeper reality: the revelation of the "truth" about God in the person and activity of Jesus. While "sign" may have referred simply to the miracles of Jesus at an early stage of the Johannine tradition, we should probably understand the terms more broadly here: to refer to the entire revelatory ministry of Jesus as witnessed by the original disciples, miracles and discourses alike, including the appearances of the risen Lord.[44]

In a concluding turn (v. 31a) to the reader ("you"), the evangelist states the purpose of it all. It is to deepen, solidify, and bring to full maturity the faith of those who were not in the eyewitness position of the original dis-

---

[43] Cf. also Francis J. Moloney, *John*, 538; Sandra M. Schneiders, "Resurrection (of the Body)," 196.

[44] Andrew T. Lincoln, *St. John*, 505–6.

ciples but have to rely on the testimony of those disciples as recorded "in this book."[45]

To state that the object of faith is that Jesus is the Messiah, the Son of God (v. 31b), may seem something of a letdown after the sublime "Lord" and "God" confession just pronounced by Thomas. Surely, mature faith has passed beyond simple acknowledgment of Jesus as Messiah. And we know from Martha's confession that even "Son of God" can be used in a sense that is merely messianic (11:27). Indeed! The conjunction and sequence of the titles suggest that belief has to move beyond simple acknowledgment that Jesus is Messiah as conventionally understood to an appreciation of his divine sonship in the unique sense that has been building up throughout the story and which has reached its climax in Thomas's sublime confession. The whole purpose of the gospel has been to bring the reader to see in the humanity of Jesus, and above all in his death in sacrificial love on the cross, the only begotten Son who is always in the bosom of the unseen God (1:18), the "I AM" (8:24) who reveals the essence of God to be love.

The goal of such perseverance in faith (cf. *pisteuontes*) is what has been stated from the outset as the goal of the entire divine project recorded and commended in the gospel: that human beings, in virtue of their believing relationship with Christ (literally, "in his name"), should have "life"—life that, beyond mere existence, involves sharing the "eternal life" of the divine communion of love. In the opening verses of the Prologue we heard that "what has come into being in him was life, and the life was the light of all people" (1:3c-4). Now, at this preliminary ending of the great sweep of the gospel, we know how that life has been made available to believers through the mission and saving death of the Son.

Appearance of the Risen Jesus in Galilee: 21:1-25

In a curious as well as delightful way the Fourth Gospel is at its most "human" when describing the risen life of the Lord. We have seen this already in John 20, especially in the appearances to Mary Magdalene and

---

[45] By referring to "deepening the faith" of those who are already believers, I am adopting the majority view according to which the purpose of the Fourth Gospel as expressed here is not to bring to faith those who are not yet believers (the "missionary" understanding) but to confirm in faith those who already are such. A finely balanced textual uncertainty—whether the aorist subjunctive *pisteusēte* or the present subjunctive *pisteuēte* is to be read—leaves the matter open (with the aorist favoring, though not necessarily demanding, the missionary interpretation). See further, Rudolf Schnackenburg, *St. John*, 3:338; Francis J. Moloney, *John*, 544; Andrew T. Lincoln, *St. John*, 506–7.

Thomas. It is even more so in the case of Jesus' final appearance, which takes place in Galilee in an extended single episode by the sea of Tiberias (21:1-25). The shyness of the disciples as they accept Jesus' breakfast invitation; the impetuosity of Peter as he jumps into the sea in his eagerness to meet his risen Lord; above all his deep emotion as Jesus draws from him a triple protestation of love: all these and several other features add human warmth and interest to the scene.

The Fourth Gospel would, then, be much impoverished without this final chapter. In several respects, however, it sits in awkward continuity with the preceding body of the gospel. This has led most scholars to regard it as an epilogue added to the "first edition" (John 1–20) by a later hand, who drew on fresh material from the wider gospel tradition.[46] The most obvious reason for regarding John 21 as an addition is the existence of the editorial conclusion at 20:30-31 that brings the narrative to a close on such a fitting theological note. While in most respects chapter 21 is thoroughly "Johannine" in tone and content, there is a notable proportion of words and phrases not appearing in the earlier chapters.[47] John 21 displays a concern for the mission of the disciples that is indeed foreshadowed but is not prominent in the earlier chapters. The disciples' bored return to their earlier occupation of fishing, their failure to recognize Jesus, and their awkwardness in his company are odd features after the joy that attended his appearance on Easter Sunday evening and their reception of the Spirit.[48] Despite the notice in verse 14 about this being the third time that Jesus appeared to the disciples after his resurrection, their responses as described in the narrative could well convey the impression that this is the first time they have seen him. Following the beatitude pronounced upon those who, unlike Thomas, believe without seeing Jesus (20:29), it is also somewhat odd to have a narrative that involves actually seeing him.[49] The new narrative set in Galilee implies that we know that the disciples, led by Peter, were fishermen, but there is no hint of this being their occupation earlier on. Nor have we heard before of "the sons of Zebedee" (v. 2), and while we have heard of Thomas the Twin and Nathanael, the absence of Andrew and Philip, granted their earlier roles, is striking.

---

[46] A notable exception to the consensus is Gail O'Day, "The Gospel of John," 854–55, who points out that all the extant manuscripts of the gospel, including the most ancient, contain chapter 21. Without any external evidence that the gospel ever circulated without the chapter, a decision has to be made on internal evidence alone.

[47] This to some extent is explained by the preoccupation with fishing, an activity that does not feature in John 1–20.

[48] Cf. Raymond E. Brown, *John XIII–XXI*, 1078; Francis J. Moloney, *John*, 545–46.

[49] Cf. Andrew T. Lincoln, *St. John*, 510.

While these considerations lead most interpreters to see John 21 as an epilogue added to an earlier "edition" of the gospel, not lacking are strong elements of continuity as well. It is perfectly fitting that a narrative devoted basically to the mission of the disciples should provide an "ecclesiological" complement to the strongly "christological" focus of John 1–20.[50] The narrative in fact puts "flesh" upon Jesus' pronouncements on the disciples' future mission at the Supper (14:12; 15:16; 16:2-3; 17:18-23).[51] Finally, it is particularly fitting that Peter who three times denied Jesus beside a charcoal fire (18:18, 25) be rehabilitated alongside a similar fire through a triple declaration of love (21:9, 15-17).

Peter, along with the Beloved Disciple, is the chief character and focus of John 21. As we have seen, the two are often paired in the latter part of the gospel, chiefly to the disadvantage of Peter, who is regularly upstaged by the disciple, the hero of the community behind the gospel and the guarantor of its tradition (21:24; cf. 19:35). Chapter 21 offers a more balanced view. The disciple may be the first to discern that the stranger who has called them from the shore is the risen Lord (21:7; cf. 20:8). But, apart from this, there is only the concluding clarification of his subsequent fate (v. 23) and the affirmation of his reliable "authorship" (v. 24). Peter, on the other hand, is the major player: he drags in the unbroken net with its abundance of fish and, following his protestations of love, is three times commissioned as pastor and chief shepherd of the church.

This realignment of relationship between Peter and the disciple probably reflects a move on the part of the Johannine community to align itself more directly with the wider community of believers in which Peter's leadership was clearly acknowledged and the memory of his heroic death revered (21:18-19).[52] While the community retained its special claim upon the witness of the one it called "the disciple that Jesus loved" (21:24), its depiction of Peter in this final chapter offers something of a corrective to the less flattering earlier portrayal. Such a move toward alignment with the wider Christian community is particularly understandable following the death of the disciple, an event that this chapter clearly presupposes and seeks to come to terms with (21:20-23).

---

[50] Cf. Raymond E. Brown, *John XIII–XXI*, 1082; Rudolf Schnackenburg, *St. John*, 3:344; Jean Zumstein, "Der Prozess der Relecture in der johanneischen Literatur," *New Testament Studies* 42 (1996): 394–411, see 404.

[51] Cf. Gail O'Day, "The Gospel of John," 854–55.

[52] On Peter's prominence in the post-Easter church see especially, Martin Hengel, *Saint Peter: The Underestimated Apostle* (Grand Rapids, MI: Wm. B. Eerdmans, 2010).

John 21 falls easily into two main divisions:

1. Abundant Catch of Fish and Breakfast Hosted by Jesus: 21:1-14

2. Rehabilitation of Peter: His Future and That of the Beloved Disciple: 21:15-24

A second formal conclusion, echoing that at 20:30-31, brings the work to a close: 21:25.

1. *An Abundant Catch of Fish and Breakfast Hosted by Jesus: 21:1-14*

This scene itself falls into three sections: a fruitless night of fishing: 21:1-3; an abundant catch at the command of Jesus: 21:4-8; and a lakeshore breakfast hosted by Jesus: 21:9-14.

A Fruitless Night of Fishing: 21:1-3. The extended scene by the lakeside in Galilee is introduced as one where Jesus "revealed" (*ephanerōsen*) himself again to the disciples (v. 1). The language recalls the comment about his "revealing" his glory when he miraculously remedied the lack of wine at the wedding of Cana (2:11), a scene at the very beginning of his ministry with which this final episode by the lakeside has much in common. First, as also at Cana (2:1b-2) the main players are introduced (v. 2). Unsurprisingly, Simon Peter leads off, followed by Thomas the Twin, who has of course featured prominently in the previous chapter. The mention of Nathanael, who we now learn stems from Cana in Galilee, establishes a further link with the sign Jesus performed in that locale. We recall also that, following Nathanael's confession (1:49), Jesus promised him that he would see "greater things" (1:51), a promise now to be fulfilled abundantly. More surprising is the listing of the "sons of Zebedee" (James and John) since, aside from the Synoptic tradition, we would not know of their existence or names from the Fourth Gospel. Making up the number to seven is the mention of "two other disciples," one of whom must be the still-unnamed "disciple whom Jesus loved" (cf. v. 7).[53] The symbolic completeness of the number seven suggests that we are to see the group as representative of the future church community as a whole.[54]

---

[53] Strictly speaking, the Beloved Disciple could be one of the "sons of Zebedee" (notably, John!); cf. C. K. Barrett, *John*, 117, 578. However, it is more likely that the author is following the practice of leaving him unnamed.

[54] Cf. Rudolf Schnackenburg, *St. John*, 3:352; Andrew T. Lincoln, *St. John*, 510.

A situation of need is set up when, following Peter's lead, the group embarks on a night of fruitless fishing (v. 3). As noted earlier, we would not know from earlier in the gospel that Peter or any of the other disciples were fishermen. This Galilean sequence, however, has drawn on this detail from the wider tradition to introduce the fishing motif which, as in that tradition, functions as a symbol of mission. Without any reference to Jesus, the disciples have gone out on the lake by themselves in the darkness. Unsurprisingly in view of his words at the Supper (cf. 15:4-5), for all their nightlong toil they have caught nothing (v. 3d).

An Abundant Catch: 21:4-8. With dawn (v. 4), the darkness recedes and there, standing unrecognized on the shore, is the Light of the world. His tone of address, "Children (*paidia*)" (v. 5), reflects the new familial intimacy of the postresurrection era (20:17). His question, "You haven't caught anything to eat yet, have you?"[55] shows awareness of their lack of success;[56] at the same time it highlights the need that he will miraculously address. Ironically, he gives the appearance of being disappointed at their inability to provide him with anything to eat, while all along knowing that it is he who will provide for them food in abundance.

This abundance comes about when the disciples, following his instruction, cast their net to the right of the boat (v. 6). The result is a catch of such quantity that they are not able to draw the net into the boat. "Draw in" translates a Greek word, *helkein*, that appears elsewhere in the gospel in relation to people's being "drawn" to Jesus by the Father (6:44) or by Jesus to himself when "lifted up from the earth" (12:32). This suggests that the "fishing" motif is already operating on a symbolic level: an image of the disciples' apostolic mission. Apart from Jesus, their efforts are fruitless (15:4-5); obedient to his command, in the light of his "day," they experience success beyond all expectation.[57]

In line with the "sign" pattern familiar from earlier in the gospel, the human need and the miraculous remedy have been described. Now (v. 7)

---

[55] The Greek sentence is in the form of a question expecting the answer "No" (*mē ti*). "Anything to eat" translates the rare Greek word *prosphagion*, which strictly speaking refers to something eaten together with bread as a kind of relish; here, it is simply equivalent to "fish"; cf. C. K. Barrett, *John*, 580; Raymond E. Brown, *John XIII–XXI*, 1071.

[56] Cf. Raymond E. Brown, *John XIII–XXI*, 1070.

[57] The miraculous catch of fish in obedience to Jesus' command, after a night of fruitless fishing, echoes—though with many differences—Luke's presentation of the call of Simon (5:1-11). On the relationship between the two traditions, and their likely origin in a single post-Easter appearance to Peter in Galilee, see Raymond E. Brown, *John XIII–XXI*, 1085–92.

follows the response in faith that sees in the miracle a sign pointing to a deeper reality. The Beloved Disciple had come to belief in the resurrection of Jesus through discerning the significance of the folded and separately placed facecloth (20:6-8). Now the same disciple sees in the abundant catch a sign that the indistinct figure who has hailed them from the lakeshore is indeed the risen Lord.

This time, however, he is not going to be first in the race (cf. 20:4). Simon Peter, on learning that it is Jesus who stands on the shore, reacts with characteristic boldness (v. 7b). He has been wearing in the boat only an outer garment. Were he to cast this off in order to swim more easily to the shore, he would arrive naked. So he simply tucks it in before diving into the water.[58] The action, which does not lack a comic aspect, displays both impetuosity and love, foreshadowing the protestations that are soon to follow (vv. 15-17). The Beloved Disciple may again have precedence in faith. But he is not going to outstrip Peter in devotion to the Lord. When the remaining disciples follow in the boat, dragging behind it the overladen net (v. 8),[59] they anticipate their future apostolic mission under the leadership of Peter, which is shortly to be reinstated and confirmed.

A Lakeshore Breakfast: 21:9-14. The breakfast hosted by Jesus on the shore is replete with symbolism of the church's life and mission. The charcoal fire (*anthrakia*), as already noted, recalls the scene of Peter's signal failure in the court of the high priest (18:18, 25). The meal that Jesus has prepared (v. 9)—fish and bread—consists of the same items that on an earlier occasion he had miraculously multiplied to feed five thousand people (6:9).[60] By bidding the disciples to add to what he has prepared some of the fish that they have caught (v. 10), Jesus conveys the sense of a single unified apostolic mission: they will fruitfully carry on what he has set in train when, as just now on the lake, they "fish" for people at his command. Simon Peter's going on board the boat (v. 11) and dragging (*helkein* again; cf. v. 6) the net to the land further points to the disciples' involvement in Jesus' "drawing all to himself" (12:32). The net, untorn despite its containing no less than a hundred and fifty-three large fish, symbolizes the capacity of the church to hold

---

[58] For this understanding of the verb *diazōnnymi* and explanation of the curious situation where Peter actually puts on clothes to go for a swim, see esp. Raymond E. Brown, *John XIII–XXI*, 1072; also Francis J. Moloney, *John*, 553.

[59] The verb *syrein* has the sense of pulling with exhausting effort; cf. Rudolf Schnackenburg, *St. John*, 3:356.

[60] Cf. Andrew T. Lincoln, *St. John*, 512.

a multitude of people together in unity under the leadership of Peter,[61] a narrative fulfillment of Jesus' prayer for unity at the Supper (14:12; 15:5; 17:18, 20-21).[62] No conclusive explanation has ever been found for the precise number—153—of fish.[63] In some respect that the author has not made explicit, though presumably intending his original readers to understand, it probably signifies perfection and completion: at the end of the age the church will have brought to Jesus all those that the Father has drawn to him for salvation (6:44).

The net brought to shore, Jesus invites (v. 12) the disciples to come and have breakfast. They do not need (literally, "dare") to ask him, "Who are you?" because, having seen the sign of the abundant catch, they now share the disciple's faith: they know that "it is the Lord" (cf. v. 7). The description of Jesus' gestures, where he "takes the bread and gives it to them and the fish likewise" (v. 13), echoes so closely his earlier multiplication of the loaves and fish in the same Galilean locale (6:11)[64] that allusion to the Eucharist here, as in that earlier account, is unmistakable.[65] He who has given "his flesh for the life of the world" (6:51) is the true host whenever the community celebrates the Eucharist, sustaining them, in Word and sacrament, with the Bread of Life.

As something of an afterthought we are told that this is the third time that Jesus revealed himself to his disciples after his rising from the dead (v. 14). The enumeration excludes the appearance to Mary Magdalene—possibly because appearances are understood here in the sense of being to the disciples collectively rather than to individuals.[66] The note is in any case a final

---

[61] This is doubtless a particularly "Catholic" view. It seems to be well grounded in the text on the basis that it is Peter, soon to be rehabilitated and installed as shepherd and pastor of the church, who activates Jesus' command, bringing the bulging net to shore untorn; cf. Raymond E. Brown, *John XIII–XXI*, 1097; Francis J. Moloney, *John*, 551.

[62] Cf. Gail O'Day, "The Gospel of John," 858.

[63] See the exhaustive discussion of Raymond E. Brown, *John XIII–XXI*, 1074–76. No explanation seems to have surpassed Augustine's mathematical one on the basis that 153 represents the sum of the numbers 1 to 17, which itself is the sum of the numbers 7 and 10, both of which separately indicate perfection and completeness; cf. C. K. Barrett, *John*, 581. An obvious explanation is that the tradition recorded the number that one of those present actually counted (Brown seems to have a certain sympathy for this, p. 1076) but such historical precision seems alien to the otherwise highly symbolic tendency of the Johannine tradition; cf. C. K. Barrett, *John*, 581.

[64] Lacking only are references to "taking" and (save for a Western manuscript variant) "giving thanks" (*eucharistēsas*).

[65] Cf. Raymond E. Brown, *John XIII–XXI*, 1098–1100; Francis J. Moloney, *John*, 551, 553; Andrew T. Lincoln, *St. John*, 513.

[66] Cf. Gail O'Day, "The Gospel of John," 859.

detail of resemblance between the miracle recorded here, the last in the gospel as a whole, and the Cana miracle recorded as the first. In both cases Jesus "revealed himself" (Cana: "revealed his glory" [2:11]) by remedying, miraculously and in extravagant degree, a human need, providing thereby a sign leading to deeper faith. Both episodes feature a revelation of the divine that for believers of subsequent generations continues sacramentally under the form of bread and wine.

2. Rehabilitation of Peter: His Future and That of the Beloved Disciple: 21:15-24

Peter Rehabilitated and Commissioned as Chief Pastor: 21:15-19. Breakast over, there is unfinished business to attend to. Peter has been the leading player in the scene just concluded but the shadow of failure at the passion remains. In a brief but intense dialogue (vv. 15-17) Jesus moves to renew the relationship at depth, confirm Peter in leadership, and point to a future where he will not fail but heroically glorify God (vv. 18-19).

The triple interrogation to which Jesus submits Peter matches—and heals—the threefold denial. By a charcoal fire (*anthrakia*, 18:18, 25) Peter had three times denied his Lord. Now, beside a similar fire (21:9), there is no recrimination, no mention of the failure, not even an expression of for-giveness—just the unspoken allusion to the denial delicately conveyed in the triple probing. Finally, there is the sense of past failure being wiped away and swallowed up in present love.

Jesus solemnly addresses Peter each time by his full name, "Simon, son of John." This is how he had addressed Peter on their first meeting before going on immediately to give him the nickname "Cephas, which is translated 'Rock' [*petros*]" (1:42). Peter had shown himself to be far from "rock" (= rocky ground) at the time of the passion. Now his capacity to be truly a "rock" for the community is being grounded on deeper self-knowledge and superior love. Jesus asks him the first time around, "Do you love me more than these?" (v. 15b). At the Supper, Peter had put himself forward, boldly protesting that he was ready to "follow" Jesus even to the point of laying down his life for him (13:37). As Jesus predicted (13:38), that boldness had evaporated in denial. Now, however, Jesus does take Peter's capacity for leadership seriously but rests it entirely on the basis of love.[67] It is only as

---

[67] "These" (*toutōn*) in the phrase "more than these" must refer to the other disciples—not, however, in the sense that Peter should love Jesus more than he loves the disciples (so, curi-ously, Francis J. Moloney, *John*, 559). Raymond E. Brown, *John XIII–XXI*, 1104, is hesitant

one who loves Jesus more—and who will demonstrate that love—that Peter is to have leadership and authority in the community.

Peter draws back from any claim to love "more"; on that score he has learned his lesson.[68] He simply throws the response back to Jesus, assuring him of his love and appealing to Jesus' knowledge of that love (v. 15c). In turn Jesus immediately commissions—or recommissions—him in his leading pastoral role: "Feed my lambs" (v. 15d). The shift from the missionary emphasis of the catch of fish in the previous scene to the pastoral language here is significant. In an extended discourse earlier in the gospel Jesus presented himself as the Good Shepherd (10:1-16), one prepared to lay down his life for his sheep (10:11, 15b). Now, for the time of his physical absence that stretches ahead indefinitely, the Shepherd is commissioning Peter to carry on the pastoral role of protecting, nurturing, and keeping united (cf. 21:11 [the untorn net]) "the flock" entrusted to him by the Father. The flock includes also those "other sheep" (converts from the wider world) that do not yet belong to the original fold but who must be brought into the one fold, under the one Shepherd (10:16). Peter does not replace Jesus as Shepherd but Jesus entrusts to him for safekeeping and nurturing the flock ("my sheep") that in obedience to his mission from the Father he has gathered for (eternal) life.[69]

Needless to say, interpreters still tend to divide along denominational lines when assessing the authority and in particular any sense of "office" that is being accorded to Peter here.[70] It seems inescapable that Peter is being singled out from the other disciples and portrayed as more than a "model" of the self-sacrificial love incumbent upon all.[71] It is a further question

---

about a greater love being expected of Peter on the grounds that in the Fourth Gospel that is the prerogative of the Beloved Disciple. But the disciple is the "disciple that Jesus loved," not the "disciple who loved Jesus"; his "prerogative" is passive rather than active.

[68] Rudolf Bultmann rather attractively observes: "He does not say he loves Jesus more than the others, but he declines—obviously with modest reserve—to pass a judgment on the others, and only affirms that he does love Jesus" (*Gospel of John*, 711).

[69] Cf. Rudolf Schnackenburg, *St. John*, 3:365. Andrew T. Lincoln, *St. John*, 518, speaks of Peter's role as that of "under shepherd."

[70] Some warn against seeing an analogy with the commissioning of Peter as the "rock" foundation of the church in Matt 16:17-19; cf. Gail O'Day, "The Gospel of John," 861. The discussion of this issue by Raymond E. Brown, *John XIII–XXI*, 1112–17, remains a model of sensitivity and fair mindedness.

[71] So, Gail O'Day, "The Gospel of John," 860–61, 864. Even a Catholic scholar such as Francis J. Moloney seems unnecessarily dismissive in stating: "Discussions of the Petrine office in the Roman tradition of Christianity are out of place in an exegesis of this passage.
. . . The person charged with that pastoral office, and all Christian pastors, like Peter, are

whether the responsibility being conferred upon Peter is something so personal to him that it ceases with his death or something that is meant to continue in the church beyond his personal lifespan. Clearly, the Catholic doctrine of the Roman primacy as it has developed over the centuries cannot be wrung in a literal sense out of the metaphorical language in which Peter is commissioned here. Nonetheless, one may ask why, when Peter had presumably been dead for some decades, the Johannine author felt it important to remind the community of the pastoral authority given to him by the risen Lord. That Peter is presented in this way suggests that the authority conferred upon him continues in the community in some significant way?[72] In this sense the commission given to Peter seems at least open to the development seen in the Catholic tradition.

The exchange between Jesus and Peter continues a second (v. 16) and a third time (v. 17) in very similar, though not identical terms. The variation in the Greek original in the terms for "love" (between *agapan* and *philein*) is purely stylistic and involves no lessening or increase of intensity.[73] The same applies to the variation in the verbs that refer to pastoral care (*boskein* and *poimanein*),[74] as also to the designation of the recipients of that care under the image of "sheep" (*arnia* and *probata*).[75] An intensification in the exchange does, however, set in when Peter responds with deep emotion to a third round of questioning (v. 17)—doubtless because allusion to his triple denial is now clear. Probed to the depth of his being, he can only protest, "Lord, you know all things; you know that I love you."[76]

---

challenged to repeat the relationship Jesus had with his flock" (*John*, 555; cf. 559). True, but Peter is being singled out and given an authoritative commission, as many Protestant scholars, including Bultmann, have acknowledged; cf. Raymond E. Brown, *John XIII–XXI*, 1113; cf. also C. K. Barrett, *John*, 584 ("a very high view of the office and importance of Peter is taken").

[72] So, Raymond E. Brown, *John XIII–XXI*, 1117. Brown also provides a helpful discussion of the theological force of the citation of John 21:15-17 (along with Matt 16:16-19) by the First Vatican Council (1870) in relation to the council's dogmatic definition of the Petrine primacy.

[73] This is the scholarly consensus today. The two verbs are used interchangeably across the Fourth Gospel: e.g., in regard to the description of the disciple "whom Jesus loved": *agapan*: 13:33; 19:26; 21:7, 20; *philein*: 20:2; and the Father's love for Jesus: *agapan*: 3:35; 10:17; 15:9; 17:23, 24, 26; *philein*: 5:20; also the parallelism between the statements in 14:23 (*agapan*) and 16:27 (*philein*); cf. C. K. Barrett, *John*, 584; Raymond E. Brown, *John XIII–XXI*, 1103; Rudolf Schnackenburg, *St. John*, 3:362–63.

[74] *Poimanein* expresses a shepherd's care in general; *boskein* has the more specific sense of "graze," "pasture."

[75] There is variation in this case too in the manuscript tradition: *probatia* instead of *probata* in various combinations; see Raymond E. Brown, *John XIII–XXI*, 1104–6.

[76] Cf. Mark 14:72, where following his third denial and the second crowing of the cock, Peter breaks down and weeps.

With a final commissioning (v. 17e) Jesus leaves off questioning Peter and points to a future where he will amply demonstrate his love (v. 19). Alluding perhaps to a known proverb, he makes a contrast between the freedom Peter has enjoyed in his "youth"—girding himself and going about where he will—and a time of constriction in his old age when he will stretch out his hands and someone else will gird him and take him where he would rather not go.[77] The later church tradition according to which Peter died by crucifixion under Nero in the early 60s has led interpreters from earliest times to find in Jesus' words, especially the phrase "stretching out your hands," a reference to this mode of execution.[78] More important, however, than the precise mode of death is the prophecy that Peter in his death would "glorify God," thereby linking his death inextricably with the supreme glorification of God that the gospel has again and again associated with the death of Jesus (12:28; 13:31-32; 17:1, 5).[79]

Jesus' final command, "Follow me" (v. 19b), reminds us of Peter's earlier protest at the final Supper: "Lord, why can I not follow you now? I will lay down my life for you" (13:37). Events later that night proved all too soon the hollowness of that claim. Now Jesus is calling Peter to a renewed discipleship, founded on his superior love that, as readers of the gospel are aware, will involve following Jesus right up to sharing his heroic death. Like the Good Shepherd, the "under shepherd" will glorify God by laying down his life in love. He will amply fulfill Jesus' claim: "Whoever serves me must follow me, and where I am, there will my servant be also" (12:26).

The Beloved Disciple: 21:20-24. So much for Peter, but where does the hero of the Johannine community, the Beloved Disciple, fit into the future life of the church? Skillfully, the author introduces this issue by having Peter, whose role has just been clarified, turn, notice that the disciple is following, and ask Jesus, "Lord, what about him?" (vv. 20-21). Somewhat unnecessarily— or at least so it seems at first sight—we are reminded that this is the disciple

---

[77] There are at least three elements of contrast: "young/old"; "girding oneself/being girded by another";"going freely/being taken"; cf. Raymond E. Brown, *John XIII–XXI*, 1107, who in fact counts the last contrast as two.

[78] A difficulty with this interpretation is the reference to Peter's being bound and led where he would not go (v. 18d) coming after the mention of stretching out his hands (v. 18c), which would seem to be the reverse order in regard to crucifixion; cf. Raymond E. Brown, *John XIII–XXI*, 1107–8. Also the Greek verb *zōnnynai* more strictly means "gird" (cf. v. 18b and *diazōnnynai* in v. 7) rather than "bind." However, very similar references to the mode of Jesus' own death in 12:33 and 18:32 would seem to tie the two deaths so closely together as to make a reference to crucifixion more or less inescapable.

[79] Cf. Andrew T. Lincoln, *St. John*, 519.

who at the Supper had had the position of closest intimacy to Jesus (leaning upon his breast and inquiring about the identity of the betrayer [13:23-24]). It is as though the Johannine community, which has been somewhat on the margins of the wider church gathered around the memory of Peter, is now asking to be noticed and have due recognition given to the intimacy with Jesus it enjoys through its legacy from the disciple.

The community has evidently preserved as part of its tradition a saying attributed to Jesus according to which the disciple would not die until the return of Jesus at the end of the age. Yet, the clear implication of the explanation provided in verse 23 is that the disciple has in fact died,[80] thereby creating considerable "dissonance" with the word of Jesus.[81] Moreover, if the disciple died from natural causes, as seems to have been the case, rather than through a heroic martyrdom like Peter, then the community may have experienced a loss of prestige when comparisons were made.[82] These matters are addressed by having Jesus issue something of a rebuke to Peter (v. 22). If the disciple is to "remain" (*menein*), that is, stay alive, until the return of the Lord—and so not experience the kind of martyrdom that awaits Peter—that is no concern of his: he should get on with his own discipleship ("You follow me!" [v. 22c]). Jesus has other plans for the disciple—no less important but different. The author is not instituting a polemic against Peter or the claims of the community that looked to his leadership, but ensuring, after Peter has been honored, that the distinctive role of the Beloved Disciple is recognized and honored alongside him.[83]

Nonetheless, the "dissonance" between Jesus' word about the "remaining" of the disciple and the fact of his death stands. The author addresses this in verse 23 with a rather casuistic clarification of what Jesus had in fact said: not that the disciple would not die but "If it is my will that he remain until I come, what is that to you?"[84] In other words, Jesus had not made a prophecy about the disciple's future but uttered a conditional expression about his own will while asserting that the matter is no concern to Peter.

---

[80] Cf. Raymond E. Brown, *John XIII–XXI*, 1118–19.

[81] Cf. Francis J. Moloney, *John*, 557.

[82] Cf. Andrew T. Lincoln, *St. John*, 521.

[83] Cf. Rudolf Schnackenburg, *St. John*, 3:368; Raymond E. Brown, *John XIII–XXI*, 1120–21; Andrew T. Lincoln, *St. John*, 520–21.

[84] The final phrase, "What is that to you?" is missing in important early manuscripts. It may be an addition to make the citation of Jesus' words match completely what he said in v. 22. In any case, the point being made derives from the conditional clause rather than from this phrase.

With a focus on the conditional element any dissonance between statement and fact falls away.[85]

There is a sense, however, in which the Beloved Disciple, despite his death, does "remain" (v. 24).[86] He "remains" and makes an irreplaceable contribution to the entire believing community through the testimony to the saving events and the written record of that testimony that he has "authored" in the shape of the gospel. "Authored" translates the Greek participle *grapsas* which, as in the case of Pilate's having an inscription drawn up and placed on Jesus' cross (19:19), does not necessarily mean that the disciple physically wrote all that is contained in the text. More likely it means that he instigated its composition as a record of his unique witness to the life-giving revelation disclosed in Jesus.[87] The sentences about the disciple then conclude with an expression of confidence from the community about the reliability of his witness: "And we know (*oidamen*) that his witness is true" (v. 24c).[88] Standing at the close of the gospel, the assertion reaches out to invite all later generations of believers to enter into that confidence and so find in their own day the life and hope that the community's witness contains.

A Second Conclusion to the Gospel: 21:25

In the final sentence of the gospel as a whole (v. 25) the author steps forward in the first person ("I think") to make the point that all that has been recorded is only a fraction of what might have been included. Flamboyant hyperbole of this nature was conventional at the end of literary works in the ancient world[89] and commentators by and large do not give high marks to this particular example.[90] In its own way, however, it does provide a memorable "signing off" for a project as immense as the revelation contained in the Fourth Gospel.[91]

[85] Cf. Andrew T. Lincoln, *St. John*, 522.

[86] Along with C. K. Barrett, *John*, 587–88, and Gail O'Day, "The Gospel of John," 862, I take v. 24 closely with the previous verse dealing with the disciple.

[87] On this sense of the participle, cf. Francis J. Moloney, *John*, 561; Andrew T. Lincoln, *St. John*, 523.

[88] Cf. a similar "intrusion" of the community voice in 19:35 with respect to the disciple's testimony about the flow of blood and water from Jesus' side.

[89] For references, see Raymond E. Brown, *John XIII–XXI*, 1130; Andrew T. Lincoln, *St. John*, 523–24.

[90] Most consider it an imitation of the preliminary conclusion at 20:30-31.

[91] In this vein, Raymond E. Brown cites the early Christian writer Origen as coming close to the writer's true purpose in stating: "It is impossible to commit to writing all those particulars that belong to the glory of the Saviour" (*John XIII–XXI*, 1130).

Looking back over John 21 as a whole, we can appreciate the attempt it represents to bring the witness of the Beloved Disciple that the community treasured into alignment with the tradition concerning Peter that prevailed in the wider church. Where Peter represented authority and unity—albeit founded totally on love—the disciple's witness, in a complementary rather than a rival way, brought a sense of intimacy between the divine and the human without which Christianity would be greatly impoverished. We can be deeply grateful that he "remained"—and remains—through his witness in the gospel down to our day.

Glossary of Select Johannine Terms

Faith/Believe	The Fourth Gospel makes copious reference to human faith in the verbal form "believe" (*pisteuein*) but never employs the noun *pistis*. This lends the sense that, rather than simply an internal disposition, faith is a dynamic personal commitment, above all to the person of Jesus (2:11; 3:16; etc.) and to the claims he makes about himself (9:35; 11:25-26), or to claims made about him in a more creedal, confessional sense (6:69; 20:31). Synonymous with believing in this sense are expressions such as "coming to" (6:35; 7:37-38), "knowing" (17:8), "receiving/accepting" (1:12; 5:43: 13:20; 17:8). The gospel recognizes different levels of faith: from the immature and unsatisfactory (especially that which does not see the miracles truly as "signs"(2:23; 7:31; 8:30-31) or which hesitates from full commitment (12:42), to the fully mature, which leads to the gift of (eternal) life (3:15-16, 36; 5:24; 6:40, 47; 11:25; 20:31). In confronting the problem of unbelief, the gospel does not resolve the tension between faith as involving human decision and commitment, on the one hand, and also being "drawn" by the Father (6:44, 65), on the other.
Flesh	"Flesh" (*sarx*) has its biblical sense in the Fourth Gospel denoting human existence (17:2), especially in its weakness and mortality over against the divine (1:13; 3:6; 6:33; 8:15). However, the divine Word, the Son of God, has "become flesh" (1:14), transforming human existence so that in his person it becomes a vehicle for the

revelation of God. The incarnate Son "gives up" his "flesh," that is, his human bodily life, for the life of the world (6:51). In a sacramental sense the eucharistic bread is his "flesh," which believers must eat in order to have (eternal) life (6:52-54).

Glory/Glorify	"Glory" (*doxa*) has the everyday sense of "reputation," "honor," or "recognition" (5:44; 7:18; 12:43). Standing alongside this sense in the Fourth Gospel is the biblical usage where "glory" denotes the presence and power of the unseen God. Human beings "glorify" (*doxazein*) God when they acknowledge the presence of God in creation and divine saving acts. In the theology of the gospel the glory of God is most notably revealed in the person and works of the incarnate Son (2:11; 11:4, 40; 17:1). Above all, Jesus is most transparent to the being of God in his self-sacrificial death upon the cross which, along with his resurrection and ascension to the Father, is the "hour" of his "glorification" (7:39; 12:16, 23, 28; 13:31-32). In this revelation Jesus "glorifies" the Father and, by the same token, is "glorified" by the Father in the sense of being revealed as the Son who has been the glory of the Father from all eternity (1:1, 14; 8:54; 17:1, 5, 24). Disciples continue Jesus' glorification of God when they faithfully follow his way (15:8; 17:22; 21:19).
Hour	While "hour" (*hōra*) can have the ordinary sense of marking the time of day (1:39: 4:6), the gospel characteristically uses the term to indicate a significant period in Jesus' life, especially the "hour" of his "glorification," that is, his return to the Father in his death, resurrection, and ascension (12:23, 27; 13:1; 17:1). Likewise, "hour" can indicate a time of particular significance or new circumstance for the disciples because of the coming or departure of Jesus (4:21; 5:25; 16:2, 25, 32).
Jew, "The Jews"	The Fourth Gospel uses "Jew" (*Ioudaios*), especially in the plural form "the Jews" (*Ioudaioi*), in a variety of ways. In the early chapters (1–4) the term has principally a neutral (or even positive [cf. 4:22]) ethnic or cultural sense, referring to members of the Jewish people (1:19; 2:6, 13; 3:1; 5:1; also 6:4; 11:19, 31, 33, 36; 12:9;

19:40). In chapters 5–11, "the Jews" refers to the dialogue partners of Jesus, in an atmosphere of increasing hostility and refusal to believe (5:10, 15-16, 18; 6:41; 7:1, 13; 8:48; 9:22; 10:31, 33; 11:8; 18:31-36; 19:7, 31, 38; 20:19). In this latter, negative sense, "the Jews" refers principally to the Jewish religious authorities, especially the chief priests, who, set in their opposition to Jesus and determined to bring about his death, have become in a symbolic sense the factual representatives of the "world" of unbelief that it is the mission of Jesus to challenge and overcome. The phrase "the Jews" no longer represents an ethnic, geographical, or even religious group but has become a symbol of the prideful human propensity to cling to status and position rather than to submit to the life-giving revelation of God that challenges such things. The Fourth Gospel's choice of "the Jews" to represent this tendency reflects the historical setting in which its narrative is necessarily cast (a quasi "life" of Jesus of Nazareth) and also the Johannine community's recent painful history of separation from and rivalry with the synagogue. Responsible interpretation of the gospel must take careful note of these factors and also of the variety of ways—positive, neutral, negative—in which "Jew"/"the Jews" can appear in the text.

Judgment/Judge

The motif of "judgment" (*krisis*)"/ "judge" (*krinein*) features prominently in the gospel because mounting hostility means that Jesus is on trial virtually from the start of his public life. Both noun and verb occur in the neutral sense of judgment as a process, the outcome of which may be either acquittal or condemnation; more usual is simply the negative sense of "condemnation." The Son's mission in the world institutes the divine process of judgment, which in the more conventional Jewish eschatology was seen as a future event but which the gospel sees as brought forward into the ministry of Jesus. Human beings enter into their own judgment—either for acquittal or condemnation—according as they come or do not come to the Light and, in faith, find life rather than condemnation (3:17-21; 5:22-24; 9:39).

Life	"Life (*zōē*) can refer to present physical (mortal) life but more characteristically, even without the attendant adjective "eternal" (*aiōnios*), refers to the share in the divine eternal life, which it is the goal of the Son's mission to impart to human beings (3:16; 10:10b). Life in this sense transcends the barrier of death and, in the realized eschatology of the gospel, is a gift already communicated to believers (5:24; 11:25-26).
Sign	For "sign" (*sēmeion*) see Excursus: "Miracles as Signs (*Sēmeia*) in the Fourth Gospel": pp. (57–58) above.
Sin	While the Fourth Gospel does take account of human sinning in the sense of particular acts of moral transgression (murder, lying, theft, etc. [cf. 8:24; 9:34; 20:23]), its primary concern is the radical evil and alienation from God in the human heart of which particular "sins" are the outward expression. Archetypal human sin (*hamartia*) has primarily a christological reference in that when God sends "the Light" (the Son of God) into the world for its salvation, human beings reject the Light, preferring to remain in the darkness lest their misdeeds be exposed (3:18-21).
Spirit	Spirit (*pneuma*) can refer to the human spirit (11:33; 13:21). In biblical thought generally, "spirit" (*pneuma*) denotes the life-giving power of God in the world. In this sense its saving impact upon human beings is contrasted in the gospel with mere human capacity denoted by "flesh" (3:5, 8; 6:63). In the gospel the Spirit is especially the divine power present uniquely in Jesus (1:32, 33; 3:34), symbolized by water (4:10-15; 7:37-39), the instrument of the rebirth of human beings "from above" (3:5, 8; cf. 1:12-13) and of their cleansing from sin (1:34; 20:23). After his death, the risen Lord imparts the Spirit to the disciples to empower them to continue his mission in the world (20:22; cf. 19:30).
Spirit (as Paraclete)	In a highly distinctive and personal usage the gospel describes the Spirit as "Paraclete" (*paraklētos*), indicating a number of roles that the Spirit will play under this guise as a replacement and compensation for the presence of Jesus after his return to the Father: comforter

(14:15-17) and ongoing revealer of the truth in the sense of bringing to mind what Jesus had done (14:26) and indicating the meaning of that for the later time (16:12-14); finally, in a more forensic sense, standing by the disciples when they are on trial before the world (15:26-27) and in fact prosecuting the judgment (condemnation) of the world (16:7-11).

Truth

"Truth" (*alētheia*), along with its cognate adjectives, (*alēthēs*, *alēthinos*) can simply be opposed to falsehood (4:18, 37; 5:31; 10:41). Especially in connection with the prominent motif of "witness," it can mean "reliable," as opposed to not being based upon or corresponding to reality (8:16; 19:35; 21:24). More characteristically in John truth is connected to revelation, specifically to the final and definitive revelation of God given in the person of Jesus as incarnate Son of God as distinct from earlier and now overtaken foreshadowings in the story of Israel (1:14, 17). In this sense Jesus is the "true Vine" (15:1), the "true Bread" (6:32), etc., in distinction from and superior to earlier types (Israel, the manna in the desert). Whereas the Law was given by Moses, "grace and truth" have come about in Jesus Christ (1:17). Likewise, the "true worshippers" (4:23) are those whose worship, in contrast to the old material worship in temples or shrines, corresponds to the new reality being brought into being by the mission of Jesus. After the resurrection and the departure of Jesus to the Father, the Spirit, in the guise of "Paraclete," will continue the "truth-communicating" role of Jesus for the benefit of the community: "reminding" them of what he had taught, and leading them to further knowledge of the "truth" (14:15-16, 26; 15:26; 16:13).

World

"World" (*kosmos*) can refer to the entire creation: all things which were "made" through the Word (cf. 1:3; 17:5). More specifically, *kosmos* denotes the entire human world (16:21) created by God to share the divine eternal life but factually fallen into the grip of forces alien to God, which is why it needs to be saved (3:16; 17:6, 11, 17). More negatively and predominantly in John, "world" refers to that part of humanity that has definitively said "No" to the saving mission of the Son and responds with unbelief and hatred (15:18-19; 17:14). Since it is to Israel that the Son's mission has in the first instance been directed ("his own"), the primary representatives of this nay-saying world are those members of Israel (chiefly the leadership: "the Jews") who have rejected him and who, by the time of the writing of the gospel, have extended that rejection to the community of believers gathered in his name.

Bibliography

Commentaries on the Fourth Gospel

Barrett, C. K. *The Gospel According to St. John*. 2nd ed. London: SPCK, 1978.

Brown, Raymond E. *The Gospel According to John*. 2 vols. Anchor Bible 29–29A. Garden City, NY: Doubleday, 1966–70.

Bultmann, Rudolf. *The Gospel of John: A Commentary*. Oxford: Blackwell, 1971.

Lincoln, Andrew T. *The Gospel According to Saint John*. Black's New Testament Commentary. New York: Hendrickson, 2005.

Moloney, Francis J. *The Gospel of John*. Sacra Pagina 4. Collegeville, MN: Liturgical Press, 1998.

O'Day, Gail. "The Gospel of John." In *New Interpreter's Bible* IX. Nashville, TN: Abingdon, 1995, 491–865.

Schnackenburg, Rudolf. *The Gospel According to St. John*. 3 vols. New York: Crossroad, 1968–1982.

Schnelle, Ugo. *Das Evangelium nach Johannes*. 4th ed. Theologischer Handkommentar zum Neuen Testament 4. Leipzig: Evangelische Verlagsanstalt, 2009.

Other Works

Borgen, Peder. *Bread from Heaven: An Exegetical Study of the Concept of Manna in the Gospel of John and the Writings of Philo*. NovTSupp 10. Leiden: Brill, 1965.

———."John 6: Tradition, Interpretation and Composition." In *Critical Readings of John 6*, edited by R. Alan Culpepper. Biblical Interpretation Series 22. Leiden: Brill, 1997, 95–114.

Brown, Raymond E. *The Epistles of John*. Anchor Bible 30. New York: Doubleday, 1982.

———. *The Death of the Messiah: From Gethsemane to the Grave: A Commentary on the Passion Narratives of the Four Gospels*. 2 vols. New York: Doubleday, 1994.

————. *An Introduction to the Gospel of John*, edited by Francis J. Moloney. New York: Doubleday, 2003.

Byrne, Brendan. *'Sons of God'—'Seed of Abraham': A Study of the Idea of the Sonship of God of All Christians in Paul against the Jewish Background*. Analecta Biblica 83. Rome: Biblical Institute Press, 1979.

————. "The Faith of the Beloved Disciple and the Community in John 20." *Journal for the Study of the New Testament* 23 (1985): 83–97.

Carter, Warren. *John and Empire: Initial Explorations*. New York: T. & T. Clark, 2008.

Catechism of the Catholic Church. 2nd ed. Vatican City: Libreria Editrice Vaticana, 2000.

Coloe, Mary. *God Dwells with Us: Temple Symbolism in the Fourth Gospel*. Collegeville, MN: Liturgical Press, 2001.

Culpepper, R. Alan. "The Pivot of John's Prologue." *New Testament Studies* 27 (1980–81): 1–31.

————. *Anatomy of the Fourth Gospel*. Philadelphia: Fortress, 1983.

————. "The Johannine *Hypodeigma*: A Reading of John 13." *Semeia* 53 (1991): 133–52.

————, ed. *Critical Readings of John 6*. Biblical Interpretation Series 22. Leiden: Brill, 1997.

Dodd, C. H. *The Interpretation of the Fourth Gospel*. Cambridge: Cambridge University Press, 1953.

————. *Historical Tradition in the Fourth Gospel*. Cambridge: Cambridge University Press, 1963.

Donahue, John R., ed. *Life in Abundance: Studies of John's Gospel in Tribute to Raymond E. Brown*. Collegeville, MN: Liturgical Press, 2005.

Donaldson, Terence L. *Jews and Anti-Judaism in the New Testament*. Waco, TX: Baylor University Press, 2010.

Freeman, Laurence. *Light Within: Meditation as Pure Prayer*. Norwich: Canterbury Press, 2008.

Hengel, Martin. *Saint Peter: The Underestimated Apostle*. Grand Rapids, MI: Wm. B. Eerdmans, 2010.

Henneberry, B. H. "The Raising of Lazarus (John 11:1-44): An evaluation of the hypothesis that a written tradition lies behind the narrative." PhD thesis, University of Louvain, 1983.

Katz, Steven T. "Issues in the Separation of Judaism and Christianity after 70 C.E.: A Reconsideration." *Journal of Biblical Literature* 103 (1984): 43–76.

Koester, Craig R. "The Death of Jesus and the Human Condition: Exploring the Theology of John's Gospel." In *Life in Abundance: Studies of John's Gospel in Tribute to Raymond E. Brown*, edited by John R. Donahue. Collegeville, MN: Liturgical Press, 2005, 141–57.

Kysar, Robert. *John: The Maverick Gospel*. 3rd ed. Louisville, KY: Westminster John Knox, 2007.

Lee, Dorothy A. "The Story of the Woman at the Well: A Symbolic Reading (John 4:1-42)." *Australian Biblical Review* 41 (1993): 35–48.

———. *The Symbolic Narratives of the Fourth Gospel: The Interplay of Form and Meaning*. Journal for the Study of the New Testament Supplement Series 95. Sheffield, UK: JSOT Press, 1994.

———. *Flesh and Glory: Symbolism, Gender, and Theology in the Gospel of John*. New York: Crossroad, 2002.

———. *Transfiguration*. New York: Continuum, 2004.

———. "Paschal Imagery in the Gospel of John: A Narrative and Symbolic Reading." *Pacifica* 24 (2011): 13–28.

Martyn, J. Louis. *History and Theology in the Fourth Gospel*. 3rd ed. Louisville, KY: Westminster John Knox, 2003.

Menken, Marten J. J. "John 6:51c-58: Eucharist or Christology." In *Critical Readings of John 6*, edited by R. Alan Culpepper. Biblical Interpretation Series 22. Leiden: Brill, 1997, 183–204.

Metzger, Bruce M. *A Textual Commentary on the Greek New Testament*. 2nd ed. London: United Bible Societies, 1975.

Moloney, Francis J. "The Function of Prolepsis in the Interpretation of John 6." In *Critical Readings of John 6*, edited by R. Alan Culpepper. Biblical Interpretation Series 22. Leiden: Brill, 1997, 129–48.

———. *Love in the Gospel of John: An Exegetical, Theological, and Literary Study*. Grand Rapids, MI: Baker Academic, 2013.

Moore, Sebastian, and Anselm Hurt. *Before the Deluge*. London: Geoffrey Chapman, 1968.

Newbigin, Lesslie. *The Light Has Come: An Exposition of the Fourth Gospel*. Grand Rapids, MI: Wm. B. Eerdmans, 1983.

Neyrey, Jerome H. "Jacob Traditions and the Interpretation of John 4:10-26." *Catholic Biblical Quarterly* 41 (1979): 419–37.

Nickelsburg, George W. E. "Son of Man." In *Anchor Bible Dictionary*, edited by David Noel Freedman. New York: Doubleday, 1992, 6:137–50.

Painter, John. *The Quest for the Messiah: The History, Literature and Theology of the Johannine Community*. 2nd ed. Edinburgh: T. & T. Clark, 1993.

Pontifical Biblical Commission. *The Interpretation of the Bible in the Church*. Vatican City: Libreria Editrice Vaticana, 1993.

Rensberger, David. *Johannine Faith and Liberating Community*. Philadelphia: Westminster, 1988.

Schneiders, Sandra M. "The Face Veil: A Johannine Sign (John 20:1-10)." *Biblical Theology Bulletin* 13 (1983): 94–97.

———."Death in the Community of Eternal Life: History, Theology and Spirituality in John 11." *Interpretation* 41 (1987): 44–56.

———. "The Resurrection (of the Body) in the Fourth Gospel: A Key to Johannine Spirituality." In *Life in Abundance: Studies of John's Gospel in Tribute to Raymond E. Brown*, edited by John R. Donahue. Collegeville, MN: Liturgical Press, 2005, 168–98.

———. "The Word in the World." *Pacifica* 23 (2010): 247–66.

Thompson, Marianne Meye. "Thinking about God: Wisdom and Theology in John 6." In *Critical Readings of John 6*, edited by R. Alan Culpepper. Biblical Interpretation Series 22. Leiden: Brill, 1997, 221–26.

Zumstein, Jean. "Der Prozess der Relecture in der johanneischen Literatur." *New Testament Studies* 42 (1996): 394–411.

Scripture Index

Modern Author Index

Subject Index

Note: **Bold** type indicates principal areas of definition and discussion